PROUST AND THE A

Proust and the Arts brings together expert Proustians and renowned interdisciplinary scholars in a major reconsideration of the novelist's relation to the arts. Going beyond the classic question of the models used by Proust for his fictional artists, the essays collected here explore how he learned from and integrated, in highly personal ways, the work of such creators as Wagner or Carpaccio. This volume reveals the breadth of Proust's engagement with varied art forms from different eras: from "primitive" arts to sound recordings, from medieval sculpture to Art Nouveau glassmaking, from portrait photography to the private art of doodling. Chapters bring into focus issues of perception and detail in examining how Proust encountered and responded to works of art, and attend to the ways art shaped his complex relationship to identity, sexuality, humor, and the craft of writing.

CHRISTIE MCDONALD is Smith Professor of French Language and Literature in Romance Languages and Literatures, and Professor of Comparative Literature at Harvard University.

FRANÇOIS PROULX is Assistant Professor of French at the University of Illinois at Urbana-Champaign.

PROUST AND THE ARTS

EDITED BY

CHRISTIE MCDONALD

and

FRANÇOIS PROULX

CAMBRIDGE
UNIVERSITY PRESS

University Printing House, Cambridge CB2 8BS, United Kingdom

One Liberty Plaza, 20th Floor, New York, NY 10006, USA

477 Williamstown Road, Port Melbourne, VIC 3207, Australia

314-321, 3rd Floor, Plot 3, Splendor Forum, Jasola District Centre, New Delhi - 110025, India

79 Anson Road, #06-04/06, Singapore 079906

Cambridge University Press is part of the University of Cambridge.

It furthers the University's mission by disseminating knowledge in the pursuit of education, learning and research at the highest international levels of excellence.

www.cambridge.org
Information on this title: www.cambridge.org/9781107501911

First published 2015
First paperback edition 2018

A catalogue record for this publication is available from the British Library

ISBN 978-1-107-10336-8 Hardback
ISBN 978-1-107-50191-1 Paperback

Contents

Figures

Notes on contributors

ANTOINE COMPAGNON is Professor of Modern and Contemporary French Literature at the Collège de France and Blanche W. Knopf Professor of French and Comparative Literature at Columbia University. In addition to editing Proust's *Sodome et Gomorrhe* (Bibliothèque de la Pléiade, 1988) and *Carnets* (with Florence Callu, 2002), he has authored several books of literary criticism, theory, and history, including *Proust Between Two Centuries* (1989; English translation 1992), *Five Paradoxes of Modernity* (1990; English translation 1994), and *Les Antimodernes: de Joseph de Maistre à Roland Barthes* (2005). He has recently edited two collections of essays on Proust, *Swann le centenaire* (with Kazuyoshi Yoshikawa and Matthieu Vernet, 2013) and *Lire et relire Proust* (2014).

JOHN D'AMICO is a Ph.D. candidate in French at Harvard University. His dissertation, "The Cults of Ennui and Attention in Nineteenth-Century France and Beyond: Baudelaire, Flaubert, Huysmans, Proust, Barthes," takes literary boredom as a point of departure to propose an alternative history of attention.

SOPHIE DUVAL is Maître de conférences at the université Bordeaux Montaigne and a member of the Équipe Proust at the ITEM/ENS (Institut des textes et manuscrits modernes, École normale supérieure, Paris). A specialist of literary irony and satire, she is the author of two books, *La satire* (with Marc Martinez, 2000) and *L'ironie proustienne: La vision stéréoscopique* (2004). She is also co-editor of *Mauvais genre: La satire littéraire moderne* (special issue of *Modernités*, with Jean-Pierre Saïdah, 2008) and *Proust et les "Moyen Âge"* (with Miren Lacassagne, 2015).

EVELYNE ENDER is Visiting Professor at The Johns Hopkins University, and was formerly at Hunter College and the Graduate Center, the City

University of New York (CUNY). Her book *Architexts of Memory: Literature, Science, and Autobiography* (2005), which won the MLA's Scaglione Prize for Comparative Literary Studies, draws from neuroscientific models of memory and cognition to read literary works by Proust, Woolf, Nerval, and others as laboratories for the study of human memory.

STEFANIE GOYETTE is a post-doctoral Fellow in Liberal Studies at New York University. She is currently working on her first book, which considers the role of space and gender in the Old French fabliaux.

VIRGINIE GREENE is Professor of French and Chair of the Department of Romance Languages and Literatures at Harvard University. A specialist of medieval literature, she is the author of *Le sujet et la mort dans* La Mort Artu (2002) and *Logical Fictions in Medieval Literature and Philosophy* (2014). She is also the editor of *Towards the Author: Essays in French Medieval Literature* (2006), the translator in modern French of the *Débat sur le Roman de la Rose* (2006), and a co-author of *Thinking Through Chrétien de Troyes* (2011). She contributed detailed biographical notices on Proust's correspondents to the anthology *Lettres* (2004).

SUZANNE GUERLAC is Professor of French at the University of California, Berkeley. She has published widely on nineteenth- and twentieth-century French literature and cultural ideology, including the books *Thinking in Time: An Introduction to Henri Bergson* (2006) and *Literary Polemics: Bataille, Sartre, Valéry, Breton* (1997), for which she received the MLA's Scaglione Prize for French and Francophone Studies. Her recent work on the articulations between literature, the visual arts, and philosophy includes her current book project, *Proust: Photographies*, which examines the relationship between time, vision, memory, and the production of experience in *À la recherche du temps perdu.*

JOHN HAMILTON is William R. Kenan, Jr. Professor of German and Comparative Literature at Harvard University. He is the author of *Soliciting Darkness: Pindar, Obscurity, and the Classical Tradition* (2004); *Music, Madness, and the Unworking of Language* (2008); and *Security: Politics, Humanity, and the Philogogy of Care* (2013).

ELISABETH LADENSON is Professor of French and Comparative Literature at Columbia University. She is the author of *Proust's Lesbianism* (1999) and *Dirt for Art's Sake: Books on Trial from Lolita to Madame Bovary* (2007).

SERAFINA LAWRENCE is a doctoral student in Comparative Literature at the Graduate Center, the City University of New York (CUNY), and Literary Manager at Cherry Lane Theatre, New York.

FRANÇOISE LERICHE is Maître de conférences HDR at the université Stendhal–Grenoble 3, where she is a member of the Litt&Arts research group. She is also a member of the Équipe Proust at the ITEM/ENS, Paris. She is the editor of the anthology *Lettres* (2004), and the director of an international research team working toward an updated, digital edition of Proust's correspondence. She co-edited a digital edition of Proust's *Agenda 1906* with Nathalie Mauriac Dyer and Pyra Wise (2015). Her publications include *Genèse et correspondances* (co-edited with Alain Pagès, 2012) and numerous works on Proust.

NATHALIE MAURIAC DYER is Directrice de recherche at the CNRS (ITEM/ENS, Paris). She is the editor of *Bulletin d'informations proustiennes* and director of the publication of Proust's *Cahiers 1 à 75 de la Bibliothèque nationale de France*. Her book *Proust inachevé: Le dossier "Albertine disparue"* (2005) addresses the implications of the discovery in 1986 of the last hand-corrected manuscript of Proust's *Albertine disparue*, which she edited for publication as *Sodome et Gomorrhe III: La Prisonnière suivi de Albertine disparue* (1993). She is co-editor of *Proust face à l'héritage du XIX*e *siècle: Tradition et métamorphose* (with Kazuyoshi Yoshikawa and Pierre-Edmond Robert, 2012), and editor of *Proust, 1913*, *Genesis* 36, 2013.

CHRISTIE MCDONALD is Smith Professor of French Language and Literature in Romance Languages and Literatures, and Professor of Comparative Literature at Harvard University. She is the author of numerous books on topics ranging from eighteenth-century French literature to contemporary theory and painting, as well as *The Proustian Fabric: Associations of Memory* (1991); her articles on Proust have appeared in *The Cambridge Companion to the French Novel* (1997), *Approaches to Teaching Proust* (2003), *The Strange Mr. Proust* (2009), and *Swann le centenaire* (2013). She has edited or co-edited many volumes of essays, including *French Global: A New Approach to Literary History* (with Susan Rubin Suleiman, 2010; French translation, 2014) and *Rousseau and Freedom* (with Stanley Hoffmann, 2010).

FRANÇOIS PROULX is Assistant Professor of French at the University of Illinois at Urbana-Champaign. He has published articles in *Nineteenth-Century French Studies* and *Bulletin d'informations proustiennes*. He was guest curator of the exhibition *Private Proust: Letters and Drawings to Reynaldo Hahn* at Houghton Library, Harvard University (2013). His current book project on *Reading and French Masculinity at the Fin de Siècle* was awarded a research fellowship from the National Endowment for the Humanities for 2015–2016.

SINDHUMATHI REVULURI is Associate Professor of Music at Harvard University. She is currently completing a book, *Sounding Empire in Fin-de-Siècle France: Exoticism, Nationalism, and Modernist Musical Thought*, examining the dual currents of exoticist representation and nationalism in music in the context of French imperial aspirations and the beginnings of modernism in France. She has published articles in numerous musicology journals as well as the *Oxford Handbook of Mobile Music Studies* (2014).

MAURICE SAMUELS is Betty Jane Anlyan Professor of French at Yale University. He is the author of *The Spectacular Past: Popular History and the Novel in Nineteenth-Century France* (2004) and *Inventing the Israelite: Jewish Fiction in Nineteenth-Century France* (2010), for which he received the MLA's Scaglione Prize for French and Francophone Studies. He co-edited a *Nineteenth-Century Jewish Literature Reader* (with Jonathan M. Hess and Nadia Valman, 2013).

ELAINE SCARRY is Walter M. Cabot Professor of Aesthetics and General Theory of Value, and Harvard College Professor at Harvard University. She is the author, among many books, of *The Body in Pain: The Making and Unmaking of the World* (1985), *Dreaming by the Book* (1999; winner, Truman Capote Award for Literary Criticism), *On Beauty and Being Just* (1999), *Thinking in an Emergency* (2011), and *Thermonuclear Monarchy: Choosing between Democracy and Doom* (2014).

SUSAN RICCI STEBBINS is an independent scholar based in Brookline, Massachusetts. She is co-author of *Life as Art: Paintings by Gregory Gillespie and Frances Cohen Gillespie* (2003) and has contributed essays to *The Lure of Italy: American Artists and the Italian Experience, 1760–1914* (1992), *In Pursuit of Refinement: Charlestonians Abroad, 1740–1860* (1999), and *The Last Ruskinians: Charles Eliot Norton, Charles Herbert Moore, and Their Circle* (2007).

CAROLINE WEBER is Associate Professor of French at Barnard College. She is the author of *Queen of Fashion: What Marie Antoinette Wore to the Revolution* (2007) and *Terror and its Discontents: Suspect Words in*

Revolutionary France (2003), and has published widely on eighteenth-century French literature and culture and contemporary theory. Her forthcoming book, *Swan Song*, is a biography of the three principal models for Proust's duchesse de Guermantes.

KAZUYOSHI YOSHIKAWA is Professor Emeritus of French at Kyoto University and a member of the Équipe Proust at ITEM/ENS, Paris. He is the author of *Proust et l'art pictural* (2010) and editor of the *Index général de la correspondance de Marcel Proust* (1998). He has co-edited collections of essays including *Proust aux brouillons* (with Nathalie Mauriac Dyer, 2011), and *Comment naît une œuvre littéraire ?* (with Noriko Taguchi, 2011). He has published numerous articles on painting and the visual arts in Proust's fiction, and is currently producing a new Japanese translation of *À la recherche du temps perdu*.

Acknowledgements

The editors express their profound gratitude to the following people, for their invaluable assistance and support:

John D'Amico, Stefanie Goyette, Violeta Banica, Kathleen Coviello, Corydon Ireland, Jessica Martinez, Leslie Morris, David Pendleton, Susan Ricci Stebbins, Matthew Rodriguez, Dennis Sears, Theodore E. Stebbins, Jr., Christina Svendsen, Caroline Szylowicz, Jessica Tanner, Akili Tommasino, and Stephan Wolohojian.

We also thank the following conference sponsors:

Cultural Services, Consulate General of France in Boston; and at Harvard University: Bacon Fund and Potter Fund, Department of Romance Languages and Literatures; Center for European Studies; Department of Comparative Literature; Department of Music; Department of Philosophy; Department of Romance Languages and Literatures; Elson Family Arts Initiative; Mahindra Humanities Center; Office for the Arts; Presidential and Museum IT Fellows Program; Provostial Fund for the Arts and Humanities; and the Reischauer Institute for Japanese Studies.

Note on the text

The chapters by Antoine Compagnon, Sophie Duval, Françoise Leriche, Nathalie Mauriac Dyer, and Kazuyoshi Yoshikawa were translated from the French by Stefanie Goyette, with the assistance of John D'Amico.

This volume follows the citation system designed by Adam Watt, editor of *Marcel Proust in Context* (Cambridge University Press, 2013). All quotations from *À la recherche du temps perdu* are taken from the Modern Library edition of *In Search of Lost Time* in six volumes, translated by C. K. Scott Moncrieff (except for *Time Regained*, translated by Andreas Mayor and Terence Kilmartin), revised by Terence Kilmartin and D. J. Enright (New York: Modern Library, 2003). References are given in the form (1: 234), i.e. volume number, followed by page number.

These are followed by a reference to the Bibliothèque de la Pléiade edition of the novel in four volumes, produced by a team of scholars under the direction of Jean-Yves Tadié (Paris: Gallimard, 1987–1989). References to the French text are given in the form (IV, 321). Modifications to the Modern Library translation (by the author or translator of the chapter in question) are signaled with the abbreviation "trans. mod."

Unless otherwise stated, references to Proust's essays and other short writings are taken from *Against Sainte-Beuve and Other Essays*, translated by John Sturrock (Harmondsworth: Penguin, 1988) and *Contre Sainte-Beuve précédé de Pastiches et mélanges et suivi de Essais et articles*, edited by Pierre Clarac and Yves Sandre (Paris: Gallimard, 1971). These are incorporated in the text with the abbreviations *ASB* or *CSB*, each followed by page numbers. Where no reference to *ASB* is given, the passage in question is not included in Sturrock: translations from these passages are by the author of the chapter in question.

Quotations from Proust's early work *Les Plaisirs et les Jours* and his unfinished novel *Jean Santeuil* are taken from *Jean Santeuil précédé de Les Plaisirs et les Jours*, edited by Pierre Clarac and Yves Sandre (Paris:

Gallimard, 1971), and identified with the abbreviation *JS*. Translations from these works are by the author of the chapter in question.

Unpublished manuscripts by Proust are cited in French, followed by an English translation. Transcriptions of passages from unpublished manuscripts are by the author of the chapter in question. For manuscripts that have been the object of scholarly editions, only an English translation is given; a reference to the relevant French edition is provided in a note. All translations of manuscript material are by Stefanie Goyette and John D'Amico.

All references to Proust's correspondence are to the *Correspondance de Marcel Proust* (abbreviated to *Corr*, followed by volume number and page number), edited by Philip Kolb, in 21 volumes (Paris: Plon, 1970–1993), with the exception of letters added or updated in the anthology *Lettres*, edited by Françoise Leriche with Caroline Szylowicz (Paris: Plon, 2004). Unless otherwise stated, translations from the correspondence, and from all other works in French, are by the author of the chapter in question.

CHAPTER 1

Introduction

Christie McDonald and François Proulx

Most readers – and even many non-readers – know Marcel Proust's *À la recherche du temps perdu* as a vast social tapestry unfolding against the scintillating background of Belle Époque France; a reminiscence of the illusions of youth and the complex ties of family; and a deep investigation of the psychology of desire and loss, remembrance and forgetting. Those who have read all the way through the final volume, *Le Temps retrouvé*, know that Proust's novel is also a prolonged meditation on the significance of art in life, and the path to becoming an artist.

Proust's novel traces the aesthetic apprenticeship of its narrator-protagonist, a figure similar to, but also crucially different from Proust himself. From an impressionable boy who reads avidly, dreams of traveling to far-off places, and wants to become a writer but who is unsure he has the talent or willpower, the protagonist transforms himself into an increasingly lucid and mature observer of society and of his own heart; at the very end of the novel he resolves to write. Along the way, he encounters the work of a number of artistic models, many of them historically real and some of them fictional – the actress La Berma, the writer Bergotte, the painter Elstir, the composer Vinteuil. Overcoming an initial failure to understand their work or appreciate it for artistically valid reasons, he eventually learns vital aesthetic lessons from each of these creators, through a series of revelations that could be distilled to this aphorism from *Le Temps retrouvé*: "you can make anew what you love only by renouncing it" (6: 525, trans. mod.; IV, 620).

Summarized in this way, Proust's relationship to the arts seems evident: it is a question of models, of lessons, and of a kind of synthesis, perhaps even transcendence. *À la recherche du temps perdu* would then constitute a summation, an imaginary museum that houses a series of great works, especially from those arts considered the highest in the nineteenth-century canon, painting and music; a paper cathedral, where artworks serve as stations leading to the protagonist's artistic apotheosis, his sacrifice and resurrection through writing.[1] This shrewd maneuver positions literature as the highest art in the emergent twentieth century, and Proust as its greatest practitioner. Much valuable scholarship has built on this seductive narrative.

The chapters collected in *Proust and the Arts* aim to extend and challenge this received conception in two related ways, and unfold the complexity behind the apparently simple conjunction of its title.[2] First, they go beyond the classic question of the models used by Proust for his fictional artists, and break new ground in exploring how he learned from and integrated in highly personal ways the work of such creators as Wagner or Carpaccio. Second, they reveal the breadth of Proust's engagement with varied media from different eras, outside questions of canon and hierarchy: from "primitive" arts to sound recordings, from medieval sculpture to *Art Nouveau* glassmaking, from portrait photography to the private art of doodling.

In his introduction to the catalogue of a major exhibition on Proust and the arts in 1999, Jean-Pierre Angremy noted the "ceaseless expansion"[3] of the Proustian realm: the great rise of Proust's critical fortune since his death, but also the continual enrichment of our appreciation of his work, with new questions that emerge from each rereading and every new study.[4] This principle of expansion is inscribed in Proust's novel, and in fact structures it. At the very end of *Le Temps retrouvé*, the narrator – right after musing about how the literary endeavor he is about to begin might mirror "what is so often done by painters" – describes this work-to-come as an attempt "to transcribe a universe which had to be totally redrawn" (6: 527–528; IV, 622–623).[5] Proust designed his cosmically expansive novel, not as something vast and embalmed (as we might sometimes think of cathedrals or museums), but as the space of a living, ever-renewed process (as cathedrals and museums ideally are). His novel's structure is not closed but open, not didactic but pedagogical: the narrator does not end up writing *À la recherche du temps perdu*, and the reader is not given readymade answers. Instead both are perpetually set in motion, toward new endeavors and in search of ever-new insights.[6]

The inverse of this expansive quality, for Proust, is idolatry. Another word for artistic complacency, idolatry is what stops the process of *recherche*. Idolaters love art for the wrong reasons, viewing it as an embellishment to their world rather than an invitation to question how they see that world. Proust borrowed the notion from John Ruskin, but eventually came to see Ruskin himself as an idolater. This evolution informs the dynamics of apprenticeship and the development of relationships to art that reverberate through the novel. When does admiration for an artist or love of an artwork turn into repetition rather than creation? Swann the connoisseur idolizes art and turns it into a process of association to enhance love and life. The hero needs to learn to evade the habits to which Swann succumbs; he must overcome his artistic loves (the novels of Bergotte, for instance) in order to become a true creator. Yet observing Swann's errors is not enough for the hero to avoid them, and he must go through his own trials. Proust was exquisitely sensitive to the blind spots of his characters, constantly adjusting their perceptions of art and social life. Through his depictions of idolatry, readers are warned not to get too comfortable with what they think they know, lest they become caught in the web of habit and routine, unable to pursue the kinds of deeper truth Proust is seeking. The same, we would argue, applies to scholarship.

Proust seems almost to have set a trap for his critics, between the experiences of the hero and the retrospective critical analyses of the narrator – the two being separated by the evolving story. Many of us who love Proust's work, and have written about it, have joyfully indulged in sheer admiration and near repetition of the narrator's thought. How not to do so with such a great work? As readers, we identify with a doubting hero, and aspire to the narrator's voice of analytical confidence. But if we allow ourselves to think we are on the side of the narrator, for whom answers have already unfolded, then we are in fact like Swann, too much at ease with our knowledge, mistaking our love of Proust for a settled understanding of his art. We are pressing Proust to our heart like Swann presses to his the reproduction of a Botticelli, deluding himself that it gives him mastery over the unknowable Odette (1: 318; 1, 222). The interplay between the narrator and the hero is a reminder that what we know constantly changes with time and perspective. The chapters collected in this volume take up this challenge, opening new interpretative avenues.

* * *

This book originated in several iterations of a seminar course on Proust in the Department of Romance Languages and Literatures at Harvard University, culminating in a semester-long celebration of the centenary of *Du côté de chez Swann* in 2013. Starting in 2008/2009, independent scholar Susan Ricci Stebbins developed a superb museum guide that linked Proust's novel to a surprising number of works at the Harvard Art Museums.[7] For instance, a painting by Manet, now on the cover of this volume (Figure 1.1), evoked a passage from *À l'ombre des jeunes filles en fleurs*:

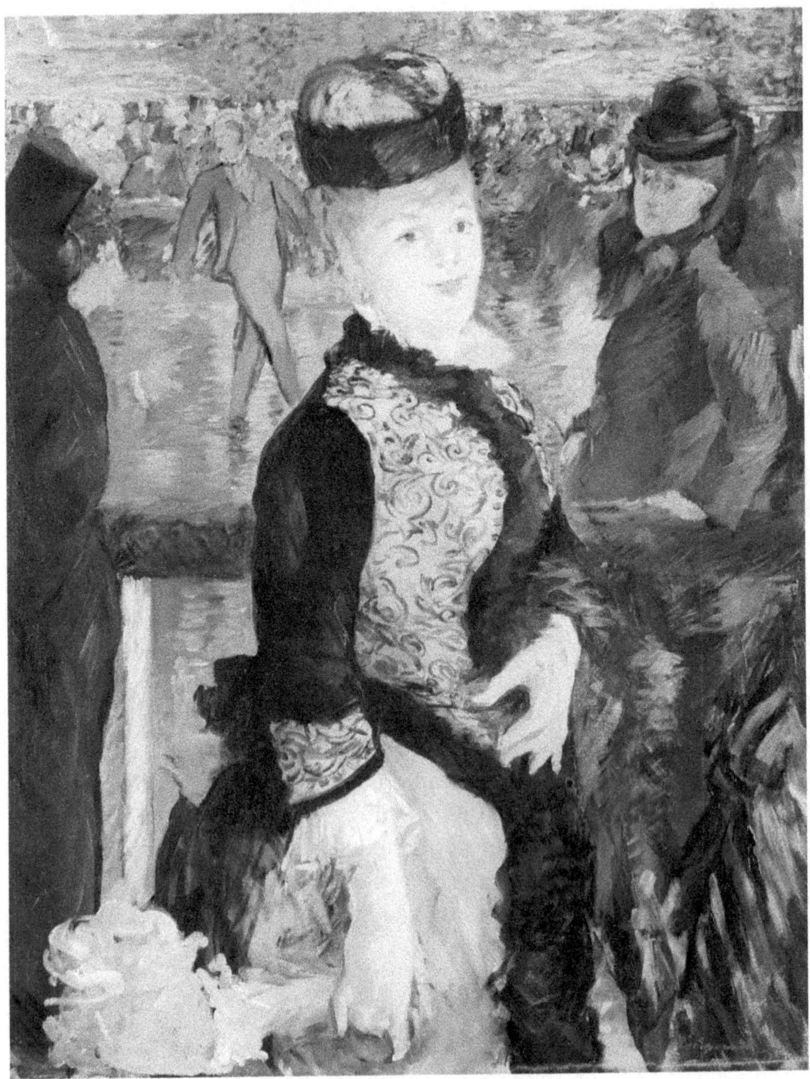

Figure 1.1 Manet, *Skating*, 1877

And this, Elstir's earliest manner, was the most devastating of birth certificates for Odette because it not only established her, as did her photographs of the same period, as the younger sister of various well-known courtesans, but made her portrait contemporary with the countless portraits that Manet or Whistler had painted of all those vanished models, models who already belonged to oblivion or to history. (2: 604; II, 218)

Although Proust may not have seen this particular work, for our students and for us, the passage and the painting came alive in an unexpected dialogue. Like Odette, the main figure in the painting is a woman of ambiguous social status (courtesan or respectably married bourgeoise?); the grey background plane is similarly open to interpretation (ice skating or roller skating?).[8] Proust saw Manet as one of "these great innovators who are the only true classics" (*CSB* 617), and a forerunner to a new generation of painters – including the fictional Elstir (3: 685; II, 790).[9] Taking students to the museum was a reminder that the relationship to art in Proust's novel goes much deeper than the representation of any given work. His invitation to readers, to explore and make connections between art and lived experience, can be taken up through different means: for Proust, this meant in person or in print;[10] for us, it can also mean online.

The conference "Proust and the Arts," on April 19 and 20, 2013, was the keystone of our celebration of *Du côté de chez Swann*. What promised to be a joyful occasion turned into a state lockdown of the entire region on April 19, during the pursuit of two men who had bombed the Boston Marathon a few days earlier. The curfew was lifted in time for a concert of music linked to Proust, eerily disturbed by police sirens.[11] The conference talks, compressed into a splendid but long event the next day, reminded everyone in attendance of how Proust's work heightens the sense of significant moments; he himself wrote – a mere three months before his death – that life would "suddenly appear delicious" if we were threatened with disaster.[12]

* * *

Proust and the Arts brings into conversation multiple strands of scholarship. In the past three decades, genetic criticism, with its meticulous studies of the immense corpus of Proust's drafts and revisions, has informed much scholarly work in France and Japan.[13] This volume makes available in English original studies by some of the leading practitioners of this critical approach, opening fascinating views into the novelist's creative process. Many of the book's contributors from North American institutions approach Proust through questions about cognition, identity, and social or art history, examining how the arts shape his relationship to the craft of writing. In Proustian fashion, these diverse research perspectives, seemingly as different as the Swann and Guermantes ways, often meet in unexpected places. Gathered here, they show how Proust's complex interactions with the arts can inspire readers today.

This collection highlights the renewed relevance of Proust's capacious attention to the arts in light of current debates, about the possibility of sustained attention in our increasingly digital era and around questions of reading in the future. It attests to the enduring richness of Proust's artistic achievement, and the ways his novel continues to speak to book and art-lovers of all kinds. We hope readers will take as much pleasure in this collection as we have in bringing it together.

NOTES

1 Jean-Yves Tadié neatly sums up this view in proposing that, "by his recomposition and integration of all the arts, Proust is [the] universal heir [of the] heritage of the West." Foreword to *Proust in Perspective: Visions and Revisions*, ed. Armine Kotin Mortimer and Katherine Kolb (Urbana and Chicago: University of Illinois Press, 2002), ix.

2 Important scholarly predecessors and interlocutors of this volume include the essay collections *Au seuil de la modernité: Proust, Literature and the Arts*, ed. Nigel Harkness and Marion Schmid (Oxford and New York: Peter Lang, 2011); *Proust and the Visual*, ed. Nathalie Aubert (Cardiff: University of Wales Press, 2012); *Marcel Proust et les arts décoratifs: poétique, matérialité, histoire*, ed. Boris Roman Gibhardt and Julie Ramos (Paris: INHA/Classiques Garnier, 2013); and *Marcel Proust in Context*, ed. Adam Watt (Cambridge University Press, 2013).

3 Jean-Pierre Angremy, "Exposer Proust," in *Marcel Proust, L'écriture et les arts*, ed. Jean-Yves Tadié with Florence Callu (Paris: Gallimard/Bibliothèque nationale de France/Réunion des musées nationaux, 1999), 9.

4 Working from a premise – "what did Proust know?" – that addresses classic questions of sources and biography, essays for that catalogue gesture toward this broadening in significant ways, including studies by two contributors to the present volume, Antoine Compagnon and Kazuyoshi Yoshikawa.

5 William C. Carter highlights the importance of this image: "Proust's *Recherche* is an open-ended novel built on the model of the universe . . . dynamic, freed from the effects of entropy, of winding down to a conclusion." *The Proustian Quest* (New York University Press, 1992), 228–229.

6 Maurice Blanchot was one of the first commentators to describe *À la recherche* as a "complete-incomplete work" ["une œuvre achevée-inachevée"] whose principal characteristic is the "movement" of writing "without end." *The Book to Come*, trans. Charlotte Mandell (Stanford University Press, 2003), 24; *Le livre à venir* (Paris: Gallimard, 1959), 36–37.

7 This guide became the basis for the digital exhibition *A Proustian Gallery: Selected Works form the Harvard Art Museums*. proust-arts.com/a-proustian-gallery.html

8 The English term used in the painting's original title, "Au Skating," evokes the novelty and fashionable status of roller-skating in Paris starting in the winter of 1875/1876. See John O'Brian, "Édouard Manet: *Skating*, 1877," in *Degas to Matisse: The Maurice Wertheim Collection* (New York: Harry

N. Abrams/Harvard University Art Museums, 1988), 66–69. O'Brian notes that Manet "calculated the impact of the . . . signifiers in this painting with considerable care" and deliberately chose "not [to] provid[e] the necessary visual information that might permit an unambiguous reading" of the background or the figure (68–69). In *Le Côté de Guermantes*, the narrator observes how Rachel finds herself, like Odette, caught between "double" identities: as she is about to board a train with her aristocratic lover Saint-Loup, "a pair of common little tarts" recognize her and exclaim, "Come on, we'll all go to the rink together" ["viens, on ira ensemble au skating"] (3: 213; II, 459).

9 Antoine Compagnon proposes that "Proust's place in literature is analogous to Manet's in painting: was he the last of the great classics or the first of the revolutionaries?" *Proust Between Two Centuries*, trans. Richard E. Goodwin (New York: Columbia University Press, 1992), 20–24. See also Yasué Kato, "Proust et Manet: à propos des 'Notes sur Manet' de Jacques-Émile Blanche," *Gallia: Bulletin de la Société de langue et littérature françaises de l'Université d'Osaka* 39 (1999), 1–8.

10 Allowing for an enhanced reading experience akin to a hypertext, a number of publications have provided marvelous guides to paintings cited by Proust, including Eric Karpeles's *Paintings in Proust: A Visual Companion to In Search of Lost Time* (London and New York: Thames & Hudson, 2008) and Yann Le Pichon's *Le Musée retrouvé de Marcel Proust* (Paris: Stock, 1990); for musical works related to Proust, the collective CD-book *Marcel Proust, une vie en musiques* (Paris: Archimbaud/Even & arts/Riveneuve, 2012) provides a similarly engaging introduction.

11 Sindhumathi Revuluri's program notes for the concert are available at proust-arts.com/program-notes.html. We thank her for organizing this event, and the musicians, Lewis Epstein, Monica Hershberger, Hannah Lewis, and Samuel Parler, for their solacing performances.

12 Response to an inquiry from the newspaper *L'Intransigeant* in August 1922 (*CSB* 645–646); cited by Corydon Ireland in "Confronting Evil, Embracing Life: Two Truncated Harvard Conferences Prove Surprisingly Relevant after a Cave-dark Week," *Harvard Gazette*, April 23, 2013, available at news.harvard.edu/gazette/story/2013/04/confronting-evil-embracing-life.

13 See for instance the illuminating essays collected in *Proust aux brouillons*, ed. Nathalie Mauriac Dyer and Kazuyoshi Yoshikawa (Turnhout: Brepols, 2011) and *Proust face à l'héritage du XIXe siècle: tradition et métamorphose*, ed. Nathalie Mauriac Dyer, Kazuyoshi Yoshikawa and Pierre-Edmond Robert (Paris: Presses Sorbonne nouvelle, 2012).

PART I

Art's way

CHAPTER 2

Primitives and primitive arts in the Recherche

Nathalie Mauriac Dyer

It is generally understood that for Proust the term "Primitives" would have referred to those European artists, precursors of the Renaissance, that art historians of his era had recently "rediscovered." Proust had become familiar with these Primitives during his Ruskinian period, through a number of exhibitions in France and abroad.[1] The traces left by these experiences in his correspondence[2] and in his work remain relatively subtle, with the exception of Giotto in the Venice episode. Following these traces would keep us within the habitual limits that bound the study of representations of plastic arts in *À la recherche du temps perdu*. I propose to take a different path.

Proust believes in the persistence of the past in the present ("The past is not fugitive, it stays put" [3: 752; II, 711]) but not in the progress of the arts: "art is no more advanced now than in Homer's day" (3: 446; II, 624). For him, as a result, the creative effort is always primary: it cannot rely on the formula of a predecessor. And if we understand by "primitivism" the preference given, in the context of artistic practices, to a return to "original" or primary sensation, prior to any intellectual correction, then there undoubtedly exists another "primitivist" Proust. In *Le Côté de Guermantes II*, the narrator is enchanted to find in the painter Elstir's canvases "a sincere return to the very root of the impression": Elstir "sought to wrest from what he had just felt what he already knew" (3: 574; II, 712–713). This approach goes back to Turner, cited in Proust's preface to his translation of Ruskin's *The Bible of Amiens* in 1904: "my business is to draw what I see, and not what I know" (*ASB* 175; *CSB* 121).[3] Transposed into a literary context, this aesthetic of a rerooting in the perceptive[4] is also found, according to the narrator, in authors like Madame de Sévigné or Dostoyevsky. The latter, "instead of presenting things in their logical sequence, that is to say beginning with the cause, shows us first of all the effect, the illusion that strikes us" (5, 510; III, 880). It is precisely this aesthetic that Proust claims for his own work: in January 1914 he explains to Jacques

Rivière that he did not seek to "analyze in an abstract fashion" but rather to "recreate" the "evolution of his thought" (*Corr* XIII, 99–100). If in *La Prisonnière* the narrator places Dostoyevsky among the ranks of the "primitives" (5: 510–512; III, 880–882), we must situate Proust there as well – with the understanding that this primitivism, even if it arises from a critique of the intellect, is a province that intellect concedes to sensation. But this type of "Dostoyevskian" primitivism will not be my object here, nor will the primitivism that posits any creator, "no more advanced than Homer," as a sort of absolute origin.

In the era when the *Recherche* was conceived and written, the terms "primitives" and "primitivism" suggested other meanings as well. "Primitives" could also designate those populations that the colonizing forces of the West understood, or found convenient to understand, as being arrested at earlier stages of cultural and anthropological development. The West likewise conceived of its own pre-historical development as a different incarnation of these populations. In contrast, Primitivist artistic approaches recognized the value of artistic artifacts created by so-called primitives, and found in them a reservoir of forms and inspiration – from Gauguin to the Fauves and the Cubists, with Picasso at the helm.[5] Was Proust aware of these debates? Are they reflected in his novel? Are those "primitives," a priori far removed from his aesthetic taste and from the punctilious and worldly societies he depicts, represented in *À la recherche du temps perdu*, and, if so, how? In what follows, my first foray into these questions, we will discover, even in an all too summary fashion, a less familiar side of Proust.

Du côté de chez Swann appeared in 1913, the same year in which *The Rite of Spring* unleashed its organic rhythms and "pagan" dances at the Théâtre des Champs-Élysées, and in which Apollinaire published *Alcools*. It is difficult to picture in Proust's bedroom the "fetishes from Oceania and Guinea"[6] evoked in the poet's chambers at the end of "Zone," or to imagine that he could have frequented the Musée d'Ethnographie du Trocadéro as assiduously as Picasso who, in the process of creating the *Demoiselles d'Avignon*, experienced a kind of epiphany looking at African masks.[7] But Proust was well aware of the presence of colonial artifacts in French society of the Third Republic, and of the newfound aesthetic attention of which they were the object. Several passages in the *Recherche* attest to it. The hero's mother humorously compares the petty social conquests of Madame Swann to "trophies" brought back from a "colonial war" ("I saw Mme Swann in all her war-paint; she must have been embarking on some triumphant offensive against the Massachutoes, or the Singhalese, or the Tromberts"; "Now that the Tromberts have been subdued, the neighboring tribes will soon surrender" [2: 120; I, 506]). Odette, when she was still a *cocotte*, collected "in the Rue La Pérouse" – and here the name of the famous navigator was perhaps not given by accident – "her animals carved in precious stones, her fetishes" (2: 261, trans. mod.; I, 604). Further, the narrator writes that certain "society people" liken the *Ballets russes*, with horror, to "Negro art" (5: 314–315; III, 741–742); this passage from *La Prisonnière* was added during the War,[8] perhaps after Proust discovered the expression *art nègre*, launched by Apollinaire in a note for the *Mercure de France* in April 1917.[9] These few occurrences, precisely because of their rarity, suggest that the question of a possible Proustian "primitivism" should not be approached through the "classic" means of artifacts.

Instead, a detour through representations of the supposed "primitives" in the *Recherche* will allow us to discover the development of a critique – albeit incomplete – of colonialism and ethnocentrism. In *À l'ombre des jeunes filles en fleurs*, we find an anecdote concerning Madame Blatin and a certain Singhalese "exhibited" at the *Jardin d'Acclimatation*: "Well, to continue, she went up to one of these black fellows with 'Good morning, blackie!' . . . this classification seems to have displeased the black. 'Me blackie,' he said angrily to Mme Blatin, 'but you, harpy!'" (2: 148, trans. mod.; I, 526). The anecdote is attested in a 1915 letter, where it concerns a Senegalese man (*Corr* XIV, 45); it shows that Proust is perfectly aware of the intellectual sophistication of the so-called "inferiors."

Elsewhere, he transposes this racial contempt into social contempt: a "royal" (the Princess of Luxembourg, often followed by a "little negro page, dressed in red satin") treats two bourgeois – namely the hero and his grandmother – as she would animals in a zoo: they are "loveable beasts," "duck[s]," or "antelope[s]," who "by a miraculous stride in evolution" have somehow attained a level "not quite so low in the scale of creation," which is to say, the level of young children (2: 379–380; II, 59–60). In a similar fashion, M. de Bréauté, quite surprised to encounter the hero at a Guermantes dinner party, considers him

> as if he had found himself face to face with one of the "natives" of an undiscovered country on which his raft had landed, from whom, in the hope of ultimate profit, he would endeavor, observing with interest the while their quant customs and without interrupting his demonstrations of friendship or forgetting to utter loud cries of benevolence like them, to obtain ostrich eggs and spices in exchange for glass beads. (3: 590; II, 724)

Yet the no less aristocratic Prince of Agrigente is soon, in turn, reduced to a state of inferiority by the hero, who goes as far as to call him a "vulgar drone" (3: 582; II, 725); likewise the Princess of Parma, who uses the same turns of phrase as the Princess of Luxembourg, finds herself "classified" by the narrator-zoologist: "from the language . . . I could discern the nature of the beast. She was a royal personage" (3: 582; II, 718). In this system, the "dominated" effectively turn back such de- or sub-humanizing gestures on the "dominators," provoking a reversal of positions, and thus an equalization. The discourse of the novel also humorously casts doubt on the existence of cultural difference between human populations, and therefore on the possibility of encountering genuine alterity. Any ethnographer exposes himself to deception and disillusion, like the hero who is finally introduced to the Guermantes circle and who believes himself able, in turn, to treat them as "natives":

> After having scaled the inaccessible heights of the name Guermantes, on descending the inner slope of the life of the Duchess, I felt . . . the same astonishment that an explorer, after having taken into account, in order to visualize the singularity of the native customs in some wild valley of Central America or Northern Africa, its geographical remoteness, the strangeness of its place-names and its flora, feels on discovering, once he has made his way through a screen of giant aloes or manchineels, inhabitants who (sometimes indeed among the ruins of a Roman theatre and beneath a column dedicated to Venus) are engaged in reading Voltaire's *Mérope* or *Alzire*. (3: 720; II, 815)

The "savage" reads Voltaire. Cultural competence, taste, refinement – these are not functions of geography, nor even of history, since, according to Proust, the same optical illusion distorts our relationship to the past: "it is as though we imagined [Homer and Hannibal] to be as remote from ourselves as an animal seen in the zoo" (3: 571; II, 710). We find ourselves adopting, with regards to figures of the remote past, the same unjustifiable perspective as the Princess of Luxembourg who, incapable of acknowledging her natural equality with so-called "inferior" races or classes, transforms them into animals. The choice of "great" figures like Homer or Hannibal comically underscores the error of her approach.

Yet this gradual refamiliarization of a world where there would exist no "inferior" or "primitive" populations appears to come up against clusters of irreducible foreignness. In the *Recherche*, two social groups are repeatedly compared to "primitives," and the term in these cases is used to connote a kind of savagery. First, the inverts: in *Sodome et Gomorrhe II* we witness an amusing mixup between Charlus and Cottard, as the baron takes the doctor's hand and – is he not, after all, a "royal" like the Princess of Luxembourg? – "caressed it for a moment with the kindly affection of a master stroking his horse's nose and giving it a lump of sugar," while the doctor, who "imagined that this stroking of his hand was the immediate prelude to an act of rape . . . rolled his eyes in terror, as though he had fallen into the hands of a savage who, for all he knew, fed upon human flesh" (4: 642; III, 458–459). The originality of this passage, in relation to others cited above, is less in the mirroring of deprecating points of view that identify the "other" with an animal or a savage, than in their simultaneity, since each character, occupied as he is with treating his neighbor as an inferior, is blind to the judgment of which he is himself the object at the same moment. It is all the more troubling to note that the narrator occupies in turn the position of Cottard: he diagnoses in Morel a "blind and primitive savagery" (4: 420; III, 303), and while about to witness the "conjunction" of Charlus and Jupien, he compares himself to a voyager shipwrecked on an island where the inhabitants "might turn out to be cannibals" (4: 9–11; III, 10). Further still, he proposes that "to form a picture of" the inverts, "we ought to think if not of the wild animals that never become domesticated, of the lion-cubs, allegedly tamed, which are still lions at heart, then at least of the negroes whom the comfortable existence of the white man drives to despair and who prefers the risks of life in the wild and its incomprehensible joys" (4: 33; III, 26). The palpable sympathy of the narrator for black people might allow us to understand, by transitivity, that which he feels for inverts; still, in order to find the means to depict their incomprehensible mores, the narrative voice resorts first to the discourse of animalization,[10] then to that of race,[11] both of which connote a fundamental sense of foreignness.

A second social group finds itself, somewhat more unexpectedly, compared with "primitive men" and "savage tribes": the servants.[12] Let us begin with Françoise:

> Françoise disbelieved me, for, like those primitive men whose senses were so much keener than our own, she could immediately detect, from signs imperceptible to the rest of us, the truth or falsehood of anything that we might wish to conceal from her. (1: 38; I, 29)
>
> She had a power, the nature of which I have never been able to fathom, for at once becoming aware of anything unpleasant that might happen to my parents and myself. Perhaps it was not a supernatural power, but could have been explained by sources of information that were peculiar to herself: as it may happen that the news which often reaches a savage tribe several days before the post has brought it to the European colony has really been transmitted to them not by telepathy but from hill-top to hill-top by beacon fires. (3: 77; II, 363)

Some readers may be troubled by the dichotomy between the *us* of the familial clan and the *she* of the servant, an opposition grounded (in the first example) in a "natural" difference between modern man and a supposed prehistoric man, and (in the second) in a "cultural" difference between the colonizing European and the colonized "savage." Here again, this double opposition (which covers the two types, historical and geographical, of so-called "primitive" populations) is not reversible, contrary to that which marks the encounter between aristocrats and bourgeois, or between "natives" and Europeans: here, no equalization is possible, places cannot be exchanged. Paradoxically, the dissymmetry is not founded on reciprocal contempt, but rests rather on the recognition of a form of *superiority* in the other race: the mysterious superiority of the "primitive" over the "civilized," a reversal carrying a seemingly fraught sense of fear.

To support this hypothesis, let us examine, as it appears in a 1921 notebook, *Cahier* 60, the following unpublished passage, which was written to complete the text of *Sodome et Gomorrhe II.* It offers a lengthy portrait of the Guermantes's servants:

> Enfin j'arrivai à l'Hôtel de Guermantes. Les entrées ~~les portes, les couloirs~~ en étaient occupées par une race <primitive> plus ancienne par conséquent plus noble que les Guermantes <eux-mêmes> et leurs invités, <par> les ~~divinités immobiles~~ <~~et silencieuses~~> immobiles divinités du foyer, les majestueux, les mystérieux domestiques.... Des valets de pied du prince, d'une époque plus récente passaient silencieusement dans les portes, sans vous frôler. De plus anciens se tenaient perchés, l'oeil perçant, sans remuer. Tous appartenaient à un peuple qui est aussi peu connu que les Étrusques. De sublimes rafales traversent sa mentalité obscure (incapable des réflexions étendues, appliquée à des arts restreints, à des divinations occultes). Ses superstitions rendent <sa charité> plus belle encore, quand on pense au mépris profond . . . qu'a pour son maître le valet de chambre qui si ce maître tombe malade le veillera <nuit et jour> avec plus de dévouement qu'un ami, qu'un frère . . . Rangés devant l'entrée les soirs de réception, c'étaient presque tous d'énormes valets de pied vieillissants que des excès <– antérieurs[–]> de champagne avaient conduit à la nécessité de l'eau de Contrexéville, et qui avec leur stature monumentale, leur épiderme de poterie préhistorique ou mexicaine faisaient entre les arcades de l'hôtel le plus impressionnant ensemble sculptural qui se puisse voir.[13]

> Finally, I arrived at the Hôtel de Guermantes. The entryways ~~the doors, the hallways~~ were occupied by a <primitive> race more ancient and thus more noble than the Guermantes <themselves> and their guests, <by> the ~~immobile~~ <~~and silent~~> ~~divinities~~ immobile divinities of the foyer, the majestic, the mysterious servants.... The prince's footmen, from a more recent era, passed silently through the doors without even brushing against you. More ancient ones stood perched above, with piercing eyes, without moving. All belonged to a people as little known as the

> Etruscans. Sublime bursts traverse their obscure mentality (incapable of sustained reflections, applied only to limited crafts, and to occult divinations). Their superstitions render <their charity> even more admirable, if one thinks of the profound contempt . . . the manservant has for his master, that same servant who, if his master falls ill, will watch over him <day and night> with more devotion than a friend, than a brother . . . Arranged before the entryway on party evenings, almost all were enormous, aging footmen whom < – earlier [–] > excesses of champagne had led to require mineral water, and who, with their monumental stature, their epidermis of prehistoric or Mexican pottery, created between the arcades of the hotel the most impressive sculptural ensemble to be seen anywhere.

The servants' primitiveness is ambivalent. On the one hand, its extreme character is the basis of a certain ontological superiority: their nature is, paradoxically, aristocratic, even divine. But this extreme primitiveness also relates the servants to pre-humanity, and not only because their "obscure mentality" (a sort of "primitive mentality" *avant la lettre*, this term being coined later in ethnological discourse)[14] implies an intrinsic limitation: perched, immobile, with their "piercing eyes," the "oldest" evoke mysterious birds of prey – one could almost imagine their totemic origin, like that given to the Guermantes clan, born from the "the mythological impregnation of a nymph by a divine Bird" (3: 602; II, 732). The subservient immobility of the footmen, with their "monumental stature," motivates the final comparison with a "sculptural ensemble," an image not without precedent: the passage (which was likely meant to be added to the arrival of the hero at the Princesse de Guermantes's soirée, at the beginning of *Sodome et Gomorrhe II*) echoes the "decorative presence" and "marmorean immobility" of the colossal servants at Madame de Saint-Euverte's in "Un amour de Swann" (1: 461; I, 318–319). But while the vehicles of comparison there belong to a familiar cultural zone (paintings by Mantegna, antique statues), here Proust uses a vehicle that is entirely exotic and which likely constitutes, moreover, a unique instance in his arsenal of artistic references ("with their epidermis of prehistoric or Mexican pottery").

According to contemporary guidebooks, a collection of "terracotta statuettes and masks" representing various major gods in the primitive Mexican pantheon were on display at the Musée d'Ethnographie.[15] This museum occupied one wing of the Palais du Trocadéro: the next wing was dedicated to the Musée de Sculpture comparée, which Proust appears to have frequented.[16] We cannot exclude the possibility of a visit, motivated by curiosity, to the adjoining museum. The reference to Mesoamerican pottery, in any case, did not make it into the definitive version of the text.

Proust rewrites the passage in the same *Cahier* 60. He places it in a different context, that of the Grand-Hôtel de Balbec, the director "having engaged a staff belonging in part to that same ancient race that served at the Hôtel de Guermantes." Here the place of the master is held by Bloch's uncle Nissim Bernard, an extremely rich invert:

> Seul il croyait l'être dans sa chambre, mais il voyait se détacher du fond un chef d'étage, monumental étrusque tout à ses ordres, prêt à appeler s'il le désirait la troupe de jeunes figurants célébrant Esther devant la salle à manger, prêt à s'offrir lui-même si le mélancolique israélite préférait une beauté plus solide et mûrie, aux tons cuivrés de poterie . . . Mais M. Nissim Bernard ne se souciait ni d'Aimé, ni des autres individus à la race étrusque, non qu'ils ne lui eussent plu par eux-mêmes. Mais les chambres étaient éclairées.[17]
>
> He believed himself to be alone in his room, but he saw a *chef d'étage* emerge from the background, a monumental Etruscan ready for his orders, prepared to call if he desired the troupe of young actors celebrating *Esther* in the dining room, ready to offer even himself if the melancholic Israelite preferred a riper, more solid beauty, with the coppery tones of pottery . . . But M. Nissim Bernard took no notice of Aimé, nor of the other members of the Etruscan race, not that they, themselves, wouldn't have pleased him. But the chambers were all lit up.

In this passage, we find inverts and servants, the two groups of irreducible strangeness – unsurprisingly, perhaps – mixing together and understanding each other, neighboring "races" of "savages" and of "primitives." In the published version of the novel, Proust combines the two passages from *Cahier* 60 in a condensed form:

> Like all the *chefs d'étage* of the Balbec hotel, like several of the Prince de Guermantes's footmen, Aimé belonged to a race more ancient than that of the Prince, and therefore more noble. When one asked for a private room, one thought at first that one was alone. But presently, in the pantry, one caught sight of a sculptural waiter, of that ruddy Etruscan kind of which Aimé was the epitome, slightly aged by excessive consumption of champagne and seeing the inevitable hour for mineral water approach. Not all the guests asked them merely to wait upon them. (4: 529; III, 379)

The "ruddy Etruscan kind" typified by the *chef d'étage* Aimé condenses antiquity and exoticism, since "ruddy" evokes the color of Mesoamerican pottery, through the "coppery tones" mentioned in the preceding passage.

Despite the work of condensation over the course of these rewritings, the definitive version preserves what I would argue is the key aspect of the original passage: the servant, that most familiar and well-known figure – in a word, the *domestic* – paradoxically contains a superlative strangeness. (Does not the word "Etruscan" connote, by way of opposition to Rome, its close neighbor, both a sort of anterior antiquity and an "interior" foreignness?) It is tempting to relate this presence of the most foreign at the heart of the most familiar to a Freudian category (a concept being elaborated during the same period, it is worth noting): the *Unheimlich* (1919),[18] in English, the *uncanny*. The figure of the servant would then be, in a certain sense, the Proustian figuration of the uncanny, allegorized through either the prehistoric or the exotic primitive. To put it differently, if Proust did not decorate his room, like Apollinaire, with "fetishes from Oceania and Guinea," it is because he did not need them: he knew that the "primitive" is already there, at home, without the necessity of resorting to the mediation of artistic artifacts in order to approach it. Lodged in the closest of proximities under the guise of the social figure of the servant (and of the invert), that irreducible strangeness is shown to already inhabit the self.

In order to accede to the power of the imaginary contained within this intimate "primitive" dimension, the Proustian world bypasses a detour through the fetish, and contents itself with the transformation – the metaphor – produced by the gaze. Consequently, the transmutation of the "servants" into statues (or into animals: immobile birds of prey in this example, "greyhounds" in "Un amour de Swann") stems less from a process of aestheticization (or idolatrous perversion, as it is too often claimed) than from an apotropaic gesture, an attempt at imaginary conjuration and domination. Art regains its magic function. Let us reexamine the end of the grandmother's agony:

> My grandmother too tried to lift up her face to Mamma's. It was so altered that probably, had she been strong enough to go out, she would have been recognised only by the feather in her hat. Her features, as though during a modeling session, seemed to be straining, with an effort which distracted her from everything else, to conform to some particular model which we failed to identify. The work of the sculptor was nearing its end, and if my grandmother's face had shrunk in the process, it had at the same time hardened. The veins that traversed it seemed those not of marble, but of some more rugged stone. Permanently thrust forward by the difficulty that she found in breathing, and as permanently withdrawn into itself by exhaustion, her face, worn, diminished, terrifyingly expressive, seemed – as in a primitive, almost prehistoric sculpture – like the rude, purplish, russet, desperate face of some savage guardian of a tomb. (3: 440–441, trans. mod.; II, 620)

The grandmother's terrifying metamorphosis into a "primitive sculpture" (and this metamorphosis is a late addition, like the passage from *Cahier* 60, which appeared in 1921 in the successive galleys and proofs of *Le Côté de Guermantes II*) thwarts any inclination towards an aestheticizing or idolatrous reading, in the Ruskinian sense; instead it lays the groundwork for the mineral descriptions of the "fierce and rudimentary old deities"[19] of the *bal de têtes*.

The narrator, necessarily, is "one of them," to use a favorite expression of his (5: 280; III, 720): he is subject to these same Primitivist paradigms. This would explain why Françoise herself – who is compared, as we have seen, to "primitive men" and to a member of some "savage tribe" – ultimately assists him in his work of creation. Let us also note that the author of the work in question, like so many primitive works, remains anonymous. From the opening of the novel, in a passage added in 1913 to the galleys of *Du côté de chez Swann*, the narrator, disoriented by his nocturnal awakenings, presents himself as inferior and anterior to even a prehistoric humanity:

> when I awoke in the middle of the night, not knowing where I was, I could not even be sure at first who I was; I had only the most rudimentary sense of existence, such as may lurk and flicker in the depths of an animal's consciousness; I was more destitute than the cave-dweller . . . (1: 4; I, 5)

At the end of the novel, meanwhile, a third image for the writer's work is introduced, much less frequently examined than the two famous metaphors of the gown and the cathedral:

> Whether it would be a church where little by little a group of faithful would succeed in apprehending verities and discovering harmonies or perhaps even a grand general plan, or whether it would remain, like a druidic monument on a rocky isle, something for ever unfrequented, I could not tell. (6: 520; IV, 618)

Between the occurrences of the "cave-dwellers" and of the "druidic monument" at the two extremes of the novel, we may draw up a catalog of the protagonist's "Primitivist" (but not necessarily exotic) practices: belief (from a "Celtic" perspective) in metempsychosis, reincarnation, the transmigration of souls, and animism; a stationary voyage through space and time; the imaginary transformation into an animal (shamanism); significant attention to dreams; the "return" of the dead; experimentation with drugs; visions, hallucinations, ecstasies; initiation rites; the dance of "masks" . . . It seems to me that these practices form a paradigm that invites another kind of reading of the *Recherche*, sure to defamiliarize a work we think we know. "The arts" in Proust's novel would no longer be limited to the fine arts of the modern western tradition (even if expanded to include the so-called decorative arts, dance, or photography), but also comprise techniques or practices of life and of the decoding of the world, forms of experience, modes of tribal inclusion, means of communing with the sacred... Picasso recalled that he came to understand, while gazing upon African masks, how the plastic practice of their makers and his own were both a kind of exorcism, a cathartic response to what he felt to be the general hostility of "everything."[20] At the risk of appearing provocative, I would claim that Proust, in his artistic practice as a writer, grappled with comparable forces, which are not only represented in his novel thematically, as I have tried to suggest all too rapidly above, but also brought into play in his very writing. This may also be why his book touches us at the most profound levels of our own human experience.

NOTES

1 For the exhibition of the Flemish Primitives in Bruges in 1902, see Kazuyoshi Yoshikawa, "Proust aux expositions," in *Proust et les moyens de la connaissance*, ed. Annick Bouillaguet (Presses Universitaires de Strasbourg, 2009), 214–215. For the rival exhibition of French Primitives that took place at the Louvre two years later, see Antoine Compagnon, "Proust au musée," in *Marcel Proust, l'écriture et les arts*, ed. Jean-Yves Tadié (Paris: Gallimard/Bibliothèque nationale de France/Réunion des musées nationaux, 1999), 73.

2 In 1906, for example, Proust dreamed of acquiring several canvases by Italian Primitives. See *Corr* VI, 337.

3 John Ruskin, *The Eagle's Nest* [1872], in *The Works of John Ruskin*, 39 vols., Library Edition, ed. E. T. Cook and A. Wedderburn (London: George Allen, 1903–1912), XXII (1906), 210.

4 In *Le Côté de Guermantes I* (3: 92–96; II, 374–377) the narrator describes the distortions that modify perception in an individual afflicted with varying degrees of deafness. Philippe Soupault and André Breton (the latter would, a few years later, advocate a Surrealist "integral Primitivism") recognized their own aesthetic in the passage, and sought to have it pre-published in *Littérature*, a Dadaist magazine.

5 From the extensive available bibliography, I would mention the classic *"Primitivism" in 20th Century Art: Affinity of the Tribal and the Modern*, ed. William Rubin (New York: Museum of Modern Art, 1984).

6 Guillaume Apollinaire, "Zone," trans. Roger Shattuck, *The Yale Anthology of Twentieth-Century French Poetry*, ed. Mary Ann Caws (New Haven, CT: Yale University Press, 2004), 14.

7 See André Malraux, *Picasso's Mask* [*La Tête d'obsidienne*, 1974], trans. June Guicharnaud (New York: Holt, Rinehart & Winston, 1976), 10–11.

8 *Cahier* X (NAF 16717), *paperole* at fo. 1.

9 *Mercure de France* 451, April 1, 1917, 559–561.

10 Albertine, a captive invert, is often compared to an animal, domesticated or tamed, whose escape will show that it had remained wild.

11 Yuji Murakami has shown how the narrator, gripped by his jealousy concerning Albertine, uses anti-Semitic and anti-Dreyfusard discourse ("Gomorrhe 1913–1915: survivance de l'affaire Dreyfus dans le Cahier 54," *Genesis* 36 (2013), 79–88).

12 See also Edward J. Hughes, "The Primitivism of Françoise," in *Marcel Proust: A Study in the Quality of Awareness* (Cambridge University Press, 1983), 69–74.

13 The < > enclose additions. *Cahier* 60 (NAF 16700), fos. 90–93 rectos.

14 The ethnologist Lucien Lévy-Bruhl would retitle as *La Mentalité primitive*, in 1922, what in 1910 he had called *Les Fonctions mentales dans les sociétés inférieures*.

15 See Nélia Dias, *Le Musée d'Ethnographie du Trocadéro, 1878–1908: anthropologie et muséologie en France* (Paris: Éditions du CNRS, 1991), 178. The American gallery was quite important, housing more than 1,000 artifacts, primarily of Mexican and Peruvian origin.

16 See *À l'ombre des jeunes filles en fleurs* (2: 322; II, 20). This museum is also evoked in the preface to *La Bible d'Amiens*: "you will find casts of these bas-reliefs at the musée du Trocadéro" (*CSB* 88, 99).

17 *Cahier* 60 (the citation is from pages torn out between folio 93 and folio 94, which are found in the *reliquat* NAF 27350, fo. 129r).

18 Sigmund Freud, "Das Unheimliche," *Imago* 5 (1919).

19 Letter to Reynaldo Hahn, [11 April 1907,] *Corr* VII, 139.

20 See Malraux, *Picasso's Mask*, 10–11.

CHAPTER 3

"Some dear or sad fantasy": Faith, Idolatry, Infidelity

Sophie Duval

In 1900, following the death of Ruskin, Proust published two articles, "Ruskin à Notre-Dame d'Amiens"[1] and "John Ruskin."[2] Augmented with a foreword and a post-scriptum, they would become the preface to his 1904 translation of *The Bible of Amiens*. In the final lines of "John Ruskin," Proust applies to Ruskin what Ruskin had written of Turner: "through those eyes, now filled with dust, generations yet unborn will learn to behold the light of nature" (*ASB* 182; *CSB* 129).[3] Proust's article reproduces, at the end of the text, Ruskin's drawing of a famous figurine from the portal of the Booksellers in Rouen cathedral, which Ruskin had offered as an allegory of the "vitality"[4] of medieval art (*ASB* 178; *CSB* 124). Adding a further layer of allegory, Proust converts the figure to an allegory of Ruskin himself, dead but his eye wide open, a symbol of the vitality of his vision.

Proustian idolatry

Yet in the post-scriptum of his preface to *La Bible d'Amiens*, Proust questions the lucidity of this vision, borrowing Ruskin's own concept of idolatry and turning it against him. Ruskin defines idolatry as "the serving with the best of our hearts and minds, some dear or sad fantasy which we have made for ourselves"[5] – in Proust's translation, "quelque chère ou triste image que nous nous sommes créée" (*ASB* 183; *CSB* 129). In a footnote, Proust explains that this statement applies better to idolatry as he himself understands it than to its original context in Ruskin: he imbues the concept with added relevance by distorting it with a touch of infidelity.

For Proust, idolatry is a voluntary moral blindness, the ruse of a conscience fooling itself, an insidious interior power that does battle, in a ceaseless psychomachia, with the capital Virtue of "intellectual sincerity" (*ASB* 183; *CSB* 129). The idolater confects pleasant fantasies for himself: he cherishes a wheedling image, a specious idea, a disingenuous discourse, all for the sake of the beauty he finds and the pleasure he takes in them, while persuading himself of their truth.[6] Such self-delusion aims for narcissistic enjoyment, for a self-valorization that is manifested in poses, in affectations, in scenes played out on the great stage of the world and within the idolater himself.

In this very manner, Ruskin twists his reasoning, adopts flashy metaphors, and solemnizes his arguments with endless citations of the Bible. He convinces himself that Christian art is superior to all others, because his faith has made him fetishize it. The very term "idolatry" is idolatrous in his work: it is drawn from the religious language he adores in the letter, and its definition is inevitably accompanied by scriptural citations.[7] According to Proust, Ruskin "was obliged to lie to himself concerning the nature of the reasons which had led him to adopt" doctrines which he professed, not because they were relevant, but because he found them pleasing (*ASB* 184; *CSB* 130).

In the religious sense, idolatry consists in adoring the representation of a deity, often a statue, as if it were the deity itself. Theologians have thus always insisted on the symbolic nature of religious representations. For Proust, the dilettante who idolizes art strips the work of art "of the spirit that is in it," leaving only "a sign deprived of its meaning, that is to say, nothing" (*ASB* 189; *CSB* 136): he reduces art to a dead letter, so that he may transpose it into reality in order to aestheticize his own life. But idolatry, "an infirmity essential to the human mind" (*ASB* 187; *CSB* 134) is above all prejudicial to the artist. Idolatry does not preclude creation: instead it inspires works that ring false, that are more or less counterfeit. It engenders brilliant failures.

In uncovering Ruskin's idolatry, it was his own idolatry that Proust recognized in the Ruskinian mirror. Subsequently, he made idolatry the key to his ethical conception of art, and endeavored to rid himself of that vice. In the *Recherche*, he represented idolatry by attributing its diverse manifestations to characters who succumbed to it, notably Legrandin, Charlus, and Swann, and to a hero who must eventually overcome it in order to become a true artist.

Legrandin illustrates above all the idolatry of the snob. The snob does not want to know he is a snob: "Never had Legrandin's snobbishness prompted him to make a habit of visiting a duchess as such. Instead, it would encourage his imagination to make that duchess appear, in his eyes, endowed with all the graces." His social idolatry is allegorized in the metaphorical arrow that pierces the eye of this "St Sebastian of snobbery" (I: 180; I, 127). Charlus practices the idolatry of the dilettante, though he principally incarnates the figure of the homosexual idolater. Charlus prefers to ignore his attraction to handsome young men, and his erotic idolatry is allegorized by the near blindness that afflicts him towards the end of his life. Swann is the archetype of the idolater. He cultivates idolatry in love, deluding himself about Odette; in art, transposing the canvases of masters onto the faces of his acquaintances; in love and art at once, recasting Odette in the image of a Botticelli in order to be able to adore her; and in relation to his Judaism, becoming "quite comically blind" (3: 798; II, 870) during the Dreyfus Affair. His polymorphous idolatry is allegorized in a gesture: confronted with what he prefers to misrecognize, he removes his *lorgnon* (his spectacles) and "dr[aws] his hand across his eyes," in order "to extinguish every particle of light in his brain" (1: 380; I, 264).[8] Swann veils his own face.

Proust symbolizes idolatry through representations of self-deception, literally signified in Swann's tic: the gesture of covering his eyes becomes an allegory of Idolatry, whose modern attribute is the *lorgnon*. Proust thus plays the virtue of allegory against the vice of idolatry: Swann's tic demands to be understood in the figurative sense, while idolatrous reading reduces the sign to the literal. The allegorization of Idolatry thwarts the practice of idolatry.

Giotto's *Idolatry*

As for the hero, he spies Albertine "tossing up and catching again at the end of a string a weird object which gave her a look of Giotto's *Idolatry*; it was called, as it happened, a 'diabolo'" (2: 637; II, 241). Here, the narrator uses an artistic analogy that strongly recalls those made by Swann, particularly his comparison of the kitchen girl with Giotto's *Charity* (1: 110; I, 80). Intriguingly, Idolatry has become the vehicle of an apparently idolatrous analogy. How should this paradox be understood? For the narrator's comparison to avoid idolatry, it must differ from those made by Swann, and not reduce a work of art to a "a sign deprived of its meaning." As we will see, Proust successfully appropriated the meaning of the allegory painted by Giotto, which must be understood in the context of the Chapel of the Arena.

On the longitudinal walls of the nave, *Infidelitas*, Infidelity to God or "Idolatry" (known also as *Idolatria*), and its opposite, *Fides*, Faith, are placed across from one another. *Fides*, represented full-face, standing upright, holds in one hand the scroll of the Credo and in the other a staff topped with a cross, with which she crushes a pagan idol. On cathedral facades, as Émile Mâle explains in *Religious Art in France of the Thirteenth Century*, a tome well known to Proust, *Fides* can be characterized by two attributes: the chalice and the cross.[9] Giotto's *Infidelitas* elevates, above the infernal flames,

Figure 3.1 Giotto, *Infidelitas*, Scrovegni Chapel, Arena, Padua, *c.* 1305

a female idol brandishing a tree (Figure 3.1). The idol binds *Infidelitas* with a cord ending in a slipknot encircling his neck. *Infidelitas*, in a posture suggesting unbalance, wears a helmet with a large brim that prevents him from seeing and hearing a prophet who, on the upper part of the fresco, reads from a scroll. At Chartres, Idolatry adores "a hairy idol resembling a monkey," a figure of the "demon."[10] Albertine handles her diabolo as *Infidelitas* does his statuette, and this toy – whose name comes from the word *diable*, or "devil" – links her with medieval figures who adored diabolical monsters.

The *trompe l'œil* frescoes of the Vices and Virtues of the Arena openly imitate statues – that is to say, idols. These images, painted in mineral shades of gray, seek to prevent idolatrous viewing: exhibited as false statues, the figures are to be understood as symbols, suggesting a proper way of reading all the images in the chapel. At the heart of this ensemble of images, the representation of *Infidelitas* offers a *mise en abyme* of the frescoes' allegorical structure: the helmeted pagan mistakes the statuette for a goddess, and the little woman in turn believes that she holds a tree animated by a spirit. But each living being – man, woman, and tree – is in fact a statue, which in reality is a painting, which is in itself an allegory. The transmissibility of idolatry is thus also made visible: by contagion, the Unfaithful venerates a smaller idolater who venerates her own tiny idol, just as Ruskin idolizes the notion of idolatry, and just as Proust venerates Ruskin, who venerates Christian art.

The fresco is constructed as embedded allegories of idolatry: the tree is an allegory of idolatry housed within the allegory of the woman adoring the tree, who is herself integrated within yet another allegory, that of the Unfaithful who deifies the woman. The viewer's awareness of idolatry depends on a complex play of gazes. The viewer gazes at the Unfaithful, who gazes at the goddess, who gazes at the tree. Only the viewer, situated outside this web of illusions, knows that all of this is false, or, more precisely, that all of this is allegorical: she believes herself to be in the same position as the prophet, who overlooks the scene and withholds the truth. But the viewer, as long as she fixes her gaze on *Infidelitas*, is unaware that she herself is being observed, and is thus a part of the spectacle. In fact, *Fides* is behind her all the while, gazing at her intently. It is only in turning around, in turning her back on *Infidelitas*, that she will behold the truth. *Infidelitas* acts as a mirror that transforms the observer into what she observes, causing her to experience the unwitting blinding and contamination of idolatry. The central position of the viewer between the two frescoes is part of the allegorical apparatus in which the viewer is herself a figure. Giotto conceived this structure on the model of irony, which Philippe Hamon defines as "the spectacle of a blinding,"[11] and which always contains the possibility of an added level of meaning.[12] Irony and allegory are similarly recursive, and Giotto's *Infidelitas* conjugates them by means of this common principle.

By inserting *Infidelitas* in his novel, Proust embeds within the *Recherche* a mirror that reveals the idolatrous delusion of those characters he chides as "celibates of Art" (6: 293; IV, 470),[13] who are "quite *comically* blind" because they are unaware of being offered as a spectacle (3: 798; II, 870, my

Figure 3.2 *Synagoga* (the Synagogue personified), Notre-Dame de Paris

emphasis). The prop for this mirror is Albertine, the "fugitive being" (5: 115; III, 600) after whom the hero creates a series of "dear or sad fantasies" that are perpetually cast in doubt. The hero will journey along his path from blindness to illusion and from disillusion to illumination, while readers will either be caught up in the malicious mirror of the Proustian text, or somehow manage to uncover their own idolatries.

But there is a detail in Giotto's fresco that gives the ensemble its full meaning: seemingly cross-eyed, the Unfaithful holds his left eye wide open, fixed on the idol, and his right eye closed tight. In his *Iconologia*, Ripa notes that Idolatry is typically blind,[14] but Giotto's figure is more nuanced: he opens one glaucous eye toward the idol and closes the other to God. His blindness is not organic, but moral.

Synagoga and *Ecclesia, Fides* and *Idolatria*

No reader of Proust will fail to make the connection with the Synagogue, whose blindness is underscored by both Elstir and Charlus (2: 574, 3: 391; II, 197 and 585). An allegory for Judaism, the Synagogue is represented as

(a)

(b)

Figure 3.3 (a) Giotto, *Fides*, Scrovegni Chapel, Arena, Padua, *c.* 1305 (b) *Ecclesia* (the Church personified), Notre-Dame de Paris

blind in medieval Christian art, because Jews did not recognize Jesus as the Messiah: Jews are supposedly blind to the truths of the New Testament, and even to those of the Old, since they fail to acknowledge its typological prefiguration of the New. *Synagoga* wears a blindfold over her eyes; at Notre-Dame de Paris, she is represented with closed eyes, and her head is encircled with a serpent that prevents her, like the helmet of *Infidelitas*, from looking up. Also like *Infidelitas*, she is staggering (Figure 3.2).

Infidelitas and *Synagoga* are markedly similar. Is this resemblance fortuitous? In order to find out, we need only to compare *Fides* (Faith) and *Ecclesia* (the Church), the other two elements of the two dyads. Both of the latter are triumphant, eyes open, brandishing the cross. *Ecclesia* is typically represented as holding a chalice, in which she catches the blood and water

Figure 3.4 *Fides* (represented as *Ecclesia*) triumphing over *Infidelitas* (represented as *Synagoga*), Notre-Dame de Chartres

flowing from Christ's side in symbolic Crucifixions (Figure 3.3b). This is also the other possible attribute for images of *Fides*. Giotto's *Fides* is without it, but she wears a papal-like crown, holds a key, and stands firmly on a stone: she is undoubtedly a figure of the Church (Figure 3.3a). *Fides* and *Ecclesia* are one, like *Idolatria* and *Synagoga*. For medieval Christians, Jews and pagans were conflated in the figure of Idolatry. Was Proust aware of this? Mâle does not make the equivalence explicit, but his work would have allowed Proust to perceive it.

Mâle notes that *Infidelitas* is represented under two aspects at Chartres. On the south portal, she becomes the man adoring a hirsute idol. However, on the north portal, where "Faith [is opposed to] Infidelity (in the form of the Synagogue),"[15] "a different conception is presented. Faith has beneath her feet the Synagogue with blindfolded eyes."[16] This *Fides* who tramples *Synagoga* catches in her chalice the blood of the sacred lamb[17]: she coincides precisely with *Ecclesia*, and at her feet lays a figure of *Idolatria-Synagoga* (Figure 3.4). In his 1900 article "Ruskin à Notre-Dame d'Amiens," Proust paraphrases the passages on the Vices and Virtues from *The Bible of Amiens*. At the mention of "Idolatry adoring a monster" (*CSB* 97), he adds a note, which later disappears in the reedition of his text as the preface to his 1904 translation, *La Bible d'Amiens*: "At Chartres, Idolatry is represented by the blindfolded Synagogue (Mâle)."[18]

The same paradigm can be found in the *Recherche*: Idolatry is represented by Swann, the Jewish dilettante, the blindfolded Synagogue. Swann's allegorical tic of self-blinding first appears when he falls in love with Odette. His aesthetic idolatry reaches its zenith in the same period, when he imagines the resemblance between Odette and Botticelli's Zipporah. At the Saint-Euverte party, he entertains himself by envisioning the household staff as figures from paintings, then embarks on his famous musings on monocles: the personalities of six guests are epitomized in the description of their monocles, symbols of their defects. The monocle of the sixth guest, M. de Palancy, resembles in Swann's view "an accidental and perhaps purely symbolical fragment of the glass wall of his aquarium, a part intended to suggest the whole, which recalled to Swann, a fervent admirer of Giotto's *Vices* and *Virtues* at Padua, that figure representing Injustice by whose side a leafy bough evokes the idea of the forests that enshroud his secret lair" (1: 465; I, 322). This last monocle gives the key to the whole series: Swann is again relating people around him to figures in famous paintings, and here transforms the six guests into six of Giotto's seven Vices, each one with a monocle as his attribute. Swann compares Palancy to Injustice. Yet it seems strange that a monocle should recall, by way of a tortuous chain of associations, a "leafy bough"; moreover, Giotto's figure of Injustice is not endowed with one single "leafy bough," but with multiple trees. Swann's analogy with Injustice does not appear wholly just.

Soon after, when he hears Vinteuil's little phrase again, Swann is overcome with sorrow:

> his anguish becoming too intense, he drew his hand across his forehead, let the monocle drop from his eye, and wiped its glass. And doubtless, if he had caught sight of himself at that moment, he would have added, to the collection of those which he had already identified, this monocle which he removed like an importunate, worrying thought and from whose misty surface, with his handkerchief, he sought to obliterate his cares. (1: 493; I, 341)

Swann cannot "catch sight of himself," just as he had been unable to see himself in the series of Giotto's Vices, of which he is the seventh. All these Vices symbolize his idolatry, allegorized in his characteristic optical attribute, here reduced to a single lens, the monocle, the single open eye of *Infidelitas*. The only "leafy bough" to be found at the Arena is the one adored by Infidelity's little idol: that bough is the "part intended to suggest the whole" of the fresco of Idolatry, which is constructed with embedded synecdoches, just as Palancy is a "fragment" emblematic of the sevenfold allegory of Idolatry. At the acme of his idolatrous crisis, Swann sees his vice reflected in all the frescoes of the Arena, without recognizing it in them or seeing it in himself: mirroring the Idolater, he only has an eye for his little imaginary goddess. Like the viewer in the Arena, Swann is unwittingly ensnared in the ironic allegorical apparatus of Idolatry, where he constitutes the central figure, the cipher to a whole series of duplications.

Infidelitas

But let us return to Albertine. She now "swing[s] her diabolo like a nun her rosary" (2: 695; II, 282). The burlesque and anachronistic comedy of the diabolo here appears charged with sacrilegious irony: in an especially perfidious reworking of Giotto's fresco, Albertine the Idolater, she who plays with the devil, is here identified with Faith. *Infidelitas* becomes virtuous. How might we read the figural sense of this paradoxical allegory, which applies the very principle of infidelity to *Infidelitas*?

The artist must triumph over Idolatry, his supreme vice; but Infidelity is the virtue that allows him to remake Giotto's fresco by renouncing it,[19] to twist the Ruskinian concept of idolatry by making it his own, to recreate within himself "what a master has felt" in order to bring his own thought to light (*ASB* 193; *CSB* 140). In art, faith and fidelity would be vices if they were not joined with treachery. The theological virtue of the artist is *Infidelitas* as it implies and inverts *Fides*. Thanks to *Infidelitas* and by way of beloved images, the artist can "make for himself" fantasies that elude idolatry. By appropriating the allegorical function of images from cathedrals and from the Arena chapel, and by endowing them with a symbolic meaning inspired by Ruskin and by the two possible translations of the Latin term *Infidelitas*, Proust developed his own ethics of art, and allegorized it through Giotto's fresco, which he characteristically read ambiguously. Giotto's *Infidelitas* duplicates, in faithful recursivity, the same allegory – that of the Idolater, whose figure retains the same meaning throughout its reflexive multiplication – but the Proustian allegories denature this principle,

Figure 3.5 Ruskin, *Sculptures from the Cathedral of Rouen*, from *The Seven Lamps of Architecture*, 1849

so that the original sense is altered with each further level of meaning that Proust adds to it. Repurposed by Proust, the medieval, Giottesque, and Ruskinian allegories undergo unexpected mutations in their symbolism.

The Proustian Virtue that triumphs over *Idolatria* is not, then, *Fides-Ecclesia*, but *Infidelitas-Synagoga*, since *Fides*, just like the viewer who turns her back to the fresco, is morally blind and unaware of being so. If *Infidelitas* can be read as the virtue of Infidelity, *Fides* becomes an allegory of the vice of Idolatry. Ruskin was thus blinded by Faith, that bad faith that made him mistake medieval Christian art for Art itself. *Fides* is deluded by the "fantasies" that she makes for herself, notably that of the blindfolded *Synagoga*, the very Synagogue that forbade the cult of images in the second commandment of her Law.[20] In place of this blind faith, Proust's artist substitutes a belief engendered by an internal "vision" (6: 299; IV, 474) that preserves metaphor from idolatrous images. In his preface to *La Bible d'Amiens*, the open eye of Ruskin's favorite little character seems to allegorize this vision.

Diabolo

On the portal of the Booksellers at Rouen cathedral, faced with over a hundred sculpted quatrefoils whose four corners are each ornamented with tiny figures that all look similar, Ruskin singled out, in a spandrel, the little creature he described and drew in *The Seven Lamps of Architecture* (Figure 3.5). Shortly after Ruskin's death, Proust went to Rouen on a "pilgrimage" and was able to find the figurine: "nothing then dies of what has once lived, the sculptor's thought any more than that of Ruskin" (*ASB* 180; *CSB* 126). In "John Ruskin," Proust translated the description of the bas-relief: "the fellow is vexed and puzzled in his malice; and his hand is pressed hard on his cheek bone, and the flesh of the cheek is wrinkled under the eye by the pressure . . . [C]onsidering it as a mere filling of an interstice on the outside of a cathedral gate . . . it proves very noble vitality in the art of the time" (*ASB* 178; *CSB* 124).[21] For Ruskin, this detail allegorized medieval art and its "vitality" because the sculptor took care to give the tiny character a physiognomy of his own, chiseling the folds of the cheek pressed by his hand in order to make his gaze communicate the somber mood of a sullen, wicked imp. Characteristically, Proust turns to allegorical recursivity in order to add a level of figurative meaning: for him, "vitality" becomes, as Diane Leonard explains, the "figure of the survival of the artist's soul in his work."[22] Ruskin, who is compared to the angel of the Last Judgment represented on the tympanum of the portal, revived the sculptor's thought; Proust revives that of Ruskin, and calls on his readers to do the same. Thanks to the drawing reproduced at the end of "John Ruskin," they will be able to find the figurine, and in turn save from oblivion the thoughts of the sculptor, of Ruskin, and of Proust himself. In order to do this, they must go to Rouen and take part, as in the Arena Chapel, in a play of gazes: on that eroded stone, the figurine has preserved the hole of its angry pupil; it has remained there "unlooked at," "caught by death in the very act of gazing"; but Ruskin said "See," and it "recovered its gaze" (*ASB* 179–181, trans. mod.; *CSB* 126–127). It is vital, then, that it be looked upon, that the life of its gaze be sustained by that of new viewers. According to Diane Leonard, it is on this model that Proust conceived the madeleine episode, and more specifically the passage on the "Celtic belief" (1: 59; I, 43–44). This little figure, lost among so many others for centuries and rediscovered by Ruskin, would thus be a prototype for *À la recherche du temps perdu*.

But is it not possible to find some idolatry – idolatry which appears deeply linked to the animist logic of "Celtic belief" – in this paradigm of resuscitation through the act of beholding, or even a chain of idolatries, as in Giotto's fresco? If Ruskin was interested in this sculpture, it was because he saw it as a work inspired by the vitality of faith, not for its artistic value; in turn, Proust poured into it all his passion for Ruskin. If Proust had been entirely honest with himself, would he have thought it necessary to go to Rouen in order to look at a stone and, in doing so, reanimate captive souls? The resurrection allegorized by the figurine may well function as an allegory of time lost and regained. But if the literal sense of an allegory can generate idolatry, grafting an allegory onto another allegory might incite one to take the second symbolic sense at its word, and hop on a train to Rouen to go perform pagan rites. Allegorical recursivity would then merely shift idolatry to the next level of meaning.

Why would Proust's idolatry have fixated on this figurine? Ruskin selected it among hundreds of others; Proust likewise chose to retain from a vastly larger whole a minuscule detail in Ruskin's monumental work. Proust read the text of the *Seven Lamps*, but he also saw the engraving representing the little creature. It is thanks to this image that he rediscovered it – this is why he reproduces the drawing at the end of his article, so that his readers might themselves find the figurine. Proust claims to have recognized it because of its gaze, yet this can only be a further symbol, since it is impossible to distinguish the little grotesque figure from its fellow creatures except by its formal particularities: its head in profile, its hand on its cheek, and its head covering, that is – along with its serpent's tail, which it has in common with plenty of other figurines – the traits that come together to characterize the "poor little monster" (*ASB* 180–181; *CSB* 127) as a Jew. Proust knew how to interpret at least one of these traits, the most important one. He would have learned it from Mâle: "Jews are known by their cone-shaped cap."[23]

Proust insists on the thought of the sculptor, but neither he nor Ruskin make the tenor of this thought explicit. In medieval iconographic codes, the hand on the cheek indicates physical or moral pain.[24] This is the iconic attitude of the melancholic, which also became that of the meditative thinker or creator[25] – a posture Proust often adopts when being photographed. Representation in profile marks figures as negative,[26] as in traditional depictions of Judas.[27] As for the serpent – the very "diabolo" found on certain figurations of *Synagoga* – its symbolism is well known.[28] The monster is even endowed with a prominent nose, emphasized by the profile view, as in many anti-Semitic caricatures. Ruskin admired "the plan of this head, and the nod of the cap," and, above all, the wrinkles of the cheek, which show that "the fellow is vexed and puzzled in his malice."[29] Significantly, Proust omits the whole passage in his citation of Ruskin.

The portal of the Booksellers follows a precise iconographic program.[30] The first register of abutments recounts the story of the Fall, from the creation of Adam and Eve to Cain's fratricide. Below, four rows of quatrefoils show grotesque and often hybrid creatures: men transformed into monsters

Figure 3.6 Jews descending into the mouth of Hell, *Bible moralisée*, Paris, mid-thirteenth century

by the sins of their ancestors and the vices they inherited. On the tympanum, the Last Judgment, the ultimate episode in the story of Salvation, divides the elect from the damned. The serpentine Jew, somber and livid, awaits the moment when the angel – Saint Michael the Archangel, charged with the weighing of souls – will send him to Hell, like his brothers shown in manuscript illuminations, hand on cheek, submitting to an apostle's sermon telling them that their Law is defeated, or already snatched up by the open maw of the Leviathan (Figure 3.6). In the scene of the Last Judgment at Notre-Dame d'Amiens, under the scale of Saint Michael, *Synagoga*, whom Proust evokes in his pastiche of Ruskin, "La bénédiction du sanglier" ["The Blessing of the Boar"] (*CSB* 205), collapses on the side of the Vices and of Hell, while *Ecclesia*, standing on the side of the Virtues and of Heaven, wrests away her phylactery.

Proust, who had seen the cone-shaped cap on the engraving and who, with that clue, had been able to recapture the "sculptor's thought" in the context of the portal of the Booksellers, returns too insistently to the open eye of this "oblique and spiteful face, now resurrected" (*ASB* 181; *CSB* 127) not to have hidden, within an explicit and apparently idolatrous allegory, some dear and ironic allegory, made by and for himself. In multiplying betrayals of the sculptor, of Ruskin, of Mâle, and of the doctrine of cathedrals, Proust reincarnated *Infidelitas* in *Synagoga*, a Synagogue with her eye

Figure 3.7 Proust, "The Church and the Synagogue (blindfolded)"

forever open, an allegory of creative Infidelity and of the personal vision of the artist.[31] During the Dreyfus Affair, Swann becomes an idolater of his own Jewishness through an inadequate fidelity to the faith of his fathers, which turns him into a caricature of the Jew (4: 121–122; III, 89). Paradoxically, he is mistaken in siding with a just cause, because he has made it into a vain "dear fantasy": like Ruskin, Swann lies to himself about the reasons that led him to adopt his stance. But Jewishness can also be turned to allegorical and poetic uses, making the "harmless and monstrous little figure" (*ASB* 180, trans. mod.; *CSB* 126) a fantasy in which the perfidy, rebellion, and obstinacy that thirteenth-century Christianity attributed to Jews are transformed into the supreme virtue of the artist's moral code.

The survival of the "little monster" is assured. By way of the ironic, chiasmic and recursive games of allegory and idolatry, the Proustian pilgrims who go to Rouen, in good faith and fidelity, to revive the figurine, imitating Proust who imitated Ruskin, find themselves beholding an oblique gaze. Like the viewer of *Infidelitas* at the Arena Chapel, they are implacably turned into idolaters by the wrathful little Jewish "diabolo" that they have so piously come to see and revive. Proust bequeathed to his worshipers a dynamic allegory in which they are the living, blind figures.

NOTES

1 *Mercure de France*, April 1900.
2 Published in two parts in the *Gazette des beaux-arts*, April 1 and August 1, 1900.
3 *Lectures on Architecture and Painting* [1854], in *The Works of John Ruskin*, 39 vols., Library Edition, ed. E. T. Cook and A. Wedderburn (London: George Allen, 1903–1912), XII (1904), 128.
4 *The Seven Lamps of Architecture* [1849], in *Works of Ruskin*, VIII (1903), 217.
5 *Lectures on Art* [1870], in *Works of Ruskin*, XX (1905), 66.
6 "He says something not because it is true but because he enjoys saying it, and listens to his own voice uttering the words as though they came from someone else" (1: 353; I, 245).
7 Ruskin's definition of idolatry goes on to incorporate citations from the Gospels of Luke and Matthew.
8 See also *Du côté de chez Swann* (1: 45, 510 and 537; I, 34, 352 and 371).
9 Émile Mâle, *L'art religieux du XIIIe siècle en France: Étude sur l'iconographie du Moyen Âge et sur ses sources d'inspiration*, new edition, revised and augmented (Paris: Armand Colin, 1902), 141.
10 *Ibid.*, 141–142. Published in English as *Religious Art in France of the Thirteenth Century*, trans. Dora Nussey (London: J. M. Dent; New York: E. P. Dutton, 1913), 113–114.
11 *L'ironie littéraire: Essai sur les formes de l'écriture oblique* (Paris: Hachette Supérieur, 1996), 11.
12 An ironist is always likely to be "ironized" by another ironist, a further level can always be added to each level of ironic meaning.
13 Critics have proposed various interpretations of *Infidelitas*: Albertine worshiping women; the hero worshiping Albertine; the hero turning away from artistic truth . . . This figure is capable of focusing a number of images in its little mirror: Swann, worshiper of works of art; Swann, caught around the neck with Odette's noose, which she uses to strangle his artistic tendencies; or Proust, idolater of Ruskin, who is in turn an idolater of Christian art.
14 Cesare Ripa, *Iconologia* [1593–1603], ed. Piero Buscaroli, with a preface by Mario Praz (Milan: TEA Arte, 1992), 179–180.
15 Mâle, *L'art religieux*, 131; *Religious Art*, 104.
16 Mâle, *L'art religieux*, 142; *Religious Art*, 114 (trans. mod.).
17 Mâle, *L'art religieux*, 141; *Religious Art*, 113.
18 *Mercure de France* 34:124 (1900), 79.
19 See *Le Temps retrouvé* (6: 525; IV, 620).
20 "Thou shalt not make thee any graven image" (Exodus 20:3–5; Deuteronomy 5:7–8).
21 Ruskin, *The Seven Lamps*, 217.
22 "Proust et Ruskin: réincarnations intertextuelles," *Bulletin d'informations proustiennes* 24 (1993), 75.
23 Mâle, *L'art religieux*, 15; *Religious Art*, 3.

24 See François Garnier, *Le langage de l'image au Moyen Âge: Signification et symbolique* (Paris: Le Léopard d'Or, 1982), 181.
25 See Raymond Klibansky, Erwin Panofsky, and Fritz Saxl, *Saturn and Melancholy* (London: Nelson, 1964), 391–393.
26 See Garnier, *Le langage de l'image au Moyen Âge*, 146.
27 See for example the Arena fresco depicting the betrayal of Judas, where his profile is caricatured in the image of a devil standing behind him.
28 See Debra Higgs Strickland, *Saracens, Demons and Jews: Making Monsters in Medieval Art* (Princeton University Press, 2003), 122–138. It was believed that Jews had horns (hidden under their hats), like Moses, and a tail (106).
29 Ruskin, *The Seven Lamps*, 217.
30 See Markus Schlicht, *La Cathédrale de Rouen vers 1300: Portail des Libraires, portail de la Calende, chapelle de la Vierge* (Caen: Société des Antiquaires de Normandie, 2005), 203–217.
31 In a drawing traced on an image from Mâle's book representing Christ crucified between the Church and the Synagogue, Proust identifies *Ecclesia* as his faithful Reynaldo Hahn (Figure 3.7). He thus semitizes *Ecclesia* who, by a sort of reverse typology, becomes a figure of *Synagoga* with her eyes open, promising resurrection and salvation. The caption reads: "L'Église et la Synagogue (aux yeux bandés) Vitrail de Bourges. Symbolise la vie aveugle se détournant avec tous ses espoirs de Marcel, et Reynaldo plein de pitié recueillant le sang de sa plaie et Konsolant" ["The Church and the Synagogue (blindfolded) Stained glass window at Bourges. Symbolizes life blindly turning all its hopes away from Marcel, and Reynaldo full of pity collecting blood from his wound and Konsoling him"]

CHAPTER 4

I am [not] a painting: how Chardin and Moreau dialogue in Proust's writing

Christie McDonald

In *À la recherche du temps perdu,* the first person "I" of the narrator asks "who am I?," and what is the relationship between art, life, and artistic creation? The questions are repeated throughout the novel, while the answers remain only partial: defining the self in, through, and against models. Proust was a master at tracking the thrill and disappointment of ideal as well as imperfect models and the work of inexorable change in time and space.

I start from the end, in a sense, by suggesting that the evocation of works and artists as models, whether musical or visual, call to mind reference points that must be left behind by the end of the novel. The question that I want to ask here is not so much *who* Proust's biographical models were for his aesthetic theory and for his fictive artists (Vinteuil, Bergotte, and Elstir): much work has been done on both. Rather, in two specific cases, I want to ask *how* Proust through his narrator and hero (who come closer and closer together) looked to the models of painters in order to then shake free from and transform their work into his own. I propose in particular to look at the way in which the art of the eighteenth-century painter Jean Siméon Chardin (1699–1779) and the nineteenth-century Gustave Moreau (1826–1898), at a century's remove and not commonly associated together, became catalysts in very different ways for thinking through the creative process.

In the beginning of *Le Temps retrouvé,* the narrator "reads" an imagined passage about the Verdurin's salon from a parody of the Goncourts's *Journal.* He is at one point reminded of Diderot (*Lettres à Sophie Voland*) and the natural beauty prized by the eighteenth century. Proust refers infrequently to Diderot, and then not directly to the *Salons,* considered to be an inaugural work in art criticism, but he shared with him and the Goncourts an important appreciation for Chardin. Like Diderot, the narrator suggests that his own thought process is close to the practice of painting on a canvas: "seeing," he writes in the same passage, cannot occur without a preliminary "sketch" ["un croquis"] having taken place in his thought, after which his imagination can take off and begin to "paint" ["peindre"]. Reflecting on a dilemma opened up by Diderot,[1] the narrator addresses the problem of how to encompass the simultaneity of feeling and perceptions, and then translate the creative expression of these through painting, music and writing. In the *Le Côté de Guermantes I*, the narrator states: "We feel in one world, we think, we give names to things in another; between the two we can establish a certain correspondence, but not bridge the gap" (3: 57; II, 349).

Diderot had been explicit in his *Lettre sur les sourds et muets* about the difference between perception, which happens all at once, and the compressed linearity of analytical language: "The state of our soul is one thing, the account we give of it – whether to ourselves or to others – is another; the instantaneous totality of sensations that constitute that state is by no means the same thing as the sequential and itemized attention that we are forced to apply to it in order to analyze it, communicate it, and make ourselves understood."[2] The disconnect between feeling and thinking, on the one hand, and expression, on the other, links Proust to Diderot in a deeper way than the *Journal* suggests: the *Recherche* explores *how to pass from life to art*, from impressions and sensations to the analysis of them, in artistic creation.[3] Chardin's painting was a strong tie in working through these issues.[4]

Proust wrote early essays on Chardin and Moreau in both of which he identified aesthetic principles that he carries through the novel. The first was Proust's essay on Chardin (a painter who particularly interested both Diderot and the Goncourts before him), written between art criticism and journalism at age 24.[5]

Chardin

The conceit in the early essay, "Chardin et Rembrandt" from 1895, begins with Proust asking his reader (who would not read this during Proust's lifetime)[6] to imagine a young man of modest fortune and artistic taste, irritated by life's domestic details. Because he can get neither to Holland nor to Italy, the young man goes to the Louvre to see the palaces and princes he envisions by a Veronese, Van Dyck, or Claude Lorrain. Our narrator, in this case Proust, stops him in front of Chardin's paintings so that he may taste "the pleasure that the spectacle of modest lives or of still life affords," describing, among others, "a sideboard already half cleared with knives left lying on the table-cloth," "a kitchen interior where a live cat is walking

Figure 4.1 Chardin, *The Ray*, *c*. 1725–1726

over some oysters, while a dead ray-fish hangs on the wall," such subjects as might revolt [répugner] a beholder (*ASB* 123; *CSB* 373).

What Proust has learned from Chardin, he writes, is that a pear is as alive as any precious stone because the painter has declared the equality of all things before the painter's thought. Chardin was great because his *magic* was to have brought alive an overlooked world of the mundane and humble.[7]

In this essay, Proust maps out not only the importance of Chardin as an artist in the history of painting, but a technique for interiorizing his work: "If when you look at a Chardin you can say to yourself, this is intimate, is comfortable, is alive like a kitchen, when you walk about a kitchen you will say to yourself, this is interesting, this is grand, this is beautiful like a Chardin" (*ASB* 124; *CSB* 374). So once the poet has seen these paintings at the Louvre, the effect would be so great that he would not need to see Chardin's paintings again, as he can see them everywhere in his own kitchen.[8] That is, Chardin's work will be integrated to the point where it infuses all space as though it were a still life. The "I" of the essay leads the younger man (his hero) to see that Chardin was more than just a painter whose work should be described. Chardin was a guide to be followed and integrated: "Here we are at the endpoint of that journey of initiation into the neglected life of inanimate nature that each one of us may make by letting himself be guided by Chardin, as Dante let himself be guided of old by Virgil" (*ASB* 129; *CSB* 380).

Proust sprinkles references to Chardin lightly throughout the *Recherche*, and in particular at three crucial moments.

First, the painter Elstir finds in Chardin's work fragments anticipating his own painting. The artist conceives of such precedent as both an opening and an obstacle because, he writes, the public was unable to put together admiration for Chardin with their distaste for the way in which Elstir's work questioned the understanding of vision. They could not fathom that what was new in Elstir *was also new* in Chardin: "Elstir for his own part, in striving to reproduce reality (with the particular trademark of his taste for certain experiments), had made the same effort as a Chardin or a Perronneau" (3: 575; II, 713).

The second example takes place in *Albertine disparue* when the hero, who is in Venice, follows in Ruskin's footsteps to St. Mark's; here, with his mother, the geographical layering of Venice and his childhood in Combray come together through a juxtaposition (already worked out in the early essay) of two painters: "the valuable instruction in the art of Chardin acquired long ago" (5: 848; IV, 205) with the grandeur of Veronese (Figures 4.3a and b).[9]

How then will the writer make the transition beyond the voyage of initiation described with Chardin? Proust does not leave Chardin behind as a model. In fact, as Kasuyoshi Yoshikawa has astutely shown, the narrator continues to see with Chardin's eyes, even when the painter's name is removed:[10] the literary transcription from an ekphrasis of Chardin's *Buffet* (Figure 4.2) written in the early essay, is recycled for a scene at Balbec in *À l'ombre des jeunes filles en fleurs.*

> Since I had seen such things depicted in water-colors by Elstir, I sought to find again in reality, I cherished as though for their poetic beauty, the broken gestures of the knives still lying across one another, the swollen convexity of a discarded napkin into which the sun introduced a patch of yellow velvet, the half-empty glass which thus showed to greater advantage the noble sweep of its curved sides and, in the heart of its translucent crystal, clear as frozen daylight . . . I tried to find beauty there where I had never imagined before that it could exist, in the most ordinary things, in the profundities of "still life." (2: 613; II, 224)

Figure 4.2 Chardin, *The Buffet*, 1728

The words about Chardin have become those of the narrator, in the close integration of this painting as it is transposed into the artist's vision.[11] But the narrator also states in a sketch from *À l'ombre des jeunes en fleurs* that if one has been too much under the influence of Chardin's *The Ray* or Rembrandt's *Good Samaritan*, there is a good antidote: looking at the *Wedding of Cana*, or paintings by Moreau like *The Young Man and Death* (Figure 4.4), "to reveal to us that if the most ordinary of things can be just as beautiful as the most opulent, even so, the most opulent ones are not excluded from the category of the beautiful and have a beauty proper to them as well."[12]

This passage expands on the early essay "La poésie ou les lois mystérieuses" where Proust wrote of the poet who should "paint" and light up equally the natural world and the world of artifacts and art. Rather than follow solely in Chardin's path, and turn away from mysterious laws and opulent objects, he has learned from Gustave Moreau (along with Robert Louis Stevenson's *The Rajah's Diamond*) to prize, and take as symbols, sumptuous garments and things lifted from the natural world.[13] Although Proust will not retain an interest in Moreau's symbols, he finds a crucial aspect of his aesthetic theory in the essay written about Moreau in 1898. If the humble is beautiful, so too can the luxuriant be: Chardin next to Veronese or Moreau; Moreau next to Chardin (Figures 4.3a and b).

I believe one can say that Chardin and Moreau constitute the two sides of an oxymoron needed to ensure a transition: the two sides coexist not only in seeing the value of both the humble and the opulent, but also in ways that help the narrator chart inclusion and exclusion, along with superimposition, as strategies out of idolatry toward creation.

Moreau

In the essay penned following Gustave Moreau's death in 1898, Proust wrote that a painting is like an apparition "of some little part of a mysterious world of which we know various other aspects, which are canvasses by the same artists" (*CSB* 669).[14] Proust repeats the word *apparition* as that which allows a glimpse into the "soul" of the poet or painter – the two being interchangeable here – who has found his homeland, or in Proustian terms his true country in art; "The country which works of art thus show us fragments . . . is the poet's soul" (*CSB* 670).[15] We the beholders may recognize an as yet unseen work from apparitions of this strange world of

Figure 4.3a Chardin, *The Return from Market*, 1739

Figure 4.3b Veronese, *The Wedding at Cana*, 1563

Figure 4.4 Moreau, *The Young Man and Death*, 1856–1865

the artist, recognition that is fundamental to the search for aesthetic truth in the novel: fragmentary glimpses are promises that a great artist's work will come together in a unitary vision. Yet, Proust states, it is only given to a few to be love-struck for a painting, whereas it seems possible for everyone to fall in love with a person, and so this kind of artistic love is very rare (*CSB* 674).[16] Proust had sensed early on the danger of loving a painting too much when he took Ruskin to task saying that he was afflicted, however deliciously, with idolatry.[17] One example he cites in his "Ruskin" is Robert de Montesquiou,[18] whose writing about Moreau Proust will admire a few years later . . .

> I am taking here as my example, when I tell them that . . . [Robert de Montesquiou] recognizes admirably the same stuff as is worn by Death in Gustave Moreau's *The Young Man and Death* . . . And as he looks at the actress's drapery or at the society woman's dress he is moved by such noble associations and exclaims: "Quite lovely" not because the material is lovely, but because it is the material painted by Moreau . . . and hence forever sacred . . . to idolaters. (*ASB* 188; *CSB* 135)

Finding beauty not simply in the thing, but because of the master, is the intellectual sin artists must avoid (and he includes an example from Balzac's *Les Secrets de la princesse de Cadignan*). In the posthumously published notes on Moreau, Proust cites the same painting (*The Young Man and Death*) and exhorts the poet to break free and look inside himself as he looks at an object or work of art (*ASB* 147: *CSB* 418) (Figure 4.4).[19]

I believe that Proust attempted to sidestep the problem of being too powerfully influenced by the aesthetic he gleaned from Moreau by displacing references to his works into lesser encounters not within his aesthetic theory. Here are two examples.

The first is found in "Un amour de Swann" when Swann suddenly remembers Odette, not as Botticell's beautiful Zipporah who made him fall in love with her, but as a kept woman.

What is striking here is that the narrator does not cite the sequence of paintings and the watercolor Proust had seen of the *Apparition*, after Moreau's death at the painter's house soon to become a museum.[20] Rather, he displaces the title into a comparison with a common noun: Odette is like an apparition of Moreau's paintings of poisonous flowers intertwined with precious jewels. There being no ekphrasis of the work, we the readers are kept away and outside of this dangerous vision, away from even visualizing the painting.

Figure 4.5 Moreau, *The Apparition*, 1876–1877

If the word *apparition* historically has multiple meanings from the religious manifestation of Christ to an appearance or phantom,[21] here the implicit comparison with Salomé, as the demonized erotic woman, intensifies the sense of danger lurking behind Odette's facade in her former life of kept woman. As so often, then, Swann turns a work of art toward the emotions of love and not toward his own creation of a work of art. Other examples include Swann's reception of Vinteuil's sonata, and its haunting little phrase, described as an "apparition" in *Du côté de chez Swann*: both as the federating emblem of his love for Odette and then a searing reminder of her absence. Gilberte and Mme Swann, La Berma, as well as the young women in *À l'ombre des jeunes filles*, all take on the quality of visual apparitions, as does Françoise's genius in cooking. Only in the first instance, with Odette, is the word connected to Moreau's work, the *Apparition* (Figure 4.5), and then cleverly only by inference: "that strange personification, the kept woman – an iridescent mixture of unknown and demoniacal qualities embroidered, as in some fantasy of Gustave Moreau, with poison-dripping flowers interwoven with precious jewels" (1: 380; I, 263).

Moreau is twice mentioned in *Le Côté de Guermantes II*, and this is my other example. First, by Saint-Loup who speaks of "stunning pictures by Gustave Moreau" (2: 457; II, 114) in the collection of paintings owned by Mme de Guermantes, though he qualifies others in the collection as insignificant and "as rather a joke" (2: 457; II, 114). The Duchess, who prides herself on liking everything new and interesting, repeats Swann and echoes Saint-Loup in a conversation with the Princesse de Parme (about the *style empire*), comparing a sculpted mermaid with a mother-of-pearl tail in a young man's sick-bed to a Moreau painting: "it was most moving, it was precisely that same composition as Gustave Moreau's *Death and the Young Man* (Your Highness must know that masterpiece, of course)" (3: 713; II, 810).

The narrator never directly evokes Moreau's painting; others – intermediaries – do: Saint-Loup, Swann, Mme de Villeparisis, or the Duchess channeling Swann. Bypassing Moreau's mythological symbolism and retrospective vision, as Theodore Johnson has shown, the narrator refers to Moreau either by indirect reporting (as with *The Apparition*) or in comic fashion – in each instance, leaving aside the deeper effects of Moreau's art that Proust writes out of the narrative. He separated out his own aesthetic vision, partially articulated in relation to Moreau in the early essay, from the allusions within the novel to Moreau, as Yoshikawa points out. In an oblique commentary on Moreau's work, Proust performs a transfer from an early description of an unnamed but identifiable watercolor (*Poète mort porté par un centaure*, in *Cahier* 5)[22] to a similar description of an early Elstir watercolor with a mythological subject – a work that is said not to be one of his best, as Elstir leaves behind his mythological period for a later Japanese and then impressionist period.

So it is that the writer Bergotte finds in Vermeer, not Moreau or Chardin, the final revelation of the "little patch of yellow wall" in his *View of Delft* and the recognition of "fragments of an identical world . . . the same table, the same carpet, the same woman, the same novel and unique beauty" (5: 508; III, 879), which signal whether in Vermeer or Dostoevsky the genius of the artist.

Yet the hero reacts to Elstir's paintings in the gallery of the Duke and Duchess of Guermantes just as Bergotte is reported to have reacted to Vermeer, and Proust did earlier to Moreau: "I had before me fragments of that world of new and strange colors which was no more than the projection of that great painter's peculiar vision, which his speech in no way expressed" (3: 573–574; II, 712).

In particular, one of the paintings speaks to him clearly ("sings" is the verb) – more than either Elstir the theoretician, the person or man of taste – about the equivalence of objects, be they hospitals, churches, even a somewhat vulgar woman at whom one might wish *not* to look. The lesson here turns out to be that what was prized in Chardin (the equivalence of objects valued only through the perspective of the painter) is shunned in Moreau, such is the ambivalence before the power of models. The painting speaks or sings to him saying: "there virtue is all in the painter's eye" in the creation of a "poetical composition" (3: 576; II, 714). The major difference between the two being that one could enter into and integrate Chardin's world whereas Moreau's was sealed off.

The final experience of involuntary memory, and its elaboration in *Le Temps retrouvé*, opens the way to the narrator's comprehension that, when early in the novel, he fixed his mind on objects (a cloud, a flower or stone), he discovered something very different: "some thought, which they translated after the fashion of those hieroglyphic characters which at first one might suppose to represent only material objects" (6: 273; IV, 457).

In a passing glance at Diderot, the narrator understands that the simultaneous and indivisible unity of creation was to be found through feeling in an emblem or hieroglyph (as the superimposition of the senses compressed into one figure). The hero must now convert impressions and sensations into a spiritual equivalent, for which the narrative formulates an aesthetic theory based on metaphor and the narrator's discovery that he is ready to write. Moreau is gone, but Chardin returns in the final pages of *Le Temps retrouvé*, as the model's model, in the much celebrated sentence: "But – as Elstir had found with Chardin – you can make anew what you love only by renouncing it" (6: 525, trans. mod.; IV, 620). The English translation does not quite reproduce the pile-on of the two names juxtaposed in French: "Elstir Chardin." If Elstir held onto Chardin, we are left not knowing exactly what the narrator, whom the hero is asymptotically joining at the end of the novel, will do with his models.

The need to take a distance from, or even discard models clearly does not mean giving them up entirely; they remain crucial. But in order to create, Elstir/Chardin like Elstir/Proust must perform an act of dissociation, separation and reconstruction to create anew.[23] Chardin and Moreau, among many others – even Diderot fleetingly – reappear only to be left behind as models and guides in the search not only for time past but for new art, now and in the future. As the narrator writes in the beginning of *Le Temps retrouvé*, after reading the Goncourts' fictionalized *Journal*, he may not have had the greatest ability to observe (a statement most readers would refute!).

> Always I was incapable of seeing anything for which a desire had not already been roused in me by something I had read, anything of which I had not myself traced in advance a sketch which I wanted now to confront with reality . . . Then and then only has my imagination been set in motion, has it begun to paint. (6: 41; IV, 297)

In learning to "see," to glimpse from models a way forward in order to invent, to imagine, and in this sense to "paint," the author, narrator and hero could in the end take off the brackets of my title and proclaim "I am [not] a painting" but a written work of art.

NOTES

1 Diderot looks to surmount the dichotomy between thought and feeling, feeling and language. Judgment is impossible in any art without comparisons extracted from simultaneous impressions. Memory assures the transition between simultaneity and the temporal succession of past, present, to future. The problem is to pass from "total and instantaneous" sensation to analytical thought in time.

2 Denis Diderot, "Letter on the Deaf and Dumb, For the Use of Those Who Hear and Speak," *Selected Writings*, ed. and intro. Lester G. Crocker, trans. Derek Coltman (New York: Macmillan, 1966), 33–34. "The formation of language demanded itemization: but to *see* an object, to *decide* that it is beautiful, to *experience* a sensation of pleasure, and to *desire* possession of that object are all parts of a single and instantaneous state of the soul" (*ibid.*, 34).

3 See Gita May, "Chardin vu par Diderot et par Proust," *PMLA* 72:3 (June 1957), 403–418; also Antoine Compagnon, *Proust Between Two Centuries* (New York: Columbia University Press, 1992), who compares Proust's idea of a "composed whole," not to a monolithic unity but to something more like Diderot's notion of a whole composed of many parts.

4 Proust read Gaston Schéfer's *Chardin: biographie critique* (Paris: Henri Laurens, 1904). The twenty-four reproductions in this book include *Le Singe peintre* (Louvre), *La Guitare* (private collection), *La Raie*, and *Le Buffet* (both from 1728 at the Louvre).

5 Diderot, *Les Salons*, ed. Jean Seznec and Jean Adhémar (Oxford: Clarendon Press, 1963), 4 vols; Jules et Edmond de Goncourt, *Arts et artistes (*Paris: Hermann, 1997), 83–95. The Goncourts published their essay on Chardin in 1864. See Proust, *Comme Elstir Chardin . . .* , postface Sylvie Pierron (Paris: Altamira, 1999). For a discussion of the trajectory of challenges to the classical aesthetic of Horace's *ut pictura poesis* in art criticism from Diderot to Proust, see Nicolas Valazza, *Crise de plume et souveraineté du pinceau: Écrire la peinture de Diderot à Proust* (Paris: Classiques Garnier, 2013).

6 The first publication of this piece was in *Le Figaro littéraire*, March 27, 1954, later published as "Chardin et Rembrandt," in *CSB*, 372–382.

7 "Being in no sense a display of special virtues, but the expression of what was most intimate in his life and what is most profound in things, it is our lives it addresses itself to, it is our lives that it comes to affect, which it inclines gently over towards things, moves closer to the heart of things" (*ASB* 130–131; *CSB* 382). Chardin's creative acts did not emerge from knowledge and laws, as Proust continues, "but from an obscure and incomprehensible power, which we do not make stronger by elucidating it" (*ASB* 131; *CSB* 382).

8 "For from the day we saw it at the Louvre and extracted its meaning by virtue of the incalculable richness of works of art, it multiplies in us, and innumerable are such Chardins presented to us daily by our humble dining rooms . . . When one is unduly influenced by Chardin's *The Ray*, which proves that the most elementary laws of relief and solidity suffice to render infinitely precious the humblest of objects, or Rembrandt's *Good Samaritan* that creates all the value of matter through the light that gives the well-cord and shadow of the door their divinity, the sight of the *Wedding at Cana* or certain works of Gustave Moreau are not useless for they reveal to us that if the most ordinary of things can be as beautiful as the most opulent, even so, the most opulent ones are not excluded from the category of the beautiful and have a beauty proper to them as well" (*À l'ombre des jeunes filles en fleurs*, "Esquisse LVI" [II, 975]). Unless otherwise indicated, translations in this chapter are by John D'Amico.

9 "And as I went indoors to join my mother who by now had left the window, on leaving the heat of the open air I had the same sensation of coolness that I experienced long ago at Combray when I went upstairs to my room; but in Venice it was a breeze from the sea that kept the air cool, and no longer on a little wooden staircase with narrow steps, but on the noble surfaces of marble steps continually splashed by shafts of blue-green sunlight, which, to the valuable instruction in the art of Chardin acquired long ago, added a lesson in that of Veronese" (5: 847–848; IV, 205).

"And for the welcoming coolness of my uncle's house there were wafts of sea-air, and shafts of sunlight streaking long shadowy expanses of marble, and expounding, as in a picture by Veronese, the counter-doctrine to Chardin's doctrine that even the most commonplace things can be beautiful" (*Marcel Proust on Art and Literature*, 85; *CSB* 111).

10 See Kazuyoshi Yoshikawa, *Proust et l'art pictural* (Paris: Champion, 2010), 262–263ff. Yoshikawa points out that Swann is not the only one to indulge in idolatry but that the entire *Recherche* is infused with it. See Thomas Baldwin, who brings together Diderot's comments about Chardin with Proust's on Hubert Robert, and deals with the issue of ekphrasis moving away from the referential: *The Picture as Spectre in Diderot, Proust, and Deleuze* (London: Legenda, 2011), 3. See also Chapter 3 in the present volume.

11 Yoshikawa, *Proust et l'art pictural*, 264.

12 "Esquisse LXXXI," in *À l'ombre des jeunes en fleurs* (II, 975).

13 See Proust, "Poetry, or the mysterious laws" (*ASB* 148; *CSB* 419).

14 Proust continues: "We are in a drawing-room, we are conversing, all at once we look up and catch sight of a picture we have never seen before and yet have already recognized, as though we remembered it from some previous existence." (*Marcel Proust on Art and Literature*, 347; *CSB* 669).

15 *Marcel Proust on Art and Literature*, 348; *CSB* 670.

16 "Perhaps if it were within everyone's capacity to be smitten with love for a work of art, as it is within everyone's capacity (or at least, appears to be) to be smitten with love for some person of another sex (I speak of true love), we might similarly know how rare a thing it is to be in love with a work of art" (*Marcel Proust on Art and Literature*, 354; *CSB* 674).

17 "When he talks he is afflicted – delightfully – with idolatry" ("John Ruskin," *ASB* 188; *CSB* 135).

18 A model for Charlus as well.

19 Proust, "Poetry, or the Mysterious Laws" (*ASB* 147; *CSB* 418).

20 Proust visited Moreau's house in November 1898, as it was under construction to become a museum, and he was writing the essay following Moreau's death. See Yoshikawa, *Proust et l'art*, 170, and Theodore Johnson, "Marcel Proust et Gustave Moreau," *Bulletin de la Société des Amis de Marcel Proust* 28 (1978), 619. See also Paul Flat, *Musée Gustave Moreau: l'artiste – son oeuvre – son influence: 18 héliogravures hors texte* (Société de l'édition artistique, 1899). Charles Hayem donated five works, four of which were watercolors, to the Museé du Luxembourg, 1899: among them were the watercolors *L'Apparition* and *Le Jeune homme et la mort* (as well as *L'Amour et les muses, Oedipe et le Sphinx). Orphée* was in the museum since 1867. Mme Straus owned *Chanteur persan* or *Chanteur indien*, now owned by the Ephrussi de Rothschild Foundation at Saint-Jean-Cap-Ferrat, which had been in the living room of Émile Straus; Proust could have seen this work. He also read with great interest a series of six articles by Ary Renan published in *La Gazette des beaux-arts* during 1899 (for which Charles Ephrussi served as editor), the same period of time when Proust writes his own fragments on Moreau. He did not go to the exhibition of Moreau works in 1906 (as the correspondence makes clear). Proust became acquainted with all the works he cites in the novel through the publication of Ary Renan (Yoshikawa, *Proust et l'art*, 181), and he read the catalogue

piece by Robert de Montesquiou, 'Un peintre lapidaire," published in *Altesses sérénissimes*, reproduced in *Gustave Moreau par ses contemporains* (Paris: Éditions de Paris, 1998), 69–89. See Yoshikawa, *Proust et l'art*, 169–191.

21 The thread of the fragmentary apparition takes its meaning from the multiple levels of the word: "French *apparition* (15th cent. in Littré), Latin *appāritiōn-em* , noun of action, *appārēre* to APPEAR *v*. . . . The senses are those of late Latin and French. Classical Latin had only the sense "attendance, service, servants," a special sense of *appārēre* "to appear at a summons, wait upon, attend": see APPARITOR *n*., APARAUNT *n*. (Etymologically, exactly = APPEARANCE *n*., and having a parallel development of senses. But now almost restricted in common use to [the] sense . . . : *spec*. 'An immaterial appearance as of a real being; a spectre, phantom, or ghost', and when used in other senses, having generally from this association some idea of *startling* or *unexpected* appearance.)" *Oxford English Dictionary*.

22 Cited in Yoshikawa, *Proust et l'art*, 184.

23 See Elstir's watercolor of Odette: "Artistic genius acts in a similar way to those extremely high temperatures which have the power to split up combinations of atoms which they proceed to combine afresh in a diametrically opposite order, corresponding to another type" (2: 601; II, 216).

PART II

Apprenticing and integrating

CHAPTER 5

Art and craft in Marcel Proust's life and work

Virginie Greene

To the memory of Dorothy Kolb.

"Good job" the English say. "Beau travail" disent les Français. The French have no work ethic. Instead, they have "la conscience professionnelle" and one phrase does not translate the other. If I had written this paper in French I would not have titled it "Art et artisanat dans la vie et l'œuvre de Marcel Proust." "Craft" and "artisanat" allegedly refer to the same thing, but don't have the same flavor.

From a broad perspective, French and Anglo-American cultures share a common history of labor, capital, industry, art, and craft, or, in one word, work. The linguistic differences I pointed out do not reveal two different cultures but two different styles within the same culture. In order to understand thoroughly the formation of these two styles, it would seem more appropriate to investigate economic, politic, and social materials than the writings of a man who never had a job in his life. However, on matters of style, one can learn much from Proust, even when style is related to work in its concrete aspects.

In *Proust and Signs*, Deleuze claims that the unity of *À la recherche du temps perdu* is not provided by memory or time past: "What is involved is not an exposition of involuntary memory, but the narrative of an apprenticeship: more precisely, the apprenticeship of a man of letters."[1] For Deleuze, this apprenticeship consists in learning how to decipher signs. The essential craft of the man of letters is semiotic, which we should not be surprised to find in a book published in 1964. I do not deny the importance of signs in Proust's novel, but I propose another way to understand the apprenticeship narrated in *À la recherche*, by shifting focus from semiotics to pragmatics, and from art to craft.

The man who could not make his bed

Proust did not know how to make his bed. Why should he have known? He did not know how to hammer a nail either, to cut or joint pieces of wood, to sweep or wax a wooden floor, to wash dishes or polish silverware, to cook, bake, or make preserves, to paint or plaster a wall, to wash, mend, or sew clothes. I could add many more items on the list of things he never made, maintained, or repaired, although he used them. It is easier to draw the list of manual and physical activities that members of the upper class could practice without demeaning themselves: sports like horseback riding, hunting, fencing, tennis, or golf, playing musical instruments such as piano or violin (not tuba or drums), practicing fine arts such as drawing, painting, or, less frequently, sculpture, gardening (with help from paid gardeners). Ladies practiced textile crafts, for decorative or charitable purposes. Some gentlemen might have known how to shave with a straight razor, probably not how to sharpen a razor blade. Two careers involving manual or physical activities were available for upper-class men: the military and medicine.

Proust did not practice any of those gentle crafts, not even shaving. Céleste Albaret recounts that a *coiffeur* came to shave him at home. When the *coiffeur* was not available or Proust was too sick, he grew a beard.[2] What about his drawings? Proust practiced drawing in a deliberately skill-less, craftless fashion, which is what makes them so endearing. Some of Proust's drawings parody specific art schools or movements. In a letter to Reynaldo Hahn, Proust explains that he has made thirty drawings which "presented a bold criticism of the various schools of painting" (*Corr* VI, 103).[3] All of them parody the art of drawing practiced in boudoirs and drawing rooms, and exhibit, to quote Françoise Leriche, "a critical eye . . . his caricatures clearly question . . . what we 'see' in works of art."[4] They may also be an ironic tribute to John Ruskin.

Proust passed on all the available opportunities to let his inner *homo faber* flourish. Most people in his close entourage, though, practiced a craft or a profession involving manual skills. His father was a medical doctor, his brother a surgeon, his friends and lovers were musicians, painters, army officers, sportsmen, scientists, or gardeners. To pick one example, Robert de Montesquiou-Fezensac could have been a competent designer, had he not believed he was a Poet and had he not inherited his mother's industrial fortune.

The only thing Proust wanted to do was to write books, which was considered a decent activity for a gentleman, but was not one involving much craft, if we take craft as a direct, physical involvement with the material world that surrounds us. However, it turned out that the man who could not make his bed was also a man who could not write a book.

The man who could not write a book

The first book Marcel Proust authored appeared in 1896, under the title *Les Plaisirs et les Jours*, published by Calmann-Lévy, the publisher of Balzac and Anatole France.[5] France provided a preface, Reynaldo Hahn the scores of four pieces for piano, and Madeleine Lemaire fifty illustrations. Each of these illustrations is signed. Twenty copies of *Les Plaisirs et les Jours*, printed on paper from the imperial manufactures of Japan, included an original watercolor by Madeleine Lemaire, signed too. In total, she contributed seventy drawings or paintings.

The book has often been described as a failure. As François Proulx suggests, it is a failure if it is considered as a "commercial venture," and not so much if it is considered as part of "an economy of the gift."[6] The problem may also be that *Les Plaisirs et les Jours* is not a book, but a breviary of 1890s aesthetics and a luxury object. It would have been more truthful to present this object as "*Les Plaisirs et les Jours*, a picture book by Madeleine Lemaire, with texts by Marcel Proust and music by Reynaldo Hahn." But Proust could not help thinking he was writing *his* book. In other words, he had picked the wrong mold and the wrong recipe for his cake.

His next writing project also failed to become his book, but in a different way. This time, Proust tried to bake a cake without a mold and with too many recipes. No book came out of it, at least during his lifetime. The manuscript called *Jean Santeuil* contains the beginning of an introduction: "May I call this book a novel? It is perhaps less and much more, the very essence of my life gathered without blending anything into it during the hours when, torn apart, it pours out. This book has never been made: it has been harvested" (*JS* 181). Precisely. In the practice of any craft, a moment comes when one has to move from the preliminary steps of gathering materials and tools, choosing patterns or designs, trying, testing, sketching, planning, or measuring toward the first decisive gesture, whether it is a cut, a stitch, a stroke, a broken egg, or a word on a sheet of paper. Proust did not reach that stage as he worked on *Jean Santeuil*. He did in a subsequent project, which seemed even more doomed to fail than *Jean Santeuil*: the "essay on Sainte-Beuve and Flaubert" morphing into a conversation with Maman, which became *À la recherche du temps perdu*.[7] Between *Jean Santeuil* and the essay on Sainte-Beuve, Proust translated Ruskin.

Translating Ruskin

No one today would deny the importance of the Ruskinian phase in Proust's life and work.[8] Several scholars consider that one important thing Proust learned during this phase is the discipline of working. Antoine Compagnon insists that on one point Proust always remained in agreement with Ruskin: "a sense of discipline and faith in work."[9] It is true that Ruskin had a long, productive career as a writer, art critic, scholar, and public figure, and that he wrote extensively about work, labor, discipline, art, and craft. There is also ample proof that Proust worked hard and productively in order to publish *La Bible d'Amiens* and *Sésame et les Lys*, which critics praised for the quality of the translation, introductions, and notes. Still, the idea of Marcel Proust learning his work ethic from John Ruskin sounds counterintuitive, if by work ethic we understand tidiness, organization, productivity, reliability, regularity, method, control, mastery, and anything else that may enable someone to deliver. Ruskin would ask "Deliver what?" Describing an "imposing iron railing" installed in front of a pub in Croydon, with the result that the tiny space thus delimited became "a protective receptacle of refuse, cigar-ends and oyster-shells," Ruskin concludes that this masterpiece of urban design "represented a quantity of work, partly cramped and deadly, in the mine; partly fierce and exhaustive, at the furnace; partly foolish and sedentary, of ill-taught students making bad designs: work from the beginning to the last fruits of it, and in all the branches of it, venomous, deathful, and miserable."[10] For Ruskin, most of the work done in England is wasteful, ugly, and unethical. On the contrary, "generally, good, useful work, whether of the hand or head, is either ill-paid, or not paid at all."[11] Moreover, "none of us, or very few of us, do either hard or soft work because we think we ought; but because we have chanced to fall into the way of it, and cannot help ourselves."[12] Ruskin praises work and rejects idleness, but never defines a clear, simple work ethic. Between deprecations and praise, Ruskin's work ethic looks like a dogged impulse to continue to work without faith in the worth or usefulness of the work, and without hope for a just reward or recognition.

What type of worker was Ruskin himself? In the words of John Batchelor, "his editors make Ruskin seem, grand, majestic and *tidy*. In reality, he was never tidy, though to be untidy is not to be incoherent."[13] Ruskin worked enormously, in part to realize the contradictory dreams of his father, John James Ruskin, a trader in sherry and a reader of Byron. Ruskin senior wanted his son to be a successful genius, an inspired capitalist, and a hard-working dilettante. This was an insane program that Ruskin junior fulfilled, insanity included. In 1852, Ruskin (who was then age 33) wrote his father to defend his project of writing about Venice instead of continuing the successful series on *Modern Painters*:

> I cannot write anything but what is *in* me and interests me. I never could write for the public – I never *have* written except under the conviction of a thing's being important, wholly irrespective of the public's thinking so too – and all my power, such as it is, would be lost the moment I tried to catch people by fine writing. You know I promised them no Romance – I promised them Stones.[14]

This romantic posture is an affirmation of Ruskin's *conscience professionnelle.* The phrase "work ethic" presents work as a social virtue, whereas *conscience professionnelle* presents work as a personal obsession. My work ethic makes me feel responsible of my work in front of others; my *conscience professionnelle* makes me continue to research, read, and write, until *I* am satisfied or throw the towel in despair. Both are necessary for the accomplishment of any difficult work, but are more often than not in conflict with one another. Such a conflict can be at once productive and destructive, as the massive and untidy *œuvre* of John Ruskin shows.

Among the travails that Ruskin's style renders so accurately, craft appears as an element of peace, joy, and stability. Ruskin practiced drawing all his life with great pleasure and talent. Craft is also the ideal form of work he envisions in his utopian writings, and the exercise of fundamental faculties such as observation, ingenuity, memory, imagination, and patience. "I am essentially a painter and a leaf dissector" Ruskin wrote in 1860.[15]

Ruskin mentions, describes, and praises many crafts, including the craft of the translator, in the chapter of *The Bible of Amiens* dedicated to "The Lion Tamer." Ruskin defends Saint Jerome, patron saint of translators, against Protestant contempt by saying that "he represents, in his total nature and final work, not the vexed inactivity of the Eremite, but the eager industry of a benevolent tutor and pastor."[16] In Proust's translation: "il représente dans sa nature entière et dans son œuvre finale, non pas l'inactivité chagrine de l'Ermite, mais le labeur ardent d'un maître et d'un pasteur bienfaisants."[17] Further, Ruskin describes Jerome's industry not as the conscious fulfillment of divine orders but as an art and a craft: "partly as a scholar's exercise, partly as an old man's recreation, the severity of the Latin language was softened, like Venetian crystal, by the variable fire of Hebrew thought."[18] In Proust's translation: "Ce fut moitié exercice d'écrivain, moitié par récréation de vieillard qu'il se plut à adoucir la sévérité de la langue latine ainsi qu'un cristal vénitien, au feu changeant de la pensée hébraïque."[19] Proust translates "scholar's exercise" as "exercice d'écrivain," and gives more agency to the translator in turning the passive "the severity of the Latin language was softened" into the active "il se plut à adoucir la sévérité de la langue latine." If I retranslate Proust's translation into English, and take it as a description of what *he* is doing, I obtain: "Partly as a writer's exercise, partly as a young man's recreation, the softness of the French language was hardened, like Venetian crystal, by the variable fire of Ruskin's thought." The French find English a little bit harsh to the ear and rough to the palate, but admire its precision. Describing a dress, Proust writes in *Le Côté de Guermantes*, "her gown, the bodice of which had for its sole ornament innumerable spangles (either little sticks and beads of metal, or brilliants), moulded her figure with a precision that was positively British" (3: 63; II, 353). Proust wrote this sentence with a precision that was positively British, and with an eye for well-crafted objects that was positively Ruskinian.

In reading and translating Ruskin, Proust found ways to resolve his own problems with work and career. Like Ruskin, he had to please his parents by demonstrating a work ethic while fulfilling his still inchoate *conscience professionnelle*. Like Ruskin, he had to transform an over-protected child into a worker without killing the child's creativity. Like Ruskin, he had to handle inner demons such as guilt, hypochondria, and unspeakable loves. Translating Ruskin meant assessing the risks of using the deep inner self as the source of a work ethic and the foundation of a work practice. Thus, the psychotic guided the neurotic, and the neurotic understood the virtue of occupational therapy.

The late mad genius could not have helped the young aspiring writer if their encounter had not involved living persons, material objects, and real places. It is not enough to read, think, or write about craft. One needs to practice and to receive advice and training. One needs to establish a workshop – even if it turns out to be one's bed.

Because of his limited grasp of English, Proust had to use consultants in order to translate Ruskin. A collaboration among artists produced *Les Plaisirs et les Jours*, but Proust, due to his age, was not the real master in this undertaking. When he decided to translate Ruskin, he became the *maître d'œuvre* of a layered process, involving collaborators whose tasks he alone determined. In this regard, Proust worked like Saint Jerome, who used numerous consultants and helpers, including Jews and women.

Encounter with a craftswoman

Among these collaborators one is particularly important from the perspective of craft: Marie Nordlinger, who was Reynaldo Hahn's second cousin. She had studied fine arts at the School of Arts in Manchester, and specialized in metalwork. Reynaldo nicknamed her "Benvenuta Cellina."[20]

Marie Nordlinger met Proust in 1896. She had come to Paris to study sculpture and painting. She was 20 and Proust was 25. They became friends and met several times at Reynaldo's parents place or in the salon of Madeleine Lemaire.[21] Marie Nordlinger played the role of an expert in English and Englishness for Proust, although she was a cosmopolitan English speaker rather than a pure "Brit." More important than her knowledge of the language was the fact that she was, according to her memoirs, "a devotee of Ruskin, steeped in Pre- and Post-Raphaelite doctrine."[22] In 1897, Robert de La Sizeranne's book *Ruskin et la religion de la beauté* appeared, making Ruskin famous in France. In December 1899, Proust wrote to Marie Nordlinger that he had begun "a small work completely different from what I usually do, about Ruskin and some cathedrals" (*Corr* II, 377).

At first, Proust did not use Marie's linguistic competence: his mother drafted a rough translation for him, and he consulted a few English or anglophone friends on specific terms or sentences. He started to consult Marie on Ruskin in early 1900, just after Ruskin's death. This led him to discuss issues related to arts or crafts with her. In a letter dated March 1900, Proust responds to her claim that she had not learned how to write: "Do not complain of not having learned. *There is nothing to know.* Even what is called technical skill is not a knowledge in the strict sense." Proust then explains that a scientific, learned relation to words does not lead to anything productive, but that technique, tact, or skill with words only starts when knowledge is forgotten (*Corr* II, 390). In this letter, Proust describes the art of the writer as a craft in opposition to a science, which allows him to privilege involuntary memory over conscious knowledge. A craftswoman is less likely to intellectualize or theorize her work than a scientist, and she is less likely to believe she has absolute control over her materials.

Marie Nordlinger, after failing to be hired by Lalique, was hired by Siegfried Bing in the metal workshop of *L'Art Nouveau*, in March 1903.[23] In June she started to help Proust correct the proofs of *La Bible d'Amiens*. She recalled that, during one of these sittings, Proust was intrigued by her Japanese cloisonné earrings: "So Ruskin was abandoned for the time being and I had to expatiate on the craft, origin, history, and the various forms of enamel."[24] She also wrote in the notes of her edition of Proust's letters to her, "In our conversations, we often talked about techniques, for we both practiced an art and loathed approximations."[25]

We can find another trace of Proust's conversations with Nordlinger in the preface to *Sésame et les Lys*, when Proust describes his bedroom in the vacation home where he locates his reading experiences as the antithesis of William Morris's theories:

> William Morris's theories, which Maple and English designers constantly apply, dictate that a room is beautiful only if it contains things that are useful to us and only if any useful thing – even a simple nail – is not hidden but made visible . . . According to these aesthetic principles, my bedroom was not beautiful at all, for it was full of useless things modestly dissimulating the useful ones, and even making them extremely difficult to use.[26]

Marie Nordlinger was not a fan of the English Arts and Crafts movement.[27] She found her aesthetic home in the "Art Nouveau" movement, which was greatly influenced by Ruskin's ideas about beauty and nature. If we accept Françoise Leriche's thesis that Proust is an Art Nouveau rather than an Impressionist writer, the role of Marie Nordlinger in the formation of his aesthetic takes an even greater importance.[28]

This role has a material dimension, for their conversations were often triggered or centered on objects, including some that Marie Nordlinger made, such as a pink enameled hawthorn flower (*Corr* IV, 61).[29] Once, she gave him a cheap toy that was available at Bing's store, the Japanese water flowers that eventually blossomed in a memorable cup of tea (*Corr* IV, 111–112).[30] But the most important thing she gave him is the realization that art – any art – is craft, and that his personal, unique contribution to literature would blossom out of the practice of a humble craft, involving scissors and glue.

Draft as craft

This pun is as bad as any of Doctor Cottard's, but, again, the linguistic differences between English and French can help us to reconsider one of Proust's singularities, his way of drafting. "Craft" comes from a Germanic root meaning "power, strength, virtue." "Draft" comes from the verb "to draw" and would correspond in French to "trait" from the verb *tirer*, but has a different semantic range. Most important is the fact that "draft" is related to the craft of "drawing" (*dessiner*), and to the skill of "sketching." This semantic field involves precision, decision, strength, and planning.

Brouillon comes from the verb *brouiller*, which comes from a Germanic root that also gives *brouet* ("brew"). We are in the semantic field of brewing, stewing, concocting, mixing, blending, fusing, confusing. When *brouillon* is used as an adjective, it signals bad working habits. "Elle est très brouillon" is not a compliment. The term *brouillon* is most often associated with elementary school exercises. Pupils use (or used?) *cahiers de brouillon* for their assignments. *Brouillon* is so childish or elementary that artists prefer to use other words, such as *esquisses, croquis*, or *premier jet*. In the most recent Pléiade edition of *À la recherche du temps perdu*, the section presenting excerpts from Proust's manuscripts is entitled *Esquisses*.[31]

The editors and authors of the essays published in the recent volume *Proust aux brouillons* had to work against the grain of the French language in order to establish the importance, dignity, and beauty of Proust's unique way of drafting.[32] The title plays on the pictorial tradition of the *Christ aux outrages*, and on the etymological sense of *travail*, which is related to torture. In parallel to this critical volume, Nathalie Mauriac Dyer directs the publication of Proust's seventy-five *cahiers* in facsimiles, presenting them as tools for research and objects of art.[33] Proust himself had realized the value of his *brouillons*, when he asked Gaston Gallimard to create a special deluxe edition of *À l'ombre des jeunes filles en fleurs*, including pages of his corrected proofs (*Corr* XVII, 443–444).

Thinking of Proust's drafting technique as a craft led me to think about its evolution. Since I have not been able to verify them in the manuscripts themselves, I will present my thoughts as a series of questions and guesses.

When and how did Proust learn to draft a piece of writing? I suggest that he learnt that technique in elementary and high school, like everyone else in the French educational system of his times. He certainly used *cahiers de brouillon*, but did his teachers check the *brouillons* or did they only assess the final stage of assignments? Did they practice a pedagogy of rewriting? How did they give feedback? My guess is that the corrections were mostly interlinear, pointing out grammatical or stylistic problems on specific words and phrases. There might have been some training in the general building of an argument involving substitution, suppression, expansion, or displacement on a larger scale. I doubt this would have involved cutting and gluing pieces of paper together; it would have more likely involved scratching off and rewriting, in order to *mettre au net*, the French expression that signifies the passage from the *brouillon* to the final version.[34] This could be checked on the *Papiers scolaires* kept in the "fonds Marcel Proust" at the Bibliothèque nationale de France, which contains samples of French compositions, translations from and into Latin, and a philosophical composition corrected by Alphonse Darlu.[35]

How did Proust draft *Les Plaisirs et les Jours*? The response also lies in the "fonds Proust," which holds manuscripts, typescripts, proofs, placards, and fragments. Yves Sandre, in his edition of *Les Plaisirs et les Jours*, remarks that neither the typescripts nor the placards include any correction by Proust, but that the various proofs show a difference in the order of the pieces in the table of contents. The differences between the earlier versions (published in literary reviews) and the version published in the book indicate minute corrections, like "il devint cramoisi" ["he turned crimson"] corrected to "il devint très rouge" ["he turned very red"] (*JS* 10 and 913). I suggest that Proust drafted and corrected these pieces in a "fine tuning" mode, without massive changes. The most important structural change he attended to (probably in consultation with Reynaldo Hahn and Madeleine Lemaire) was the order of the pieces in the volume.

How did Proust draft *Jean Santeuil*? Yves Sandre's notes show that he used notebooks and loose sheets, that some pages are not corrected at all, that the pages corrected are often difficult to read, and that he copied some parts of the manuscript in an attempt to move from *brouillon* to *mise au net*, but not in a neat fashion. Besides fine tuning, Proust uses another type of drafting: he seems to write by fragments or blocks of texts not yet definitely assigned a clear position in a final design. But what was the final design?

How did Proust draft his translations of Ruskin? The materials preserved in the "fonds Proust" include Madame Proust's rough translation with annotations and corrections by Proust, manuscripts by Proust, corrected typescripts, corrected proofs, and numerous documents including corrected placards of George Elwall's translation of *The Crown of Wild Olive* and *The Seven Lamps of Architecture*. I suggest that, in his translations, Proust developed an extremely demanding method of rewriting, in which the text can be at any stage subjected to transformation on a small or large scale, and is constantly connected to other texts, through cross-referencing.

When and how did Proust learn to cut paper with scissors and to glue a piece of paper on the top of another? He most probably learnt at home with his mother or a domestic when he was very young. The same thing could be said about the few other material crafts that Proust practiced: handwriting, drawing, and tracing.[36] The fact that Proust learned all these manual skills as a child is important. Crafting and drafting were probably a way for him to induce an unconscious labor, rooted in deep memory. When did he start to practice this method of collage with his manuscripts? Céleste Albaret claims that she suggested that technique to him, for additions, and she did the cutting and gluing operations.[37] This accounts for some additions (the longest paperolles), but cannot account for displacements such as those described by Isabelle Serça in her study of interpolations in Proust's manuscripts. Serça assumes that Proust himself performed the cutting and gluing.[38] If he learned the craft at a very young age, he came to use it late in his life. Was it before he engaged in his final writing project (perhaps during his Ruskin phase), or during the project itself? When did he transform drafting into a craft, or an art?

I ask questions I cannot answer, but which I trust are answerable. It may be of particular importance in our times to retrace an aesthetic and pragmatic history of literature that integrates all levels of planning and execution, from the most material to the most spiritual level, in order to better understand our own culture of cutting and pasting, workshops, and virtual realities.

NOTES

1 Gilles Deleuze, *Proust and Signs: The Complete Text* [1964], trans. Richard Howard (Minneapolis: University of Minnesota Press, 2000), 3.

2 Céleste Albaret, *Monsieur Proust* [1973], trans. Barbara Bray (New York: New York Review of Books, 2003), 85.

3 Cited in Caroline Szylowicz, "Les dessins dans les lettres de Marcel Proust à Reynaldo Hahn," in *Cher ami . . . Votre Marcel Proust. Marcel Proust im Spiegel seiner Korrespondenz: Briefe und Autographen aus der Bibliotheca Proustiana Reiner Speck*, ed. Jürgen Ritter and Reiner Speck (Cologne: Snoek, 2009), 47. Unless otherwise specified, translations in this essay are by Virginie Greene.

4 See Chapter 12 in the present volume, page 164.

5 Marcel Proust, *Les Plaisirs et les Jours* (Paris: Calmann-Lévy, 1896).

6 See Chapter 17 in the present volume, page 244.

7 See Françoise Leriche's description of the different stages leading from the 1908 essay on Sainte-Beuve and Flaubert to the novel emerging in 1910, in Proust, *Lettres: 1879–1922*, ed. F. Leriche with Caroline Szylowicz, preface and afterword by Katherine Kolb (Paris: Plon, 2004), 429–430.

8 See for instance Diane R. Leonard, "Proust and Ruskin 2000: 'Ces étoiles éteintes dont la lumière nous arrive encore'," in *Proust in Perspective: Visions and Revisions*, ed. Armine Kotin Mortimer and Katherine Kolb (Urbana and Chicago: University of Illinois Press, 2002), 213–226.

9 Antoine Compagnon, "Introduction: A hue et à dia," in John Ruskin and Marcel Proust, *Sésame et les Lys* précédé de *Sur la lecture* (Paris: Editions Complexe, 1987), 22. See also Cynthia Gamble, *Proust as Interpreter of Ruskin: The Seven Lamps of Translation* (Birmingham, AL: Summa Publications, 2002), 9.

10 John Ruskin, *The Crown of Wild Olive*, in *The Works of John Ruskin*, 39 vols., Library Edition, ed. by E. T. Cook and A. Wedderburn (London: George Allen, 1903–1912), XVIII (1905), 387–388.
11 *Ibid.*, 422.
12 *Ibid.*, 419.
13 John Batchelor, *John Ruskin: No Wealth but Life* (London: Chatto & Windus, 2000), xi.
14 Letter of February 18, 1852, quoted by Batchelor in *John Ruskin*, 96.
15 Ruskin, *Time and Tide*, in *Works*, XVII (1905), 415, quoted by Batchelor in *John Ruskin*, 96.
16 Ruskin, *The Bible of Amiens*, in *Works*, XXXIII (1908), 105.
17 Ruskin, *La Bible d'Amiens*, trans. Marcel Proust (Paris: Mercure de France, 1926), 217.
18 Ruskin, *Bible of Amiens*, 109.
19 Ruskin, *Bible d'Amiens*, trans. Proust, 228.
20 P. F. Prestwich, *The Translation of Memories: Recollections of the young Proust* (London: Peter Owen, 1999), 55–56, 108–109.
21 See my biographical notice on Marie Nordlinger in Proust, *Lettres*, 1269–1270.
22 Prestwich, *Translation of Memories*, 60.
23 *Ibid.*, 120.
24 *Ibid.*, 125.
25 Marie Nordlinger, notes to Marcel Proust, *Lettres à une amie: recueil de quarante-et-une lettres inédites adressées à Marie Nordlinger, 1889–1908* (Manchester: Éditions du Calame, 1942), 118.
26 Proust, preface to Ruskin, *Sésame et les Lys* précédé de *Sur la lecture*, 45–46.
27 Prestwich, *Translation of Memories*, 174.
28 Françoise Leriche, "Proust, an 'Art Nouveau' Writer?," trans. Jane Kuntz, in *Proust in Perspective*, 202.
29 See Marie Nordlinger's note on this letter in Marcel Proust, *Lettres à une amie*, 118.
30 *Ibid.*, 118–119.
31 See the Pléiade edition, for instance I, 631.
32 *Proust aux brouillons*, ed. Nathalie Mauriac Dyer and Kazuyoshi Yoshikawa (Turnhout: Brepols, 2011).
33 Marcel Proust, *Cahiers 1 à 75 de la Bibliothèque nationale de France*, ed. dir. Nathalie Mauriac Dyer (Turnhout, Paris: Brepols/Bibliothèque nationale de France, 2008–).
34 French culture may be different from Anglo-American culture in this regard. The importance of the *brouillon* could be related to the emphasis that, until recently, French schoolteachers set from the start on the formal, aesthetic qualities of writing and *presentation* (formatting) in school exercises.
35 See *Catalogue des Nouvelles acquisitions françaises du département des Manuscrits, 1972–1986, Nos 16428–18755*, dir. Florence Callu and Annie Angremy (Paris: Bibliothèque nationale de France, 1999), 20.

36 Proust traced many of his drawings for Reynaldo Hahn. See Szylowicz, "Dessins dans les lettres," 49–50.
37 Albaret, *Monsieur Proust*, 276–277.
38 Isabelle Serça, "Genèse de l'interpolation: l'art du montage," in *Proust aux brouillons*, 45.

CHAPTER 6

"Those blessed days": Ruskin, Proust, and Carpaccio in Venice

Susan Ricci Stebbins

John Ruskin wrote in his autobiography, "Tintoret was virtually unseen, Veronese unfelt, Carpaccio not so much as named, when I began to study them."[1] Vittore Scarpaccia (*c.* 1465–1525), the Venetian painter called Carpaccio, was well patronized in his day, though largely forgotten thereafter. Yet his work became a great favorite of Ruskin (1819–1900) and of his disciple Marcel Proust, who made numerous references to it in his novel. I propose to explore the multiple ways in which Proust's use of his work and that of other Venetian painters, frequently influenced by Ruskin, enriches his characterization of people, objects, and events in the novel, while contributing to a larger framework of desire and loss symbolized by Venice itself.

Proust became keenly interested in art during his youth. While still in school he haunted the Louvre in the 1880s and early 1890s, when museums were gaining in popularity. He developed a taste for the pastoral landscapes of Paulus Potter and Albert Cuyp, and for the work of Watteau and Van Dyck. In addition, at the Louvre he admired Fra Angelico and the early Florentine masters. As a young man, Proust briefly aspired to a museum career, publishing critical reviews on exhibitions and writing several essays, unpublished in his lifetime, on Chardin, Watteau, Moreau, Monet, and Rembrandt.[2]

Though he never worked for a museum, Proust would instead curate his own vast, carefully selected, collection of works of art within his novel. In *Du côté de chez Swann* alone, we find references to a wider range of painters, as by the time this volume appeared Proust had seen numerous exhibitions and private collections in Paris, had visited Holland and Belgium, Venice and Padua, and had immersed himself in Ruskin's writings. Proust's repertoire came to include most of the major masters of the Italian Renaissance from Giotto to Titian, together with Hals and his Dutch contemporaries; he also expanded his range to include Turner, so much admired by Ruskin early in his career, and Carpaccio, whom the critic came to favor later in his life.

All of these artists were well known in Proust's day except for Carpaccio, who won numerous commissions and had been "held in great esteem" in his day, but has been generally considered a minor figure since his death – except by Ruskin and Proust. The "canon" of Italian Renaissance painters in Proust's time still generally reflected the views of Giorgio Vasari (1511–1574), the Florentine architect, painter, and historian, who favored the artists of his own city. When he considered Venice in his *Lives of the Artists* of 1568, Vasari focused on Titian, Giorgione, and the Bellini family, and two masters of the following generation, Tintoretto and Veronese. What he valued most were the painters whom he saw as remaking art, taking it from the medieval period to what he called the "modern": Giorgione, whom he valued for "copying the freshness of the living form" and his follower, Titian, whom he praised for his naturalism and his color. Vasari mentioned Carpaccio only briefly, as a follower of the Bellinis; he would have recognized that his paintings recall the tapestries and mosaics of the medieval period, that they make less advanced use of perspective than the best of his contemporaries and perhaps most importantly, that they lack the humanist underpinnings, the interest in character, of a Giorgione or a Titian.[3]

During the seventeenth and eighteenth centuries Venice became a fixture on the Grand Tour, though it was always second to Rome and Florence, as it lacked the classical ruins, ancient sculpture, and baroque architecture of Rome, or the artistic treasures of Florence. However, Richard Lassels in his *Voyage of Italy* (1670) found Venice "one of the fairest Cities in Europe." Nearly a century later, Thomas Nugent praised St. Mark's and its mosaics, and considered Venetian paintings at length, though he mentioned Carpaccio only in passing. The city's pageants, regattas, carnivals and masked balls became a major attraction, and the allure of its courtesans, many of whom were painted by leading artists, was well known. The English writer Joseph Addison in 1705 speaks fondly of "the Amours of Venice," while Thomas Nugent was even more explicit, proclaiming that "Venice is fitter for a mistress than a wife."[4] Both Ruskin and Proust, in their very different ways, echo this tradition, with Venice becoming the site of romantic dreams and sensual allure. Proust's narrator, in the novel, speaks of going out alone in the afternoons, without his mother, on "this passionate quest [recherche] of mine for Venetian women" while exploring the humble campi of the city (5: 848; IV, 205).

The reputation of Venice declined in the later eighteenth century. Edward Gibbon described its "generally ill-built houses, ruined pictures and stinking ditches . . . and a large square decorated with the worst architecture I ever yet saw." Multiple invasions from Austria and France had left buildings in ruins. However, after Napoleon's final defeat in 1815, continental travel resumed and the city's image began to improve. Goethe and Byron among others contributed to the modern, romantic vision of Venice. In Goethe's diary of his *Italian Journey* (1816) he writes, "the architecture rises up out of its grave like an ancient ghost and bids me study its principles like the rules of a dead language."[5] Byron in *Childe Harold's Pilgrimage* (1812–1818) spoke of the city's decline – "Thy wreck a glory, and thy ruin graced / With an immaculate charm which cannot be defaced" – while mythologizing the melancholy beauty of its ruins. Thus they both foreshadow Ruskin, who instead of merely lamenting the destruction of Venice, began a crusade to preserve the city. His *Stones of Venice* (1851–1853) more than any other text reestablished the importance of the city as one of the glories of western civilization.

By the mid nineteenth century increased rail travel led to growing numbers of middle-class tourists to Italy. John Murray, whose publications were among the first to serve the new, expanded class of travelers, commissioned Ruskin in 1845 to supply revisions to the handbook for travelers in northern Italy. Before heading to Italy, Ruskin prepared himself by reading Franz Kugler's *Hand-Book of the History of Painting* (1842), which brought new attention to the Venetian painters, and their importance as colorists. One of the first to treat Carpaccio's work with respect, Kugler noted that he "had successfully introduced the daily life of the Venetians of his time in the greatest variety," an element Proust would later make use of in his novel. Ruskin at this time was also influenced by a book devoted entirely to Italian painting, *De la Poésie Chrétienne* (1836), another important attempt to bring about a new appreciation of Venetian painting, by the French art historian Alexis François Rio.[6]

Ruskin's writings, from *Stones of Venice* (1851–1853) to *St. Mark's Rest* (1877) may be seen as continuations of the Grand Tour literature that had existed since the sixteenth century; they demonstrate how his own priorities changed from architecture to painting, paralleling the evolution of Grand Tour interests in the seventeenth and eighteenth centuries. Ruskin's taste in painting, moreover, evolved from his early embrace of the purity of Fra Angelico and the Florentines, seen in the first two volumes of *Modern Painters* (1843–1846), to his growing appreciation of the sophisticated colors of Titian and the Venetian painters in the later volumes (1856–1860). Influenced by his reading and travels, as well as by the personal turmoil he experienced in 1858, what he called his "unconversion," Ruskin turned from a highly puritanical, evangelical faith to a more liberal acceptance of the Roman Catholic Church and the sensual world. He could now write of "the sacredness of color" and its association with passion.[7]

Curiously, Proust's enthusiasm for Venice and its art stemmed primarily from his reading of Ruskin, rather than from any of a number of French writers who had written about the city. French writers of the early nineteenth century including Madame de Staël and Chateaubriand were relatively slow to recognize either the beauty of Venice or the importance of its painters, while Stendhal, who was admired by Proust, described Venice as "that voluptuous paradise of sensuality," but preferred Rome and Michelangelo.[8] However, by mid century the French came increasingly to embrace the city, as one sees in the work of two of Proust's favorite writers of his youth, George Sand and Théophile Gautier, both of whom are referred to in the *Recherche*. Sand, who wrote at least six novels with Venetian settings, expressed her delight with the unceasing songs and the "Moorish palaces" of the city, as well as "the delights of the night."[9] Quite different was Gautier's *Voyage en Italie* (1852), published a year after *Stones of Venice*; devoted largely to Venice and its art and architecture, it served as a guide for travelers in much the way Ruskin's volumes did. Gautier had highest praise for Titian, Veronese, and Tintoretto, but was surprised to discover a "whole new world" in the work of earlier, little-known masters of "Venetian brilliance in the naïve gothic" including Carpaccio; he wrote that "nothing is more elegant, more youthfully gracious, than Carpaccio's *Life of Saint Ursula*" and was "astonished that Carpaccio's name isn't more generally known."[10] Though Proust knew Gautier's work well, the evidence indicates that it was Ruskin's writings that inspired his trips to Venice and his appreciation of the city.

Numerous scholars have examined the influence of Ruskin on Proust, describing how he immersed himself in Ruskin's writings even before the critic's death in 1900. Shortly after Ruskin's death, Proust embarked on a series of projects devoted to Ruskin, including articles about him and translations of his work, as well as pilgrimages to the critic's favorite medieval sites, including Amiens, Chartres, Abbeville, and finally, Venice. Even though Proust was familiar with Italian paintings at the Louvre, it was Ruskin's compelling prose that lured him to Venice. Proust described how "Ruskin's books had created in us a kind of fever and desire" to visit that city. His initial motive was to see its palaces, rather than the art. Always suffering from poor health, and now believing that he was mortally ill, he went to Venice "in order, before I died, to approach, to touch, to see embodied, in palaces that were decaying but still upright, still pink,

Ruskin's ideas on the domestic architecture of the Middle Ages" (*ASB* 191; *CSB* 139).

Proust later described his visit to Venice of May 1900, writing of "those blessed days when . . . in spirit and in truth of the master, we would go about Venice in a gondola listening to his teachings by the water's edge."[11] In his 1906 review of Ruskin's *Stones of Venice*, Proust mentions stopping at all the churches and dwellings with *Stones* in hand to study each capital and relief that the writer had pointed out (*CSB* 521). In the "Séjour à Venise" section of *Albertine disparue*, a remarkable homage to Ruskin in both style and content, Proust's narrator describes the ogival window as "one of the supreme achievements of the domestic architecture of the Middle Ages," sounding like Ruskin himself (5: 846; IV, 204). Recalling the English writer's own words, he describes the city's "palaces of porphyry and jasper" (5: 845; IV, 203), echoing Ruskin's "porches . . . of jasper and porphyry."[12]

Ruskin's friend the painter Burne-Jones, another champion of the medieval, had drawn his attention to Carpaccio in 1862, but it was only in 1869 that Ruskin studied the painter with care, reporting that he "had never once looked at him" before then. He took up Carpaccio suddenly and wholeheartedly, writing that he "is a new world to me."[13] Ruskin's discovery of Carpaccio occurred during a period of increasing emotional strain, much of it the product of his tormented relationship with a young Irish girl, Rose La Touche (1848–1875), whom he pursued over many years. In Venice in 1870, he devoted himself to studying Carpaccio's scenes from the life of Saint George, with whom he identified, taking on the saint's mantle of chivalry and courage as he sought to slay his own personal dragons. The following year, Ruskin, having suffered Rose's latest rejection and increasingly aware of her weakening health, became obsessed by another series by Carpaccio, the nine large canvases devoted to the life of Saint Ursula.[14] The story of Ursula, as recounted in the *Legenda aurea*, took place in an imagined late antiquity and became "one of the best-loved virgin martyr legends" of the Middle Ages.[15]

Ruskin in August 1872 wrote a tender, detailed description in *Fors Clavigera* of *The Dream of Saint Ursula*, which pictures the youthful princess lying asleep in her canopied bed (Figure 6.1). In *Fors* for January 1875, he announced, "The woman I hoped would have been my wife is dying."[16] After Rose's death in May, Ruskin returned to Venice and devoted the fall and winter of 1876/1877 to making several copies of Carpaccio's painting.[17] It became increasingly clear from his letters and publications that in his mind Ruskin had merged his memory of Rose with Carpaccio's image of Ursula. He would associate Rose with other Renaissance paintings as

Figure 6.1 Carpaccio, *The Dream of Saint Ursula*, 1495

well; in the same publication of 1872 he compares Botticelli's Zipporah, the intended wife of Moses, to Carpaccio's Ursula, and implies that she is another symbolic figure for Rose.

With his thorough knowledge of Ruskin's writings, Proust surely knew of the personal crises in Ruskin's life, and would have been aware of his idealization of Rose and his use of Carpaccio's Ursula figure as her symbolic substitute. Notwithstanding his criticism of Sainte-Beuve's emphasis on the importance of biography, Proust was keenly interested in Ruskin's life and praised Collingwood's biography as "the finest book ever written about him."[18] Proust had read and quoted from both *Praeterita* and *Fors*, where the critic often alluded to Rose; in turn, Proust in his novel greatly expands on Ruskin's use of paintings and their details to trigger memory and emotion. Explaining why he chose to use Carpaccio in the *Recherche*, Proust wrote in 1916 (in a letter to Reynaldo Hahn's sister Maria), "I translated everything Ruskin wrote on each of his paintings . . . From the point of view of my novel, another painter, Venetian or Paduan, would have been more convenient, but there isn't a day that I don't look at reproductions of Carpaccio, and therefore I will be on familiar ground" (*Corr* xv, 58).[19]

Much has been written about Proust's use of artists and their works in his novel. Carpaccio, along with Vermeer, Giotto, and Botticelli, plays a larger role than others, but every artistic reference contributes to the multilayered textual fabric. Even the slightest mention of an artist or his work, whether familiar or not to the reader, engages the reader's imagination, reinforcing the tone, color, or veracity of Proust's scene. Regularly juxtaposing or merging past and present, Proust often relied on references to art to anchor both the narrator's and the reader's shifting perspective of time and space.

Proust found in Carpaccio's work a rich source of medieval imagery, one he mined repeatedly for use in his novel. He frequently employs Carpaccio's name as a modifier, as an evocation of the quality or atmosphere of a given scene or object, as when he describes a color, a pageant, or a view that he associates with his work. Secondly, he uses specific details or figures from Carpaccio's work as visual metonyms that trigger memories for the narrator – as when he sees the Fortuny-like cloak, or the image of the mourning woman in "Séjour à Venise." We recall that Proust noted to himself in his *Cahiers* that instead of simply describing things, he should "Use something concrete," and Carpaccio provided many of the images he needed.[20]

Proust makes his initial use of Carpaccio in *Du côté de chez Swann*, when the hero sees the Duchesse de Guermantes for the first time at a wedding in Combray. His first impression is one of disappointment, as she looks more ordinary than he had imagined, but as she glances at him and the sun's rays "shed a geranium glow over the red carpet," she smilingly advances, and he feels a "solemn sweetness in the pomp of a joyful celebration" that to him recalls "certain paintings by Carpaccio" (1: 251; 1, 176). For the reader who knew Carpaccio's work, the reference would have been clear, for Carpaccio was the master of crisply detailed religious and civic processions and ceremonies, that frequently include a group of richly dressed figures arranged, frieze-like, in the foreground, as in his *Arrival of the English Ambassadors* (Figure 6.2). Carpaccio became for Proust a synonym for the pomp and ceremony of Venetian festivities. Moreover, his paintings would occasionally be used in tandem with musical memories, as when Proust

Figure 6.2 Carpaccio, *Arrival of the English Ambassadors* (central scene, detail), 1495

links Carpaccio's paintings with the sound of a trumpet, "certain pages of Wagner's *Lohengrin*," or the reception in *Tannhäuser* (4: 66; III, 49).

In *À l'ombre des jeunes filles en fleurs*, Proust writes of Venetian gondola regattas, often held "in honor of some Embassy," as reminding Elstir of the ones "Carpaccio shows us in his *Legend of Saint Ursula*" (2: 652–653; II, 252). Elstir makes a minor error here, for there actually are no regattas in the Ursula series: is the mistake also Proust's? This would be understandable in view of the fact that he had spent barely a month in Venice in 1900. More than a decade later, as he wrote the novel in Paris, he necessarily relied on black and white photographs and illustrated Carpaccio monographs such as those by the Rosenthals and Pompeo Molmenti, who himself frequently referenced Ruskin.[21] In using Carpaccio and other painters, Proust was not seeking literal connections, but rather was trying to establish atmosphere while grounding his fiction in reality. As he wrote to Maria de Madrazo, his novel was "a work not of [art] criticism, but of life" (*Corr* XV, 56).

At a dinner given by the Guermantes, during a discussion of ancestral roots, the hero finds himself "lost in contemplation of a reliquary such as Carpaccio or Memling used to paint" (3: 735; II, 825). Only a few readers would have been familiar with this reference to an extraordinary fifteenth-century work of art, Hans Memling's *Reliquary of Saint Ursula*, which depicts the Ursula story much as Carpaccio does. The Memling is a work Proust likely saw on his visit to Bruges in 1902, and he surely knew it from the excellent illustration in Molmenti's book. For Proust,

Memling's reliquary carries associations with both history and legend, and here he convincingly intermixes both with present time. Proust used works of art such as Memling's reliquary as another writer might use adjectives or descriptions, the way painters use highlights or glazes. As he wrote elsewhere, "my historical curiosity was faint in comparison with my aesthetic pleasure" (3: 743; II, 831).

Carpaccio, like Proust, combines the real and the imaginary, as one sees in the *The Patriarch of Grado exorcising a demoniac* (Accademia, Venice). Here, the artist's accurate rendering of the old wooden bridge at the Rialto, the gondolas, and the two-story colonnade at the left of the Ca' del Papa (the actual residence of the Patriarch of Grado),[22] would have convinced any viewer of the verisimilitude of the scene, while the condensing and flattening of the space, the inclusion of hyper-realistic figures and details, and jewel-like color all confirmed its fictional qualities. Proust himself described the picture as one in which the painter "evoked the Venice of his time most freely and realistically" (*Corr* xv, 62). As Patricia Brown suggests, in other works where Carpaccio depicted Middle Eastern cities he had never seen, his architecture becomes even more fanciful.[23] Ruskin recognized this, writing in his *Guide to the Academy* that Carpaccio often painted "his fancy, or phantasy; the notion he has of what architecture should be"[24] (see Figure 6.3).

Proust, following Ruskin, reverses Vasari and the traditional canon. Carpaccio becomes the key Venetian artist for him, while Titian plays a secondary role, Giorgione, Veronese, and the Bellinis lesser ones, with Ruskin's favorite, Tintoretto, being mentioned only once in the novel. Proust uses the Venetian painters primarily to evoke the narrator's dream of Venice, both its sensual and its physical allure; his visions of the city excite his narrator as "profoundly . . . as if it had been love, love for a person" (1: 556; I, 384). Titian in the novel becomes an artist representing desire, evoking both a longing to visit the dreamed-of Venice and a complementary erotic desire. Early in *Du côté de chez Swann*, the narrator describes "the idea which I formed of Venice, from a drawing by Titian," even though in actuality few of Titian's paintings or drawings give more than a hint of Venice in literal terms (1: 54; I, 40). On occasion, Carpaccio is mentioned together with the younger painter, as when the narrator says that if he could see La Berma in Racine's *Phèdre*, "he should enjoy the same rapture as on the day when a gondola would deposit me at the foot of the Titian of the Frari or the Carpaccios of San Giorgio della Schiavoni" (2: 14; I, 432).

Proust also associated Titian with the ideal of feminine beauty, an idea he likely formed from the exquisite *Woman with a Mirror* at the Louvre

Figure 6.3 Carpaccio, *Ambassadors Meeting King Maurus* (detail), 1495

(Figure 6.4). The hero at one point tells Albertine, "you have the tresses of Laura Dianti," referring specifically to the Louvre picture, both a portrait and an allegory of vanity (2: 683; II, 273). Once in Venice, he is struck by a young woman selling glassware, and thinks of taking her back to Paris: "the beauty of her seventeen years was so noble, so radiant, that it was like acquiring a genuine Titian before leaving the place" (5: 868; IV, 219). Titian's teacher, Giorgione, plays a similar role: mere mention of his name

Figure 6.4 Titian, *Woman with a Mirror*, *c.* 1515

brings Venice to mind (3: 584; II, 719), and on one occasion Saint-Loup describes an alluring woman as "wildly Giorgionesque" (4: 129; III, 94).

The younger Venetian master, Veronese, is typically characterized by Proust as a painter of opulent fêtes, and is often linked with Carpaccio in this regard. The narrator in *À l'ombre des jeunes filles en fleurs* mentions "the festivities" that Veronese and Carpaccio "so loved to depict" (2: 652; II, 252) and later in the novel he compares the splendid soirée given by the Princesse de Guermantes to the same painters (4: 66; III, 49). In reality, their works are hardly comparable: Carpaccio typically depicted the stately receptions of ambassadors and other formal events, while Veronese's two lavish "dinner" scenes, *The Wedding At Cana* (Figure 4.3b) and the *Feast at the House of Levi* (Accademia, Venice) are richly detailed and extravagant.

It was Carpaccio's paintings above all that Proust chose to bring his imagined Venice to mind. To Maria de Madrazo, he announced his plan to use Carpaccio in a structural role for what he called his "Fortuny leitmotif." Knowing that the popular designer in Paris, Mariano Fortuny (1871–1949), was making use of ancient Venetian materials in his own designs, Proust wrote that he was planning to include a Fortuny dress in the novel to "above all evoke Venice, and the desire to go there." He explained that this leitmotif will play a role "in turn sensual, poetic, and sorrowful" (*Corr* XV, 57). The narrator describes Fortuny's gowns as "faithfully antique but markedly original," as representing "Venice saturated with oriental splendor." Proust writes, "everything of those days had perished, but everything was being reborn," speaking on one hand of Fortuny's revival of ancient designs, while on the other announcing one of the central themes of his novel (5: 497–498; III, 871). Later, Albertine has died, and the hero has at last arrived in Venice. Admiring Carpaccio's *Patriarch of Grado* at the Accademia, he recognizes that one of the noblemen in the foreground is wearing a cloak embroidered with gold and pearls that reminds him "down to the last detail" of the Fortuny cloak that Albertine had worn on their last evening together. The narrator states, "It was Carpaccio who almost succeeded one day in reviving my love for Albertine" (5: 876–877; IV, 225).

Carpaccio again becomes a unifying factor merging memory and mourning, as when Proust overlays the narrator's memory of his mother at St. Mark's, dressed in mourning for her own mother, with an image of the mourning woman in black who kneels, isolated on the right, in Carpaccio's *Martyrdom of the Pilgrims and the Funeral of Saint Ursula* of 1493 (5: 876; IV, 225) (Figure 6.5). Proust likely read Molmenti's explanation that medieval painters typically represented a deceased person as separated from the living mourners in such scenes.[25] In another instance, the hero sees an eagle in one of Carpaccio's paintings at San Giorgio degli Schiavoni and it recalls his painful memories of Albertine's two rings with eagle motifs, about which she had lied to him (5: 868–869; IV, 220).

Figure 6.5 Carpaccio, *The Martyrdom of the Pilgrims and the Funeral of Saint Ursula* (detail), 1493

Proust was a master of social satire, and in one incident, he may well have had both Ruskin and Carpaccio in mind. Carpaccio's painting *Two Venetian Ladies*, also called *the Courtesans*, pictures two Venetian women surrounded by their pets (Figure 6.6). Ruskin writes of the painting in *St. Mark's Rest*: "To mark the satirical purpose of the whole, a pair of ladies shoes are put in the corner," and goes on to say that these high-stilted red shoes "were the grossest and absurdest means of expressing female pride."[26] Proust himself knew the painting, mentioning it once specifically (5: 508; III, 879), while making a satirical allusion to it elsewhere. In the scene that closes *Le Côté de Guermantes*, the Duchess enters her carriage wearing black shoes, and her husband demands that she switch to red ones to match her dress. Swann has just related to the Guermantes that he has a mortal illness, and the Duchess is torn between two social duties, showing concern for her ill friend, or attending to her fashionable appearance; hesitating for only a moment, she chooses to ignore Swann, changes her shoes, and drives off to dinner (3: 815–818; II, 882–884).

Ruskin often praised Carpaccio's accents of color, noting his frequent use of varied reds in details such as the crimson flowers and cloth in *The Dream of Saint Ursula*, or in "comic" details such as the "scarletest . . . of Parrots."[27] Proust himself regularly employs Venetian colors, adding numerous red and pink details such as the Duchesse de Guermantes's red satin dress, her "cloak of a magnificent Tiepolo red" (4: 83; III, 61), her collar of rubies, and Albertine's cloak lined with a cherry pink, "so peculiarly Venetian that it is called Tiepolo pink" (5: 531; III, 896).

Both Ruskin and Proust initially described Venice as a kind of terrestrial Eden. When Ruskin first encountered Venice in 1835, he saw the "enchanted world of Venice," hardly able to believe that "the fairy tale should come true;" in 1841 he named it "the paradise of cities."[28] On Ruskin's penultimate visit to Venice in 1876–1877, burdened by his almost unbearable grief for Rose, his increasing dismay at the pace of modernization, and his bouts of mental illness, the city had lost meaning for him. Then, in 1888, two years before his death, the aging critic set out on the last of his "Grand Tours." Visiting the Louvre on a day in August when he might have crossed paths with the young French art lover Marcel Proust, he spotted Carpaccio's *The Sermon of Saint Stephen*, a picture that Proust never mentions. As Ruskin wrote his friend Charles Eliot Norton, the painting, one "totally unknown to me," was hung "sky-high," and seemed "utterly forgotten and neglected." He told Norton, "I have not said my last word of Veronese yet – nor of Carpaccio."[29] A few weeks later he visited Venice briefly for the last time, but now very ill "he could scarcely look at the Venetian architecture [and] could not explain what the buildings were."[30] As John Pemble writes, "Ruskin for forty years waged a feverish battle against the flight of time and the failure of memory, striving to fix in words and drawings some record of Italy's fugitive glory."[31]

In 1916 Proust wrote to Gaston Gallimard that "the penultimate . . . volume of *À la recherche*" was to be "almost entirely about death and survival in the memory" (*Corr* XIX, 728). In *Albertine disparue*, he

Figure 6.6 Carpaccio, *Two Venetian Ladies*, 1490–1495

describes the hero's dream of Venice as ending in disillusion, having played out its familiar theme of desire and loss. With the hero's final realization of the loss of Albertine and his mother's imminent departure, he finds himself alone, in a state of "irrevocable solitude," and feels that all the enchantment of the palaces, the Rialto, and the paintings was gone; they had only been "mendacious fictions." The narrator states, "The town that I saw before me had ceased to be Venice . . . things had become alien to me" (5: 884; IV, 231).

In *Le Temps retrouvé*, Proust skillfully orchestrates two last refrains of his Venetian motif. In the first, on an evening walk through wartime Paris, that city becomes for the narrator "a whole imaginary exotic city, an oriental scene . . . arbitrarily fanciful when it came to the background, just as out of the town in which he lived Carpaccio made a Jerusalem or a Constantinople by assembling in its streets a crowd whose marvelous motley was not more rich in color than that of the crowd around me" (6: 106; IV, 342). Later, the paving stones on which he stumbles in the Guermantes's courtyard awaken in him his memories of Venice and the feeling of happiness he had felt long ago as he stood upon two uneven stones in the baptistery of St. Mark's. Ironically, it was standing in the baptistery of St. Mark's, studying Ruskin, that Proust himself first began to acknowledge his disenchantment with Ruskin's "idolatry," the critic's confusion of aesthetics and morality (*ASB* 186–190; *CSB* 132–137). Years later, he wrote that he did not feel he had the strength to return to Venice since it was "too much of a graveyard of happiness" for him (*Corr* VI, 75). As his narrator observes, "the true paradises are the paradises that we have lost" (6: 261; IV, 449).

NOTES

1 *Præterita: Outlines of Scenes and Thoughts Perhaps Worthy of Memory in My Past Life*, in *The Works of John Ruskin*, 39 vols., Library Edition, ed. E. T. Cook and A. Wedderburn (London: George Allen, 1903–1912), XXXV (1908), 156.

2 For a selection of these essays in English, see *Marcel Proust on Art and Literature, 1896–1919*, trans. Sylvia Townsend Warner (New York: Carroll & Graf, 1997).

3 Giorgio Vasari, *Lives of Seventy of the Most Eminent Painters, Sculptors, and Architects*, ed. E. Blashfield and A. Hopkins (New York: Charles Scribner's Sons, 1896), II, 344–348, III, 1–3.

4 Richard Lassels, *The Voyage of Italy* (Paris: Vincent du Moutier, 1670), 365; Thomas Nugent, *The Grand Tour*, 3rd edn. (London: J. Rivington, 1778), III, 62 and 48; Joseph Addison, *Remarks on Several Parts of Italy*, 2nd edn. (London: J. Tonson, 1718), 73.

5 *The Letters of Edward Gibbon*, ed. J. E. Norton (London: Cassell Publishers, 1956), I, 193; J. W. Goethe, *Italian Journey, 1786–1788*, ed. Thomas P. Saine and

Jeffrey L. Sammons, trans. Robert R. Heitner (New York: Suhrkamp, 1989), 82.

6 Franz Kugler, *A Hand-Book of the History of Painting* (London: John Murray, 1842), 149–50; see Robert Hewison, *Ruskin on Venice: The Paradise of Cities* (New Haven, CT: Yale University Press, 2009), 90–93.

7 Hewison, *Ruskin on Venice*, 269–270 and 253.

8 Stendhal, *Life of Rossini*, trans. Richard N. Coe (New York: Criterion Books, 1957), 192.

9 George Sand, *Lettres d'un Voyageur*, vol. 1 (Brussels: Meline, Cans, 1838), 81–82 and 88.

10 Théophile Gautier, *Italia: Voyage en Italie*, ed. Marie-Hélène Girard (Paris: La Boîte à Documents, 1997), 22, 188, and 208.

11 Proust, translator's note to John Ruskin, *La Bible d'Amiens* (Paris: Mercure de France, 1904), 245; *On Reading Ruskin: Prefaces to* La Bible d'Amiens *and* Sésame et les Lys *with Selections from the Notes to the Translated Texts*, ed. and trans. Jean Autret, William Burford and Philip J. Wolfe (New Haven, CT and London: Yale University Press, 1987), 82.

12 See Peter Collier, *Proust and Venice*, trans. Daniela Fink (Cambridge University Press, 1989), 45–46.

13 Ruskin, *Modern Painters*, in *Works*, VI (1903), 356, n.

14 *St. George* series (*c.* 1502–1507), S. Giorgio degli Schiavoni, Venice; *Life of St. Ursula* (*c.* 1490–1500), Academy, Venice.

15 Carole M. Cusack, "Hagiography and History: The Legend of Saint Ursula," in *This Immense Panorama: Studies in Honour of Eric J. Sharpe*, ed. Carole M. Cusack and Peter Oldmeadow (Sydney: School of Studies in Religion, University of Sydney, 1999), 91–92.

16 Ruskin's series of letters were published in the form of pamphlets during the 1870s. See *Works*, XXIX (1907), letters 74 and 75. See also Cynthia J. Gamble, "Zipporah: A Ruskinian Enigma Appropriated by Marcel Proust," *Word & Image* 15:4 (1999), 381–394.

17 Charles Herbert Moore (1840–1930), a colleague of Professor Charles Eliot Norton at Harvard, worked alongside Ruskin to assemble a teaching collection for the university. See for instance his "Study of the Head of the Sleeping St. Ursula, after Carpaccio, in the Academy of Venice" (1877–1878), Harvard Art Museums, Harvard University, available at www.harvardartmuseums.org/collections/object/231694. Their correspondence is preserved in the Charles Eliot Norton Papers, Houghton Library, Harvard University.

18 Proust praises Collingwood's biography in a translator's note to *La Bible d'Amiens* (306) and his preface to *Sésame et les lys* (*CSB* 172); see *On Reading Ruskin*, 91, 111. Proust wrote in October 1907 that he owned all the volumes of the Library Edition published to that date, which would have included volume XXIV with E. Cook's description of Ruskin's despair over Rose (*Corr* VII, 260–261). He was eagerly awaiting the publication of volume XXXIII, the *Bible of Amiens*, which was to appear in 1908 (*Corr* VII, 274–275).

19 Ruskin wrote extensively on Carpaccio in *Fors*, *St. Mark's Rest*, and the *Academy Notes*.
20 See Kazuyoshi Yoshikawa, *Proust et l'art pictural* (Paris: Champion, 2010), 30. See also 25–33 on Proust's Fortuny leitmotif; as well as Christie McDonald, *The Proustian Fabric: Associations of Memory* (Lincoln: University of Nebraska Press, 1991), 132–141.
21 Proust made a second trip to Venice in October 1900, about which little is known. On Molmenti and Rosenthal, see Yoshikawa, *Proust et l'art pictural*, 26–29.
22 J. Schulz, *The New Palaces of Medieval Venice* (University Park, PA: Penn State University Press, 2004), 91.
23 Patricia Brown, *Venetian Narrative Painting in the Age of Carpaccio* (New Haven, CT: Yale University Press, 1988), 196–216.
24 Ruskin, *Guide to the Academy*, in *Works*, XXIV (1906), 169.
25 Pompeo Molmenti and Gustav Ludwig, *The Life and Works of Vittorio Carpaccio*, trans. Robert H. Hobart Cust (London: John Murray, 1907), 109; Philip Kolb explains that Proust likely borrowed a French translation of this book (*Vittore Carpaccio, la vie et l'œuvre du peintre*, trans. H. L. Perera [Paris: Hachette, 1910]) from Maria de Madrazo in 1916 (*Corr* XV, 62–63).
26 Ruskin, *St. Mark's Rest*, in *Works*, XXIV (1906), 365.
27 *Ibid.*, 341.
28 Ruskin, *Præterita*, in *Works*, XXXV (1908), 293, 296.
29 Ruskin, letter to Charles Eliot Norton, September 11, 1888, in *The Correspondence of John Ruskin and Charles Eliot Norton*, ed. John Lewis Bradley and Ian Ousby (Cambridge University Press, 1987), 503.
30 Tim Hilton, *John Ruskin: The Later Years* (New Haven, CT: Yale University Press, 2000), 566.
31 John Pemble, *The Mediterranean Passion: Victorians and Edwardians in the South* (Oxford: Clarendon Press, 1987), 169.

CHAPTER 7

"Cette douceur, pour ainsi dire wagnérienne": musical resonance in Proust's Recherche

John Hamilton

Le Côté de Guermantes, the third volume of Proust's great novel, starts off at dawn with a new beginning, which is, so to speak, also an ending. The narrator's family has moved into a new apartment, launching a fresh phase in the young man's life but also sealing off another. The change in residence is both an overture and a fermata, opening like a window onto fresh vistas to be explored, while also retaining, willfully or not, old experiences within. The premise of every window is a wall. Yet walls, even those carefully lined with thick cork, may still allow some sounds to leak through.

"The twittering of the birds at daybreak sounded insipid to Françoise" (3, 1; II, 309). With this opening sentence we find the family's servant to be out of sorts, anxious and easily bothered, unappreciative of nature's gentle welcome. In the description that ensues, the narrator deftly evokes the nervous bustle and frantic agitation of setting up a new home by emphasizing the acoustic disturbances focalized through Françoise's general unease.

> Every word uttered by the maids upstairs made her jump; . . . True, the servants made no less commotion in the attics of our old home; but she knew them, she had made of their comings and goings something friendly and familiar. Now she listened to the very silence with painful attentiveness. (3: 1; II, 309)

The quotidian clamor, perfectly normal in the former house, is now out of place. The change in location renders the once familiar, even friendly ["amicales"], sounds uncanny – *unheimlich* – no longer at home. Whereas houses are usually haunted by an invasion of something new, unexpected or unnerving, here the uncanny effect has to do rather with the old and familiar emerging in a domestic space not yet domesticated, causing all auditory phenomena, including silence, to be troublesome. Fresh surroundings intensify attentiveness. Recontextualization gives occasion to reevaluation. The noises, which once adhered to a well-defined, locatable source, no longer or not yet contribute to the comforting commotion of the home, again, not because the audible content is new but because the frame has changed. The *déménagement* dislocates all phenomena from their former resting place and transforms them from being a source of reassurance to a sourceless source of anxiety. The new home, at least initially, is haunted by the acousmatic.

Françoise's hyperacoustic reactions quickly infect the narrator himself. Yet, what captures his attention is not the barrage of trifling sounds that disturb the household from within and without, but rather the magical resonance of the family name attached to the new quarters. For the new apartment belongs to the "hôtel de Guermantes." Thus, the long paragraph that opened with innocent chirping ends decisively on this majestic tonic, with a fermata, so to speak, that will reverberate long after the chord is struck. Unlike Françoise, whose ears are pricked up by random noises that seem terribly out of place, the hero attends to the enchanting power of the name that will lend the new place an intriguing aura. Whereas Françoise must come to terms with the household racket, he loses himself in the onomastic music that the property evokes.

The two modes of listening that this opening paragraph engages depend on two distinct practices of reception. Françoise, the harried servant, simply registers the sonorous material that impinges on her perception, material that may or may not be intelligible; while the narrator, in search of time lost, filters out everything that is extraneous, so as to focus on the singular sound of the name "Guermantes," a name that participates in a broad and highly nuanced symbolic and indeed musical network. In a decisive way, Françoise's ear takes in a full range of acoustic phenomena – or more precisely, *acoumena* – which may or may not be located into a consciously intelligible scheme. Her auditory system is therefore analogous to a phonograph, which registers the soundscape of the new and not yet familiar domestic space. Here, the phonograph should be understood as a machine that lacks the capacity of consciousness and therefore cannot relate present sensations with ones now absent. The phonograph neither thinks nor remembers; it simply records the given, preserving the sound waves that are otherwise evanescent. In contrast, the narrator consciously attends to the sonic implications of the name, pursuing any number of associations that lend intelligibility to experience. His mind processes the sounds received, which are thereby endowed with significance. All the same, as readers of Proust's novel already know, the great accomplishments of memory are not based on consciousness, not on the voluntary filtering of experience, but rather on the involuntary links that are triggered when subjective intention is suddenly interrupted. As we shall see, the resonance produced by this circumvention of consciousness is, so to speak, no less musical.

The narrator, who already knows how this mechanism works, offers an illustrative example in the paragraph that directly follows. After summoning the magic word, "Guermantes," we turn to a reflection on the "Name" in general.

> At the age when Names, offering us an image of the unknowable which we have poured into their mould, while at the same moment connoting for us also a real place, force us accordingly to identify one with the other to such a point that we set out to seek in a city for a soul which it cannot enshrine but which we have no longer the power to expel from its name. (3: 3; II, 310)

As Aristotle emphasized, resonance is the result of one body striking another hollow body, including the case where the soul forcefully directs air against the windpipe to produce a voice.[1] In the Proust passage, the process is far less physical, far more idealized, more phantasmatic: it is a Name that serves as the resonant chamber and the subject's soul that pours the "image of the unknowable" into it. At the same time, names are attached to a "real place" ["un lieu réel"], which forms the basis for identification and for those personal identities who should occupy this place but alas seldom do. This failure becomes all too clear, as the passage continues to explain, when we come to know the "real person" ["la personne réelle"] to whom the idealized identity corresponds. The encounter with the real destroys the meaning of the ideal; and the Name *Guermantes*, once so enigmatically evocative and full of unimaginable promise, becomes nothing more than a dead, mute sign. The music of the past yields to the emptiness of the present.

> But should a sensation from a bygone year – like those recording instruments which preserve the sound and the manner of the various artists who have sung or played into them – enable our memory to make us hear that name with the particular ring with which it then sounded in our ears, we feel at once, though the name itself has apparently not changed, the distance that separates the dreams which at different times its same syllables have meant to us. (3: 4; II, 311)

A storage device like the gramophone would have recorded the tone, the sound, and the style, that once colored the pronunciation of the name before it came to be revised or filtered through conscious memory. The technology, which boasts no consciousness, would remind memory of a lost resonance. As the narrator continues to reflect, by means of a mechanical apparatus, "the name 'Guermantes' [would resume] for a moment, after all these years, the sound, so different from its sound today" (3: 5, trans. mod.; II, 312). In the imagined playback, the hero is momentarily liberated from his present location within the walls of the new Paris apartment, freed from the confines of his relocated and therefore dislocated position, and thus permitted to return to Combray, specifically to the day of Mlle Percepied's marriage, when the Duchesse de Guermantes glowed in her billowy scarf. For a moment, the recorded soundtrack conjures the country air:

> I breathe the air of the Combray of that year, of that day, mingled with a fragrance of hawthorn blossom blown by the wind from the corner of the square, harbinger of rain, which now sent the sun packing, now let it spread itself over the red woollen carpet of the sacristy, clothing it in a bright geranium pink and in that, so to speak, Wagnerian sweetness. (3: 5; II, 312)

The evocation of Wagner, qualified by the phrase "so to speak" – *pour ainsi dire* – points to the musical quality of the reminiscence awakened by the imagined gramophone. The sunlight on the carpet conjures Wagner, but what is the sense of this conjuration? How should we read this *pour ainsi dire*? Is it expressed in the subjunctive as opposed to the indicative mood, in the mode of the "so to speak," which colors the music as somehow unreal, as a personal judgment, wish, or desire? Or is the stated observation of Wagnerian sweetness an attempt "to speak thus (and not otherwise)," concretely identifying "the particular timbre," "the sound and the style" of that special time and that special day?

When we return to Mlle Percepied's wedding, described in the "Combray" section of the novel's first volume, we recall that the sun, bursting forth from a threatening cloud, transformed the woolen carpet into rosy violet, lending it an air of "solemn sweetness in the pomp of a joyful celebration, which characterize[s] certain pages of *Lohengrin*" (1: 251; I, 176). The event that a gramophone recording of the name "Guermantes" would summon was therefore not "so to speak, Wagnerian" but rather Wagner straight and simple, namely the very familiar Bridal Chorus, which accompanies Elsa of Brabant and her newlywed husband, whose name is not to be revealed. The narrator's recording instrument speaks in this way, because the name of Brabant was initially associated with the young boy's magic lantern in the early pages of the novel, linked, that is, to the legendary figure of Geneviève de Brabant, whom the Duchesse de Guermantes fancies to be her ancestor. His gramophone, unlike Françoise's recording device, is perfectly conscious, capable of making connections between what is present and what is absent to the senses, between the heard and the unheard.

Across the novel, allusions to Wagner's compositions far outnumber those to any other artist.[2] Even the "petite phrase" from Vinteuil's sonata, which plays a crucial role throughout Swann's story, ultimately comes to be related to *Tristan*, when the narrator, later in life, performs it at the piano. Wagner's compositional method, which finely weaves leitmotifs into a complex musical fabric, offers an artistic strategy for accumulating pieces of experience over time. What the passing flirtation with the gramophone suggests is that Wagner names a means of speaking-so or speaking-as, *pour ainsi dire*, disrupting the conscious agency of the current self, short-circuiting the voluntary memory, in order to let the former self be heard. Involuntary memory operates on the basis of a recording instrument, insofar as it reminds the conscious memory of what it has lost. Preserved in gramophonic inscription, musical resonance speaks thus and thus achieves what Daniel Melnick identifies as the novel's primary task, namely to serve as "both a defense against and a transcendence of negating, impermanent, corrupt reality."[3]

Decades before Proust meditated on the reactivation of stored data, other writers considered how the new technology of sound recording might disclose the way memory operates. In 1880 the Epicurean philosopher who incidentally coined the term *anomie*, Jean-Marie Guyau, published a brief essay entitled "Memory and Phonograph," in which he employs the figure of phonographic inscription to describe how "invisible lines are incessantly carved into the brain cells."[4] Guyau then reflects, "If the phonographic disk had self-consciousness, it could point out while replaying a song that it remembers this particular song." That is to say, if the phonograph could hear itself, it would exhibit the capacity of memory. Writing in the late nineteenth century, only three years after the wizard of Menlo Park introduced his new device, Guyau must admit, "The principal difference between the brain and the phonograph is that the metal disk of Edison's still rather primitive machine remains deaf to itself; there is no transition from movement to consciousness." The human brain, however, is not deaf to itself; it is capable of synthesizing perception and memory, willfully or not. As Guyau concludes, the brain is, so to speak, a "conscious phonograph."

Prerequisite for the narrator's success as a writer is phonography in general, preserving the traces that would otherwise dissolve into complete oblivion; and it is specifically prerequisite for storing the music, Wagner above all, which establishes the brilliant continuity that produces a single novel out of episodic fragments. Music's privileged role in the *Recherche* rests on its capacity to open language up to productive overdetermination. As Eric Prieto observes, "Music provides a model for that aspect of literary semantics identified not with denotation or direct predication but with *signifiance*, with the secondary meanings of larger syntactical units that cannot be analyzed in terms of denotative values of the individual words that make up the text."[5] Accordingly, in Proust's novel, the name "Guermantes" functions like a sublime recording of days long past, accessible for playback at any point, whereby the minutest details and the singular tonalities of that time may be heard again and thus trigger a string of further associations.

To be sure, Proust clearly draws on a rich and profound familiarity with performed music, from his childhood devotion, inculcated by his mother, to Mozart and Gounod, Massenet and Chopin, to his later, efflorescent relationship with Reynaldo Hahn, who introduced him to an inspiring range of contemporary composers.[6] Despite their shared tastes, the close friends strongly differed on the case of Wagner, whose mythic excesses were distasteful to Hahn. In 1895, following a performance of *Tannhäuser* at the Paris Opéra, Proust attempted to justify his fascination with the German psychopomp:

> The essence of music is to awaken in us the mysterious depths (inexpressible both in literature and in general in all modes of finite expression that use either words and consequently ideas, which in that case are determined, or determined objects – painting, sculpture) of our soul, which begin there, where the finite and all the arts that have the finite for its object stop, there where science, too, stops, and which one can for that reason call religious. (*Corr* 1, 386–387)

For Proust, music's formidable potential to arouse what otherwise remains dormant within the recesses of our souls – a potential exemplified by Wagner's mystical force – transcends our cognitive faculties, which remain tethered to determinate and hence finite experience. Music thus furnishes an ideal method for the composition of the *Recherche*. As Jean-Jacques Nattiez expresses it, "Thus Wagner emerges as a principal source for Proust's thinking. He provides him with a mirror-image of his own poetics and – in a slightly narcissistic way – of a creative *alter ego*."[7] Yet, if the Wagnerian leitmotif supplies the methodological basis for Proust's literary endeavor, it is arguably the gramophone that establishes the technological ground for the conversion from the musical to the literary.

This artistic conversion depends on the physical recording – *enregistrement* – of acoustic phenomena, which are filed away, forgotten, and only thus eligible for recall. It is then at this final, eminently literary stage, that meaning is produced. In structural terms, the sounds must first undergo a kind of materialization, as though inscribed into the cerebral cortex, like the lines drawn upon a wax cylinder or disc, before they become available for reactivation through a process of dematerialization. Proust explicitly describes this acoustic itinerary, this passage between the gramophonic and the narrative voice, through the figure of Swann and his experience as a listener. Relaxing at the home of the Verdurins, Swann is treated to a piano performance. After the pianist had finished, it is clear that Swann is far more affected than the other guests. The narrator gives the following explanation:

> The year before, at an evening party, he had heard a piece of music played on the piano and violin. At first he had appreciated only the material quality of the sounds which those instruments secreted. And it had been a source of keen pleasure when, below the delicate line of the violin-part, slender but robust, compact and commanding, he had suddenly become aware of the mass of the piano-part beginning to emerge in a sort of liquid rippling of sound, multiform but indivisible, smooth yet restless, like the deep blue tumult of the sea, silvered and charmed into a minor key by the moonlight. (1: 294; 1, 205)

When he first heard Vinteuil's sonata a year ago, Swann's ears merely received "the material quality of the sounds," attentive to the pleasurable shape and flow of the melodies. Musicologists have rightly connected this description to the Impressionist music aesthetics developed by Claude Debussy in relation to the Symbolist poetry of Paul Verlaine, as the reference to the moonlight ["le clair de lune"] makes perfectly clear.[8] The result is a quasi-Baudelairean synesthesis:

> But then at a certain moment, without being able to distinguish any clear outline, or to give a name to what was pleasing him, suddenly enraptured, he had tried to grasp the phrase or harmony – he did not know which – that had just been played and that had opened and expanded his soul, as the fragrance of certain roses, wafted upon the moist air of evening, has the power of dilating one's nostrils. (1: 294; 1, 205)

For Swann, the musical waves evade cognition; they overwhelm his capacity to comprehend. Proust, however, is not content to linger with these passing impressions, which are powerful and confused ("il ne savait lui-même"); and instead demonstrates how they enter the subconscious, not despite but precisely because they bypass the cognitive faculty. In this way, Proust engages music in order to set up his own approach to literary narrative. For it is Swann's prior auditory experience, when the music was materially impressed into the psyche, which permits the second performance to work in concert with recollection:

> And this impression would continue to envelop in its liquidity, its ceaseless overlapping, the motifs which from time to time emerge, barely discernible, to plunge again and disappear and drown, recognized only by the particular kind of pleasure which they instill, impossible to describe, to recollect, to name, ineffable – did not our memory, like a labourer who toils at the laying down of firm foundations beneath the tumult of waves, by fashioning for us facsimiles of those fugitive phrases, enable us to compare and to contrast them with those that follow. And so, scarcely had the exquisite sensation which Swann had experienced died away, before his memory had furnished him with an immediate transcript, sketchy, it is true, and provisional, which he had been able to glance at while the piece continued, so that, when the same impression suddenly returned, it was no longer impossible to grasp. (1: 295; 1, 206)

The primary impressions would evanesce, generating a momentary pleasure yet eluding the cohesive grasp that Proust admired in Wagner's *Gesamtkunstwerk*, if it were not for the memory's laborious capacity to transcribe these material traces, capturing them and thus redeeming them from complete oblivion. As an amateur in every sense, Swann has but "provisional" access to these recorded impressions. Like Françoise, Swann fails to place the sonic material into a meaningful context. As for the narrator, he too will remain incapable of writing until he discovers that the objects of his search have not disappeared entirely, but rather lie dormant in the gramophonic recesses of his mind, that the "Names" recorded there have indeed captured the sounds, the musical timbre and pleasure, that speak thus and do not speak otherwise, ready to play back, so to speak, what would otherwise remain impossible to describe, recollect or name, in order that he, the writer, might speak.

NOTES

1 *De anima*, 2.8, trans. Hugh Lawson-Tancred (Harmondsworth: Penguin, 1986), 176–179.

2 For a critical account of Wagner's influence on Proust, see Eric Bedriomo, *Proust, Wagner, et la coïncidence des arts* (Paris: J.-M. Place, 1984).

3 Daniel Melnick, "Proust, Music, and the Reader," *Modern Language Quarterly* 41 (1980), 189.

4 Jean-Marie Guyau, "Memory and Phonograph" (1880), cited in Friedrich Kittler, *Gramophone, Film, Typewriter*, trans. G. Winthrop-Young and M. Wutz (Stanford University Press, 1999), 30–31.

5 Eric Prieto, *Listening In: Music, Mind, and the Modernist Narrative* (Lincoln: University of Nebraska Press, 2002), 49.
6 For a comprehensive overview of Proust's engagement with music, see Jean-Yves Tadié, "L'univers musical de Marcel Proust," *Revue de littérature comparée* 67 (1993), 493–503.
7 Jean-Jacques Nattiez, *Proust as Musician*, trans. D. Puffett (Cambridge University Press, 1989), 31.
8 See for instance Cormac Newark and Ingrid Wassenaar, "Proust and Music: The Anxiety of Competence," *Cambridge Opera Journal* 9 (1997), 163–183 (168–169).

PART III

Expanding the arts

CHAPTER 8

Proust and archeological discovery

Kazuyoshi Yoshikawa

Under the sway of imperialism and orientalism, the second half of the nineteenth century witnessed a succession of archeological excavations that brought to light the great civilizations of antiquity, at Pompeii and in Egypt, Assyria, and Greece. Proust would not remain indifferent to the archeological discoveries of his era. Hence the narrator, during his stay at Doncières, counters the claims of "poets" who affirm that "we recapture for a moment the self that we were long ago when we enter some house or garden in which we used to live in our youth." He suggests, rather, that "[t]here is no need to travel in order to see [this garden] again; we must dig down inwardly to discover it. What once covered the earth is no longer above but beneath it; a mere excursion does not suffice for a visit to the dead city: excavation is necessary also" (3:115; II, 390–391).

The city of Pompeii, entirely covered in ash following the eruption of Mount Vesuvius, was the object of several dig attempts going back to 1709. It did not truly become the object of scientific research until 1860, when Giuseppe Fiorelli conceived the idea of pouring plaster into the gaps between the ash layers. This method allowed him to reconstitute the shape of human and animal bodies. Proust enjoyed perusing a volume from a collection on "famous cities of art" titled *Pompéi: Histoire – Vie privée*, which includes several illustrations of Fiorelli's results.[1] In *À l'ombre des jeunes filles en fleurs*, we find an allusion to these reconstructed human bodies: "The features of our face are hardly more than gestures which force of habit has made permanent. Nature, like the destruction of Pompeii, like the metamorphosis of a nymph, has arrested us in an accustomed movement" (2:667; II, 262).

After Schliemann's rediscovery of the Greek site of Troy (the legendary city of Homer's *Iliad*) in 1873 and of the city of Mycenae in 1876, excavations of the Athenian Acropolis in 1886 unearthed a number of Korai in an archaic style dating to the sixth century BCE. In "Autour de Madame Swann,"

Bergotte suggests an analogy between La Berma's art and the "Korai of the old Erechtheum" (2: 183; I, 550). In 1900 the British archeologist Arthur John Evans discovered the palace of Knossos in Crete. We find an echo of this discovery in *Le Côté de Guermantes*, in a description of flowering pear trees that form "great quadrilaterals – separated by low walls – of white blossom," compared to "airy roofless chambers which seemed to belong to a Palace of the sun, such as one might find in Crete" (3: 204; II, 453). The numerous mentions of the excavations of ancient Greece in Proust's novel deserve a complete study, which I intend to undertake in the near future.

Assyria was also the object of archeological digs in the nineteenth century, notably under the French consul Paul-Émile Botta who, beginning in 1843, excavated the site of Khorsabad, the ancient Dur-Sharrukin, Sargon II's capital city. Among the numerous allusions to Assyrian excavations in the *Recherche*, it is essential to mention the minor character Nissim Bernard, "this figure from Susa" whose Jewish first name "set[s] hovering above it the pinions of an androcephalous bull from Khorsabad" (2:483; II, 132). In an illuminating article on the trope of the "Assyrian profile," Antoine Compagnon has examined the role of Assyrian archeology and its Jewish representations in Proust's work.[2]

In what follows I will show how Proust integrated the discoveries of Egyptian archeology into the *Recherche*, in light of the development of this field by French scholars in the nineteenth century. In 1822 Jean-François Champollion uncovered the mysteries of Egyptian hieroglyphs in front of the Académie des Inscriptions et Belles-Lettres; in 1824 he published a *Précis du système hiéroglyphique*. Auguste Mariette (1821–1881) arrived in Egypt in 1851 to direct work at several archeological sites, including the temple of Edfu, and to oversee the opening of an archeological museum, which would become the Museum of Cairo in 1902. Gaston Maspero (1846–1916), the second director of the Museum of Cairo and a professor at the Collège de France, was the face of Egyptian studies in Proust's era.

À la Recherche contains several rather unoriginal allusions to the Pyramids. Odette confides to Swann that she is going to Egypt with Forcheville: "Yes, my dear boy, we're starting on the 19th; we'll send you a view of the Pyramids" (1:506; I, 350). Upon returning from Doncières, the hero is stupefied to see in his grandmother "an overburdened old woman" that he no longer recognizes, "like a sick man who, not having looked at his own reflection for a long time, and regularly composing the features which he never sees in accordance with the ideal image of himself that he carries in his mind, recoils on catching sight in the glass, in the middle of an arid desert of a face, of the sloping pink protuberance of a nose as huge as one of the pyramids of Egypt" (3:185; II, 439–440).

Just as descriptions of churches in *À la Recherche* owe much to Émile Mâle's works on the religious art of the Middle Ages, so Proust draws on the works of Gaston Maspero for information on Egyptian civilization. In *La Prisonnière*, Brichot cites "his colleague M. Maspero" alongside "his masters M. Mérimée and M. Renan" (5:441; III, 831). In a manuscript passage written for his review of the *Mémoires* of the Countess de Boigne, but edited out of the published text by *Le Figaro* for its March 20, 1907 issue, Proust remarks that "the most trivial details" of life in antiquity are now "the subject of our scholars' most serious work." In support of this assertion, he cites the names of Assurbanipal's guests at "a hunt in honor of Ummanigas, Ummanappa, Tammaritu and Kudourru," of "Tiglath-Pileser, who boasted of having killed a hundred and twenty lions" at the Assyrian court, and of the greyhounds "Abaïkaro, Pouhtes, Togrou" at a castle in ancient Egypt (*CSB* 925).[3] Each of these references comes from Maspero's *Au temps de Ramsès et d'Assourbanipal*,[4] where we find the very passages cited by Proust: "These young men with barbarous names and uncouth speech – Ummanigas, Ummanappa, Tammaritu, Kudourru, Paru – are the legitimate heirs to the Susian throne";[5] "The times are past when old Tiglath-Pileser could boast of having killed one hundred and twenty adult lions";[6] "others hold the large greyhounds with strange names – Abaïkaro, Pouhtes, Tongrou – in a leash."[7]

Maspero's work is in fact a textbook describing Near Eastern civilizations, reedited several times after its initial publication in 1890. Philip Kolb notes that Marie Nordlinger recalls borrowing the book from Proust, which confirms he owned a copy. Kolb also cites Proust's evocation of the book's return in a letter from December 7, 1906 to Nordlinger, his collaborator on his translations of Ruskin: "What strange folly to have returned this little schoolbook! If I went out during the day [,] I would love to see this Assyrian and Egyptian art that seems so beautiful to me" (*Corr* VI, 308). Cut by *Le Figaro*, these lists – the names of guests at Assurbanipal's hunt, or of large Egyptian greyhounds – were meant to support the thesis that Proust inferred from the *Mémoires* of the Countess de Boigne: that "the most trivial details" of quotidian life in the past nonetheless come to engrave themselves in memory, and to find, as a consequence, their place in history.

Proust often reworked elements from his earlier writings into his novel. The passage inspired by Maspero's book appears again in "Autour de Madame Swann": "I was as marvelously surprised as on the day on which

I read for the first time, in one of Maspero's books, that there existed a precise list of the sportsmen whom Assurbanipal used to invite to his hunts a thousand years before the birth of Christ" (2: 68; 1, 469). In this scene from the novel, the precision of the "list of the sportsmen" is underscored, as was the case in the review of the Countess de Boigne's *Mémoires*, but their names are no longer listed. The significance is no longer found in the names themselves, but rather in an improbable circumstance that surprises the hero. Immediately before this passage, he had questioned Norpois at length about Madame Swann and Gilberte, confiding in him his admiration for the mother and daughter. When the diplomat announces his intention to relate his admiration to them, the hero can barely restrain himself from "kissing his soft, white, wrinkled hands," but believes that he "alone had noticed" the "impulsive movement" that he had scarcely begun to sketch. Quite the contrary: "some years later," Norpois confides to one of the most faithful friends of the hero's family that he had "seen the moment in which [the hero was] about to kiss his hand." It is this very moment that sets up the reference to the precision of Maspero's "list of the sportsmen," and allows Proust to highlight "the incalculable proportions of absence and presence of mind, of recollection and forgetfulness, of which the human mind is composed" (2: 67–68; 1, 468–469). The minor details reported by the illustrious scholar thus illustrate the *Recherche*'s exploration of one of the unsuspected truths of the human mind.

It is Egyptian civilization in particular that provides Proust's novel with images for the theme of the "double." The importance of metempsychosis in Egyptian culture was known in Proust's time, and we find it referenced, for example, in the volume devoted to Cairo in the same "famous cities of art" series as the volume on Pompeii.[8] Maspero's book *Au temps de Ramsès et d'Assourbanipal* contains a more detailed explanation of the Egyptian funeral rite that consisted of mummifying the body: "The soul does not die at the same time that the breath expires upon the lips of man: it survives, but with a precarious life, of which the duration depends upon the corpse, and is measured by it." Men died "twice, first in the body, and then in the double." Therefore, "to deliver the double from . . . agony uselessly prolonged, . . . the flesh must be rendered incorruptible. This is attained by embalming it as a mummy."[9] If the Egyptians mummified the body, it was in order to avoid physical decay and to enable the survival of the double. This conception of the "double" is developed in another book by Maspero: "left to itself, the double was unable to obtain the food and all the other objects which were as necessary to it now as before. These, consequently, had to be supplied by the living."[10]

Proust calls on this understanding of the "double" in *Le Côté de Guermantes*, in relation to La Berma's performance of *Phèdre*. Not having been nourished for some time, the hero's admiration for La Berma has withered:

> My faith and my desire no longer coming forward to pay incessant worship to the diction and the presence of La Berma, the "double" that I possessed of them in my heart had gradually shriveled, like those other "doubles" of the dead in ancient Egypt which had to be fed continually in order to maintain their originals in eternal life. That art had become a poor and pitiable thing. It was no longer inhabited by a deep-rooted soul. (3: 39, trans. mod.; II, 336–337)

Here again, knowledge of Egyptian civilization is mobilized to bring to light a universal law governing human psychology.

The mummy, that is to say, the "double," for the ancient Egyptians, plays an even more central role in the final scene of *À l'ombre des jeunes filles en fleurs*. Françoise, removing the window coverings and opening the curtains in the hero's room, reveals the summer day:

> Twelve o' clock struck, and Françoise arrived at last. And for months on end, in this Balbec to which I had so looked forward because I imagined it only as battered by storms and buried in the mist, the weather had been so dazzling and so unchanging that when she came to open the window I could always, without once being wrong, expect to see the same patch of sunlight folded in the corner of the outer wall, of an unalterable color which was less moving as a sign of summer than bleak as the color of a lifeless and factitious enamel. And when Françoise removed the pins from the top of the window-frame, took down the cloths, and drew back the curtains, the summer day which she disclosed seemed as dead, as immemorial, as a sumptuous millenary mummy from which our old servant had done no more than cautiously unwind the linen wrapping before displaying it, embalmed in its vesture of gold. (2: 730, trans. mod.; II, 306)

The sumptuous image of the day transformed into a mummy "embalmed in its vesture of gold" is a fitting end to the stay at Balbec. But this image raises two questions. First, what is meant by the comparison of a dazzling summer day to a mummy, which is not merely embalmed, but completely inanimate? And second, given that this scene, where Françoise uncovers the light of day as she opens the curtains, seems to have been performed repeatedly from the beginning of the stay at the Grand-Hôtel de Balbec, why is her gesture only described for the first time at the end of the summer visit?

I will begin by responding to the second question. In the definitive text, Françoise's opening of the curtains is absent from the description of the "next morning," after the arrival at Balbec (2: 341; II, 33). It is evoked once, in the very middle of the stay: "in the morning when Françoise undid the blankets that shut out the light" (2: 566; II, 191), but it is not followed, in that instance, by the appearance of the summer day. And yet the Grasset proofs, established in 1913 – at which time the stay at Balbec was already planned for a second volume, then still called *Le Côté de Guermantes* – placed Françoise's action and the apparition of the summer day as a mummy toward the beginning of the summer season, right before the carriage ride with Madame de Villeparisis. Here is the passage, already quite similar to the definitive text:

> Mais parfois aussi, et pendant des semaines de suite, le beau temps fut si éclatant et si fixe que quand Françoise venait ouvrir la fenêtre, j'étais sûr de trouver le même pan de soleil plié à l'angle du mur extérieur, et d'une couleur immuable qui n'était plus émouvante comme une révélation de l'été, mais morne comme celle d'un émail inerte et factice. Et tandis que Françoise ôtait les épingles des impostes, détachait les étoffes, tirait les rideaux, le jour d'été qu'elle découvrait semblait aussi mort, aussi immémorial qu'une somptueuse et millénaire momie que notre vieille servante n'eût fait que précautionneusement désemmailloter de tous ses linges, avant de la faire apparaître, embaumée dans sa robe d'or.
>
> But sometimes, and for weeks on end, the fine weather was so dazzling and so unchanging that each time Françoise came to open the window, I was sure to find the same patch of sunlight folded in the corner of the outer wall, of an unalterable color which was no longer moving as a revelation of summer, but rather bleak as the color of a lifeless and factitious enamel. And when Françoise removed the pins from the top of the window-frame, took down the cloths, and drew back the curtains, the summer day which she disclosed seemed as dead, as immemorial, as a sumptuous millenary mummy from which our old servant had done no more than cautiously unwind the linen wrapping before displaying it, embalmed in its vesture of gold.[11]

This passage is identically transcribed, still just preceding the scene of the carriage ride with Madame de Villeparisis, in an excerpt from the forthcoming second volume about the stay at Balbec published by the *Nouvelle Revue Française* in its June 1, 1914 edition (Figure 8.1).[12] Therefore, both the opening of the curtains by Françoise and the appearance of the summer day were attached, up to the 1914 version of the novel, to the beginning of the stay at Balbec, and thus inscribed as a daily ritual put in place right from the arrival at the seaside hotel.

946 LA NOUVELLE REVUE FRANÇAISE

campagne, de la contiguïté de cultures différentes, le réseau de la lumière ou de l'ombre qui uniformisait tout ce qu'il contenait dans ses réseaux et supprimait toute démarcation entre la mer et le ciel assimilés que l'œil hésitant faisait, tour à tour, empiéter l'un sur l'autre, les inégalités âpres, jaunes, et comme boueuses, de la surface marine, les levées, les talus qui dérobaient à la vue la barque où une équipe d'agiles matelots semblait moissonner, tout cela, par les jours orageux, faisait de l'océan quelque chose d'aussi varié, d'aussi consistant, d'aussi accidenté, d'aussi populeux, d'aussi civilisé que la terre carossable d'où, en voiture avec Mme de Villeparisis, nous le regarderions.

Mais parfois aussi, et pendant des semaines de suite, — dans ce Balbec que j'avais tant désiré parce que je ne l'imaginais que battu par la tempête et perdu dans les brumes,— le beau temps fut si éclatant et si fixe que quand Françoise venait ouvrir la fenêtre, j'étais sûr de trouver le même pan de soleil plié à l'angle du mur extérieur, et d'une couleur immuable qui n'était plus émouvante comme une révélation de l'été, mais morne comme celle d'un émail inerte et factice. Et tandis que Françoise ôtait les épingles des impostes, détachait les étoffes, tirait les rideaux, le jour d'été qu'elle découvrait semblait aussi mort, aussi immémorial qu'une somptueuse et millénaire momie que notre vieille servante n'eût fait que précautionneusement désemmailloter de tous ses linges, avant de la faire apparaître, embaumée dans sa robe d'or.

La voiture de Mme de Villeparisis nous emmenait. Parfois comme la voiture gravissait une route montante entre des terres labourées, je voyais — rendant les champs plus réels, les prolongeant jusque dans le passé, — quelques

Figure 8.1 *La Nouvelle Revue Française*, June 1, 1914

But why was this summer day compared to a mummy? The answer can likely be found in the expression, "for weeks on end, the weather had been so dazzling and so unchanging." In the hero's eyes, already accustomed to the fine weather that continued for "weeks on end," even a brilliant summer day (since one effect of habit, in Proust's work, is to change the aspect of all things) is destined to lose its radiance, its vivacity, to become "bleak as the color of a lifeless and factitious enamel," reducible to something as inanimate as a mummy. In order to strengthen this comparison with the mummy, the writer plays with phonic recurrence. The consonant *m* and the vowels *o* and *i*, taken from the root word *momie*, expand into the series of adjectives applied to the summer day: *mort* and *morne* ["dead" and "bleak"], but also *millénaire*, *immémorial*, and *immuable* ["unchanging"], all derived by the same paradigm.

But is the care taken to prepare the image of the "mummy" sufficient? Could the perceived fixity of the fine weather, which lasted "for weeks on end," really justify this premature evocation, at the very start of the summer season, of an image of gloom – the death of the summer sun? It seems to me that this sense of prematurity motivated Proust to move this scene to the end of the stay at Balbec. That displacement, made on the Gallimard proofs around 1917, has been noted by multiple editors of *À l'ombre des jeunes filles en fleurs*,[13] but the concerns to which it responds have never been sufficiently explained.

By examining the last page of the Gallimard proofs (Figure 8.2),[14] we can see clearly how the writer performed this displacement. The basic text describing the metamorphosis of the day into a mummy has not been changed at all: it is in every way identical to the text published in 1914 in the *Nouvelle Revue Française*. Towards 1915, Proust cut this page from the excerpt published in the *Nouvelle Revue Française* – see the identical typography – and pasted it onto the Gallimard proofs. (This is the same method that Nathalie Mauriac and I have made evident in our recent critical edition of *Cahier 53*, one of the first drafts of *La Prisonnière*, from which Proust tore several pages, also around 1916 or 1917, in order to paste them into the fair copy of the manuscript for that part of the novel.)[15]

What is new here are the handwritten additions appearing in the margins of the proofs. One of the most important changes is that Françoise's opening of the curtains is no longer a scene described during the stay at Balbec, but is now only evoked later, in a narration of memories of the summer season:

> J'oubliai d'ailleurs presque immédiatement ces dernières semaines [du séjour à Balbec]. Ce que je revis invariablement quand je pensai à Balbec, ce fut

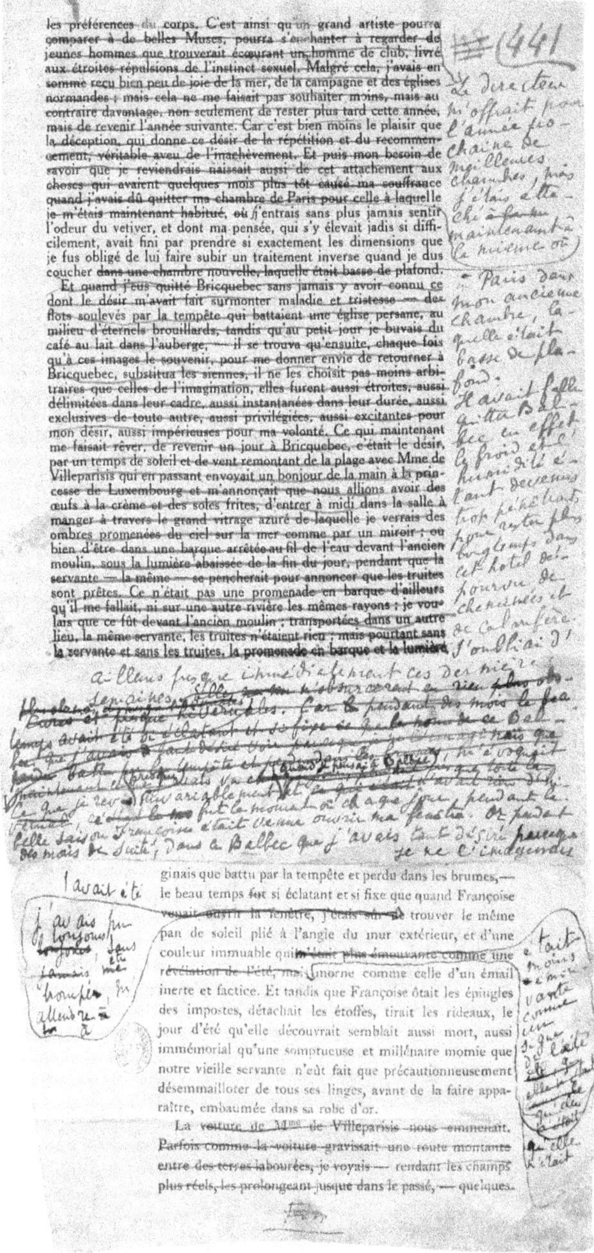

les préférences du corps. C'est ainsi qu'un grand artiste pourra comparer à de belles Muses, pourra s'enchanter à regarder de jeunes hommes que trouverait écœurant un homme de club, livré aux étroites répulsions de l'instinct sexuel. Malgré cela, j'avais en somme reçu bien peu de joie de la mer, de la campagne et des églises normandes ; mais cela ne me faisait pas souhaiter moins, mais au contraire davantage, non seulement de rester plus tard cette année, mais de revenir l'année suivante. Car c'est bien moins le plaisir que la déception, qui donne ce désir de la répétition et du recommencement, véritable aveu de l'inachèvement. Et puis mon besoin de savoir que je reviendrais naissait aussi de cet attachement aux choses qui avaient quelques mois plus tôt causé ma souffrance quand j'avais dû quitter ma chambre de Paris pour celle à laquelle je m'étais maintenant habitué, où j'entrais sans plus jamais sentir l'odeur du vetiver, et dont ma pensée, qui s'y élevait jadis si difficilement, avait fini par prendre si exactement les dimensions que je fus obligé de lui faire subir un traitement inverse quand je dus coucher dans une chambre nouvelle, laquelle était basse de plafond.

Et quand j'eus quitté Bricquebec sans jamais y avoir connu ce dont le désir m'avait fait surmonter maladie et tristesse — des flots soulevés par la tempête qui battaient une église persane, au milieu d'éternels brouillards, tandis qu'au petit jour je buvais du café au lait dans l'auberge, — il se trouva qu'ensuite, chaque fois qu'à ces images le souvenir, pour me donner envie de retourner à Bricquebec, substitua les siennes, il ne les choisit pas moins arbitraires que celles de l'imagination, elles furent aussi étroites, aussi délimitées dans leur cadre, aussi instantanées dans leur durée, aussi exclusives de toute autre, aussi privilégiées, aussi excitantes pour mon désir, aussi impérieuses pour ma volonté. Ce qui maintenant me faisait rêver, de revenir un jour à Bricquebec, c'était le désir, par un temps de soleil et de vent remontant de la plage avec Mme de Villeparisis qui en passant envoyait un bonjour de la main à la princesse de Luxembourg et m'annonçait que nous allions avoir des œufs à la crème et des soles frites, d'entrer à midi dans la salle à manger à travers le grand vitrage azuré de laquelle je verrais des ombres promenées du ciel sur la mer comme par un miroir ; ou bien d'être dans une barque arrêtée au fil de l'eau devant l'ancien moulin, sous la lumière abaissée de la fin du jour, pendant que la servante — la même — se pencherait pour annoncer que les truites sont prêtes. Ce n'était pas une promenade en barque d'ailleurs qu'il me fallait, ni sur une autre rivière les mêmes rayons ; je voulais que ce fût devant l'ancien moulin ; transportées dans un autre lieu, la même servante, les truites n'étaient rien ; mais pourtant sans la servante et sans les truites, la promenade en barque et la lumière

ginais que battu par la tempête et perdu dans les brumes,— le beau temps fut si éclatant et si fixe que quand Françoise venait ouvrir la fenêtre, j'étais sûr de trouver le même pan de soleil plié à l'angle du mur extérieur, et d'une couleur immuable qui n'était plus émouvante comme une révélation de l'été, mais morne comme celle d'un émail inerte et factice. Et tandis que Françoise ôtait les épingles des impostes, détachait les étoffes, tirait les rideaux, le jour d'été qu'elle découvrait semblait aussi mort, aussi immémorial qu'une somptueuse et millénaire momie que notre vieille servante n'eût fait que précautionneusement désemmailloter de tous ses linges, avant de la faire apparaître, embaumée dans sa robe d'or.

La voiture de Mme de Villeparisis nous emmenait. Parfois comme la voiture gravissait une route montante entre des terres labourées, je voyais — rendant les champs plus réels, les prolongeant jusque dans le passé, — quelques

Figure 8.2 Gallimard proofs of *À l'ombre des jeunes filles en fleurs*, c. 1917

> le moment où chaque jour, pendant la belle saison, Françoise était venue ouvrir ma fenêtre.
>
> Moreover, I forgot almost immediately these last weeks [of our stay at Balbec]. What I saw invariably in my mind's eye when I thought of Balbec was the moment, repeated each day of that summer season, when Françoise came to open my window.[16]

Another addition, of equal importance, prolongs the duration of the fine weather: "weeks on end" ["des semaines de suite"] in the *Nouvelle Revue Française* excerpt, becomes "months on end" ["des mois de suite"] in the Gallimard proofs: "And for months on end, in this Balbec . . . the fine weather had been so dazzling and so unchanging" ["Or pendant des mois de suite, dans ce Balbec . . . le beau temps avait été si éclatant et si fixe"].

To summarize these major changes: the summer day uncovered by Françoise, unchanging "for months on end" in Balbec, no longer appears directly during the stay at the hotel, but is instead evoked later, in a memory of the summer season. The comparison of the day to a mummy, even though the text remains identical from one version to the other, is rendered more convincing, it seems to me, thanks to these two late changes. The retrospective vision of a summer day unchanged for "months on end" robs it of its radiance, its vibration, rendering it irrevocably something *morne* and *mort*, "bleak" and "dead." Françoise's opening of the curtains, because this action is transcribed in the past through the memory of that long-ago summer vacation, is more clearly related to the undressing of a corpse, "unwind[ing] the linen wrappings" in order to reveal the nudity of a "mummy." As the handwritten addition confirms, this summer day becomes, along with the sea of the summer resort, what the narrator "invariably" saw "when [he thought] of Balbec." Through this act of recollection, the summer day itself becomes a "double" in the hero's mind, like the mummy to whom the Egyptians brought "food and all the other objects" needed to keep it alive. The metaphor of the mummy that sumptuously closes *À l'ombre des jeunes filles en fleurs* is thus promoted to the status of illustration, drawn from the discoveries of Egyptian archeology, of the theory of recollection explored in Proust's work.

NOTES

1 Henry Thédenat, *Pompéi: Histoire – Vie privée* (Paris: Laurens [Les villes d'art célèbres], 1910), 25–27.

2 Antoine Compagnon, "Le 'profil assyrien' ou l'antisémitisme qui n'ose pas dire son nom: les libéraux dans l'affaire Dreyfus," *Études de langue et littérature françaises* (Université de Kyoto) 28 (1997), 133–150.

3 The manuscript of this article is preserved at the BnF: NAF 16634, fo. 92r.
4 Pierre-Louis Rey traces this source in a note for the Pléiade edition of *À l'ombre des jeunes filles en fleurs* (1, 1352, note 2).
5 *Au temps de Ramsès et d'Assourbanipal: Égypte et Assyrie anciennes*, 6th edn. (Paris: Hachette, 1912), 284. Published in English as *Life in Ancient Egypt and Assyria* (no translator credited) (New York: Appleton, 1892), 253.
6 *Temps de Ramsès et d'Assourbanipal*, 300; *Life in Ancient Egypt and Assyria*, 268.
7 *Temps de Ramsès et d'Assourbanipal* 114; *Life in Ancient Egypt and Assyria*, 108.
8 "Moreover, with their belief in a new life in another world, the *double* required a body. They endeavored to prolong the existence of the body by means of embalming" ["D'ailleurs avec leur croyance à une nouvelle vie dans un autre monde, il fallait au double, un corps. Son corps, on essayait bien d'en prolonger l'existence par l'embaumement"]. Gaston Migeon, *Le Caire* (Paris: Laurens [Les villes d'art célèbres], 1909), 116.
9 Maspero, *Temps de Ramsès et d'Assourbanipal*, 134; *Life in Ancient Egypt and Assyria*, 124.
10 Gaston Maspero, *Guide du visiteur au musée du Caire*, 4th edn. (Cairo: Imprimerie de l'Institut Français d'Archéologie Orientale, 1915), 10. Published in English as *Guide to the Cairo Museum*, trans. J. E. and A. A. Quibell (Cairo: Printing-office of the French Institute of Oriental Archaeology, 1910), 6.
11 From "bleak" ["morne"] onwards, the passage is identical to the published version of the novel (2: 730; II, 306). NAF 16753, fo. 83r.
12 Marcel Proust, "À la recherche du temps perdu," *La Nouvelle Revue Française*, June 1, 1914, 921–969, with this editor's footnote on page 921: "These fragments are taken from the second volume of *À la recherche du temps perdu*, titled *Le Côté de Guermantes*, to be published by Bernard Grasset in the near future" ["Ces fragments sont extraits du deuxième volume de *À la recherche du temps perdu*, intitulé *Le Côté de Guermantes*, qui doit paraître prochainement chez l'éditeur Bernard Grasset"]. Our passage, where the mummy appears, is found on page 946, with the following addition placed just after "for weeks on end" ["pendant des semaines de suite"] "– in this Balbec to which I had so looked forward because I imagined it only as battered by storms and buried in the mist –" ["– dans ce Balbec que j'avais tant désiré parce que je ne l'imaginais que battu par la tempête et perdu dans les brumes –"].
13 See for example the GF edition, vol. 1 (1987), 34, as well as the Pléiade edition (II, 1490).
14 BnF, Rés. m.Y^2 824, 441 (Proust's pagination).
15 Marcel Proust, *Cahiers 1 à 75 de la Bibliothèque nationale de France: Cahier 53*, ed. Nathalie Mauriac Dyer and Kazuyoshi Yoshikawa (Turnhout: Brepols and Bibliothèque nationale de France, 2012), 2 vols.
16 See note 14 above.

CHAPTER 9

Swann's gift, Odette's face: photography, money, and desire in À la recherche du temps perdu

Suzanne Guerlac

We are at the hôtel de Guermantes. Swann has brought a gift to his friend Oriane, just as she prepares to go out to an elegant dinner party with her husband. The focus of this much commented-upon scene (which marks the end of *Le Côté de Guermantes II*) is the Guermantes's intractable denial when confronted with the news, reluctantly acknowledged by Swann, that he is dying. Their attention is taken up with other things: Oriane is concerned about her shoes, the Duke has plans to see his mistress after dinner and is eager to get out the door.

What interests me in this scene is Swann's gift: a gigantic photograph, so big it does not fit through the door. Swann has had it delivered to the hôtel de Guermantes and it sits downstairs in the vestibule. On her way out, the Duchess asks her valet to remove the envelope so she can see the photograph. Not tonight, her husband pleads, concerned about being late for dinner. He signals to the protagonist his horror at the gigantic size of this object, and asks his wife: "But where are you going to stick a toy that size?" In my bedroom, she replies: "I want to have it before my eyes" (3: 814; II, 881). We never see the photograph and we never hear another word about it.

What would Oriane have seen if she had removed the photograph from its envelope? Swann has abandoned his study of Vermeer and taken up research on the Templars. Oriane has expressed a desire to see portraits of the Knights of Rhodes because, as the Duke confides to the hero, "our family is very much mixed up in the whole story" (3: 787; II, 862). As the Duke explains, the photograph is an image of portraits of Knights of Rhodes impressed upon ancient coins of Malta, a composite print that presents both sides of a number of coins (Figure 9.1). The photograph belongs, then, to the series of photographic reproductions of artworks (or cultural artifacts) that Swann has offered the hero in "Combray." It also serves as a kind of family photograph since the Guermantes's bloodline goes back this far, which is why Oriane is curious to see the portraits.

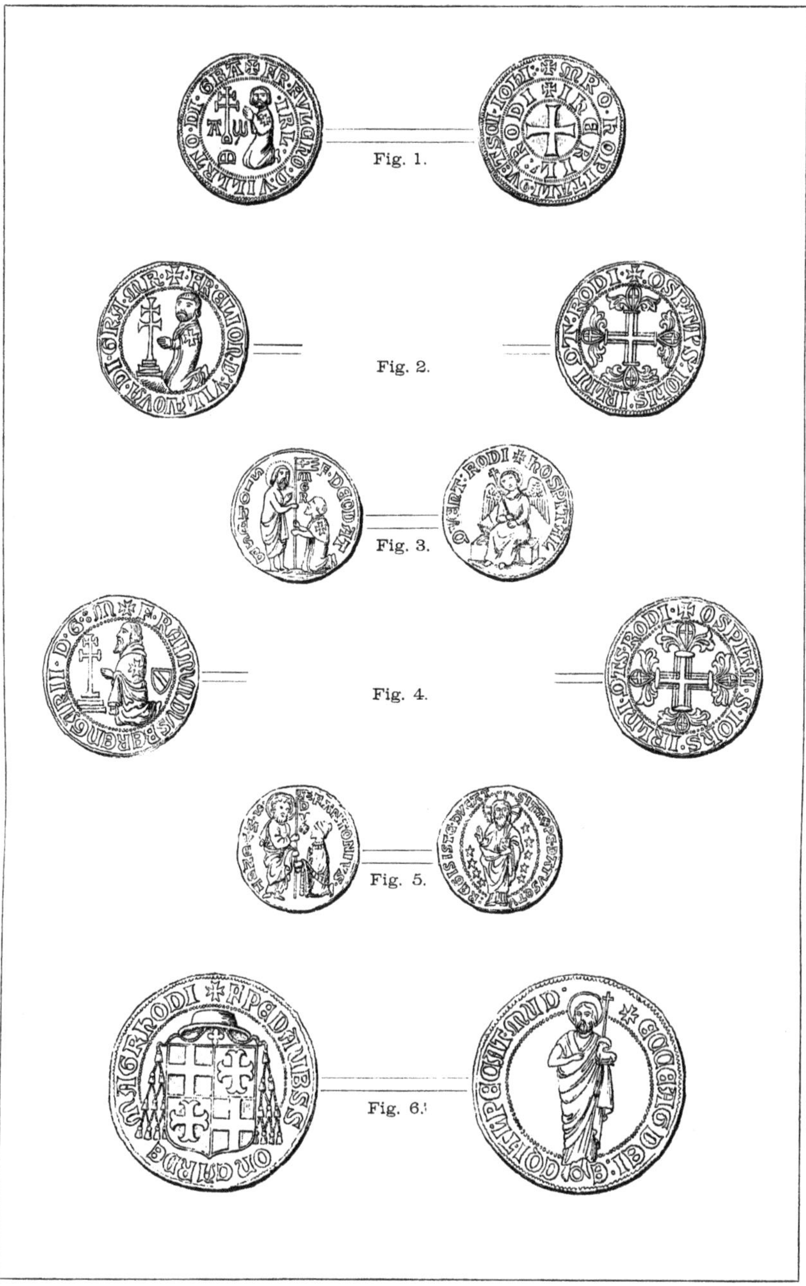

Figure 9.1 "Coins of the Grand Masters of Malta," from *American Journal of Numismatics*, 1882

As these are impressed on ancient coins, however, it has been necessary to vastly enlarge the images for her to make out the faces. This would explain why the photograph is so huge. But by enlarging the images of the knights, Swann has also enlarged the flip side: the coins themselves. His last gift to Oriane, then, is, among other things, a comically enlarged photograph of money. Swann's gift presents a photographic image that both documents the glorious past of the noble class to which the Guermantes proudly belong, shoring up their sense of privilege, and, as a grotesquely enlarged photograph of coins, suggests the modern money economy that is hastening the decline of this class.[1]

As a sign of the decadence of the times, Oriane complains about a visitor who passed by that morning and, apparently all out of calling cards, tore off part of an envelope addressed to herself and left it in lieu of a proper card. Wittily, Oriane imagines returning the favor (and getting her revenge) by leaving the immense envelope in which Swann delivered his gigantic photograph as her calling card.

There is a certain logic to this joke, one that takes up all the themes that converge in Swann's gift: class, money, and photography. Since the mid nineteenth century, when Eugène Disdéri found an economical way to produce small photo images that could be printed in series and pasted individually on cards, photo *cartes de visite* had become all the rage (Figure 9.2).[2] Disdéri made a fortune in this new, hugely profitable, industry of commercial photography that produced inexpensive photo portraits, art reproductions and pornography, all of which circulate in the *Recherche*.

Because of its size, Swann's final gift to Oriane calls attention to its material being *as photograph*, even as it displays immense images of coins. It presents an articulation of money and photography that can be historically situated in the second half of the nineteenth century, when photography becomes an "image machine."[3] Modernity involves a circulation of money and of images in the new market economy – "photography allows and accomplishes the interiorization of money in the image," writes André Rouillé, speaking of the rise of commercial photography, "It crystallizes the double logic of technology and monetary economy."[4] Commercial photo portraits operate like coins, putting faces into circulation and exchange, just as the coins of Swann's gift once did with their engraved portraits – "*cartes de visite* are in many ways akin to monetary currency."[5]

If money reduces the value of aristocratic distinction, so do commercial photo portraits, which generate the new factitious distinction of celebrity. "Have you noticed," Michelet wrote to the Goncourt brothers, "how in our times, famous men do not have the signification of their physiognomy?

Figure 9.2 Eugène Disdéri, *Madame Kann*, 1858

See their portraits, their photographs . . . In our times . . . our physiognomy is less ours. We are portraits of a collectivity rather than of ourselves."[6] As Philippe Ortel remarks (glossing Michelet's comment), with photography the analogical relation between the face and the soul, hallmark of a good painted portrait, is replaced by "a metonymic and horizontal relation between faces, which have become sensory surfaces, matrixes for reproducible traits."[7] When money and technology come together in commercial photography, social forces affect the image of the self. In the *Recherche*, Odette de Crécy claims this situation as an opportunity, producing her social identity through manipulations of her "countless photographs" (2; 601; II, 216), imprinting the effects of society on her face and body in a meticulous appropriation of her photographic image.

In his *Essai sur l'art de la photographie* (1862), Eugène Disdéri theorizes the "logic of the pose" as it pertains to commercial portrait photography.[8] He explains that, to stay in business, the photographer must satisfy a paying customer in his or her dual role as subject and viewer of an image intended for social circulation. This requires balancing the sometimes conflicting demands of truth and beauty: truth without beauty loses clients while beauty without truth is discrediting. Disdéri resolves this dilemma with a subtle theory of resemblance.

Unlike the term *imitation*, which belongs to the discourse of photography since the days of the daguerreotype, resemblance is not objective. It requires recognition, not only the individual – or self – recognition of the photographic subject after the fact, but recognition by a third party, the subjects' friends and associates. "Those who know the person to be represented," Disdéri explains, "produce a clear idea of the person, the result of all the various appearances that have been noted thousands of times."[9] Resemblance, in other words, is a social operation that determines the truth of the subject as type, a type that is not empirically given but is produced by a collective imaginary.[10] The truth of the type reflects the truth of the market. Its fictive dimension concerns social desire.

The first task of the good portrait photographer, then, is to discern "the real type and the true character"[11] of the model by putting oneself imaginatively into the social milieu of the photographic subject and intuiting the social idea to which he or she corresponds. It is on this basis that the pose – the entire *mise en scène* of the portrait, the "attitude and gesture and expression, together with distance, lighting, clothing and accessories"[12] – will be artfully devised, constituting the reality that the photograph will capture and fix in a portrait. This is no simple task, Disdéri explains, because ultimately it is the *physiognomy* of the photographic subject that "finishes and completes the resemblance," and "the muscles of the face, completely interconnected, form a network of infinite complexity and mobility."[13]

Disdéri has an appreciation of the nuances and complexity of the physiognomy of the face second only to that of Deleuze and Guattari, who emphasize the social dimension of this kind of physiognomic practice when they theorize "the social production of the face."[14] This includes not only the production of a face but also a "facialization [visageification]"[15] of the body and its surroundings. Proust has Odette perform just this when he writes that, "disciplining her features, [Odette] had made of her face and figure that creation the broad outlines of which her hairdressers, her dress-makers, she herself – in her way of holding herself, of speaking, of smiling, of moving her hands and eyes, of thinking – were to respect throughout the years to come" (2: 601; II, 216). Proust suggests not merely that Odette controls her facial expression at the moment her photos are taken, but that she disciplines her entire being, turning it into what Deleuze and Guattari theorize as a face. She has trained her whole body – even her ways of thinking and speaking (we remember her charming Anglicisms) – to consistently perform the pose in her life. When (adopting Swann's point of view) Proust refers to "the countless photographs of the 'definitive' [ne variatur] Odette who was his charming wife," his slippery syntax merges Odette with her photographic image: she *was* her "countless photographs" (2: 601; II, 216). This is the work of subjectification that Deleuze and Guattari attribute to the "machine" of facialization – "you've been recognized," they write, "the abstract machine has you inscribed in its grid."[16]

Odette *ne varietur* is the triumphant Odette, the one we see strutting along the allée des Acacias like a supremely chic automaton at the end of *Du côté de chez Swann*; she is the flower of the Elysian Garden of Women in the elegiac closing of this volume of the *Recherche*. Odette de Crécy has transformed herself into Mme Swann. She has traded in her Japanese robes for silk peignoirs in the manner of Watteau; when it comes to furnishings, "the Far East was retreating more and more before the invading forces of the eighteenth century." The woman who "was reckoned a fool . . . at the Verdurin's" can now "[be] regard[ed] as a superior woman" (3: 261–263; II, 605). Only the flowers she surrounds herself with as a kind of signature trait hearken back to the private quarters of the "very odd little house with a lot of Chinese stuff" (1: 597; I, 413) where Odette de Crécy used to receive her gentlemen friends.

The most striking feature of Odette's transformation into Mme Swann, however, is that "she seemed to be so much younger" (2: 263; I, 606). Older now – on the allée des Acacias we glimpse a locket of grey hair, folded into her now blonde coiffure – she appears much younger. Various explanations are given for this fact: changes in fashion, a slight weight gain, and so on. But the most compelling is that Odette has found her style. More than that, she has found her type, which is to say her face:

> Odette had at length discovered, or invented, a physiognomy of her own, an unalterable "character," a "style of beauty," and on her uncoordinated features – which for so long, exposed to the dangerous and futile vagaries of the flesh, putting on momentarily years, a sort of fleeting old age, as a result of the slightest fatigue, had composed for her somehow or other,

> according to her mood and her state of health, a disheveled, changeable, formless, charming face – had now set this fixed type, as it were an immortal youthfulness. (2, 264; 1, 606)

Before her transformation, her features were "uncoordinated," her face "disheveled . . . formless"; she resembled the "infinitely mobile"[17] physiognomies of Disdéri's photographic subjects before he constructed their pose and fixed their images in the photographic portrait. If Odette appears younger now (though she is older), it is because she has applied, like rose powder, the image of her social type, over her chaotic features "as . . . an immortal youthfulness." The mask has become her face.

Swann, Proust writes,

> had in his room, instead of the handsome photographs that were now taken of his wife, in all of which the same enigmatic and winning expression enabled one to recognize, whatever dress and hat she was wearing, her triumphant face and figure, a little daguerreotype of her, quite plain, taken long before the appearance of this new type, from which the youthfulness and beauty of Odette, which she had not yet discovered when it was taken, appeared to be missing. (2: 264; 1, 606)

He prefers an old daguerreotype image – Odette as a "frail young woman with pensive eyes and tired features" – to the "handsome photographs" (2: 264; 1, 606) that produce a fixed and unvarying image of her, giving her a face, facializing her body and producing her as a subject. It is the immunity to time, the impenetrability of this face – permanently young and beautiful – to any lived experience, that renders Odette at once grotesque and glamorous, and permanently so. Swann "had difficulty in identifying her face, either in the flesh or on the paste-board [la figure de chair ou de bristol][18] with the painful and continuous anxiety which dwelt in his mind" (1: 438; 1, 303). It does not seem to matter anymore whether Swann sees Odette in person or sees her photograph – "a jump" has been made "from the organic strata to the strata of signifiance and subjectification."[19]

We will not see much more of Odette until after Swann's death, when she reappears as Mme de Forcheville at the matinée Guermantes in *Le Temps retrouvé*. The hero will hardly recognize her there, not because she has changed (like all her contemporaries, who have fallen into decrepitude) but because she has *not* changed. Odette alone is strangely immune to the destructive force of time: "Only . . . Mme de Forcheville, as though she had been injected with some liquid, some sort of paraffin with the property of inflating the skin but protecting it from change, might have been an old-fashioned cocotte 'stuffed' [naturalisée] for the benefit of posterity" (6: 376; IV, 526). She inhabits the dead time of her image: "because she had not changed she seemed scarcely to be alive" (6: 380; IV, 528). Her beauty intact, she graces the bitter *bal de têtes* with her immortal youthfulness.

Her timeless beauty strikes the narrator here as a "miraculous . . . defiance of the laws of chronology" (6: 377; IV, 526), but Odette has been defying chronology narratively all along. It is with some effort that Swann and the narrator piece together the elements of her story. Swann learns that her mother sold her on the streets of Nice from the age of 16. Thanks to the little watercolor by Elstir, in which Odette appears as "Miss Sacripant," the reader grasps that she has been a *lorette*, a figure of the prostitute that engaged in cross-dressing as a manifestation of autonomy and social ambition.[20] Writers of the period associate the *lorette* with the forces of capitalism, and specifically the figure of the stockbroker; "the lorette's unscrupulous business habits" find their counterpart in illegal practices of financial speculation such as *l'agiotage*.[21] Swann, of course, is the son of a stockbroker and at home in the world of credit, speculation, and exchange, and Proust characterizes his erotic adventures in these terms:

> Swann was so fond of women that, once he had got to know more or less all the women of the aristocracy . . . he had ceased to regard those naturalisation papers, almost a patent of nobility, which the Faubourg Saint-Germain had bestowed upon him, except as a sort of negotiable bond [valeur d'échange], a letter of credit . . . which enabled him to improvise a status for himself in . . . some obscure quarter of Paris, where the good-looking daughter of a local squire or town clerk had taken his fancy. (1: 269–270; I, 188)

As improbable as the union of Swann and Odette might appear at first glance, the two are, in this sense, made for each other.

On the very first page of "Un amour de Swann," Proust refers to Odette as "*la cocotte*" (1: 266; I, 186). Whereas a mistress is financially dependent on the man who keeps her, and so can reasonably be expected to be faithful to him (or at least to appear to be), the *cocotte*, a variant on the figure of the *lorette*, is conventionally supported by several lovers at once.[22] Pleased by the power his wealth affords him, Swann makes a sort of category mistake: he takes Odette for his mistress. He remains in denial concerning her real status. Readers and critics tend to follow suit, speaking of Odette's promiscuity, or her "mediocrity," instead of acknowledging that Swann's jealousy is a structural problem linked to Odette's status as a *cocotte*, a figure of the prostitute who achieves power and success by manipulating the desires and resources of a number of men simultaneously. Swann forgets, it seems, what he must have already known on some level: Odette is, from the start, entangled with money.

Simmel writes in his *Philosophy of Money* (1900) that "the economic counterpart of the relation of prostitution is money."[23] By this he means not simply that prostitution implies money exchange but that it reveals something essential about money: its pure instrumentality. There is, as he puts it, "an ominous analogy between money and prostitution."[24] Odette is the emblem of both.[25] Money, like Odette, never grows old. Simmel associates it with an absence of memory and with "the domination of an immediate 'now' time."[26] Money is formless – "absolutely formless"[27] – as well as timeless. Like a liquid, it "lacks internal limits"[28] and "adjusts with equal ease to every form and every purpose the will wishes to imprint it with."[29]

In a fit of jealousy, Swann reproaches Odette in just these terms: "you are not even a person," he rages at her, "a clearly defined entity . . . you are a formless water that will trickle down any slope that offers itself, a fish devoid of memory . . . you are not a person . . . you are beneath everything in the world" (1: 412; I, 285–286). He objects to her formlessness, her absence of memory, her willingness to mold herself to any external contour and to respond to the solicitations of other men. He rages in other words, against her emptiness, the "complete emptiness" that Simmel attributes to the purely formal, and irreducibly social, structure of money.[30] Whereas "most other objects are used up" by time, Simmel writes, "money, with its almost unlimited durability remains unaffected by this change of individual objects."[31] So we find Odette gleaming like a gold coin in the rubble of the Guermantes salon.

At the matinée in *Le Temps retrouvé*, the hero sees Odette, in her bright beauty, as "the embodiment of the Universal Exhibition of 1878." He seems to hear her announce: "I am the Allée des Acacias of 1892" (6: 380; IV, 528). According to a contemporary account, the World's Fair of 1878 announced a new civilization, "quite different from the one whose tradition has been preserved through monuments and history."[32] With its ironwork buildings that "seemed to open willingly to the desire and the rush of the crowd," it announces the new civilization of the money economy.[33] The year 1892 was when Jacques Reinach, the financier accused of bribing public officials on behalf of the Panama Canal Company, committed suicide in the course of the worst monetary corruption scandal of the century. Jean Jaurès, who headed a parliamentary commission of inquiry into the scandal (authorized by the Loubet ministry), declared that "the power of money" had taken control of French institutions. He announced a "dying social order," emphasizing that "It is impossible to clearly distinguish with certainty between what is honest and what is dishonest, between fair . . . practices and fraud. We are witnessing a kind of social decomposition."[34] This is the state of the Guermantes world after the war: "though the names were unchanged . . . the people . . . had become different" ["sous les mêmes noms c'était . . . d'autres gens"] (6: 389; IV, 534). Thanks to their money, Mme Verdurin and Gilberte Swann have both married into the Guermantes family.[35] Odette, now Mme de Forcheville, looks younger than her daughter, Gilberte. In the absence of cultural memory, Proust writes, returning to the trope of the Panama scandal, it is impossible to know whether "M. Loubet and M. Reinach are brigands or . . . great patriots" (6: 401; IV, 542) and "ministers with a tarnished reputation and women who had started life as prostitutes were now held to be paragons of virtue" (6: 391; IV, 536).[36] Simmel notes the "complete independence of money from its origins and its eminently ahistorical character";[37] Proust attributes the difficulty of discerning who is who and what is what in the new world of the Guermantes to "this forgetfulness, which with its vigorous growth covers so rapidly even the most recent past" (6: 398; IV, 540). What is lacking in the new world of the Guermantes, Proust writes, is "the sense of History" (6: 403; IV, 542). This is the leveling effect not of time but of the money economy.

In the *Recherche*, Proust explores not only the time of individual memory and experience but also the time in which "as in some transforming fluid, men and societies and nations are immersed" (6: 355; IV, 510). Odette brings these two levels together, and Simmel helps us analyze them both.

* * *

At the end of the novel Odette is the only one left standing, untouched by time, in the world of the Guermantes. She has successfully climbed from the abject margins of the social world to its center. Her subjectification through the "abstract machine of facialization" that commercial photography operates has endowed her with the "inhuman" face of a coin; she figures the modern money economy that has both enabled her ascent and altered the world she arrives into.[38] The "face" in the sense of Deleuze and Guattari, "is a politics" to the extent that facialization means subjectification: "what chooses the face is not the subject . . . it is the face that chooses the subject."[39] "Certain assemblages of power . . . require the production of a face."[40] And yet it seems clear that Odette is not merely a victim of the social assemblages of power that "trigger" the abstract machine of facialization; she is complicit with them, precisely as a *cocotte*, which is also to say, precisely because she is, in Simmel's terms, a stranger. "The stranger," he writes, "is predominantly interested in money for the same reason that makes money so valuable to the socially deprived . . . it provides chances for him that are open to fully entitled persons."[41] Simmel emphasizes the "sociological importance" of the relation between money and the stranger: "The role that the stranger plays within a social group directs him, from the outset, toward relations with the group that are mediated by money."[42]

In the world of Proust's novel both Odette and Swann are strangers.[43] It is precisely as a stranger (a *cocotte*) that Odette also becomes the object of Swann's passionate desire, in a love story that Proust sets up as paradigmatic for the novel as a whole. Odette thrives at the intersection of money and desire, and it is because this is so that she hinges the individual and social levels of Proust's novel. In "Un amour de Swann," Swann wrestles with the idea that Odette might be a "kept woman" in an amusing scene that concludes when, still in denial on this point, he resolves to substantially increase the amount of money he gives her each month (1: 380–381; 1, 263). Proust suggests that Swann not only pays more to Odette because he wants her more, but that he pays her more *in order to* want her more.[44] We take this to be the logic of Proustian desire, one that will be played out in Saint-Loup's fraught relationship with Rachel and the hero's tug of war with Albertine. But it is also the logic of money. "We desire objects only . . . to the extent that they resist our desire," Simmel writes in *The Philosophy of Money*, appearing to ventriloquize Proust *avant la lettre*: "the mere withholding of a desired object often endows it with a value quite disproportionate to any possible enjoyment that it could yield . . . the remoteness, either literal or figurative, of the objects of our enjoyment shows them in a transfiguring light and with heightened attractions."[45] The logic of money informs not only Proust's social novel but also what critics have often taken to be a quintessentially Proustian structure of desire. For Simmel, money implies at once a (socioeconomic) historical structure and a psychological structure, a logic of desire associated with an epistemology of relativism.[46] Similarly, in Proust, money informs both the social novel of *déclassement* and *reclassement*, and the story about the narrator's "search for lost time."[47]

Critics who focus on the narrator tend to emphasize the vocation story, reading desire metaphysically. They tend to see time itself as the problem, and the *bal de têtes* in *Le Temps retrouvé* as a dramatization of the way time undoes individuals. As if, by accessing essences through art, one might be spared this destructive power of time to undo things, to grotesquely alter them, and to eventually make them vanish. As a "rose that has been sterilized" and a "mechanical doll," however, Odette stands as a warning against this kind of reading of the *Recherche* (6: 377, 380; IV, 526, 528). Untouched by time, she represents an entirely factitious version of transcendence. She amounts to a pastiche of essence, standing as she does for the essence of nothing, that is, for the purely quantitative economy of money exchange that is altering the social world of the Guermantes.

If we take Odette seriously (as we must for reasons that I hope are now obvious), another reading comes into view. Perhaps the structure of Proustian desire should not be taken as a vindication of the superiority of art over life, or even read in terms of snobbism or distinction; perhaps it should be read as a symptom of the effects of the new money economy that will gradually dissolve those barriers of class to which the Duc de Guermantes so nostalgically alludes when he beholds the portraits of his ancestors on the coins of Malta, and reads Swann's gift not as a photograph of money but as a family portrait – "our family is very much mixed up in the whole story."[48] Surely it is a coincidence, but in Simmel's *Philosophy of Money* it is the coins of Malta that exemplify the fiduciary value of money – the same coins Swann has photographed, enlarged, photo collaged, printed, and offered to the Guermantes as his final gift.[49]

NOTES

1 Money "removes the distinctive formations of aristocratic classes." Georg Simmel, *The Philosophy of Money* [1900], ed. David Frisby, trans. Tom Bottomore and David Frisby (London and New York: Routledge, 2004), 424.

2 See Elizabeth Ann McCauley, *A.A.E. Disdéri and the Carte de visite Portrait Photograph* (New Haven, CT: Yale University Press, 1985), and Peter Hamilton and Roger Hargreave, *The Beautiful and the Damned: The Creation of Identity in Nineteenth Century Photography* (Burlington, VT: Lund Humphries, 2001).

3 André Rouillé, *La Photographie: entre document et art contemporain* (Paris: Gallimard, 2005), 59. Unless otherwise noted, translations in this chapter are by Suzanne Guerlac.

4 Rouillé, *Photographie*, 63.

5 *Ibid.*, 62.

6 Cited in Philippe Ortel, *La Littérature à l'ère de la photographie: enquête sur une révolution invisible* (Nîmes, Chambon, 2002), 318.

7 *Ibid.*

8 Eugène Disdéri, *Essai sur l'art de la photographie* (1862), ed. Fabrice Masanès (Paris: Séguier, 2003), 71–72.

9 *Ibid.*, 63–64.

10 During this same period, Arthur Batut produced photographic visualizations of statistical averages, by superimposing images, to produce the visualization of an empirical (or statistical) type.

11 Disdéri, *Essai*, 65.
12 *Ibid.*
13 *Ibid.*, 77–78.
14 Gilles Deleuze and Félix Guattari, *A Thousand Plateaus, Capitalism and Schizophrenia*, trans. Brian Massumi, (Minneapolis: University of Minnesota Press, 1987), 181.
15 *Ibid.*, 181 and 185–186.
16 *Ibid.*, 177. Deleuze and Guattari do mention Proust's Odette in relation to facialization (185–186), but only in relation to Swann's investment in aesthetics, his coding of Odette's face in relation to Botticelli.
17 *Ibid.*, 78.
18 "Bristol" refers to the cardboard on which photographs were mounted.
19 Deleuze and Guattari, *Thousand Plateaus*, 181.
20 Proust does not use this term but it is implied by Elstir's image. See Courtney Ann Sullivan, "Classification, Containment, Contamination, and the Courtesan: The *Grisette, Lorette*, and *Demi-Mondaine* in Nineteenth-Century French Fiction," Ph.D. thesis, University of Texas at Austin, 2003, available at repositories.lib.utexas.edu/bitstream/handle/2152/982/sullivanca032.pdf
21 *Ibid.*, 110.
22 Sullivan, citing Dumas, gives the figure of between six and twelve lovers supporting her at the same time (*ibid.*, 109, n. 96).
23 Simmel, *Philosophy*, 408.
24 "we experience in the nature of money itself something of the essence of prostitution, the indifference to its use . . . the objectivity inherent in money as a mere means . . . " *Ibid.*, 407.
25 In an incident crucial to Swann's jealous suffering, Odette, identified not only with fashion but also with luxury, frequents a restaurant called the *Maison Dorée* [Golden House]. See Simmel, *ibid.*, on fashion and luxury.
26 Simmel, *Philosophy*, preface, xxiii–iv.
27 *Ibid.* 294.
28 *Ibid.*, 537.
29 *Ibid.*, 351.
30 *Ibid.*, 351.
31 *Ibid.*, 199.
32 Charles Blanc, *Les Beaux-Arts à l'Exposition Universelle de 1878* (Paris: Librairie Renouard, 1878), 41.
33 *Ibid.*, 61.
34 Jaurès also declares that "a financial state has taken control within the democratic one." Jean Jaurès, "L'Affaire Panama. Le Devoir du Gouvernement," discours parlementaire, séance du 8 février 1893. Available at www.assemblee-nationale.fr/histoire/jaures/discours/panama_08021893.asp
35 Marriage for money, Simmel writes, can be considered "a variation on prostitution" (*Philosophy*, 413).
36 Reinach was the financier of the Panama Company, Loubet the minister who authorized the investigation into the scandal and then blocked its progress.

37 Simmel, *Philosophy*, 334.
38 Deleuze and Guattari speak of the "inhumanity" of the face socially produced by facialization (*Thousand Plateaus*, 181).
39 *Ibid.*, 108.
40 *Ibid.*, 175.
41 Simmel, *Philosophy*, 241.
42 *Ibid.*, 240.
43 The issue of anti-Semitism, built into Simmel's reflections on the stranger, is of central importance in the scene (and meaning) of Swann's gift, a question I cannot enter into here but treat elsewhere.
44 Simmel writes that "objects are not difficult to acquire because they are valuable, but we call those objects valuable that resist our desire to posses them" (*Philosophy*, 69).
45 Simmel, *Philosophy*, 68–69.
46 "Money is the pinnacle of a cultural historical series of developments," writes Simmel (*Philosophy*, 302).
47 The terms *déclassement* and *reclassement* appear in the scene of Swann's gift, with reference to Swann and the issues of anti-Semitism and his marriage to Odette (3: 798; II, 870).
48 For another possibility, see René Girard's theory of "triangular desire" in *Deceit, Desire, and the Novel: Self and Other in Literary Structure*, trans. Yvonne Freccero (Baltimore: Johns Hopkins University Press, 1965). This approach neglects the economic (and historical) dimension that Simmel contributes to our understanding of Proust's novel, through his analysis of a structure of desire that belongs to the social psychology of money that is historically framed. Another social theorist of imitation (contemporary with Proust) is of course Gabriel Tarde, whose work informs Proust's novel in important ways. See Gabriel Tarde, *Les Lois de l'imitation* [1890] (Paris: Kimé, 1993).
49 Simmel, *Philosophy*, 191. Forty pages of *The Philosophy of Money* were translated into French and published in 1912 as *Mélanges de philosophie relativiste: contribution à une culture philosophique* (Paris: Alcan). Various articles by Simmel were published in French from 1894 to 1896.

CHAPTER 10

Oriane's artful fashions

Caroline Weber

> Compared with those ideas, the image of Mme de Guermantes at the Opéra was a very insignificant thing, a tiny star twinkling beside the long tail of a blazing comet . . .
>
> *Le Côté de Guermantes* (3: 72, trans. mod.; II, 360)

Proust assigns to the Duchesse de Guermantes a major presence throughout the *Recherche* – most notably, in the extended dinner-party scene in *Le Côté de Guermantes*, but also at the very beginning and the very end of the novel. Playing with his magic lantern as a child in Combray, the hero admires Geneviève de Brabant, a medieval "daughter of the House of Guermantes" (1: 143; I, 103) from whom Oriane descends, luminously projected on his bedroom wall: a first instantiation of the ancient, aristocratic phantasm that, when it resurfaces soon afterward in the Guermantes forebears figured in the tapestries and stained-glass windows of the village church, activates one of the first stirrings of his literary vocation. He dreams of chatting with the Duchesse about the poems he vaguely hopes someday to compose, then abandons the fantasy when he realizes he does not know what those poems would say. This lack of follow-through, of course, dogs his creative ambitions for the next several thousand pages – until the new Princesse de Guermantes's afternoon party (the so-called "bal de têtes"), when the narrator, enfeebled and middle-aged, has the epiphany that brings his story to its circular conclusion: he will regain the myriad, seemingly lost or wasted moments of his past by transmuting them into literature. Beset on all sides by his old friends' ravaged faces, each memento mori more harrowing than the last, he seizes with justifiable excitement on the idea that "art [is] the most real of all things, the most austere school of life, the true Last Judgment" (6: 275; III, 880). As if to underscore this notion, meanwhile, a lone voice pierces through the ambient party noise, striking the narrator's ears "like the trumpet of the Last Judgment" (6: 346; III, 927, trans. mod.): the voice of the Duchesse de Guermantes, prompt and foil to his burgeoning artistic consciousness.

As the alpha and omega of the hero's narrative, Mme de Guermantes occupies a privileged position with regard to his *venue à l'écriture*, to his sense of himself as an artist and of art as the ultimate form of reality and means of redemption ("the most real of all things . . . the true Last Judgment"). In a novel with no shortage of artist characters, the Duchesse is manifestly not the only figure who inspires the narrator to ponder the nature and the stakes of the creative enterprise. But she offers a different perspective on the matter, precisely because she is not an artist as such. Though one dowager countess claims that "Oriane de Guermantes . . . does water-colors worthy of a great painter, and writes better verses than most of the great poets" (3: 613; II, 447), the Duchesse does not channel her talent into the Time-defying work of a Bergotte, a Vinteuil, or an Elstir. Rather, like her fellow *mondain* Swann – who instead of working on his Vermeer monograph contents himself with noting piquant resemblances "between living people and the portraits in galleries" (a kitchen-maid and Giotto's Charity, Odette and Botticelli's Zipporah) (1: 459; I, 317) – Mme de Guermantes presents a cautionary tale about the limits of superficial, pseudo-artistic modes of expression.

Tellingly enough, the narrator never sees, and the *Recherche* never again mentions, the original paintings and poems ascribed to the Duchesse by her dowager friend. Instead, the text shows Oriane's visual artistry to consist chiefly in her elegant style of dress, and her principal verbal talent to reside in her original conversational style (defined on the one hand by her snappy, quintessentially modern and Parisian "Meilhac and Halévy" wit, and on the other by an earthy, antiquated Champenois vocabulary and pronunciation [1: 475; I, 328]). In both her clothing and her speech, Oriane's inventive impulses negotiate a series of antithetical terms: sacred and profane, *vieille France* and *Ville Lumière*, past and present, everlasting and ephemeral.[1] In so doing, they appear to hold out a promise of transcendence, an intimation of immortality implicit as well in the metaphors attending her first and last cameos in the novel: Geneviève de Brabant, suffused with "the mystery of the Merovingian age," and the trumpets of the Last Judgment, heralds of a world without end (1: 242; I, 169). Ultimately, however, neither of the Duchesse's preferred art forms succeeds in defying Time. At best, they inspire the narrator to think creatively in turn, and to consider how a product of the imagination might "bring out the opposed facets" (6: 507; IV, 609) of human experience: "[the ones] that were outside time" and "the ones relating to Time" (6: 355; IV, 510).[2] For the sake of (relative) brevity, this chapter will focus only on the Duchesse's fashion statements, as they unfurl between the twin poles of the timebound and the timeless. For the narrator, Oriane's artful sartorial flourishes serve as signposts along a road that she herself does not take nearly far enough: the road to art – and from there to eternity.

* * *

The Duchesse's first appearance as a fashion-plate occurs in "Combray," before the young hero has ever laid eyes on her. Because of the romanticizing ancestral portrayals he has seen through his magic lantern and in church, he has come to envision Mme de Guermantes, too, as a kind of historical relic, imbued with "the colors of a tapestry or a stained-glass window" (1: 246; I, 172) and evoking the primordial French fatherland: "the ancient heritage, the poetic domain from which the proud race of Guermantes, like a mellow, crenellated tower that traverses the ages, had risen already over France, at a time when the sky was still empty at those points where later were to rise Notre-Dame of Paris" (3: 7; II, 313). But these notions of feudal-age grandeur square ill with the depiction Dr. Percepied, from whom the narrator "had heard most about Mme de Guermantes," shows him one day: "the number of an illustrated paper in which she was depicted in the costume she had worn at a fancy dress ball given by the Princesse de Léon" (1: 245; I, 172). This illustration abruptly transports the Duchesse from the poetic domain of Frankish prehistory to the bustling "capital of the nineteenth century," two eras as incommensurable as their respective, emblematic creations: the lone, crenellated tower and the mass-produced magazine.[3] When depicted in the latter, Oriane reveals her unexpected affiliation with a thoroughly modern species of woman: the well-heeled *Parisienne*.

Referenced just before the account of Dr. Percepied's daughter's wedding, where the hero first beholds the Duchesse in person, the current-day magazine illustration prefigures the disappointingly non-Merovingian mien she presents on that occasion, with her "billowy scarf of mauve silk, glossy and new and bright" (1: 245; I, 172), a detail that undermines his *vieille France* ideal in two ways. First, like the magazine, the scarf belongs not to the past but to the present – in both its newness and its stylish hue. (Mauve so dominated fin-de-siècle women's fashion that the era was sometimes called "the mauve nineties.")[4] Second, "stylishness" is a quality to which anyone with access to a shiny mauve cravat can lay claim – a quality that is innately reproducible, not irreducibly original. Indeed, the hero has seen the same accessory on Mme Sazerat, a middle-class neighbor in Combray more notable for her dog (whose comings and goings Aunt Léonie discusses with Françoise) than for any exalted pedigree. (In fact,

Mme Sazerat's sole connection to the nobility lies in her late father's having squandered his fortune on a "cruel" young Mme de Villeparisis.) The rapprochement the mauve cravat effects between *bourgeoise* and *duchesse* thus strikes the narrator as unthinkable – "Never had it occurred to me that she [Mme de Guermantes] might have . . . a mauve scarf like Mme Sazerat" (1: 246; I, 172) – and strips Oriane of her historic glamour: "So that's Mme de Guermantes – that's all she is!" (1: 247; I, 173). In bowing to the democratizing dictates of modern chic, she loses her singular heraldic distinction.[5]

As chronicled in the press, her voguish persona further subverts the hero's *vieille France* ideal by referring back to a criticism voiced by Swann earlier in "Combray," when he decries the media's treatment of the Faubourg's every diversion as front-page news, a practice that impels readers to

> take interest in some fresh triviality or other every day, whereas only three or four books in a lifetime give us anything of real importance. Suppose that . . . a transmutation were to take place, and we were to find inside it – oh! I don't know, shall we say Pascal's *Pensées*? . . . And then, in the gilt and tooled volumes which we open once in ten years . . . we should read that . . . the Princesse de Léon had given a fancy dress ball. (1: 34; I, 26)

The chiasmic reversal of values Swann proposes here rests on an explicit devaluation of the *mondanités* defining social life as he – and his friend Oriane – know it. Although it is precisely "to just that sort of amusement that he devoted his life" (1: 136; I, 97), Swann dismisses the Princesse de Léon's costume ball as a "triviality," the antithesis of things of "real importance" contained in timeless works of literature. In addition to exposing the hypocrisy of his own conduct ("I found all this contradictory," the narrator says of the older man's harangue), Swann's assertion that "the balls given by the Princesse de Léon [were] of no importance" (1: 136; I, 97) proleptically disparages the clothes-conscious frivolity of the Duchesse herself. In garnering media attention with her party costume, she aligns herself with "trivialities" rather with things of "real importance."

In *Le Côté de Guermantes*, the hero, now a young man, considers this tension at greater length. Having moved with his parents into a dependency of M. and Mme de Guermantes's Parisian *hôtel particulier*, he has ample opportunity to study her up close. Against the backdrop of the modern metropolis, he stops focusing on the lady's "Merovingian" persona, and starts worshiping her instead for her exalted position in Parisian society: blessed with "the highest position in the Faubourg Saint-Germain" (3: 28; II, 328), "the Duchesse is one of the noblest souls in Paris, the cream of the most refined, the choicest society" (3: 67; II, 356). He has trouble reconciling this information, though, with what he discovers to be the Duchesse's intense preoccupation with fashion. To the hero, the avid curiosity with which Mme de Guermantes regards a well-heeled actress in the street, or the anxious concentration she brings to bear on her reflection in the mirror at home, betrays an insufficient respect for her own stature as the Faubourg Saint-Germain's reigning goddess. Indeed it is this very stature that she jeopardizes, he thinks, by entering into a crass mimetic competition with "ordinary" women, and playing "the role, so unworthy of her, of a fashionable woman . . . like a queen who has consented to appear as a servant-girl in theatricals at court" (3: 29; II, 329).

Needless to say, in the caste hierarchy upheld by the denizens of the Faubourg, the social distance between a soubrette and a queen is impossibly vast; when bridged, dire *déclassement* ensues. Which condition, as the mature narrator of the *Recherche* – versus the still-young hero of *Le Côté de Guermantes* – knows full well, awaits the Duchesse herself in *Le Temps retrouvé*, where he finds that she has undermined her once unassailable social position by befriending actresses, a group as far removed from duchesses, in *mondain* principle, as soubrettes are from queens. But already in *Le Côté de Guermantes*, the narrator affirms Oriane's self-abasement through fashion by noting that in her inordinate concern for the latter, she recalls not only a queen posturing as a soubrette, but a mythological deity who, in metamorphosing into a swan (in English, one notes the homonym for her friend Charles's surname), has forgotten her celestial origins: "She checked whether her veil was hanging properly, smoothed her cuffs, adjusted her cloak, as the divine swan performs all the movements natural to his animal species . . . and darts suddenly after a button or an umbrella, as a swan would, without remembering that he is a god" (3: 29; II, 329). This second metaphor reinforces the idea that the Duchesse's interest in clothes compromises her divine, *sui generis* essence – not incidentally described in *Le Côté de Guermantes* as the product of "the union of a goddess with a bird" (3: 100; II, 379).[6] In reintroducing this conceit here, the narrator stresses the degree to which the goddess demeans herself by obeying the instincts of her "animal species." To fuss over her sleeves and veil, as Mme de Guermantes does, is in his view to behave as brutishly as a swan pecking at a button.

The hero reverses this judgment, however, when he spies the Duchesse one night at the Opéra-Comique, entering the box of her cousin, the Princesse de Guermantes, whose flamboyant ensemble (decorated with seashells, pearls, and plumes galore) has already caught his eye and put him in mind of a Nereid. In stark contrast to her cousin, the Duchesse is turned out in an exquisitely simple white muslin gown – the bodice tailored "with a precision that was positively British" – that challenges the narrator's opinion of her chic as an all too human flaw: "the Duchess, goddess turned woman . . . appear[ed] in that moment a thousand times more lovely" (3: 63, 69; II, 353, 358). In this case, Oriane's style does not detract from her superiority, but confirms it:

> It was as though the Duchess had guessed that her cousin, of whom, it was rumoured, she was inclined to make fun for what she called her "exaggerations" . . . would be wearing this evening one of those costumes in which the Duchess considered her "dressed up," and that she had decided to give her a lesson in good taste. (3: 62; II, 353)

This elevating sartorial display even includes some touches that recall the narrator's swan analogy and undo its previous, negative valence:

> The Duchess wore in her hair only a simple aigrette which, surmounting her arched nose and prominent eyes, reminded one of the crest on the head of a bird. Her neck and shoulders emerged from a drift of snow-white chiffon, against which fluttered a swansdown fan . . . (3: 63; II, 353)

The lady's swanlike elegance now strikes her young admirer as "the materialisation, snow-white or patterned with color, of [her] inner activity," the lofty form with which, like an artist, she has endowed an original idea. In the process, the Duchesse has reasserted her divinity – "I did not believe that any other woman could usurp that spangled bodice, any more than the fringed and flashing shield of Minerva" – and has even imparted it to the Princesse's other guests: looking up at the box, the narrator writes, "it was as though I had seen . . . the assembly of the Gods . . . between two pillars of Heaven" (3: 68; II, 357).

And yet, this effulgent vision of the Guermantes crowd as so many "Immortals" (3: 68; III, 357), metonymically sanctified by their proximity to the resplendent Oriane, assumes an ironic cast if one again looks ahead to *Le Temps retrouvé*, which finds many of these selfsame "Gods" reappearing at the *bal de têtes* as cadaverous

> puppets which exteriorised Time, Time which by habit is made invisible and to become visible seeks bodies, which, wherever it finds them, it seizes upon, to display its magic lantern upon them . . . Life at such moments seems to us like a theatrical pageant [féérie] in which from one act to another we see the baby turn into a youth and the youth into a mature man, who in the next act totters towards the grave. (6: 342–345; IV, 503–504)

While the Duchesse's vestimentary triumph at the Opéra may offer a fleeting glimpse of transcendence, then, the experience does not last; it is not enshrined in an enduring work of art (such as a book, a painting, or a sonata). In this respect, too, the narrator's designation of Mme de Guermantes and her companions as "Immortals" carries an ironic inflection, even without any foreknowledge of the *bal de têtes*; for her "lesson in good taste" is hardly the sort of aesthetic achievement in which a real *immortel* – a member of the Académie française – would glory. And its "artistic" value diminishes even further when one recalls that, as with the mauve cravat, any fashion statement is subject to appropriation – to vulgarizing pastiche – by lesser mortals: copied soon afterward by the arriviste bumpkin Mme de Cambremer, Mme de Guermantes's masterpiece of good taste imparts to her imitator the look of a "provincial schoolgirl, mounted on wires, rigid, erect, desiccated, angular, with a plume of raven's feathers stuck vertically in her hair" (3: 64; II, 354).

Similarly, the hero himself cannot, at this stage in his literary *Bildung*, do full justice to the Duchesse's sartorial sublimity; the elation the Opéra tableau triggers in him exceeds his ability to give it meaningful expression, though it does inspire him to try:

> From time to time, the scintillating smile of Mme de Guermantes, and the warm feeling it had engendered, came back to me. And without exactly knowing what I was doing, I tried to find a place for them (as a woman studies the effect a certain kind of jewelled buttons that have just been given her might have on a dress) beside the romantic ideas which I had long held . . . for instance of being loved by a woman . . . (3: 71–72; II, 359)

In attempting to meld Oriane's image with his own imaginings, the hero engages in a rudimentary effort to wrest art from life. Pursued, however, with insufficient focus ("without exactly knowing what I was doing") and endowed, as yet, with no concrete form, his creative experiment is of fleeting duration – not unlike the Duchesse's own sartorial *coup de théâtre*. He emphasizes this parallel by comparing himself to a woman evaluating a given clothing detail for its aesthetic potential – the very exercise to which Mme de Guermantes devotes so much energy – and by specifically mentioning "a certain kind of jewelled buttons," the demeaning obsession of the divinity turned swan. With these implicit analogies, the hero underlines his artistic failure and the Duchesse's alike: his inchoate flights of "novelistic" fancy no more count as literature than her one-woman fashion show qualifies her for admission to the Académie française.[7]

Many years later, in *La Prisonnière*, the narrator again examines Mme de Guermantes's "art of dressing" with an eye to its artistic viability. Having heard Elstir describe the Duchesse, now a friend of the adult hero, as "the best-dressed woman in Paris" (5: 33; III, 543), he seeks her counsel in choosing for Albertine one of the lavish Fortuny house-dresses Oriane has recently taken to wearing, and for which she has launched a craze in Paris. First introduced by the textile artisan Mariano Fortuny in 1907, these garments eschewed the cumbersome shaping devices (bustles, crinolines, boning) that had hitherto underpinned women's luxury apparel; with their relatively relaxed cut, Fortuny's gowns modernized the feminine silhouette.[8] At the same time, they were made from materials – intricately embroidered with patterns inspired by "old Venetian models" – that exuded a palpable "historical character" (5: 34; III, 543). It is this evocative commingling of antiquity and modernity that the narrator, again citing Elstir as an authority, accentuates in describing Oriane's new *peignoirs*:

> These Fortuny gowns . . . were those of which Elstir, when he told us about the magnificent garments of the women of Carpaccio's and Titian's day, had prophesied the imminent return, rising from their ashes, as magnificent as of old, for everything must return in time, as it is written beneath the vaults of St Mark's, and proclaimed, as they drink from the urns of marble and jasper of the Byzantine capitals, by the birds which symbolise at once death and resurrection. (5: 497; III, 871)

In this passage, the narrator hints at the potential of the Duchesse's Fortunys to defy Time; for in recreating the vestments of Carpaccio's and Titian's female subjects, they have revived those sartorial wonders "rising from their ashes, as magnificent as of old."[9] These ashes, moreover, suggest one self-resurrecting bird, the phoenix, while the Byzantine architectural iconography evokes another, the pelican, which, because early Christians construed its practice of regurgitating food for its young as an act of nourishing its children with its own flesh, became a favored symbol of Jesus's crucifixion and resurrection.[10] Echoing the prospect of renewal heralded by its pagan *confrère*, the phoenix, the Son of God's avian avatar, as embroidered in a Fortuny dress, would thus appear to extend His promise of eternal life – "everything must return in time" – to the wearer: here, Mme de Guermantes. "Hinting, through the extreme modernity [dernier cri] of [her] appointments, at the forms of an earlier day" (1: 595; I, 411), the trend-setting Duchesse once more evinces a creative play of opposites, and is thereby reborn in an arresting new guise.[11]

Thus constructed, Mme de Guermantes's Fortuny persona seems "to respond to a specific intention, to be endowed with a special significance" (5: 34; III, 543). Crucially, however, the aesthetic intention she figures forth is Fortuny's, not her own; while she does not diminish its beauty, she does not create it, either – she merely, with her reputation for elegance, consecrates its desirability among her fellow *Parisiennes*.[12] And setting such a fashion is a process (assimilating ancient and durable creations – Byzantine columns, Renaissance paintings – to a passing fad) that directly inverts that of a genius like Elstir (who captures the ephemera of modern life – "the delicate gesture with which [milliners] give a last refinement, a supreme caress to the bows or feathers of a hat after it is finished" [2: 659; II, 256] – for the purposes of timeless art).[13] In fact, this very principle of inversion explains why transcendence eludes Oriane in her Fortuny mode as well. For any style's value *as* fashion lies in its putative newness, in the contrast it presents to the style that came before it (or, in the case of the Duchesse's sartorial performance at the Opéra, the style that stands beside it – the Princesse de Guermantes's overwrought getup, pointedly used by Oriane as a *repoussoir*). While no artwork is impervious to changing tastes and trends (still less to that most inexorable of human forces, forgetting), fashion more than any other form of cultural expression relies for its very existence on negating in the present the same look it deemed "*le dernier cri*" in the past; the pursuit of stylishness is, in its essence, lost or wasted time.[14]

Mme de Guermantes herself proves this point by trading yesterday's understated, strictly tailored evening gown for today's unstructured, hyper-ornamented house-dress – the latter arguably just as "dressed up" as anything ever sported by the Princesse de Guermantes, and just as antithetical to the Duchesse's own, erstwhile minimalism. As unlike one another as a pagan swan pecking at a button and a Christian pelican feeding her young from her own gullet, Oriane's fashion statements have no consistency except for their own, immanent obsolescence. Or, viewed in Derridean terms, they have no consistency except their own, inherent *différance*: their propensity to mutation in time ("fashion" differs from one moment to another: for instance, from the period of *Le Côté de Guermantes* to that of *La Prisonnière*) as well as in space ("fashion" differs from one wearer to another: for instance, from the Duchesse to Mme de Cambremer).[15]

The incompatibility of such mutation with any conventional idea of immortality is dramatically confirmed by Albertine's premature death at the end of *La Prisonnière*. Because, like Mme de Cambremer, Albertine is eager to model herself on the Duchesse, she duly takes to wearing the Fortuny house-dress given to her by the hero, decorated, like Oriane's, with "the oriental birds that symbolised alternatively life and death" (5: 531; III, 896). So wholeheartedly does Albertine embrace this aesthetic, in fact, that the narrator conflates her metonymically with its avian motifs: "I kissed her . . . pressing to my heart . . . the mating birds, symbols of death and resurrection" (5: 538; III, 900). On one level, this metonymic play effects a palimpsest, with Albertine overwriting the Duchesse as the latest and greatest epigone of modern style. (The Duchesse is dead, long live Albertine.) But on another level, the rhetoric of death and rebirth proleptically signals Albertine's own looming demise. Because the narrator is already aware, though the hero is not, that death will not be long in claiming Albertine, an ironic pall hovers over his descriptions of Fortuny's resurrection imagery, which proves powerless, of course, to save the girl from her fate.

In much the same way, the Fortuny aesthetic also betrays the Duchesse, and not just because Albertine, for a time, makes it her own. Despite surviving to the end of the *Recherche*, Mme de Guermantes too falls prey to the mortal depredations of Time. In *Le Temps retrouvé*, she turns heads at the *bal de têtes* with her wizened "salmon-pink body" swathed in black lace and ropes of precious gems. But such "marvellous artifices of toilet and aesthetic" cannot disguise, much less reverse, the disfiguring impact old age has had on her. Considering this newest (and last) of her incarnations, and playing on the adjective *saumoné*, the narrator likens the Duchesse to another early Christian resurrection symbol, the fish (ΙΧΘΥΣ): "With its hereditary sinuosity of line," he notes, one discerns "some archaic sacred fish, loaded with precious stones" (6: 346; IV, 505).[16] The Fortuny frocks of *La Prisonnière*, though, having no more conferred immortality on Oriane than they did on Albertine, this overdetermined allusion to the Christian miracle of "Death swallowed up in victory"[17] is again fraught with irony. And that irony is heightened by the fact that Mme de Guermantes has, consistent with fashion's periodic abandonment of its own best-loved styles, traded her Fortunys of yore for the heavy jewels and "fins of black lace" (6: 346; IV, 505) of the dowager she has now become. Whether because they are no longer in vogue, because they no longer fit her, or because they do not suit a lady her age, the Duchesse's Fortuny robes have been defeated by Time – just like her pared-down Opéra ensemble, and just like her own, once bedazzling beauty.[18]

"Ainsi tout passe, tout s'élève, tout s'avilit, tout se détruit" [Thus all comes to pass, all rises, all decays, all is destroyed]: this maxim from Saint-Simon, a touchstone for Proust, finds paradigmatic illustration in the arc of Mme de Guermantes's "artful" costumes.[19] And yet, when discussing her gowns of yesteryear with the narrator at the *bal de têtes*, the Duchesse remains surprisingly optimistic about their lasting import as art. Although "today . . . nobody wears" the type of dress she favored in an earlier time "simply because it isn't done," she declares, "they will come back, as fashions always do – in clothes, in music, in painting." Insofar as it echoes the message of Christian resurrection figured in Fortuny's bird-patterned peignoirs – "everything must return in time" – Mme de Guermantes's comment itself recycles or revives an earlier fashion statement. For this very reason, she is clearly wrong to find "a certain originality in this philosophic reflexion" (6: 474; IV, 588), as the narrator wryly puts it. The *différance* intrinsic to fashion performs its signature, deforming gesture by repackaging the news of Jesus's – and humanity's – eternal rebirth as banal party chatter: yet another study in Saint-Simonian "vilification," courtesy of a fallen fashion icon.

Nonetheless, Oriane is *not* wrong to speculate that her *démodé* outfits might attain the same kind of enduring afterlife as a painting or a piece of music. For the narrator's own artistic epiphany is nigh, and it will enable him to see even the disappointments and losses of his life – including those associated with Mme de Guermantes's sartorial sensibility – as vital components of his art. In his future book, composed "I dare not say ambitiously like a cathedral, but quite simply like a dress" (6: 509; IV, 610), Oriane's lost styles will be found again, preserved in all their flawed, unstable, differential glory, in the sinuous lines and complex patterns of the narrator's alternately celebratory and ironic prose. Woven into the text of his *Recherche*, the Duchesse's vestimentary experiments will hover forever, like the lady herself, on the precarious threshold between exaltation and abasement, resurrection and destruction, divinity and bird. The swan is dead; long live the swan.

NOTES

1 Borrowing terminology from Gilles Deleuze's *Proust and Signs* [1964], trans. Richard Howard (Minneapolis: University of Minnesota Press, 2000), one might add to this list of antitheses "spiritualized" and "material," "transparent" and "opaque," and so on. Deleuze's account of "worldly signs," however, merely notes that they replace "action," and produce at best a "nervous exaltation" – and disqualifies them from consideration as "signs of art" (5–14).

2 See also *À l'ombre des jeunes filles en fleurs*, where the strangely uplifting vision of three old trees – a precursor of the narrator's mature artistic consciousness – makes him "waver between some distant year and the present moment," and gives him the impression that the trees "were phantoms of the

past . . . who . . . like ghosts . . . seemed to be appealing to me to take them with me, to bring them back to life" (2: 404–407; II, 77–78).

3 Proust further underscores the modernity of this image by ascribing it to a *mondain* party that actually took place: the Princesse de Léon's costume ball, held in honor of Isabella II of Spain on May 26, 1891. For one contemporary account of this party, see Sarah Spottiswood Mackin, *A Society Woman on Two Continents* (London: Transatlantic, 1896), 150–162. In fact, the *bal de têtes* of *Le Temps retrouvé*, too, references a real-life highlight of the fin-de-siècle Faubourg's social calendar: the Princesse de Sagan's notorious, animal-themed costume ball, *le bal de bêtes*, of June 2, 1885.

4 Raymond Rudorff, *The Belle Époque: Paris in the Nineties* (New York: Saturday Review Press, 1973), 225.

5 For a reading of this passage that subsumes the mauve cravat into the more general problem of the Duchesse's physicality, see Judith Oriol, *Femmes Proustiennes* (Paris: EST, 2009), 160–161.

6 On the ornithological imagery associated with the Guermantes, see Marie Miguet-Ollagnier, *La Mythologie de Marcel Proust* (Besançon: Presses Universitaires de Franche-Comté, 1982), 29–31.

7 Again for the sake of concision, I do not discuss here the "red shoes" scene in *Le Côté de Guermantes*, though this episode too posits a damning opposition between "trivialities" (the Guermantes' overriding concern with appearances), and things of "real importance" (Swann's terminal malady). The appalling hollowness of Oriane's value system surfaces again in *Le Temps retrouvé*, when, reminded by the hero of her red shoes from that long-ago evening with Swann, she remembers her shoes as having been gold. So inconsequential, in other words, is the matter of shoe color that Oriane herself cannot recall it correctly; and yet, in *Le Côté de Guermantes*, she assigns to it more importance than she does to the tidings of Swann's impending doom.

8 See Guillermo de Osma, *Mariano Fortuny: His Life and His Work* (New York: Rizzoli, 1985), 86, 90–99, 137.

9 For important analyses of the trope of Fortuny fabrics and designs in the *Recherche*, see Christie McDonald, *The Proustian Fabric: Associations of Memory* (Omaha: University of Nebraska Press, 1991), 133–144; and Valerie Steele, *Paris Fashion: A Cultural History* (New York: Berg, 2001), 214–218.

10 On the Christian symbolism of the pelican, see Frederick Edward Hulme, *The History, Principles, and Practice of Symbols in Christian Art* (New York: Sonnenschein, 1910), 188–190.

11 This play of opposites recalls Antoine Compagnon's formula about Proust's own productively liminal position "between two centuries": "tradition and revolution, the two impulses are always closely linked." See Antoine Compagnon, *Proust Between Two Centuries*, trans. Richard E. Goodkin (New York: Columbia University Press, 1992), 23.

12 As Jean-Yves Tadié has noted, in contacting Madrazo Fortuny's sister for details of these dresses' designs, Proust told her that Fortuny would be "the only living artist" to whom the *Recherche* would refer. See Jean-Yves Tadié, *Proust et le roman* (Paris: Gallimard, 1971), 93–94, n. 7.

13 "The *Recherche* or the great book of inversion," Laure Murat notes in her astute essay, "Les souliers rouges de la duchesse, ou la vulgarité de l'aristocratie française," in *D'Après Proust*, ed. Philippe Forest and Stéphane Audeguy (Paris: Gallimard/NRF, 2013), 96–105.

14 Proust himself describes this phenomenon at the end of *Du côté de chez Swann*, when the narrator searches in the Bois de Boulogne for the simple little hats of an earlier age, only to find that massive, extravagant confections have taken their place.

15 See Jacques Derrida, *Writing and Difference* [1967], trans. Alan Bass (University of Chicago Press, 1978).

16 For a canonical explanation of this Greek acrostic, see Gerard O'Daley, *Augustine's City of God* (Oxford University Press, 1999), 187.

17 I Corinthians 15:54.

18 Whereas *Le Temps retrouvé* presents the Duchesse's dress and appearance as manifestations of her decline, these same attributes endow Odette with a look of eternal youth: "Mme de Forcheville was so miraculous that one could not even say that she had grown young again – it was more as though, with all her carmines and her russets, she had bloomed for a second time . . . And indeed, for me she seemed to say . . . 'I am the Allée des Acacias of 1892'" (6: 380; IV, 528).

19 Louis de Rouvroy, duc de Saint-Simon, *Mémoires complets et authentiques du duc de Saint-Simon, sur le siècle de Louis XIV et la Régence*, vol. XIV (Paris: H. L. Delloye, 1840), 59. On the importance of this line in and to Proust, see Sylvaine Landes-Ferrali, *Proust et le Grand Siècle* (Tübingen: Gunter Narr Verlag, 2004), 275–276. In *Albertine disparue*, Proust references the line when describing "this world of ours where everything withers, everything perishes" (6: 7; IV, 270).

CHAPTER 11

Glass and clay: Proust and Gallé

Elaine Scarry

The substance we call clay has such remarkable features that an array of scientists today believe that clay may have served as the worktable on which life learned to live. Clay has the capacity to replicate itself not quite in the way that crystals grow, and not quite in the way that DNA replicates itself, but in lattice-works that are a hybrid – or something in between – crystals and DNA. NASA scientist Leila Coyne describes the "startling electronic properties," of clay, "defects" in its lattice-work that enable it to store energy and information "and then reemit it." She states: "If you take a lump of clay and hit it with a hammer it blows ultraviolet energy for a month."[1]

The theory that clay is the worktable on which life learned to live is relatively new. But two features of this account have been with us for millennia. First, the association of clay with replication. On this northern European vase from the year 1900 (Figure 11.1), a simple ginger leaf is repeated across the base. But if we scan across Babylonian, Egyptian, Chinese, Islamic, Greek, Roman, North and South American pottery, we inevitably find lines and images imprinted on the surface in repetitive streams. Clay invites and incites repetition. The second feature of clay saluted across millennia is its association with aliveness: the claims that it is alive, that while wet it seems to move, that the "inert ball . . . acquire[s] a coiled spring of energy,"[2] or even, as is said by potters in the Andes, that "it is sensitive . . . and gets upset easily"[3] are claims we have heard all our lives.

For Proust, clay was a worktable for the creation of both cities and persons. In "Noms de pays: le nom," the narrator pictures Balbec "as on an old piece of Norman pottery that still keeps the color of the earth from which it was fashioned." He asks us to inscribe two vivid pictures on the surface of this clay vase. The first is of an innkeeper welcoming the young hero to Balbec: "the inn-keeper who would serve me coffee on my arrival" (1: 552; 1, 381). The image, in other words, is that of a man holding a serving vessel,

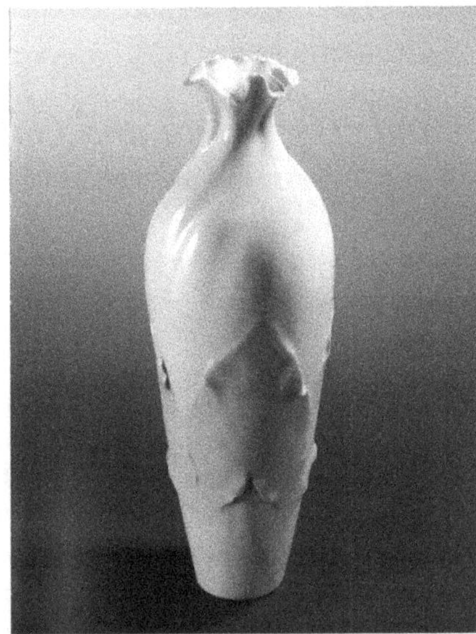

Figure 11.1 Algot Eriksson, *Vase with Arum Leaves*, 1897, porcelain

a piece of pottery, from which he pours coffee. Clay replicates clay on its own surface.

The second picture – let us say the picture we must now inscribe on the other side of the vase – requires us to imagine the innkeeper escorting the hero down "to watch the turbulent sea, unchained, before the church" (1: 552; 1, 381). The welcoming civility of the first picture has been magnified in the upheaval of civilization out of the foundational rock – the eruption of a Norman stone church out of the seabed floor.[4] Once again clay replicates clay, this time not in a local act of civility but in geological events.

The kinship between pottery-making and geological creation was one appreciated by porcelain-makers and scientists alike, as historian Robert Finley makes us aware. The picture in Figure 11.2 is not the bay of Balbec, but the bay of Naples. It is the frontispiece of Charles Lyell's *Principles of Geology*,[5] showing the ruined pillars of a Greco-Egyptian temple that Lyell believed have been lifted up by volcanic action from the seabed floor.[6] The Wedgewood House, to which Darwin belonged and which funded the voyage of the Beagle, believed the interior of the earth acted like "a titanic kiln, a heat-generating engine disgorging molten lava."[7]

Emile Gallé was immersed in geology. His genius as a glassmaker was preceded by fifteen years in which he performed color experiments on the

Figure 11.2 "Temple of Serapis," from Charles Lyell, *Principles of Geology*, 1875

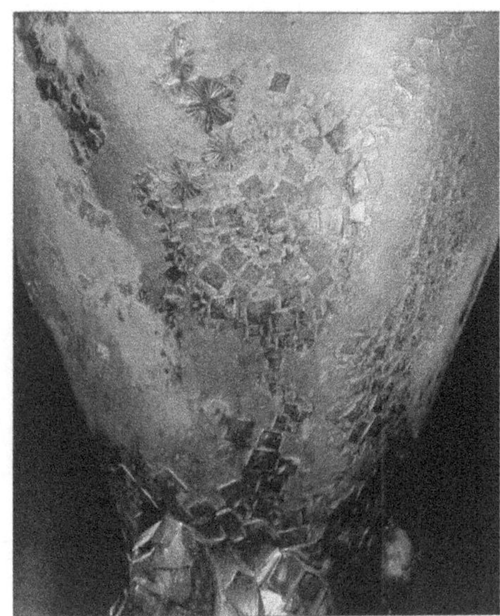

Figure 11.3 Gallé, *Geology*, 1900–1904

local clays around Nancy.[8] One of his masterworks in glass from the year 1900 is entitled *Geology* (Figure 11.3).

It depicts the gradual formation of crystals as one moves down its surface, from the radial and rectangular crystals halfway down, to the three-dimensional jewels at the base. The rayed crystals halfway down are of particular interest because when x-rays were first invented in 1895, clay was a favorite subject of scientific inquiry; soon after, the major porcelain houses in Europe began creating crystalline glazes in which the radial structure of particles under heat emerged into view, as one can see in vases emerging from Sèvres, the leading porcelain house in France, and again from Rörstrand, the leading porcelain house in Sweden.

As important as clay is to Proust in the invention of places, it is more important in the creation of persons, as we can see by turning to the high priestess of porcelain, Aunt Léonie. Bed-ridden, Aunt Léonie takes events occurring outside her bedroom window as narrative prompts for the invention of stories. But she is quite insistent that no distracting event should take place outside her window when she is holding a clay plate in her hands, a clay plate over which a story is hovering.

> These were the only plates which had pictures on them, and my aunt used to amuse herself at every meal by reading the caption [la légende] on whichever

Figure 11.4 Royal Doulton, *The Arrival of the Unknown Princess*

> one had been sent up to her that day. She would put on her spectacles and spell out: "Ali Baba and the Forty Thieves," "Aladdin and his Wonderful Lamp," and smile, and say: "Very good, very good."' (1: 77; 1, 56)

"The Arrival of the Unknown Princess." Very good, very good. Figure 11.4 shows a plate made by Royal Doulton in their 1909 series on the *Arabian Nights*. Like Proust's Balbec vase with its depiction of clay events on its own surface, here we see – on either side of the princess and her escort – huge clay vessels. They announce clay's habit of self-replication. Equally important, they suggest the immense unknown interior of the Unknown Princess, the secret and sovereign interior that we see again depicted on the Royal Doulton pattern for Ali Baba (Figure 11.5): clay replicates clay and conjures up the unknowability of other persons.

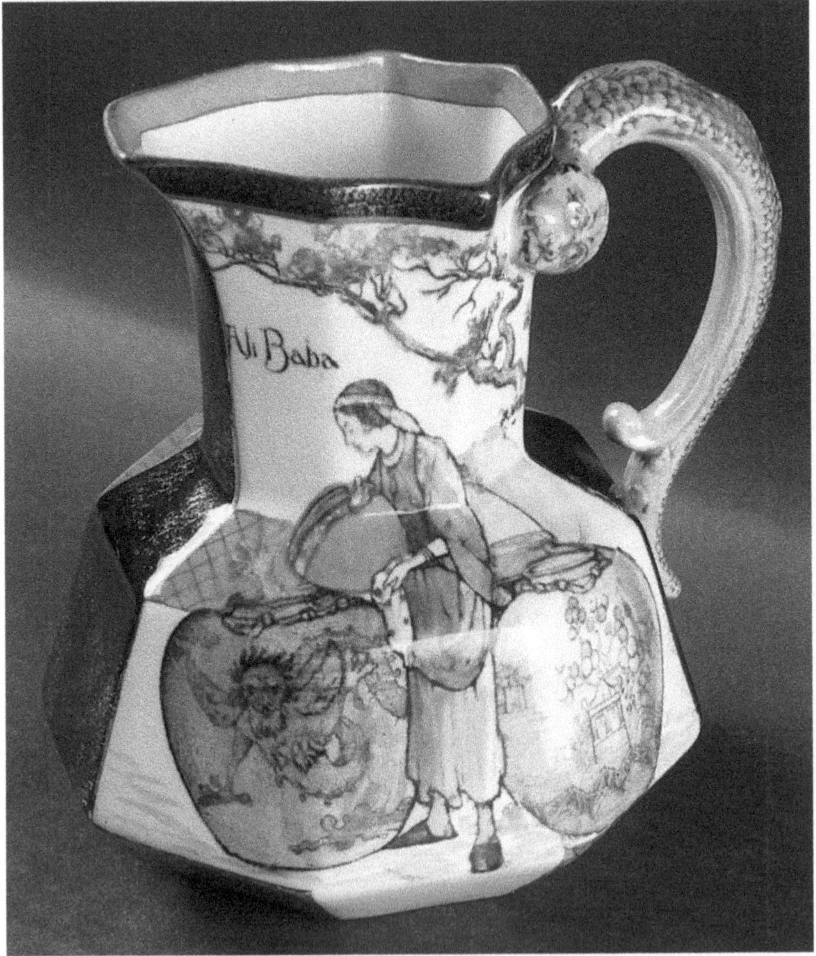

Figure 11.5 Royal Doulton, *Ali Baba*

In fact, the first time we hear about Aunt Léonie's *Arabian Nights* plates is not in the episode just cited, but in the opening section of "Combray," where the narrator first describes the mysterious interior of Swann, his "almost secret existence of a wholly different kind," aspects of his life that no one in the Combray household could ever have inferred. To know about his bohemian-aristocratic life would have been as shocking to them as finding out that after dinner Swann entered the pages of Virgil and "plunge[d] deep into the realms of Thetis." But now the narrator rejects that Virgilian story for one more familiar to Aunt Léonie:

> or – to be content with an image more likely to have occurred to her, for she had seen it painted on the plates we used for biscuits at Combray – as the thought of having had to dinner Ali Baba, who, as soon as he finds himself alone and unobserved, will make his way into the cave, resplendent with its unsuspected treasures. (1: 21–22; 1, 17–18)

But if it is fair to call Aunt Léonie the High Priestess of Porcelain, it is less because of the *Arabian Nights* plates than because of the madeleine passage.

When we think about the biscuit that prompts memories and narratives, we sometimes forget that there is a substrate, a worktable that is prior even to the tea-soaked madeleine, and that is the porcelain teacup.

> And as in the game wherein the Japanese amuse themselves by filling *a porcelain bowl* with water and steeping in it little pieces of paper which until then are without character or form, but, *the moment they become wet, stretch and twist* and take on color and distinctive shape, become flowers or houses or people, solid and recognisable, so in that moment all the flowers in our garden and in M. Swann's park, and the water-lilies on the Vivonne and the good folk of the village and their little dwellings and the parish church and the whole of Combray and its surroundings, *taking shape and solidity, sprang into being, town and gardens alike, from my cup of tea.* (1: 64; 1, 47, my emphasis)

Proust makes certain we do not miss this small porcelain lap of creation by likening the Combray teacup to the Japanese porcelain bowl. Three points deserve our notice. The specific clay mineral used in porcelain is kaolin; and kaolin's major use is the making of paper. Almost every time Proust speaks of porcelain, paper resides nearby. Here what happens to the small bits of paper reenacts the making of the porcelain itself: when wet, the paper morsels swell and bend, just as the moistened clay did in the making of the bowl. Second, the madeleine that has infused into its surface the lime blossoms itself reenacts the Asian clay bowl that traditionally has a blossom inscribed on its surface. The analogy between dough and clay, kneading dough, kneading clay, is universally recognized: clay that has been fired but unglazed is called the "biscuit." Proust was acutely aware of the analogy, as we can appreciate it we lift ourselves out of *Du côté de chez Swann* for a moment and go to *À l'ombre des jeunes filles en fleurs* where the young girls in bloom are described first as dough, then as clay.

> . . . *very young girls*, in whom the *unleavened flesh, like a precious dough, has not yet risen* [*comme une pâte précieuse travaille encore*]. They are malleable, *a*

Figure 11.6 Agathon Léonard, *The Game of the Scarf*, 1905 and 1914 editions

> *soft flow of substance kneaded* [*un flot de matière ductile pétrie*] by every passing impression that possesses them. Each of them looks like *a brief succession of little statuettes*, representing gaiety, childish solemnity, fond coquettishness, amazement, every one of them modeled by an expression that is full and frank, but fleeting. *This plasticity* lends much variety and great charm to a girl . . . (2: 662; II, 259, my emphasis)[9]

Conceivably, Proust could have been influenced here by the twenty-inch high group of biscuit (unglazed porcelain) figures of Agathon Léonard's *The Scarf Dance*, which received the gold medal at the 1900 Universal Exposition (Figure 11.6).[10]

As we learn in *À l'ombre des jeunes filles en fleurs*, Aunt Léonie underwrites the narrator's creations by leaving him her estate: her money, her furniture, her collection of antique Chinese porcelain vases. Proust chooses to focus on the last, describing a moment when the hero decides to sell a large porcelain vase so that he will have the money to give Gilberte endless days of pleasure, endless bouquets of roses and lilacs. How Proust must have longed to say, give her 1,001 days of pleasure. In fact he almost does: the hero surmises that the antique dealer will give him 1,000 francs for the vase; instead he receives 10,000 – enabling one thousand and zero days of pleasure.

We should perhaps not speak about porcelain without invoking that other high priestess of porcelain, Odette, that hallucinogenic, hypnagogic priestess of porcelain whose early relation with Swann revolves around a cup of tea that is to this moment in their love affair what "doing a cattleya" soon will be, and that Proust repeatedly links to the madeleine teacup. Dressed in "pink silk dressing-gown," Odette moves around her apartment kissing each ceramic creature, then pours Swann some tea, then adds some cream which causes her to laugh and exclaim, "A cloud!" (1: 311–313; 1, 217–218). Like the Combray teacup which produces villages, gardens, and rivers, this teacup has just produced a cloud, as clouds, in turn, throughout the novel shape shift into chariots, horses, and gods. Porcelain in Odette's world is phantasmagoric because it is shape-changing. Teacups and bowls become huge Chinese porcelain pots in which palms are planted, or glow from within because they are lanterns, lanterns that – because they are placed on floor, tables, and mantles – keep rising and falling, space-shifting as well as shape-shifting. It is, in fact, a teacup that first leads the narrator to the story of Swann and Odette: what carries us from "Combray" to "Un amour de Swann" is the "perfume – of a cup of tea" that prompts "a story which . . . had been told me of a love affair in which Swann had been involved before I was born" (1: 262; 1, 183–184). And many years later, as the narrator walks in the Bois de Boulogne, his longing for Odette and the world she represents is focused on that same small porcelain terrain:

> I should have liked to be able to pass the rest of the day with one of those women, over a cup of tea, in an apartment with dark-painted walls (as Mme Swann's were still in the year after that in which the first part of this story ends) against which would glow the orange flame, the red combustion, the pink and white flickering of her chrysanthemums in the twilight of a November evening . . . (1: 605; 1, 418)

If we rush too quickly by Odette, it is only because she is central to the account of glass coming in the second half of this chapter.

But we cannot leave clay without attending to the extraordinary moment when Proust – in describing the hero's grandmother – presents her as a clay vessel coming into being on a potter's wheel. The grandmother is walking in rapid circuits around the Combray garden in a storm, her head thrown back like an open vessel to receive the rain. She is coming to life, and reports, "At last one can breathe!" (1: 12; 1, 11). Meanwhile the mud is climbing up her plum-colored skirt, in the same way a vase or pot on a potter's wheel gradually gains altitude. Proust interrupts the description for a page, then resumes her ceaseless circuits, this time out in the fields, her face still thrown back, open to the sky, a drop of moisture on her face; and now it is this upper part of her torso that acquires the purple ("presque mauves") and brown coloration "of tilled fields in autumn." While in the first passage it was only her feet, then her hemline, then the lower half of her skirt that were coated in clay, now her whole figure is from the earth.

And what of the space in between the two passages? It is dedicated to a description of her unknowability, her foreign spirit, that makes the other residents of the Combray household tease her cruelly: "she had brought so different a type of mind into my father's family that everyone made fun of her" (1: 13; 1, 11). Like the Ali Baba plates that convey the profound and unknowable interior of Swann, so clay is here again used to summon a vast and sovereign interior. Because Proust has created here a vase-in-the-making rather than a finished vase, it is hard to locate a material equivalent – but perhaps Gallé's extraordinary "Orpheus and Eurydice" vase (Figure 11.7) provides a kindred thought.

Here Eurydice's face is thrown back to the sky, like the grandmother's, and Gallé has described Eurydice as created out of the materials of the earth: "Eurydice . . . lies faint in a sooty brown crystal."[11] Bathilde, like Eurydice, is beloved of a god, for her last name is Amédée.

The "Orpheus and Eurydice" vase carries us to Proust's reliance on glass for achieving the sovereignty of individual interiors, for sequestering an aura and atmosphere around persons, and for carrying out color experiments. We have just traced an arc *in clay* from Balbec's "old piece of Norman pottery" to the grandmother rising into life on a mystical potter's wheel; we will now see the same arc from places to persons *in glass*.

In "Noms de pays: Le nom," Florence, Venice, and Parma, along with the towns of Brittany, are all designated glass vases. Parma seems to the hero "compact, smooth, violet-tinted and soft"; he then repeats the description, "I was to inhabit a dwelling that was compact, smooth, violet-tinted and soft." Like a Gallé vase with a botanically accurate lily on its surface, Florence is "a town miraculously embalmed [embaumée] and flower-like, since it was called the City of Lilies, and its Cathedral, Our Lady of the Flower." The acute accent on Vitré "barred its ancient glass with wooden lozenges." The rivulets of Quimperlé "thread[ed] their pearls in a grey iridescence like the pattern made, through the cobwebs on a church window, by rays of sunlight changed into blunted points of tarnished silver." Lamballe hovers between glass and kaolin: "gentle Lamballe, whose whiteness ranged from egg-shell yellow to pearl grey" (1: 550–553, trans. mod.; 1, 380–382).

Figure 11.7 Gallé, *Orpheus and Eurydice*, 1888–1889

Each town name in Italy and northern France is not "an inaccessible ideal but . . . a real and enveloping substance into which I was about to plunge," an enclosed package of air. The narrator imagines entering the vase either by shrinking himself into a "minute personage" or – as in the case of azure-emerald-amethyst Venice – by retaining his human size and shouldering his way through the tight aperture, "penetrating indeed between those 'rocks of amethyst' . . . by a supreme muscular effort . . . divesting myself, as of a shell that served no purpose, of the air in my own room . . . I replaced it by an equal quantity of Venetian air, that marine atmosphere" (I: 554, 558–559; I, 383, 386).

When the young hero becomes too sickly to travel, he regards his Parisian home as a prosaic space of loss. But in fact, the retinue of vaselike distant cities will prove to have been just been a rehearsal for Proust's tour de force evocation of Paris. Waiting for Gilberte on the Champs-Elysées, the boy never knows when, or from what direction, she will appear. When she suddenly does materialize, it is always as though she has arrived upon the lustrous surface of a glass vase. At one moment, out of nowhere, the reddish-haired girl turns up against the background of a glistening fountain, as though she were another Eurydice bodied forth on its silver spray (I: 560; I, 387). Another time she slips on a sheet of ice and glides on the silver ground toward him with her arms outstretched:

> Suddenly the sky was rent in two; . . . I had just seen, like a miraculous sign, Mademoiselle's blue feather. And now Gilberte was running at full speed towards me, sparkling and rosy beneath a cap trimmed with fur, animated by the cold, her lateness and her desire for a game; shortly before she reached me, she slid along the ice and . . . it was with outstretched arms that she smilingly advanced, as though to embrace me. "Bravo! Bravo! that's splendid" . . . exclaimed [a nearby] old lady, uttering, on behalf of the voiceless Champs-Élysées, their thanks to Gilberte for having come . . . (I: 566; I, 391)

Paris, like a piece of spun barley-sugar, and like Lamballe, Vitré, Venice, and Parma, has glassy contours, contours magnified by the treasured objects Gilberte bestows on the hero – the agate marble that duplicates the color of her eyes, the frothy package "tied with mauve ribbon and sealed with white wax" that, vaselike, encloses the essay on Racine (I: 572; I, 395).

When historian Albert Sorel reviewed Proust's translations and introductions to Ruskin, he wrote a description of Proust's prose that moved Proust to write a letter expressing elation and thanks (*Corr* IV, 176–178): Proust, Sorel said, "writes a flexible French, free in movement and all-enveloping, with countless bursts of hues and colors, yet it remains translucent and, at times, puts you in mind of the glass work in which Gallé encloses his leafy traceries."[12] As Gilberte on the Champs-Élysées makes clear, by the time of *Du côté de chez Swann*, it is not just Proust's sentence style but his conception of persons and places that are vaselike.

From the first section of "Combray" forward, Swann is pictured as a glass vessel, "a transparent envelope":

> We pack *the physical outline of the person* we see with all the notions we have already formed about him . . . In the end they come to fill out so completely *the curve of his cheeks*, to follow so exactly *the line of his nose*, they blend so harmoniously in the sound of his voice *as if it were no more than a transparent envelope*, that each time we see the face or hear the voice it is these notions which we recognize and to which we listen. (1: 23–24; 1, 19, my emphasis)

Into this transparent envelope (as though Swann were a vase waiting to be filled), Proust immediately positions a bouquet of herbs and leaves and berries, for the sentence after next ends: "this early Swann abounding in leisure, fragrant with the scent of the great chestnut-tree, of baskets of raspberries and of a sprig of tarragon."

Though Proust's reliance on Gallé is vast, spirited, and loving, it can be briefly sampled here by a single place, the aquatic gardens of the Vivonne, and then a single person, Odette. Proust describes the pleasure the hero takes watching a glass jar suspended in the stream. The jar looks like solidified water; conversely the water (both within the jar and without) looks like flowing crystal:

> *I enjoyed watching the glass jars* which the village boys used to lower into the Vivonne to catch minnows, and which, *filled by the stream, in which they in their turn were enclosed, at once "containers" whose transparent sides were like solidified water and "contents" plunged into a still larger container of liquid, flowing crystal*, conjured up an image of coolness more delicious and more provoking than they would have done standing upon a table . . . showing it as perpetually in flight between the impalpable water . . . and the insoluble glass . . . (1: 237; 1, 166, my emphasis)

– a passage that at once summons Gallé's underwater vases like this early example from 1876 where it is not clear whether the vase is in the water or the water in the vase (Figure 11.8).

The lithe body of the self-delighting carp makes three turns to accommodate the upward swirl of the water, a unitary silver rotation of liquid that seems to make the vase – along with its gossamer fins and aquatic grasses – spin before our eyes (while the fish itself, like a kestrel hovering in the wind, holds steady). Chaste arrays of blacks, grays, and bronzes only

Figure 11.8 Gallé, *Carp Vase*, 1876

very rarely give way to peach (the center of the carp's eye), to violet-blue (an occasional bubble or petal), and to aqua (the bottom-most plane of glass).

A puzzling feature of the aquatic garden is Proust's account of the solitary water lily that the current never allows to rest:

Figure 11.9 Gallé, *White Water Lily against Sky-blue Glass*

> *it would drift over to one bank only to return to the other, eternally repeating its double journey.* Thrust towards the bank, its stalk would uncoil, lengthen, reach out, strain almost to breaking-point until the current again caught it, its green moorings swung back over their anchorage and brought the unhappy plant to what might fitly be called its starting-point, since it was fated not to rest there a moment before moving off once again. (1: 238; 1, 166–167, my emphasis)

I have not, nor has anyone I know, ever seen a water lily caught in a current, dragged back and forth between two banks, "eternally repeating its double journey." But its strange fatality becomes immediately comprehensible if one looks to Gallé (Figure 11.9), for indeed the gorgeous white water lily pressing up against one bank, will when the vase is rotated 180 degrees, drift to the other side of the vase, where Gallé will inevitably have placed an identical blossom, only altering slightly its posture or perspective. And when one continues to rotate the vase another 180 degrees, back to the original bank comes the water lily. The flower appears to be relentlessly ferried back and forth from one side to the other.

The exquisite botanical precision of Gallé's meadow flowers, garden flowers, and hothouse flowers is *not* what he writes about in his submission notes to the exhibition jurors. What he instead documents are his astonishing achievements in sequestering color, and Proust reenacts Gallé's techniques in his own acts of sequestering color. The passage above continues with an array of water lilies that have precise equivalents in Gallé's many water lily vases:

> I have seen in its depths a clear, crude blue verging on violet, suggesting a floor of Japanese cloisonné. Here and there on the surface, blushing like a strawberry, floated a water-lily flower with a scarlet centre and white edges . . . Elsewhere a corner seemed to be reserved for the commoner kinds of lily, of a neat pink or white like rocket-flowers, washed clean like porcelain with housewifely care . . . (1: 239; 1, 167)

From places-as-vases, we now turn to a solitary instance of a person-as-vase. We last saw Odette moving amidst her porcelain teacups, giant palm pots, glowing porcelain lanterns. Swann repeatedly watches Odette through glass, both at the Verdurin's and at her own apartment, as though she were in a vase. Proust's full reliance on Gallé becomes most clear when Odette enters the contracted envelope of air provided by the carriage.

Gallé by his own account spent more than thirty-five years studying orchids, even writing a scholarly article on the orchids specific to the Lorraine region of France. This particular one – regarded by museum curators as one of his great masterpieces – is a specific kind of orchid whose name is known to all readers of Proust: it is a cattleya (Figure 11.10). As William Warmus observes, the vase is comprised of multiple acts of glassmaking: the vase is "blown, overlaid, cut, engraved" – in order to create a sense of "deep space" with some flowers reaching out and others "falling back" into the depths beyond our reach,[13] depths we encounter again on the other side.

In the cattleya passage, Swann and Odette together inhabit the enclosed space of a carriage. The aura of cattleyas envelopes Odette, who is dressed in black velvet with inserts of white silk, swan feathers, and lace. The aura is achieved by placing the cattleyas at *three exactly-registered distances* from her body, the first a cluster held in her hand that reaches out to us and to Swann; a second resides beneath her veil but is raised three inches from her body, for the blossoms are poised on the tips of swan feathers; the third, falls back in "deep space," for it resides next to her skin.

> He climbed after her into the carriage . . . *She was holding in her hand a bunch of cattleyas, and Swann could see, beneath the film of lace* that covered her head, *more of the same flowers fastened to a swansdown plume.* She was dressed, beneath her cloak, in a flowing gown of black velvet, caught up on one side to reveal a large triangle of white silk skirt, and with a yoke, also of white silk, *in the cleft of her low-necked bodice, in which were fastened a few more cattleyas.* (1: 328–329; 1, 228, my emphasis)

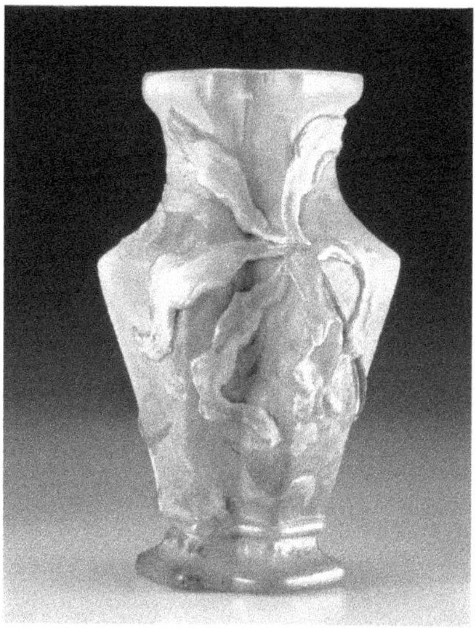

Figure 11.10 Gallé, *Cattleya Vase*, 1900

Gallé in a speech to the Stanislas Academy gave a description of orchids that may be not only the single best description that has ever been given of an orchid, but perhaps the single best description that has ever been given of Odette:

> We avow preferences for good old plants, the kinds beloved by our grandmothers. Yet the rapid modern current is deeper and more powerful than the quiet brook of our predilections. It washes everything away. *It tosses us – as Ophelia's last bouquet* – the orchid, with its richness, its inconceivable strangeness of forms, of species, of scents, of colors, of caprices, of pleasures and of troubling mysteries.[14]

Odette and the cattleya are each like the last bouquet of Ophelia. The color of orchids and violets cling to her, envase and envelop her. Even when there is no glass, no lace veil, no lavender parasol. Even when she walks in the open air of the Bois . . .

> I met Mme Swann on foot . . . *enveloped also in the artificial warmth of her own house, which was suggested by nothing more than the bunch of violets crushed into her bosom, whose flowering, vivid and blue against the grey sky, the freezing air, the naked boughs, had the same charming effect of . . . living actually in a human atmosphere, in the atmosphere of this woman, as had, in the vases* and jardinières of her drawing-room, beside the blazing fire, in front of the silk-covered settee, *the flowers that looked out through closed windows at the falling snow* . . . (1: 604; 1, 418, my emphasis)

Figure 11.11 Auguste and Antonin Daum, *Blackbirds in Snow*

a passage that then carries us to Odette's porcelain teacup, the orange-red-pink shooting star of chrysanthemums at twilight, and the narrator's longing for the pleasure of her presence.

When Proust, who repeatedly commissioned vases from Gallé as presents for friends,[15] at last names him in his pages – as he does late in *À l'ombre des jeunes filles en fleurs* (2: 522; II, 160), and again in *Le Côté de Guermantes* – it is in each instance a moment of fallen snow, passages that summon the work of Auguste and Antonin Daum, who, after Gallé died, continued his virtuosity in glass, sometimes, as here, eliminating all color, relying solely on black and white (Figure 11.11).

In no time, winter; at the corner of a window, as in a Gallé glass, a vein of crusted snow; and even in the Champs-Élysées, instead of the girls one waits to see, nothing but solitary sparrows. (3: 538; II, 687)

NOTES

1 Leila Coyne, quoted in and summarized by James Gleick, "Quiet Clay Revealed as Vibrant and Primal," *New York Times*, May 5, 1987. Gleick describes the work of the University of Glasgow's Graham Cairns-Smith, a leading scientist investigating the link between clay and the origin of life.

2 Daniel Rhodes and Robin Hopper, *Clay and Glazes for the Potter* (Iola, WI: Krause Publications, 2000), 76.

3 Andrew Roddick and Elizabeth Klarich, "Arcillas and Alfareros: Clay and Temper Mining Practices in the Lake Titicaca Basin," in *Mining and Quarrying in the Ancient Andes: Sociopolitical, Economic, and Symbolic Dimensions*, ed. Nicholas Tripcevich and Kevin J. Vaughn (New York: Springer Verlag, 2012), 116.

4 Proust repeatedly stresses Balbec's continuity with the geology beneath it. Legrandin twice speaks of "Balbec! the most ancient bone in the geological skeleton that underlies our soil," "that oldest ossature of the earth" (1: 183, 547; I, 129, 377). Norman Gothic architecture, the narrator realizes, expresses the moment when "the great phenomena of geology" suddenly blossom into a plant – suddenly making the transition to aliveness: "and gothic art seemed to me a more living thing now that . . . upon a reef of savage rocks, it had taken root and grown until it flowered in a tapering spire" (1: 548; I, 378). Clay once more acts as the worktable upon which life learns to live.

The sense of life emerging out of clay is visible in Gallé's jardinière of 1880 in which the faint green surface of the clay vase is covered with fern shaped stem-and-leaf ridges on top of which are painted thistles in green, ash blue grey, and burnt sienna. Life emerging out of clay is dramatically visible in the work of Bernard Palissy, a sixteenth-century Huguenot potter who deeply influenced Gallé: out of the surface of a large ochre basin, for example, emerge what momentarily seem all the early creatures of the earth – lizards, frogs, ferns, worms, crayfish, lobsters, and fish. For an image of this basin, see Howard Coutts, *The Art of Ceramics: European Ceramic Design 1500–1830* (New Haven, CT: Yale University Press, 2001), 43. Gallé expresses his admiration for Palissy in "Le Décor Symbolique," his address to the Stanislas Academy, reprinted in Philippe Garner, *Émile Gallé* (London: Academy Editions, 1976), 160–161. Tim Newark describes Palissy's influence on Gallé in *Émile Gallé* (Secaucus, New Jersey: Chartwell, 1989), 109.

5 Lyell's book was first published in 1830; many reprintings and editions followed throughout the nineteenth century.

6 Robert Finlay, *The Pilgrim Art: Cultures of Porcelain in World History* (Berkeley: University of California Press, 2010), 77. Finley writes, "Lyell's examination of black discoloration on the columns of the temple [of Serapis] had persuaded

him that they had been underwater for centuries and that eruption by Vesuvius, followed by earthquake, had raised them to the surface once again" (77).

7 *Ibid.*, 78–79.

8 Gallé's work with clay is richly described by Philippe Garner (*Émile Gallé*, 64–76).

9 The transition from dough to clay in this passage, though audible in all translations, is most emphatic in James Grieve's *In the Shadow of Young Girls in Flower* (Harmondsworth: Penguin, 2002), 482, cited here.

10 Liana Paredes observes that, like many other artists in Paris that year, Léonard was inspired by the American dancer Loïe Fuller (*Sèvres Then and Now: Tradition and Innovation in Porcelain, 1750–2000* [London: Hillwood Museum, 2009], 106).

11 Gallé writes of the vase in *Écrits* (his notes submitted to the Jury of the 1889 Universal Exposition), "It has caught my fancy to work with awesome onyxes and to wrap a vase in streams of lava and pitch . . . to use a flaming meteor and the gases of hell to separate Orpheus from Eurydice who lies faint in a sooty brown crystal" (cited by William Warmus in *Émile Gallé: Dreams into Glass* [Corning, NY: Corning Museum of Glass, 1984], 31).

12 Cited in "Introduction," *Marcel Proust: the Critical Heritage*, ed. Leighton Hodson (London: Routledge, 1989, 1997), 7.

13 William Warmus, *Émile Gallé: Dreams into Glass* (Corning, NY: Corning Museum of Glass, 1984), 100.

14 Émile Gallé, "Discours de Réception," L'Académie de Stanislas, May 17, 1900, reprinted in Garner, *Émile Gallé*, 161. My emphasis.

15 Garner, *Émile Gallé*, 128. Robert de Montesquiou's 1897 essay "Orfèvre et Verrier: Gallé et Lalique" invokes Florence and Venice, chrysanthemums and *A Thousand and One Nights*, and conveys his sense of how one should regard "the gift" of a Gallé vase: "Such Gallés are the only gifts we still deign offer to kings, who are proud and pleased to receive them, and whisk them away jealously for the immortal honor of their museums. Indeed – this is worth mentioning in passing, since the noble modesty of their creator is content to leave the fact more or less ignored – it was two vases by Gallé that France offered to the tzar, in order to abolish painful memories, like two priceless lachrymatories, where tears could at last flow" ("Orfèvre et Verrier: Gallé et Lalique," in *Roseaux pensants* [Paris: Bibliothèque-Charpentier, 1897], 176).

PART IV

Perceiving and transforming

CHAPTER 12

Proust's eye

Françoise Leriche

The question of Proust's relationship to the visual arts is usually posed through discussions of the role of painting, or sometimes architecture, in *À la recherche du temps perdu*, examined from two perspectives that occasionally meet. The first approach, one of erudition and the most practiced in Proustian exegesis, consists in rediscovering the actual works Proust mentions or to which he alludes in the novel, researching the *sources* of this aesthetic knowledge before examining and interpreting the (poetic or symbolic) *use* that the author makes of them.[1] The other, a hermeneutic and structural approach, concerns literary *discourse* on painting or architecture in its *auto-reflexive* dimension: the art of Giotto or Elstir, the gothic cathedral offer the protagonist an initiation, providing aesthetic models that the novel puts into practice, creating an effect of specular circularity.[2]

But *how* did Proust look at works of art? What did he see (or not see), feel (or not feel) as he beheld a given painting, fresco, or stained-glass window? It seems this question of the *eye* of the beholder has rarely been posed until now in an explicit fashion[3] – although the ways the novelist used works of art can implicitly tell us something about how the biographical man, Marcel Proust, looked at a work of art (that is, when he did not substitute his own personal impressions with an iconographic knowledge acquired after the fact in art books . . .). It is this question of the gaze I will investigate here, the question of Proust's specifically visual relationship to the plastic arts, *prior to*, in a way, the symbolic or metaphoric roles he would later have these arts play in his literary work.

How can we get to the source of that which struck his eye, stirred his emotion or sparked his critical mind? How do we know which elements, which details captured his attention? In this regard, his drawings offer a crucial object of reflection.

Unevenly studied drawings

The corpus of Proust's "drawings" is a heterogeneous ensemble. By examining their medium and function, we can distinguish within them two principal categories. One the one hand, there are the drawings that "unfold like a dream"[4] in Proust's manuscript *cahiers* and notebooks, where these cursory and more or less identifiable figures, when they are not markers of reference or location, appear to be the traces of the writer's mechanical, *unintentional* scribbling; on the other, there are the structured, captioned drawings, addressed by Proust to a specific recipient, his friend Reynaldo Hahn,[5] drawings that attest to a deliberate graphic endeavor with a particular intention. I will select my examples from this second group. These drawings are sometimes grouped as a genre under Proust's portmanteau term *dessindicace* ["dedicadrawing"], but it is preferable to reserve this notion of "dedicated drawings" for those where the initials "RH" appear, or those which are explicitly glossed as being a *casdeau* ["psresent," in the whimsically modified spelling of Proust's letters to Hahn] or a *don* ["gift"].

Proust's drawings remain little studied, and it seems significant that many pioneering studies have come from America[6] – as if, in France and Europe, strongly held aesthetic prejudices have robbed scholars of the freedom of thought necessary to see these drawings as something more than anecdotal sketches or scribbles devoid of intellectual or artistic interest.[7] Indeed, if we compare his drawings to those of other writers, Proust's seem clumsy, purely playful, without aesthetic effort. At the auction of Pierre and Franca Belfond's collection in February 2012, it was possible to compare his drawings to those of Lamartine, Sand, Hugo, Mérimée, Cocteau, and Max Jacob.[8] The encounter brought to light a striking difference: the plastic works of writers like George Sand, Max Jacob, or Jean Cocteau express personal visions or represent landscapes or social scenes (even in comic or caricatural form) endowed with intrinsic meaning, whereas those of Proust are not graphic representations intelligible in and of themselves. Accompanied by captions and comments that are necessary to explain their intent, they are produced not only as caricatures but also as images in the second degree: their interest resides precisely in the *eye* through which Proust beholds the works he ridicules. His drawings are *images of images*.

Virginie Greene and Caroline Szylowicz's excellent study conclusively showed – verifying a hypothesis put forth by J. Theodore Johnson[9] – that the medieval drawings sent to Reynaldo Hahn were literally *traced* from illustrations in the historian Émile Mâle's *L'Art religieux du XIIIe siècle en France*,[10] which testifies to their status as "secondary" images.[11] (See

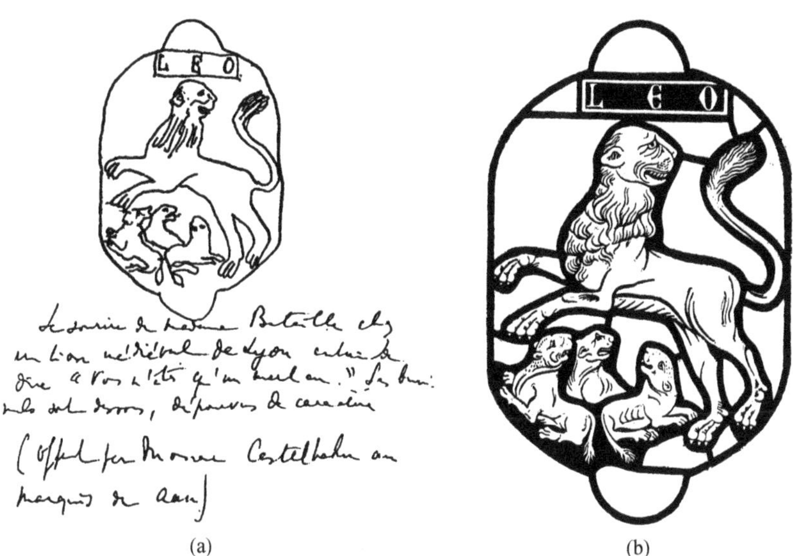

(a) (b)

Figure 12.1 (a) Proust, "Madame Bataille's smile on a medieval lion from Lyons . . . " (b) "Lion and its Cubs," from Émile Mâle, *L'Art religieux du XIIIe siècle en France*

Figure 12.1a, Proust's drawing[12] and the image it reproduces.)[13] But why does Proust entertain himself by tracing reproductions of works of art and providing them with burlesque commentary, as in his drawing of a stained-glass window from Lyons (Figure 12.1b)? Under the drawing is a strange caption, well analyzed by Greene and Szylowicz for its parodic nature:[14]

> Le sourire de madame Bataille chez un lion médiéval de Lyon entrain [*sic*] de dire "vous n'êtes qu'un merlan." Ses buninuls sont dessous, dépourvus de caractère (offert par Monsieur Castelhahn au marquis de Aan)
>
> Madame Bataille's smile on a medieval lion in Lyons saying, "you're just a whiting." Its buninuls are below, devoid of character (offered by Monsieur Castelhahn to the Marquis de Aan)

Above the drawing, Proust adds a comment, placed between quotation marks as if it were Reynaldo Hahn's response: "Et Madame de St Paul faisant la bouche de Me de Guerne dit: 'il m'a fait comme ça avec sa queue.'" ["And Madame de St. Paul imitating Madame de Guerne's mouth says: 'he did it to me like that with his tail.'"][15]

The studies devoted to these drawings consider them to be caricatures, a sort of "pastiche" of the captions typically found in art books, or else parodies of high society that mix multiple discursive forms,[16] and in either case, as a recreational activity that Proust allowed himself during his serious readings of art books. Could not the Proust of these drawings be, like Brichot, a scholar who uses his erudition to make farcical jokes in social conversation? Might he not also resemble Swann, who, perverted by "the prevailing frivolity of the world of fashion," loves "tracing in the paintings of the old masters . . . the individual features of men and women whom he knew" (1: 315; I, 219–220)?

Without denying that one can find in Proust's drawings the same foibles he would later denounce in the characters of Brichot and Swann, what emerges most strikingly from these drawings is a critical eye. Proust's magnification of *certain* details in his caricatures (see also Figure 12.2a: Carlyle, by Whistler)[17] clearly questions what we "see" in works of art. In other words, considering their humor as a form of critical distance, I propose to analyze the *metacritical* dimension of his drawings.

Images of images: a mediological reflection on the visual arts and their spectator

In modern aesthetics, as Marcel Duchamp has taught us, the artist is not (or is no longer) defined by the mastery of an artisanal know-how, but primarily by a certain propensity for looking, for exercising a critical eye on the cultural conventions and aesthetic discourses of the time. By situating my remarks within the perspective of a *cultural history of the gaze* – as it has been practiced for the past twenty or thirty years by art historians such as Georges Didi-Huberman or Hans Belting – I aim to show how Proust's irreverent drawings interrogate the legibility of works of art, by staging his own experience of beholding.

Hans Belting's *Anthropology of Images* offers a valuable theoretical framework (in German, *Bildwissenschaft*, the science of images) for my reflections on Proust's drawings. In his foreword, Belting notes that

> in our Western culture, the most frequently used and most significant paradigm of the image remains that of the painting hung on a wall, an image devoid of corporeality or movement, which we go see in museums[18]

and he argues that this recent development in human history should be contextualized in a general anthropology of the image:

> What is an image? Philosophers have approached the image as a concept in itself that is universal, without taking in consideration the various historical and medial conditions of its appearance. Conversely, mediologists and structuralists have considered these circumstances exclusively, and as a

> result they have underestimated the difference between these conditions of possibility of the image and *its specific aim*.[19]

Belting proposes a "different path":

> analyzing the image in a triangular configuration . . . *image – medium – gaze*, or *image – visual device – living body*, insofar as an image cannot be envisioned without placing it in close relation with a body looking and a medium looked upon.[20]
>
> For images to function, their production depends on two conditions . . . *our capacity to animate images that are inanimate*, as if they were . . . able to partake in a dialogue; and . . . the transformation of medium into image.[21]

These terms, "*aim*" (of the image) and "*dialogue*," or elsewhere "*interaction*," are particularly interesting: they clearly denote that Belting's "anthropology of images" in fact rests on a *pragmatics* of looking – or a pragmatics of the production and reception of visual works.

Belting thus insists on the fact that "the image exists through a double history, of its material production and its mental production," and he underscores the idea that "the image – body – medium triangle is almost always imbalanced" in various disciplinary discourses, since, according to the whims of trends or ideologies, one of these terms is usually favored to the detriment of the others.[22]

By examining the manner in which Proust envisions works of art, we can observe that while he recognizes the essential role of the body and the gaze as the "locus of images," in Belting's formulation[23] (both for the reception and the production of images), he rarely takes into account the medium (the visual device), often reducing it to a strange transparency. In the gallery of the Guermantes, Elstir's paintings appear to the protagonist as "fragments of that world of new and strange colors which was *no more than the projection* of that great painter's peculiar vision . . . The parts of the walls that were covered by paintings of his . . . were like the *luminous images of a magic lantern which* in this instance *was the brain of the artist*" (3: 574; II, 712, my emphasis). Within Belting's triangle, Proust thus emphasizes the role of the living body (the artist's head) as the site of the mental image that the painting brings into existence, but he seems to forget the *medium*: the artist's manipulation of the paint, the layering of brushstrokes, the nuances of the color palette, the material support, the dimension of the canvas and whether it be small or large. The painting, exclusively seen as a representation, is analyzed like the *projection of a mental image*, readymade in the painter's mind and simply transposed as is onto the canvas, as if a visual work were not also in part the result of the artist's gestural work in a struggle with his materials.

As Kazuyoshi Yoshikawa handily demonstrates in *Proust et l'art pictural*, Proust visited a number of museums, important exhibitions, and private collections during his youth; in spite of this, it later seems as if Proust barely made a distinction, when he was writing his novel, between the contemplation of actual works of art seen in the uniqueness of their own particular aura, and reproductions of these works in art books. It appears that these reproductions provided him with significant pleasure and sensory experiences that were just as physical as a direct encounter with the work of art itself. Indeed, in an unpublished *cahier* of drafts dating to 1910–1911, Proust delivers a surprising encomium of the identical benefits produced by illustrated art history books and . . . brothels:

> les maquerelles nous permettent de ~~mettre~~ remplacer par ~~une notion individuelle~~ un visage individuel [un] type abstrait. ~~Par là leur~~ *Elles nous rendent le même service que . . . ces autres bienfaiteurs qui leur sont analogues* et qui sont d'origine plus récente, *les auteurs d'histoire de l'art illustré, les organisateurs d'auditions <et> de représentations de chefs d'œuvres de la musique, ou de voyages aux ~~pays~~ cités fameuses*, tous ceux qui ~~à l'idée vague~~ ajoutent à notre esprit qui admirait froidement en l'imaginant avec ce qu'il connaissait déjà l'art de Wagner, ou de Mantegna, le charme individuel de ces œuvres. Comme eux elles nous alimentent, nous fournissent de ce genre de plaisir particulier qu'est la connaissance d'une œuvre . . . individuelle que nous ne connaissions pas . . . on a beau nous dire: « Elle a une chair blonde, des cheveux roux, . . . » c'est avec les femmes que nous connaissons déjà que nous imaginons celle dont on nous parle comme quand on nous parle d'un tableau ou d'une musique nouvelle c'est d'après les anciens que nous les imaginons. Il ne leur manque à l'une comme aux autres, que cette chose que nous [ne] pouvons inventer, que nous sommes obligés de demander à la réalité et dans laquelle seule nous pourrons jouir, de la chair, et des yeux, et *des harmonies de sons et de couleurs, un individu.*[24]
>
> madams allow us to ~~put~~ replace [an] abstract type with ~~an individual notion~~ an individual face. ~~Therefore their~~ *They render us the same service as . . . those other benefactors who are their analogues* of a more recent vintage: *authors of illustrated histories of art, organizers of auditions <and> of performances of musical masterpieces, or of excursions to ~~countries~~ famous cities*, all those who ~~to a vague idea~~ add to our mind, which before coldly admired, while imagining it through what it already knew, the art of Wagner, or of Mantegna, the individual charm of these works. Like them, madams nourish us, provide us with the particular type of pleasure that consists in encountering an individual work . . . with which we were not previously acquainted . . . While we can be told: "She has fair skin, red hair, . . . " it is through women we

> already know that we try to imagine the person someone is describing, just as when we are told about a new painting or piece of music, we imagine them through older ones. The only thing missing from the one as from the others, is that thing we can[not] invent, which we must demand from reality, and in which alone we can take pleasure: flesh, eyes, *harmonies of sounds and colors: an individual.*

In this passage, Proust seems to recognize the importance of the *medium* (the color, the play of light we appreciate in a painting), but it is nevertheless astonishing that he credits art history books for producing aesthetic pleasure, in the same way he praises the organizers of concerts for the music! For the art books Proust consumed with such appetite (as Yoshikawa has shown), and among which I have consulted several, *only contain black and white photographs* – that is to say, a jumble of gray nuances in which nothing can be seen – even if certain works include one or two color plates. In order to produce an effective comparison with madams (who select and assemble readily consumable young beauties in their establishments), Proust could have instead mentioned museums and collectors (who gather together works in order that they be experienced in their materiality).

To twenty-first-century consumers of images accustomed to high-quality color photographs and film, who experience black and white illustrations as a frustration, Proust's praise of mass-produced books in black and white suggests a rather limited interest in the *medium* and the particular aesthetic emotion it produces. Can we possibly imagine an art lover who could be satisfied with black and white reproductions of paintings by Mondrian, Klee, or Kandinsky? Marshall McLuhan's famous dictum, "the medium is the message," nicely sums up the credo of artistic modernity and its innovations in formal and material experimentation. But for Proust, who did not venture outside the bounds of figurative art, the *transmediation* of a painting into a black and white image (whether a photograph or an engraving) seems to procure sufficient knowledge of the work as long as it adequately shows the *scenic treatment* of a theme and its *graphic style*. The recourse to illustrated art books did not simply aid his remembrance of paintings or monuments he had already seen, as one might think; rather, as the passage from *Cahier* 64 explicitly indicates, art books helped him experience works *he did not know*. Generally speaking, it appears it was through the *mediation* of didactic books that Proust beheld most works of art, before he went to see some of them in person. In fact, it was only *after* having read Ruskin's works (and beheld their illustrations) that he visited Amiens, Venice, and Padua. In the novel, when the protagonist travels to Padua, it is "in order *to see again* [*revoir*] the 'Virtues' and 'Vices' of which M. Swann had given me reproductions" (5: 878, trans. mod.; IV, 226, my emphasis) whereas, since this will be his first (and only) voyage to Italy, one would expect the phrase "in order to see [*voir*] . . . " Put differently, it is through the mediation of *images* (whether *captioned* and/or *annotated*) that the hero, like Proust, first encounters works of visual art.

Un/intelligible works requiring cultural mediation

A scholarly art book allows one to see, and thus appreciate and understand, that which risks escaping a purely "aesthetic" contemplation. While an art book is incapable of fully representing the thickness and texture of the paint on a canvas, or the colors of a fresco or stained-glass window (and even less capable of reproducing the experience of the depth and atmosphere of the buildings that house such works), it compensates for these shortcomings by offering a multitude of close-ups of certain details of the painting, fresco, or window. Proust's constant recourse to the mediation of scholarly works shows that he is aware of the limited validity of a direct, personal, purely sensory experience of works of art, especially when dealing with works from older eras.

Hence the importance of Émile Mâle for learning to "read" medieval sculpture and stained glass. As Mâle explains, medieval religious art does not represent the sensory world (what we call "reality") in order to produce a realist illusion, as the visual arts from the Renaissance to the end of the nineteenth century have accustomed us to see. In the Middle Ages the world is defined as "a thought of God realized through the Word":

> in each being is hidden a divine thought; the world is a book written by the hand of God in which every creature is a word charged with meaning. *The ignorant see the forms – the mysterious letters – understanding nothing of their meaning*, but the wise pass from the visible to the invisible, and in reading nature read the thoughts of God. True knowledge, then, consists not in the study of things in themselves – the outward forms – but in penetrating to the inner meaning intended by God for our instruction . . . All being holds in its depths the reflection of the sacrifice of Christ, the image of the Church and of the virtues and vices. The material and the spiritual worlds are one.[25]

Since "the whole world is a symbol,"[26] theologians consider bestiary fables to be scientific truths in the same way as scriptural teachings. As such, the faithful are invited to "see" in each element of nature or history represented in the stained glass, statuary, and frescoes of medieval churches, a sign of the Creation, Fall, and Redemption. Derived from bestiaries, the lion and its cubs traced by Proust (Figure 12.1) symbolize the resurrection of Christ:

"It is said . . . that the lioness gives birth to lifeless cubs, but that after three days the roaring of the lion brings them to life. Even so the Savior lay in the tomb as dead but on the third day He rose awakened by the voice of His Father."[27]

When he saw this image in the book, Proust was able to understand its symbolic meaning *through the explanations of the historian*. But his caption on the traced drawing to Reynaldo makes clear that, without the aid of this expert interpretation, he is like the "ignorant," whose immediate reaction is to merely see a lion (or is it a lioness?) with a strange smile. As Proust comically demonstrates, a typical nineteenth-century man would ask the question, what can this smile mean?, and scrutinize the details of the image from a psychological perspective, applying anachronistic codes of interpretation because he is too far removed from medieval art to understand it.

This "smile," moreover, was barely visible to the medieval public, since the medallion, of modest size, flanks the primary panels of a stained-glass window situated a dozen meters above the ground.[28] Even if Proust had visited Lyons cathedral and seen this window, it would have been impossible for him to notice the expression on the lion's mouth. The assiduous reading of Mâle's scholarly book therefore cannot be a self-preparation prior to visiting the cathedral, to better appreciate the works of medieval art housed there, nor a memory aid used after such a visit: instead, it substitutes an interposed knowledge to the personal experience of a visit or its remembrance. The zoom effect that blows up minuscule graphic details leads the modern reader to focus on features not meant to be seen or questioned.

When looking upon the representation of a face, the nineteenth-century spectator, whose gaze is trained in the humanistic tradition of the portrait, seeks to uncover the character and moral particularities of the person depicted. Whether a contemporary or an inheritor of the aesthetic philosophy of Schelling and Ravaisson, of idealism, or of theories of physiognomy, this spectator believes – like Swann with Zipporah – that a portrait captures the "clearly intelligible type" of its model (1: 316, trans. mod.; I, 220). Art seems to offer ways of reading fugitive reality, to better seize it.[29] One might think that when Proust glimpses Madame Bataille's smile on the medieval lion, he is acting like Swann, who finds in Zipporah's portrait the "intelligible type" of an unreadable Odette, erring on the side of idealism through a belief in an ontology of physiognomies. On the contrary! Whereas Swann wants to use art in order to grasp the real, Proust does the reverse: he whimsically proposes that it is the fleeting smile (or rictus?) of Madame Bataille (the reality he knows) that allows him to interpret the strange expression of the stained-glass lion (the work of art).

The lion, roaring to bring his cubs to life, would need a wide-open maw. But the art of the Middle Ages is not a realist art; iconographic conventions dictate the representation of the main symbols, while minute details, devoid of religious meaning, are left to the artisan's fantasy. Did the medieval glassworker, by lining up a row of large teeth, try to evoke the ferocity of this exotic animal? By interpreting the lion's expression as a smile, Proust enacts a deliberately anachronistic psychological analysis that separates the image from its allegorical context: in the lion's smile, he does not see a stable clue to an *immediately intelligible* type, but rather an expression *that gains meaning only in a specific situation* (Madame Bataille's particular smile *when she says*, "you're just a whiting"). Indeed, it is because Reynaldo shares with Proust a certain set of memories of *specific* scenes (Belting would say: a common "iconic reserve")[30] that he is able to understand the moral nuance that Proust *lends* to this "smile." That nuance completely escapes us, since we are not familiar with Madame Bataille or the situation to which Proust refers (is it the rage of a furious woman, forced to smile because of social niceties? a sneer addressed to an uncouth gentleman? the look of a woman at her wits' end?). The second caption, Madame de Saint-Paul spouting an "involuntarily obscene" remark,[31] offers another interpretative model that suggests an offended smile – or perhaps a titillated one. In any case, nothing in this drawing is universally intelligible, which is what – according to idealist theories – art is supposed to be.

The parodic captions of this drawing reveal that Proust is perfectly aware that

1. there is a cultural history of art and *of the gaze*, that renders illegible to him most works from past eras, unless he approaches them with the aid of works of erudition;
2. these works are thus neither universal nor intelligible *a priori*, on first viewing;
3. it is not the work of visual art that allows us to see the world; rather, on the contrary, lived and sensory experiences make us attentive to a work's most minute details, even non-symbolic ones. The work of art therefore functions as a mirror onto which the viewer's gaze is projected. According to the Proustian theory of reading, are we not always our own reader? (6: 508; IV, 610)

The graphic projection of a sensory experience

In his drawings addressed to Reynaldo Hahn, Proust shows himself to be well aware of his personal bias by shamelessly staging the mechanics of his own gaze, his own particular eye. What does he see, for example, in

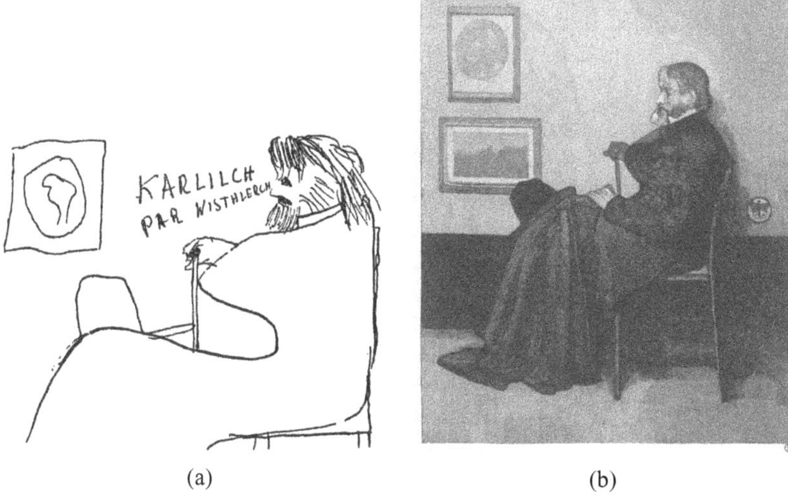

Figure 12.2 (a) Proust, "Karlilch by Wisthlerch" (b) Whistler, *Portrait of Thomas Carlyle*, 1872–1873

Whistler's portrait of Carlyle (Figure 12.2b)? He sees a strongly eroticized representation of a "man-woman," all the more surprising given that the portrait is an echo of Whistler's portrait of his mother, who is represented in the same posture and in the same room, painted from the same angle and in the same tones, but entirely austere, her chest a concave surface. It is as if all the forbidden femininity of the mother-virgin was shifted on to Carlyle, who (involuntarily?) exhibits sexual ambiguity and desire.

Indeed, it is the body on display, often shown in painful situations, that seems to draw Proust's eye. In stained-glass windows representing a man laid out on a bed (Figure 12.3), Christ crucified,[32] or the Descent from the Cross,[33] Proust "sees" his own calvary of illness, with Reynaldo as a figure of consolation. Philippe Sollers highlights the perverse eroticism of religious iconography, which Proust's blasphemous transpositions only serve to emphasize: "Christianity, with its sculptures and paintings (those of the Catholic variety), is a marvelous school for fleshing out the drives. Sadomasochism abounds for those who know how to see it from the inside: its churches are brothels."[34] In these drawings, the concept of *scenario* is essential. Proust does not reproduce isolated figures, but *scenes* where bodies, particularly the suffering body, play a central role, and undergo various interactions.

In his reading of art books, Proust privileges those images that his eye can "animate" (following Belting's expression) by recalling memories that

Figure 12.3 Proust, "Marcel is still in bedsch . . . "

are not visual, but physiological. In other words, certain images strike Proust because they reactivate in him a lived corporeal experience, perhaps occasionally agreeable, but most often painful.

For instance, in the earliest draft where Proust describes it, Giotto's Envy – where a serpent *emerges* from the figure's mouth (Figure 12.4) – spontaneously evokes the memory of a traumatic physical experience of *insertion*:

> le serpent qui lui siffle dans la bouche a l'air d'y être effectivement ~~et de la gêner surtout elle-même~~ ~~elle est obligée de fa~~ il l'oblige à ouvrir la bouche d'une manière aussi incommode que l'instrument que nous introduit dans le pharinx un opérateur . . .[35]
>
> the serpent that hisses in her mouth actually seems to be there ~~and to stifle her most of all~~ ~~she is forced to ma~~ it forces her to open her mouth in a manner as uncomfortable as the instrument that a surgeon inserts into our pharynx . . .

This account is likely the memory of medical and surgical procedures the young Proust underwent in order to treat his asthma.

Another, less commented upon drawing presents itself as a parody of a humorist's drawing, and cannot be fully appreciated unless the viewer

Figure 12.4 Giotto, *Invidia* [*Envy*], *c.* 1305

relates it to a rather disagreeable kinetic experience. This drawing of a motorcar plowing across the countryside (Figure 12.5) is captioned:

> Avec les pneus Michelin l'intrépide sportman et sa frêle épouse peuvent faire du 50 à l'heure en gardant la position étendue, telle qu'on la pratique aujourd'hui dans tous les sanatoriums.
>
> With Michelin tires, the intrepid sportsman and his frail wife can reach speeds of 50 kilometers an hour while maintaining a reclined position, like the one favored in all our sanatoriums today.

This caption is, as Proust himself writes above the drawing, a "pastiche of the *texts* of Caran d'Ache,"[36] a famous humorist (and notorious anti-Semite) of the era. Proust's drawing indeed represents a driver and his wife (more voluptuous than "frail") who appear to be reclining comfortably in the vehicle, as it races on at top speed. Country roads at the time being

Figure 12.5 Proust, "With Michelin tires, . . . "

rather poorly paved or covered in gravel, full of bumps and potholes, a velocity of 50 km/hour (a fast speed for the period) in no way made for a relaxing drive: even with good tires, the passengers would be unpleasantly shaken by the lurching of the car.

Proust denounces the falsehoods of Caran d'Ache, and, in so doing, doubtlessly alludes to one of the humorist's clearly anti-Semitic drawings. That drawing, published during the Dreyfus Affair, featured a bicycle equipped with enormous tires that supposedly permitted rapid travel between "traitors" (Figure 12.6a). But Proust also caricatures an enthusiastic publicity image that appeared in *Le Petit Journal* on the occasion of the *Décennale du Salon de l'automobile* (the tenth edition of the Paris auto show) at the Grand Palais in December 1907 (Figure 12.6b): his drawing does not exactly trace the one published in the paper, but seems to have been recopied freehand from its main elements (seat, position of the couple, woman's muff, steering wheel with its spokes, lateral headlights). Since Proust had traveled through Normandy by automobile during the summer of 1907, he seems to have been struck by this fallacious image of comfort in *Le Petit Journal*, and wanted to protest against such false advertisement.

***

A l'Exposition automobile

— Grâce à cet outil, monsieur Joseph, vous pouvez déjeuner à Paris avec Piquart et dîner chez Schwarzkoppen le soir même.

Figure 12.6a Caran d'Ache, "At the Auto Show," *Psst . . . !*, June 25, 1898

Au Grand-Palais : Le cortège de la locomotion à travers les âges
Le Présent regardant défiler le Passé

Figure 12.6b "At the Grand-Palais," *Le Petit Journal*, December 22, 1907

The way in which Proust's eye "animates" works of visual art is deeply embedded within a cultural history of the gaze: it is no longer the idealistic gaze of the nineteenth century, represented in his novel by that of Swann. Proust's gaze belongs instead to the nascent field of phenomenology, where the body (and in Proust's case, the sensitive and suffering body) becomes the measure of experience, and the criterion for a new reading of images.

NOTES

1 See the copious bibliography in Kazuyoshi Yoshikawa's recent book, *Proust et l'art pictural* (Paris: Champion, 2010). Systematizing and extending the scholarly work of its predecessors, Yoshikawa's book is an authoritative resource that offers an inventory of the pictorial references and allusions found in Proust's writings, and identifies the (generally textual) sources from which Proust drew his pictorial knowledge.

2 For example, Elstir's famous "metaphors," notably in the painting of the Port of Carquethuit (2: 567–572; II, 192–196), or the concept of the novel-cathedral in *Le Temps retrouvé* (6: 508; IV, 610). From the pioneering thesis of J. Theodore Johnson, Jr., "The Painter and his Art in the Works of Marcel Proust" (Ph.D. thesis, University of Wisconsin, 1964) to that of Yasue Kato, *Étude génétique des épisodes d'Elstir dans* À la recherche du temps perdu (Toyko: Surugadai-Shuppansha, 1998), numerous scholarly works rely on the hermeneutic approach. For example, Proust's predilection for Giotto's allegorical art (see T. Johnson, "Proust and Giotto: Foundations for an Allegorical Interpretation of *À la recherche du temps perdu*," in *Marcel Proust: A Critical Panorama*, ed. Larkin B. Price [Urbana: University of Illinois Press, 1973], 168–205) is reflected in the symbolic dimension of the Proustian novel, just as Elstir's art serves to theorize the aesthetic of the "metaphor" in the novel.

3 Chapters in the present volume by Sophie Duval, Christie McDonald, and Suzanne Guerlac each approach (from a specific point of view) the question of Proust's gaze. This convergence likely attests to a shift in Proust studies.

4 Nathalie Mauriac Dyer, "Dessins," *Dictionnaire Marcel Proust*, ed. Annick Bouillaguet and Brian G. Rogers (Paris: Champion, 2004), 298.

5 Philip Kolb published some of these drawings in *Lettres à Reynaldo Hahn* (Paris: Gallimard, 1956) before they were scattered at auction. Their layout in that volume can lead to confusion, as certain drawings are reproduced in the body of the letters, whereas, in reality, they were traced on separate sheets of paper.

6 The first analyses of Proust's medieval drawings by Johnson ("Painter and his Art"; "Proust and Giotto") date to 1964 and 1973; Claude Gandelman's discerning survey, "The Drawings of Marcel Proust," was published in *Adam International Review* in 1976 (40:394–396, pages 21–57). It was while working on facsimiles housed in the Kolb-Proust Archive at the University of Illinois, Urbana-Champaign that Virginie Greene and Caroline Szylowicz came to elaborate on Johnson's intuitions (see note 11 below). Rubén Gallo's recent study

of the "dessindicaces" to Reynaldo Hahn ("Reynaldo Hahn: Proust's Latin Lover," in *Proust's Latin Americans*, 25–72) was published by Johns Hopkins University Press in 2014.

7 Thus, according to Richard Bales, "these drawings are of no far-reaching importance" (*Proust and the Middle Ages* [Geneva: Droz, 1975], 145). As for Philippe Sollers (*L'Œil de Proust* [Paris: Stock, 1999]), he is more interested in the dreamy sketches in the notebooks, and judges the drawings to Reynaldo to be "amorous prattle," the "gibberish" of a "Marcel . . . who had long been a bit backwards" (46–48).

8 Catalogue available online at www.artcurial.com/pdf/2012/2129.pdf; see lots 19, 20, 22 (Cocteau), 51 and 53 (Hugo), 59–63 (Max Jacob), 69–70 (Lamartine), 76–79 (Mérimée), and 111–119 (Sand), in comparison with Proust's drawings (lots 97–100).

9 Johnson, "Proust and Giotto," 181–182.

10 Emile Mâle, *L'Art religieux du XIIIe siècle en France: Étude sur l'iconographie du Moyen Âge et sur ses sources d'inspiration*, new edition, revised and augmented (Paris: Armand Colin, 1902); trans. Dora Nussey as *Religious Art in France of the Thirteenth Century* (London: J. M. Dent; New York: E. P. Dutton, 1913).

11 Virginie Greene and Caroline Szylowicz, "Le miroir des images: étude de quelques dessins médiévaux de Proust," *Bulletin d'informations proustiennes* 28 (1997), 7–29 (see, notably, 10–11). A table of concordances (18–21) provides a reference for all the illustrations from Mâle's book that Proust copied in his drawings.

12 This drawing was first published by Greene and Szylowicz ("Miroir," 25).

13 Mâle, *L'Art religieux*, 57, fig. 11 "Le lion et les lionceaux (Lyon)," or *Religious Art*, 40, fig. 13 "The lion and his cubs (Lyons)." It is interesting to note, for our purposes, that Mâle's illustrations of stained-glass windows are not photographs but *drawings* made by archeologists.

14 Greene and Szylowicz, "Miroir," 14–15.

15 For a decoding of the references regarding these two members of Parisian high society, see *ibid.*, 15.

16 See Gandelman, "Drawings of Proust," 32–47 (caricatural dimension); Johnson, "Painter and his Art," 139–145 (pastiche); Greene et Szylowicz, "Miroir," 15 (parody and discursive mixing: society conversations, art book captions, lists of wedding presents published in society papers).

17 A partial reproduction can be found in *Lettres à Reynaldo Hahn*, 163.

18 Hans Belting, *Pour une anthropologie des images*, trans. Jean Torrent (Paris: Gallimard, 2004), 9. I cite the foreword written for the French translation; markedly different forewords precede the English translation of this work (*An Anthropology of Images: Picture, Medium, Body*, trans. Thomas Dunlap [Princeton University Press, 2011]) and the original German version (*Bild-Anthropologie: Entwürfe für eine Bildwissenschaft* [Munich: Wilhelm Fink, 2001]). Likewise the text of many chapters has been significantly reworked or condensed in the English version (see Belting's note on the translation, *Anthropology of Images*, 8); for this reason I usually cite the French version.

19 Belting, *Pour une anthropologie*, 9, my emphasis.
20 *Ibid.*
21 *Ibid.*, 8, my emphasis.
22 *Ibid.*, 42.
23 *Ibid.*, 37.
24 *Cahier* 64, fos. 139r–140r, my emphasis.
25 Mâle, *Religious Art*, 29, my emphasis.
26 *Ibid.*, 31.
27 *Ibid.*, 40–41. See Greene and Szylowicz, "Miroir," 14.
28 See the reproduction of the full window in Mâle, *L'Art religieux*, 55, or Mâle, *Religious Art*, 38.
29 On the topic of Odette-Zipporah and the incompatibility of Swann's philosophical idealism with reality, see my analyses in "La Question de la représentation dans la littérature moderne," doctoral thesis, Université de Paris 7, 1991, I, 74–75.
30 Belting, *Pour une anthropologie*, 31.
31 On Madame de Saint-Paul and her "involuntary" obscenity, see Greene and Szylowicz, "Miroir," 15.
32 This drawing is reproduced in the present volume (see above, Figure 3.7).
33 "Esquisse d'une descente de croix (Pierre Le Bourget)," reproduced in *Lettres à Reynaldo Hahn*, 81.
34 Sollers, *L'Œil de Proust*, 44–45. In his recent study, Rubén Gallo emphasizes the sadomasochistic component of Proust and Hahn's relationship, as staged in these "medieval" drawings (*Proust's Latin Americans*, 48–55).
35 *Cahier* 8, fo. 57v. In the definitive text, the surgical comparison disappears: the serpent who fills the figure's mouth is "so huge" that "the muscles of her face are strained," but the comparison with a child blowing up a balloon effaces any idea of violation or suffering (1: 111–112; I, 80).
36 See Figure 12.6a; Proust's emphasis.

CHAPTER 13

Sound and music in Proust: what the Symbolists heard

Sindhumathi Revuluri

This chapter proposes that sound is a critical sensory mode in the experience of reading Proust. From sonatas in salons to doorbells, from footsteps to utensils on plates, the text is constantly illuminated and enlivened by invocation of sounds. Though Proust's novel is unique in its degree of detail and the invention of an entire and realistic world for many reasons, I proceed from the idea that it is the sounds and smells and tastes – the ephemeral senses to which Proust commits himself – that distinguish the experience of reading his text.

Much previous scholarly and popular attention has been focused on music in Proust's novel, as well as the musicality of Proust's prose or the possibility of the novel itself having a musical structure.[1] Certainly, we know that music figures largely throughout the narrative as well as the manner of narrating it. As was seminally demonstrated by Jean-Jacques Nattiez, music in Proust's novel is configured not only as musical works, but performance, memory, and musical experience.[2] With this broad definition of music's presence, it is easy to see how music continually punctuates the sonic textures of Proust's world, alternately as memory, event, community, and shared experience.

But music is only one of many ways of heard communication, and furthermore, a unique and narrow way of approaching the power of ephemeral sound. Thinking more broadly about ways of hearing Proust, we begin to notice just how *loud* the pages of Proust become. There are chimes, rustling, whistling, rattling, clanking, and so much more on nearly every page – often described with compelling aural detail and conjuring vivid sonic pictures. In the context of all Proust's aural detail, descriptions of music stand out as unique. But this is not because of its potential characterization as organized sound or aural poetry. In fact, compared to the specificity with which other sounds are usually deployed in Proust's text, "music" becomes a vague notion: when music is experienced by a group of people or as a singular memory, the language used to describe it is highly metaphorical and includes very little sonic detail. Without expecting a play-by-play announcement, a listening guide, or a program note, it is still surprising to notice how much power is accorded to the experience of music and its memory (by Proust and by scholars since) with such a small amount of descriptive detail. In other words, what is striking, given the acknowledged role of music in Proust's life and writing, is the degree to which the passages in which a musical performance is narrated are often themselves remarkably silent.

The pattern of according music a potentially transcendent or hyper-expressive power while remaining silent about its sonic properties is a common one among Symbolist writers and poets of Proust's time. The Symbolists valorized music's suggestive ability that nonetheless did not commit to a single representation or interpretation. Proust's invocation of music – but also his general silence about specific characteristics – offers a chance to reflect on how the entity of "Music" could be used in the expressive arts and to what ends. In this chapter I explore the tension between sound and silence, between the suggestion of music and its actual hearing in Proust's text. I begin with a close reading of a musical event in *Du côté de chez Swann*, look at the invocation of other sounds in the text, and move finally to music and silence in the music of Claude Debussy, Proust's contemporary and a composer admired by French Symbolists.

As a scholar of music, my investment in Proust's musical imagery stems from the fundamental questions his novel inspires: what is happening within us when we listen? What is a performance and what does it mean for a musical work? In other words, music's role in Proust's novel asks us to reflect on the very nature of musical experience.[3] In this sense, it is by way of Proust that aspects of music and our language about it can be illuminated, and that our assumptions about what music is, how it is meant to work, and how we are meant to communicate about it can be newly interrogated.

For example, thinking about music in Proust's text reminds us that music is not a single thing or even a set group of sounds. If such uniqueness were a requirement of discussions of music, Proust's invocation of music would carry very little power indeed. In most cases, in Proust's text and otherwise, music is much more than what we hear but also includes what we feel, what experiences it engenders, and what communities it brings together. Such ideas have been explored in recent scholarship in musicology and ethnomusicology,[4] yet were already present in the ways in which music functions within Proust's novel.

Proust's text is prescient in a sense, as it deploys music in ways that current scholars have only begun to grapple with.[5] In Proust's texts, all of the above possibilities are explored, even without a single note sounding, so to speak. As is well known, Proust was a great lover of music; he admired the works of specific composers, and he also invested much potential in the abstract idea of music's expressive power. The link between these two aspects of Proust's admiration of music is not as self-evident as it may seem. Loving Wagner's *Parsifal* does not necessarily endorse the power of "music" as an entity. (Certainly the reverse may be easier to imagine.) Thus, the archeology of Proust's musical sources – hearing what he heard – is neither possible, nor does it necessarily illuminate the role of music in Proust's text.[6] I would even go so far as to suggest that in some ways the specificity of works and gestures does not matter to the larger understanding of how music functions within the novel. In a sense, discussing what musicologists affectionately call "the music itself" – meaning actual works, notes, meters, rhythms, expressive markings, and so on, as opposed to historical or cultural context – gives us both too much and the wrong kind of information in the context of reading Proust.

Instead of providing descriptions of "the music itself," Proust exploits numerous other narrative possibilities via musical performance: it can be an event, a character in the novel can have encounters that we can observe and understand, the audience at a concert is bonded through that experience, or it can give rise to a memory space. In all of this, the music itself matters – and it does not. The Symbolist conception of music proves to be a useful context and important backdrop: the way in which music is invoked by Symbolist poets has little to do with how it actually sounded or with its aesthetics. For the Symbolists, music was at its most powerful when it was suggestive. In writing about music, then, knowing too much about the music distracts from its suggestion and focuses instead on the exactness and realism of what we hear. Focusing on the specificity of the music (which sonata, what key, tempo markings) thus takes away from the possibilities engendered by musical space and, in fact, detracts from its abstract power. Music was most useful to the Symbolists as an abstract and expressive form; writing about music would therefore prove a special challenge. For some scholars, the very metaphors Proust uses become part of a musical structure that allows for intratextual experiences.[7] Yet I suggest that it is not music itself but the idea of music that makes this possible; put another way, it is the silence with which Proust describes music that allows it to speak across pages, scenes, and volumes of his novel.

In Proust's text, discussions of music mirror exactly the power attributed by the Symbolists. For example, early in "Un amour de Swann," we witness a musical performance at the home of the Verdurins. After some protests from Mme Verdurin, a pianist plays the pianoforte arrangement of a sonata in F sharp (which we later learn is Vinteuil's sonata for piano and violin). Mme Verdurin's protests have to do with her own reaction to the work – she insists that it moves her to tears in such a violent way that it might cause her to fall ill. So it is decided that just the *Andante* movement will be played, a suggestion she finds equally appalling, for it is ostensibly the *Andante* that carries the most emotional charge. (Perhaps from a less hysterical point of view, we might think that excerpting the *Andante* from the rest of the work does it a kind of violence, too.)

After much build-up about the work, its beauty and power, and how much Swann might enjoy it – and after the promise that he will be "caressed aurally" by the performance – we are treated not to an experience of hearing the work in the moment, but a *memory* of a previous instance, where a "little phrase" haunted Swann's memory (I: 294; I, 205). We later understand that this performance solved that earlier mystery, that this work contained the same little phrase. But all we have heard so far about this performance is, "After the pianist had played, Swann was even more affable towards him" – with the ensuing memory given as the reason for that new affability (I: 294; I, 205). In other words, the live event was not only completely silent, but completely absent. It is only a vehicle by which to get to memory.

In this familiar passage, the memory takes the place of the real event – and occupies the time and narrative space that the performance would have otherwise: we return to the present after the narration of the memory, just at the moment when the piece has ostensibly concluded. Since music unfolds in time, it would seem to be particularly useful for Proust's forays into memory and playing with time. Within the hearing of music, time ebbs and flows, passes quickly and more slowly, yet the entire experience is governed by a relatively fixed temporal frame: the duration of the piece. Near the end of the memory, past and present intersect as we are offered a tiny glimpse into the live performance, and we come to realize that the little phrase was part of both performances – a chronology that mirrors the very manner in which the realization may have occurred. But even with the foregrounding of the "little phrase" and the details provided throughout the memory and in the return to the present, there is little to hold on to in a musical sense. The description of the high note sustained through two bars only leads to the memory of a woman Swann had once seen; the slow rhythmical movement leads him to a state of happiness. In other words, the details of music are unimportant, withheld, or merely vehicles by which to access something else.

Though clues like the sustained high note and the rhythms have led to compelling arguments for what the music might have been,[8] what is remarkable is how much is left to imagination and allusion – a quality the Symbolists prized in music (as an art), even as they involved few composers in their philosophy and ideology. Proust avoids description of the sort that might give away too much about what was heard. Some scholars have called this Music, rather than music, and have suggested that it is entirely a literary construct.[9] We hear instead via memory and experience, almost skipping over sounded music directly into what it engenders. Even in the moments that seem like actual description, Proust's language is dominated by metaphors that may suggest a family of sound behavior, but never specific enough to extrapolate a definitive musical work as model. Indeed, this is what makes the project of decoding Proust's sources so fascinating: we know that there may have been inspirations, but the ways in which they are conflated and combined reflect upon his own narrative and artistic process. We know that he admired Wagner, loved Hahn, and despised Saint-Saëns – yet no one of these men or their music appears wholesale in the novel, even encoded. (Traces of each of them show up in the characterization of Vinteuil.) As any study about Proust's musical sources has found, we are nearly always beholden to metaphor in our description of music – making the identification of musical sources a nearly impossible task.

By way of contrast, I turn now to two moments in which sound – rather than music – figures largely. The distinction has not usually been taken seriously in the study of Proust, and works that attempt to "hear" Proust focus primarily on musical moments, like the one I discuss above. Yet, if we listen to Proust with open ears, we are bound to hear everyday sounds foregrounded, and loudly so, not piano sonatas or septets. There is certainly a case to be made that music marks important narrative moments, and that sound is part of the quotidian. I do not intend to deny such an analysis. In fact, I believe that music takes it potential narrative power from the density of other kinds of sound: it is able to stand out and mark important moments because of its difference.

My first example of the significant use of sound is at the very opening of the novel, as the narrator attempts to sleep. In these first few pages we learn about his night-time habits, and in this introduction sound is an important aspect of his orientation in time and space. The candle and the watch orient him, but he also relies heavily on hearing in this nighttime reverie – train whistles, compared to birds in the forest, which then conjure a hurried traveler and the new sounds that might echo in his ears. The recognition of midnight leads him to another imagining: that of an invalid in a hotel who could ring the bell and hear the footsteps approaching. In his own world he hears the creaking of the wainscoting. We learn that the dinner bell rescues him from the intrusion of the magic lantern whose charm he appreciates but finds discomforting all the same. We hear the dialogue of the grandmother and her friend. We know the young hero's mother is coming by the sound of her footsteps. Swann is recognized by the doorbell – not the alarm but the visitor's bell – and then by his voice. The lines between imagination and memory are already blurred, yet each world is full of sights, sounds, and smells. We are thus immediately drawn in to a world that we first imagine to be dark, yet nonetheless alive, through what we hear with the narrator, together.

In another example the invalid aunt Léonie – essentially alone in her bedroom – is agitated by the noises of regular life, from the knock of the postman to the chiming of church bells. The workman down the street asks permission to use his hammer, in case she is "resting" (1: 114; 1, 82). When the hero is sent to check on his aunt, the morning after the kitchen maid has given birth, it is through Aunt Léonie's snores that he is aware of her breathing – and her change in breath. While the story of Léonie's adherence to routine – and its scheduled Saturday changes – is told with both humor and pity, her isolation is marked. The sounds that punctuate this story may seem unremarkable in certain regards, yet the connection to the outside world through sound reminds her – and us – that she is not alone. The narrator's night-time listening is similarly connective – those sounds not only orient him in time, but in a world in which there are others, despite what the physical isolation might otherwise suggest.

I offer these moments in order to show the intricate counterpoint between allusion and specificity, between the description of the experience of a musical performance and the language used to discuss natural or quotidian sounds. In both of these examples the sounds are relatively specific – a knock at the door, a train whistle, a hammer, bells chiming. These, as well as many others in the text, such as the rustling of leaves or plates clattering, all contrast starkly with the metaphor-laden, allusive language used to talk about music. From the language alone, an opposition emerges, whereby music is not just a special category of sound but almost its very opposite. Proust's natural, man-made, and everyday sounds may punctuate a scene or enliven it; they are rarely further dwelled upon, though they sometimes act as a trigger for a memory. The musical passages, however, engage multiple senses – sight, smell, and sometimes taste – in metaphor, memory, and allusion. (I believe this is possible exactly because they are rarely discussing the music itself, but the experiences it might engender.) Though both experienced aurally, sounds are captured in documentary style, whereas music is left almost entirely to imagination. The remarkable contrast produces music's transcendence: without the specificity of language about sound – without that sense of concrete, grounded, shared experience – the allusive language about music would not communicate so powerfully. We need to know what is being avoided, in a sense, if we are to appreciate the spaces of memory, transcendence, and shared experience that music opens. Ultimately, the musical passages become *silent*.

To return to the question of "the music itself" and what kind of information musically specific details provide, I would like to highlight two details in the "little phrase" passage I discussed earlier: "F sharp" and "Andante" (I: 290–291; I, 203). In the context of metaphor and silence, these descriptors almost shock the system with their specificity. Yet, read against the context of other sounds, they serve as a kind of reminder that whatever their individual experience, everyone in the scene did, indeed, hear the same piece. These two details do refer to "the music itself," but they do so without offering very much aural information. We know that simply telling us the key, tempo, or a characteristic of rhythm ultimately tells us little about what was heard, or how and why that music made such an impression on Swann, Odette, Mme Verdurin, and others. We are forced instead to focus on the experience related to us, and less on the music itself. Even more, despite the experience of this music in a group, the silence of the narration allows us to imagine an *individual* experience – in the passage quoted earlier, it was Swann's experience, not Mme Verdurin's. The other sounds I discussed – despite having been experienced by single characters – are nonetheless shared in the possibility of being heard, then or at another time, by anyone, therefore creating a common shared memory.

I am not suggesting that all sonic punctuations are signs of human connection for an otherwise isolated character. Of course, there are hundreds of other sounds that permeate the text and are simply background noise. However, the two examples of the narrator and Aunt Leonie reveal how our own sonic vocabulary is often a shared one; indeed, little description is offered of the quotidian or natural sounds, the assumption being that a reader would not necessarily need further detail either to imagine them or to understand their importance for the narrative. The musical passages suggest otherwise, where even a detail like key or tempo does little to suggest specific sounds, and as much as we are drawn into its metaphor, we remain outside its performance.

There is certainly much more to say about sound in Proust's novel and a much more comprehensive study to be undertaken, perhaps even on the scale of Nattiez's *Proust as Musician*. For now, however, I would like to move to an analogous question in a contemporaneous musical work, Claude Debussy's *Pelléas et Mélisande*. Premiered in 1902 at the Opéra-Comique, Debussy's only completed opera employs Symbolist playwright Maurice Maeterlinck's play as libretto. I turn to this work because I believe it forms a productive corollary with the musical silences and resonant sounds of Proust's text, through its own conventions of the expressive language of music and opera.

Debussy had searched for a libretto that would allow him to pursue his ideal operatic form for a long time. Influenced in part by his trips to Bayreuth and his hearing of Wagner's operatic works, Debussy sought a more economical approach – one that would allow his characters to yield to destiny, to pursue mystery, and where their singing would be closer to speech. In Maeterlinck's play, Debussy found all of this: in the allusion of language, all that is not said, and the explicit interplay between light and dark. In his later comments on the opera, Debussy highlighted his own use of silence as an expressive device, and it is to this feature that I would now like to turn.

After a frustrating phase of composition in 1893, Debussy wrote to his friend Ernest Chausson, "I have been looking for the music behind all the veils that she accumulates, even for her most ardent devotees! . . . I am using, quite spontaneously, the all-too-rare resource of silence as a means of expression (don't laugh) and as perhaps the only way to point the emotion of a phrase."[10] It is possible that Debussy was referring to the specific moment of the star-crossed lovers Pelléas and Mélisande's last encounter. Pelléas decides he must leave, and allow Mélisande to be with his suspicious and jealous brother Golaud. He asks Mélisande to meet him so that he can say goodbye. He ends his sparsely accompanied soliloquy by saying, "I must tell her everything that I have not yet said," which is followed by silence (Figure 13.1). Both the suggestive lyric and the fermata over the rest suggest the power of silence, narratively and literally. The audible silence of that fermata makes a strong impression, one that can be further attenuated in nuanced performances.

Later in the life of the opera, Debussy would still insist on the importance of silence – not just to the work, but to its performance. When his friend, the conductor Eugène Ysaÿe, offered to program extracts in a concert hall setting, Debussy protested, "If this work has any merit, it is above all in the connection between its scenic and musical movement. In

Figure 13.1 Debussy, *Pelléas et Mélisande*, Act IV, scene 4 (measures 36–37)

concert performance this quality would disappear and no one could be reproached for seeing nothing in those eloquent silences which abound in the opera."[11]

Indeed, Debussy's protest seems valid in connection with another powerful moment of silence: at the opening of Act III, we meet Mélisande in her tower, brushing her hair. Each verse of her song – one of the most lyrical moments in the entire opera, and meant as an onstage song – is preceded by a compelling pause and then sung mostly a cappella (Figure 13.2). Knowing that Debussy invested silence with expressive power, the fermata over the barline before the second verse becomes more meaningful. Indeed, we may be able to hear this moment as full of anticipation and mystery, saying many things that cannot themselves be said.

Given the Symbolist context of the opera – Maeterlinck's libretto and Debussy's influences – it is worth pursuing what role or function silence plays in these two moments and more broadly.[12] Music may have been valorized by the Symbolists, even called the ideal medium by which to achieve their expressive ideals. Yet, for composers who set texts, but also for those who did not, music was not necessarily the abstract entity the Symbolists imagined and celebrated. Even Debussy, arguably a Symbolist composer

Figure 13.2 Debussy, *Pelléas et Mélisande*, Act III, scene 1 (measures 25–26)

in his networks and philosophy, found moments where it was not music, but its absence – silence – that was most able to express that allusive, illusory complex of emotions and suggestions.[13] In other words, within a given medium, whether it is narrative or fragmented, prose or poetry, written or declaimed, the most abstract, broadly suggestive, and least previously endowed with aesthetic or cultural meaning is what appeals in the way the Symbolists intended.

The two above moments from *Pelléas et Mélisande* thus illuminate ideas about sound, music, and expressive power in Proust. Where Proust uses metaphor – which I read as a kind of silence – to do the expressive work attributed to the power of music, Debussy uses silence, in the realm of music, to do that same work. Indeed, the two seem to be approaching the issue of what is beyond expression from two different perspectives, rooted in their respective media. For where Debussy says that in his dramatic form, "music begins at the point where the word becomes powerless as an expressive force; music is made for the inexpressible,"[14] Proust is bound to the word. The philosopher Vladmir Jankélévitch would later say, "Music was not invented to be talked about."[15] Proust follows this line, suggesting that "[Music] is like a possibility that has come to nothing" (5:344; III, 763). He exploits its undeveloped possibility, allowing it to stand in for numerous narrative turns and to play with time. He believes in its power to communicate, for sure, but he does not "talk about it." In other words, what Proust invests in music and then describes only through its effects, Debussy invests in music and then inserts silence.

Like Debussy's silence, we may read Proust's text as an interaction between music, sound, and silence. This triangulation, apart from simply employing a sense not always primary in our reading of Proust's novel, also suggests that the multisensory elements of the text have layers and nuance still to be explored. For Proust, whose prose is often described as itself musical and whose verbosity might prevent us from ever thinking of him as "silent," the quiet spaces in the text may open similar interpretative possibilities as Debussy's silences – they are meaningful absences in an otherwise saturated expressive form.

NOTES

1 Famous interventions on this topic include Antoine Compagnon, "Fauré and Unity Recaptured," in *Proust Between Two Centuries*, trans. Richard E. Goodkin (New York: Columbia University Press, 1992), 43–52; Kazuyoshi Yoshikawa, "Vinteuil ou la genèse du septuor," *Études proustiennes*, 3 (Paris: Gallimard, 1979), 289–347; and Jean-Jacques Nattiez, *Proust as Musician*, trans. Derrick Puffett (Cambridge University Press, 1989). See also Mauro Carbone, "Composing Vinteuil: Proust's Unheard Music," *RES: Anthropology and Aesthetics* 48 (2005), 163–165. For a selective summary of related scholarship through 1989, see Nattiez, *Proust as Musician*, 1–11. More recent scholarship is cited throughout this chapter.

2 See Nattiez, *Proust as Musician*.

3 I am not alone among musicologists in being inspired by Proust to ask philosophical questions about the nature of music. See Cormac Newark and Ingrid Wassenaar, "Proust and Music: The Anxiety of Competence," *Cambridge Opera Journal* 9 (1997), 163–183.

4 For just two examples, see Carolyn Abbate, "Music: Drastic or Gnostic?," *Critical Inquiry* 30 (2004), 505–536; and Christopher Small, *Musicking: The Meanings of Performing and Listening* (Middletown, CT: Wesleyan University Press, 1998).

5 Eve Norah Pauset takes a similar lesson from Proust's text, using it to reflect on the current state of French musicology and informing questions about the very nature of music and musical study. Pauset, "Proust musicologue? Le positivisme ambigu ou: De sentir pour écrire à sentir est écrire," *International Review of the Aesthetics and Sociology of Music* 40 (2009), 63–79.

6 Similar debates have been waged in the realm of historical performance practice. See Peter Kivy, *Authenticities: Philosophical Reflections on Musical Performance* (Ithaca, NY: Cornell University Press, 1995).

7 Naomi Perley, "The Language of an Unknown Country: Intratextuality in Proust's *In Search of Lost Time*," *19th-Century Music* 36 (2012), 136–145.

8 A popular and extremely thorough archeology has been completed by James Connelly (Proust Society of America): www.proust-ink.com/proust_playlist.pdf.

9 Newark and Wassenaar, "Proust and Music," 164. Positioned against archeological approaches, music as literary construct reminds us of the expressive power retained by non-specific sound. Still, I hesitate to go this far in my own analysis because we lose the possibility of music engendering community and music giving way to memory *in time*, which are clearly key features of the novel as a whole.

10 Cited in Robert Orledge, *Debussy and the Theatre* (Cambridge University Press, 1982), 52. Orledge also refers to Act IV, scene 4 as a possible reference point, though his interest in silence is more directed at the presence or absence of orchestral accompaniment, not full silence, as I discuss here.

11 As quoted in Orledge, *Debussy and the Theatre*, 59.

12 I take my cue in thinking about Debussy as a Symbolist from Stefan Jarocinski's arguments in *Debussy: Impressionism and Symbolism*, trans. Rollo Myers (London: Eulenburg Books, 1976).

13 Throughout his writings on *Pelléas* and compositional process, Debussy refers to silence as an integral feature of the opera. See Orledge, *Debussy and the theatre*, 48–101.

14 Cited *ibid.*, 49.

15 Vladmir Jankélévitch, *Music and the Ineffable*, trans. Carolyn Abbate (Princeton University Press, 2003), 79.

CHAPTER 14

Inside a red cover: Proust and the art of the book

Evelyne Ender and Serafina Lawrence

Pediatrics Group to Recommend Reading Aloud to Children From Birth

New York Times, June 24, 2014

In memory of Gregory T. Polletta (1929–2012) and the gentle crease on page 460 of his Pléiade vol. IV (E.E.).

Our thanks go to Professor Kyoo Lee and the students of "What is Reading?" at the CUNY Graduate Center. We are forever grateful for the privilege of learning from Helen Tartar (1951–2014), whose deep love and knowledge of books fueled our seminar conversations. Thanks also to Yulia Nazvanova and Nora Carr, for the translation of a section of Lionel Naccache's book, and to Nelly Furman, for her insightful suggestions.

In an age of seamless reading for some – on tablets, computers, and phones as well as, still, books – and at a time of increasing concern about the challenges faced by others in achieving literacy, one might well want to hear from an expert reader. What can Proust, a man who devoted his life to writing a book and is himself the inspiration for hundreds of books, teach us about the act of reading and its value? In placing a book among the objects that, in the famous scene of *Adoration perpétuelle* near the end of the *Recherche*, prompt involuntary memories, he seems to give us important cues – though without a theory, choosing instead an aesthetic form. To offer a theory would be as vulgar, his narrator tells us, as leaving a price-tag on an object (6: 278; IV, 461), but like all disclaimers this one hints at some deeper revelations, which are hidden behind the veil of nostalgia wrapped around the reddish volume of *François le Champi*. At the author's own prompting then, we are impelled to ask not only what lesson can be uncovered from a fictional scene of reading staged around George Sand's novel, but also what lies hidden inside a book besides lines, or words, or images, or ideas. While literary critics, phenomenologists, as well as cognitive psychologists explore the intricacies of reading through research models and protocols, we will argue here that Proust's *Recherche* offers its own powerful empirical model.

What is there to be found inside a book? As a work of art in the form of fiction, Proust's *Recherche* provides its own answer: a whole universe or the sum total of an experience. Indeed, of the memories recounted in this climactic episode, only this one, prompted by the apparition of the beloved book, can cross the mirror that shows "the child who for the first time spelt out [the book's] title in the little bedroom," and whose memory "must not be buried in oblivion" (6: 289, trans. mod.; IV, 466). On the other side lies the book in the making – that is a world and a life born from the child's initiation to another book, a long time ago in Combray. In casting the arch of his cathedral across an interval of many years (and hundreds of pages) so as to reunite the soon to become writer with the reading child, the author points at the crucial significance of what turns out to be a "primal scene" for the literary *Bildungsroman* that is the *Recherche*. The reminiscence prompted by a book, involuntary like the others lined up in this episode and yet different, opens the gates to the potentially infinite space of a biography about to be cast into words. For in Proust's conception, the child drawn to the book is in fact learning to spell out the elements of a world that the book helps him read, which means that reading is a form of writing.

Indeed, from the moment Proust approached the subject of books and reading in preparation for his novel, he focused on the way the books we love with passion can expand our intelligence of what constitutes our life or, more precisely, our experiences. The memories prompted by the book's red binding, his hero says, "illuminated for me not only the old groping movements of my mind [les tâtonnements anciens de ma pensée], but even the whole purpose of my life and perhaps art itself" (6: 287, trans. mod.; IV, 465). In placing the image of the reading child at this nodal point of the *Recherche*, the memories also tell us about the book's crucial role in an aesthetic education which, for Proust, can only happen at the convergence between knowledge and affect.

A phenomenological approach suggests, meanwhile, that Proust's inspired literary descriptions of reading experiences, though perhaps still beyond the reach of rigorous empirical studies, can be of value to contemporary scientific investigations. Even if Proust's (older) "wisdom" about reading cannot be converted into numbers or scientific protocols, this analysis might speak to our current concerns. For if not now, as we are steeped in conversations about the value of books and of early reading, when? In this essay, we pry away, from what is a work of art, intuitions as well as conceptual materials that might enrich or complement science driven models of the reading process, and we probe into what is hidden inside the red cover of *François le Champi*, to enrich our understanding of what is at stake when a child learns to read fiction. But because Proust's lesson cannot be simply lifted off the page as if from a didactic manual, it must be reconstructed piecemeal from what constitutes, in the vocabulary of literary studies, an allegory; its central item being a book, this is where we pick up the thread.

What is a book? *Une leçon de choses*[1]

François le Champi, the book with the red cover, is not only the last object to open the door to the past in this crucial episode of the *Recherche*; it is also by far the most complex, as shown in the four densely knit pages devoted to unpacking its meaning. The philosopher Jean-Luc Nancy provides us indirectly with an explanation, in outlining the kind of associative chain a book can prompt: "In the end, the Idea of the book will always, from the very first conception, have been the Idea of its reading and, through that reading, the Idea of another book, of another writing that continues from the first," he writes.[2] Though a worthy foil when it comes to assessing the full scope of Proust's model, Nancy's statement makes us stumble right away on a discrepancy, since the writer's idea of a book does *not*, in this case, involve reading it, at least not in any obvious, literal sense.[3] *François le Champi* remains unopened beyond its title page, its essential qualities being distinct from the words it carries. So if it invites or, more emphatically, *demands* reading, it is only in a more extended sense defined to us in these very pages as the decipherment of "a material impression, material since it came through our senses, but that we can nevertheless interpret [dont nous pouvons dégager l'esprit]" (6: 273, trans. mod.; IV, 457). Meanwhile, Proust's finely calibrated analysis, filled with qualifications and unafraid, at times, of contradictions, can best be summed up in the linear, didactic form of what would have been called, in his day already, *une leçon de choses*. Here is what it teaches us about the book. A book is:

A material thing on par with paving stones, spoons and napkins, or bread The book with its red cover is aligned with those other objects, and like them it serves as a sensory memory prompt; most notably, it "retains something of the eyes which have looked at them" and "brings back to us . . . all the images with which at the time those eyes were filled" (6: 283; IV, 463). The paving stone, a starched napkin, a spoon chiming against a cup, a whistling heating pipe, and now a book, these are the various, distinctive objects singled out in this episode because they provide "celestial nourishment" (6: 264; IV, 451). Indeed, when trying to frame this presentation in an earlier draft, Proust affixed to it the title "*Adoration perpétuelle*" so as to highlight the movement from matter to spirit or mind (*esprit* is the word he chose) that these objects permit. Yet the nearly sacramental qualities attributed to these objects, and to the book above all, are best understood in reference to a pronouncement by the author. Asked late in his career by a journalist for alternatives to his current profession, Proust suggested, teasingly, that he could have been a baker – as "giving humanity its daily bread is surely an honorable job" (*CSB* 604–605). But isn't it the case that, like a baker's, his was a manual labor done at night? And then, like bread, a book provides nourishment (albeit of a spiritual kind), allowing for the transsubstantiation of matter into spirit.

A valuable object As the narrator's gaze scans the shelves of the Duc de Guermantes's collection filled with "precious volumes" and "beautiful original editions," he is drawn to the most humble, but promising item. In fact, *François le Champi*, in Proust's description, embodies what Nancy identifies as the "modest and empirical" nature of a book and "the assemblage represented by its material oneness. Its binding and stitching create its volume."[4] If there is a type for this book lover, it would not be the bibliophile, as the text tells us, but rather the *bibliomaniac* who is driven to search "an original edition that first determined his impression of a novel." So the binding only matters because it singles out and asserts the book's physical presence, giving it a value beyond any aesthetic or monetary considerations. "Books," the narrator insists (and this would include the red one just picked up from the shelf in the Guermantes's library), "behave like things: the manner in which the cover of a binding opens, or the grain of the paper, may have preserved a memory" (6: 285, trans. mod.; IV, 464). Because of its visual and tactile features, *François le Champi* holds the precious and rare ability to trigger synesthetic, aesthetic experiences. Indeed, just as a certain volume by Bergotte might recall "snow on the Champs-Élysées," this book holds "between its syllables" a host of sensations and images.[5] It can then call upon the child the narrator once was, "wanting to be seen only by his eyes, to be loved only by his heart, to speak only to him" (6: 283, trans. mod.; IV, 463). Alone, it beckons our hero, looking back at him – in the same way that the proverbial can of sardines, in Lacan's scenario of desire, calls out to a man at sea. What then distinguishes this book from all the other objects in the series is how powerfully it acknowledges a subject and his desire. But what desire?

A mnemonic device Like the other objects of the *Adoration*, this one preserves personal memories, similar to "a vase filled with scents, sounds, moments." However, in the whole of the *Recherche*, there is only one other cue, the "petite madeleine" and linden tea, that similarly opens the wellsprings of reminiscence to decisive childhood experiences:

> A child rises within me, who takes my place, who alone has the right to spell out the title *François le Champi*, and who reads it as he read it once before, with the same impression of what the weather was like then in the garden, the same dreams that were then shaping themselves in his mind about faraway lands and about life, the same anguish about the next day. (6: 285, trans. mod.; IV, 464)[6]

Through the book, a man who acutely feels the touch of earthly years is reunited with the young child he once was, in a mnesic experience that fulfills a deep desire for an identity connected to this object. *Champi* thus feeds the desire for memories that shapes the geography of the whole book, though in order to nourish such nostalgia, the way has to remain clear. Only a straight line of images can lead to the cherished moment of a child's enchantment by a book. Hence the paradox: a scene of reading in which the book remains closed, and the text unread because the addition of Sand's words to this intimate scene would warp the trajectory of the hero's reminiscence.

A way of placing art in life Memories more meaningful than the story it tells endow the red book with overwhelming emotional power. Irrepressible tears greet an unassuming object, an object that summons up, in succession, images of a father's funeral, the picture of a mother reading that same book to the hero, and a vignette of the child who once upon a time learned to read its title. Steeped in these "tenderly intertwined memories of childhood and family" and evoking "a night, the sweetest and saddest of [a] life," the book is the receptacle of affects (6: 283, 287; IV, 462, 465). Hence, what Barthes would have called its "punctum"; the piercing, heartfelt nature of its return. Hence also its aura, which places it in a virtual library filled with works chosen for their private associations, works that "memory enriches with rich illuminations" (6: 288; IV, 466). The volume that embodies, we are told, "the essence of fiction," becomes a literary emblem: through its very existence it opens the door to a world of storytelling (6: 282, trans. mod.; IV, 462). This is why the text *inside* the book no longer matters: what it conveys are material impressions that belong to an *outside*, as reading spreads outward, from the page to the world.

Here Proust rejoins Nancy, who similarly conceives of reading as being intertwined with writing and speaks of the "the Idea of another book, of another writing that continues on from the first."[7] Proust's complex scenography serves one crucial purpose, namely a change of focus – a change deemed to show us, its readers, the role played by books in scripting our world and making sense of its signs. *François le Champi* thus marks the beginning of a long apprenticeship that leads to the decipherment of the hieroglyphics hidden in the *grimoire compliqué et fleuri* that is "a life" (6: 274; IV, 457). That this first book should be placed next to that symbolic *grimoire* that dispenses *leçons de vie* should not surprise us, nor should Proust's indirect invocation of the familiar analogies of the book of life or the book of nature.[8] Proust's ideas about the book take on, sometimes, a surprisingly contemporary aspect, as here for example with this *grimoire* (mistakenly rendered in the standard English translation as "a magical scrawl"). Proust's words evoke a cryptic, image-filled Book of Spells, as if our author had envisaged, much ahead of his time, what sociological studies of reading or Tumblr websites of the early twenty-first century will no doubt reveal: scores of pictures of a child engrossed in a Harry Potter volume.

Proust the pedagogue: a primal scene of reading

With the return of *François le Champi*, another important arch of the Proustian cathedral emerges into view; it leads us to the earlier scene, in "Combray," of the hero's initiation to reading as well as, it turns out, to writing.[9] Before he gets to see the book, the hero is shown in the act of writing – feverishly hoping to call his mother to his bedside for a kiss, through a note entrusted to Françoise. These are the first signs we have of how writing and reading are intertwined in Proust's conception, an insight we will reconsider in our conclusion. For now, we must explore more fully the psychological and mental space of reading, when the red book is part of an early apprenticeship into the mysteries of grown life. To rely on a psychoanalytic concept and speak of a "primal scene of reading" seems appropriate, given the wide range of the initiation *Champi* provides. But here again, decoding its text is not what matters; the meaning of this early lesson lies in the reverie that accompanies the experience of being read to by the mother. In his preface to Ruskin's *Sesame and Lilies*, Proust wrote that "reading is at the threshold of our spiritual life; it can lead us into it, but does not constitute it" (*ASB* 211, trans. mod.; *CSB* 178). Here we learn about a shift of focus, a shift of attention from the decoding of the words on the page, as, carried away by the maternal voice and yet inspired by it, the child maps out and builds an inner world.

Years have elapsed since the protagonist last set eyes on this book, which takes him back to the familial home at the heart of Combray, and to a child's anxieties about bedtime. The red cover has called forth the earlier scene –

when *maman* in a soothing gesture had brought out one of the volumes of Sand's rustic tales promised for the child's birthday by the grandmother, and had read him the tale. And thus, instead of the desired kiss, the child received from her a different *viaticum*, a book that, symbolically, marks the beginning of his journey away from her into the world. In reading aloud from Sand's book, the maternal voice does more than substitute the magic of literature for the pains of life; it shows the way into a different universe. Carried by the mother's voice, the words of the text open up another space, away from the anguish and the too proximate desire of this shared bedroom.

In the social world of Proust's novel, learning one's letters and discovering a book would naturally have begun outside of school, at home with a mother, who, just as she would teach the child his prayers, would also read to him at the bedside. *Maman*'s gesture of reaching for a story that can distract the child and lull him into sleep is unexceptional. So is, it would seem, the choice of this book: often beautifully illustrated, Sand's rustic novels made of simple stories told in simple words seemed designed to introduce a child to the pleasures of fiction. Moreover, as the hero's grandmother knows, *François le Champi* is the proper choice for a child's literary education in a well-heeled bourgeois family.[10]

Historically meaningful as this account may be, it is nevertheless blind to what Proust knew when he replaced what had been his first choice, *La Mare au Diable*, with *Champi*, whose story seemed better suited to latent erotic content of a scene of reading that grants the child the privilege of spending the night with his mother. When it was first staged in Paris as a play, *François le Champi* – the story of a foundling child who ends up marrying the unhappily married, beautiful Madeleine who had rescued him from abject poverty when he was a child – created quite a stir. What better choice for an initiation to the pleasures of fiction than to tease this early reader's curiosity with a book filled with half-forbidden love! A book instead of a kiss, a book in the place of a kiss, this is how things appear in the framework of the hero's sentimental education. It is left to the mature adult hero to articulate, through an analogy, the erotic nature of that first encounter with reading: like the red dress worn the first time by a woman we fall in love with, we are told in *Le Temps retrouvé*, the cover of that red book stands for what cannot yet be grasped, and tells us that reading is born of desire.

Indeed, as she censors the incriminating love scenes, *maman* leaves it to the child to "find out for himself,"[11] thereby fueling the child's curiosity about what the book reveals and prompting him to elaborate his own constructions of what lies in between the words read to him. *Champi* becomes a placeholder for all those half-forbidden volumes that drive a young person's curiosity towards unknown territories. But more meaningfully, in reading with the mother, the Proustian child is insensibly carried over the threshold, into an "inner life" built from words yet fed by his imagination. Here lies then, in substance, another Proustian lesson: the desire to read, and the meaning of reading itself lie in what the object hides, namely a subjective world that cherished books will render legible. Isn't this ultimately what Proust's narrative articulation of the theme of the red book suggests? "Combray": lured into the mysteries of reading by his mother, the child begins his education as he learns to decipher the book's title. *Le Temps retrouvé*: the emotion felt on recognizing the book of his childhood leads to a crucial revelation, namely that the words in the book are of less significance than what lies between them or even, as he tells us, "between the syllables." A simple homely phrase springs to mind here: having once upon a time learned this book "by heart," the grown reader now uses it to map out his own world and to master it.[12]

Building on his own experience, Proust conceives of a child's introduction to literacy as a blend between affect and cognitive, epistemological processes. As a doorway to an outside world, reading reaches beyond the text into a context, so that what lies inside the cover of *François le Champi* is in effect a whole universe open to intellectual investigation. Thus, the same red book, seen for itself and not merely as a mirror to the past, can be folded into a literary project to become, crucially, the *prop* and the *symbol* of a perceptual, mnemonic, imaginary transfiguration in which reading morphs into writing. The key notion is that of transmutation (Merleau-Ponty defines it as a chiasm) that will occur in between the words: "A name read long ago in a book contains *between* its syllables the *brisk wind* and *bright sunshine* that prevailed while we were reading it," Proust writes (6: 284, trans. mod.; IV, 463, our emphasis). The book we read helps us write the world, that is, it prompts an aesthetic experience that defines or creates (or remembers) a perceptual universe – for example, what it felt like that day when the book was open on our lap and we were reading it. Singled out among the other objects celebrated here (the paving stone, the spoon, the starched napkin), the book offers a script for the creation of a world, actual or virtual. A new subjective life is thus born from the succession of images from the book: a child, a young man, and a host of lifelike statues hewn in imagination out of raw stone and *disjecta membra*.

This message, delivered in the novel with the unmistakable fervor borrowed from the Gospel ("je dis," says the narrator) finds its echo in Peter Schwenger's book, *At the Borders of Sleep*, in a comment about the dreamlike, hypnagogic moment that serves as overture to Proust's *œuvre*: "Such moments bring to the foreground a background that has always been necessary for our reading. Intellectually, no doubt, we have always known that reading takes place as much in the spaces between the words as it does by means of the words themselves." Schwenger also quotes Philippe Sollers's words in *Logiques*: "we must become aware of what we write unconsciously by our reading."[13] *François le Champi* shows that the book's cognitive yield far exceeds the mere decoding of words. To use a contemporary image, reading, in Proust's conception, cannot be reduced to a system of codes designed to transcribe ideas into the brain, the way DNA gets transcripted into RNA, complex as this process may be. Meanwhile, in reaffirming, through the paradox of the unread book, the value of a waywardness of the imagination or a drift of attention away from syllables and words, the Proustian scene invites further investigation on our part, into more specialized research. Availing ourselves of the bridges between fiction and science that phenomenology allows us to build, we will explore this hypothesis and connect Proust's first-person account to a third-person, empirically driven model of reading.

Reading out of focus

Counterintuitive as they may seem, the definitions of reading that emerge from the narrator's encounters with the red book appear to align themselves with current scientific models. This is in two ways. First, in the emphasis they place on visual experiences, and second, in relying on a binary structure involving a shift of focus between an optical and a semantic apprehension of the word – a shift embedded in the reading process. Indeed, true to *Gestalt* theory, the Proustian model relies on a ground–figure relation, in which the figure vanishes to reveal the ground or the text morphs into context. In line with what neuroscientists discussing "attentional networks" describe as "a see-saw in the brain," Proust describes an alternation between visually focused and defocused states of reading (with the latter being more central to his "philosophy").[14] In articulating a space of reading in terms of a passage or switching mechanism between inside–outside, focus–periphery, he invites us in subtle but cogent ways to reconsider what might be too stark an opposition between attentive and "distracted" (or unconscious) aspects of reading. The Proustian model assumes, instead, parallel processes, so that alongside a focused, direct gaze of reading, which would seem to pin or *fix* the words on the page, there exists an indirect gaze, which in a different vocabulary might be described as dreaming, drifting, imagining as one reads.[15]

In his book *Reading in the Brain*, Stanislas Dehaene offers a detailed scientific description of the optical mechanics by which the reading eye meets this first and simplest of items, the word to be deciphered on the page on its way to making sense. As he explains, in reading a line of text, the eye moves across the page in a series of rapid jumps. Each time the gaze lands upon the page, the focusing center of the eye locks onto the corresponding unit of text (its focal range being limited to a mere 7 to 9 letters at a time), performing what is called an "eye fixation." In order for the brain to begin processing text, almost all words must be "fixated" in this way.[16]

Accordingly, the prime mover in the reading process is what we might call the *direct* gaze of the reader, formed when the eye and conscious mind unite into a single focusing force upon the text. What underwrites this model turns out to be a dual conception of bringing into focus, where optics joins up with semantics: as our eyes bring the words on the page into the literal focus of our vision, so our consciousness, in response, brings the ideas these words signify into the realm of understanding (*l'esprit* in Proust's vocabulary). This conception was indeed already present in Proust's earliest ruminations on reading, in the preface to his translation of John Ruskin's *Sesame and Lilies*. There, we encounter a quintessential image of the direct reading gaze as Proust offers his own memories of reading, as he puts it, "so lovingly" as a child (*ASB* 195; *CSB* 160).[17] The image he paints is a familiar one: a child with his nose buried in a book, his eyes locking eagerly onto one word after the next, while his mind, echoing the tight focus of his gaze, anxiously decodes the unfolding narrative.

Although this portrait of absorption – the child, nose in a book – is perhaps the emblematic expression of the traditional concept of reading understood as focusing, it overlooks a counter, yet fundamental component of the reading process, namely defocusing. Focusing on a word, which Dehaene shows to be a precondition for its mental processing, is in fact inseparable from an act of defocusing. As he notes, although while reading we have the impression from one moment to the next of perceiving around the eye's point of focus an entire page of legible text, in fact, tests show that the conscious brain is blind to what lies in the periphery and proves incapable of distinguishing the difference between a page that shows, beyond the point of fixation, a set of actual words or, as in the example he offers, "a string of x's."[18] The reader's direct gaze is like a spotlight that, in order to illuminate its point of focus, must create around it a contrasting darkness, necessarily plunging all extraneous stimuli into a defocused realm.

In his early preface to Ruskin, Proust lays out the first elements of his theory of peripheral reading, in which the reader's focus shifts from the words of the page to the life (i.e. the sensations and perceptions) that physically surrounds the book the reading child holds in hand. Not that this child is inattentive, it is merely that, in this early incarnation of the Proustian hero, he has shifted his focus from text to context (giving way to what is now an episode of his "inner life" or, in our vocabulary, a cognitive experience). Thus, in Proust's conception of what reading is like, while the narrative on the page unfolds for the direct gaze of eye and mind, a second, usually unremarked narrative emerges in the periphery of focus, quietly channeled through all five perceiving senses. In this way, he identifies for us a second, complementary gaze of reading: a defocused, *indirect* gaze, whose relative lack of conscious focus derives from the acute attention the reading child pays to the first. This second narrative rehearses the many tiny experiences that the Proustian reader mistakenly presumed to have "left behind without living them." These are of the order of sensory interferences or distractions (he calls them "vulgar impediments to a heavenly pleasure"): "the bothersome bee or sunbeam that forced us to look up from the page" or, particularly evocative of the way outside perceptions supplement a focused apprehension of words, the grandfather clock, "whose quiet remarks are void of meaning and do not, unlike human speech, substitute a different meaning for that of the words you are reading" (*ASB* 195, trans. mod.; *CSB* 160–161).

Reading is described here as a point of tension between focusing and defocusing, until, it turns out, Proust offers, in a passage that prepares his later novel, a *theory* for what will be shown with the red book. "Reading should have prevented us from perceiving all this as anything other than importunity," he writes in his preface,

> but, on the contrary, *so sweet is the memory* it engraved in us (and so much more precious to us now than what we read so lovingly at the time) that if, today, we chance to leaf through these books from the past, it is only as the sole *calendars* we have preserved of those bygone days, and in the hope of finding reflected in their pages the *houses and ponds* which no longer exist. (*ASB* 195, trans. mod.; *CSB* 160, our emphasis)

The lesson spelled out here, which finds its more radical presentation in the *Adoration*, is that the greater value of reading, as an act of bringing into focus, lies in its power, realized over time, to bring this second, defocused narrative into new, and more importantly, *meaningful* focus for the reader's understanding: by eventually revealing within it "memories much more valuable to us now than what we were reading with such passion at the time." In Proust's shorthand as already laid out in his preface to *Sesame and Lilies*, this operation involves a "mental optics" [optique des esprits], whereby "the end-point of their [books'] wisdom appears to us as only as the beginning of our own" (*ASB* 210; *CSB* 177). Reformulated in the current vocabulary of "mind," the Proustian reading experience highlights a passage from semantic operations to forms of cognition. Indeed a vision (that is, an optics) makes way for meaning (*esprit* or spirit being Proust's word for intelligence and sense). The Proustian inversion, whereby "obtrusive demands" reveal themselves, as if in after-image, as "happy memories" is of crucial significance, in identifying a switch-point or threshold where an optical process opens the way to cognition "semantically" – that is through reading.

In Proust's uncommonly long view of the reading experience, which does not end when a reader closes a book, but continues into these future years, the greatest work of reading appears to take place here, in the periphery of focus, as, through a slow process of accretion, the words in the books teach us how to attend to the world and decipher it. Thus in the pages devoted to the red book the subtle attention of an indirect gaze is what provides access to the riches of an inner world and what enables creation. As a forgotten world reemerges, prompted by the rediscovery of the book, it is indeed born "between the syllables" of the printed words and illuminated, poetically nourished even, by the experiences born in the dark periphery of his reading focus. The words of Sand's pages have vanished altogether to make way for the emergence in the mind's eye, as it were, of the new images.

The essayist had concluded, in his preface to the translation of Ruskin, that reading cannot be equated with mere consumption. When Ruskin argues that books provide us with necessary spiritual enrichment, Proust retorts that in feeding on them "as something material" or like "honey," we compromise "the intimate progress of our thought and the efforts of our own heart" (*ASB* 214; *CSB* 180–181). In the *Recherche* this intuition has been honed into a striking paradox, which says that unreading is the necessary condition for our encountering a world beyond the text, a world of artful memories for which we have names, names learned in the books that served as entry points into our inner world. This radical reversal of ground and figure alone is what enables a spiritual, quasi-mystical experience that inflects life with meaning and that supplants the child's perception with the storyteller's creation. Hence the Proustian lesson that the best and richest of reading occurs when, leaving the books we once read unopened, we attend to the after-image we inherit from them, that is, our memories. In helping decipher "life" or "reality" they serve as a ground to experiences that exist as figures in Proust's writing.[19] His mission as a reader is indeed to interpret or translate *ces vérités écrites à l'aide de figures* (i.e. "truths inscribed as figures"). There it would seem that the defocused reading gaze not only prepares us to attend to and "intentionally read" (that is perceive/remember) an outer world, it helps us create the script of what constitutes our individually coded world – where, in Proust's famous formulation, "every reader is, while he is reading, the reader of his own self" (6: 322; IV, 489).

Thresholds to a legible world

In developing the two narratives we have just identified (one born from a direct gaze of eye and mind, and the other emerging in the periphery of focus), Proust's model offers us a complex, though compelling description of how his young reader begins to make sense of words and things, namely in a crucial back and forth between a rudimentary level of reading (where the eye focuses on decoding a string of letters) and that moment, no more than a flicker, in which an inner eye or the mind applies itself to deciphering what exists invisibly "between the words." This intuition too finds its echo in recent scientific research. What Proust modestly calls, in these decisive pages, "les tâtonnements anciens de ma pensée" (in a phrase that recasts his inductive method as a set of progressive readjustments towards a discovery) relates to research on the semantic aspects of reading analyzed recently in two contrasting contexts.

We can only summarize the direction these take, by highlighting the results of two studies that build on experiments that bear on how semantic flexibility relates to focus. Reading, Proust had warned in his preface, "becomes dangerous . . . when, instead of awakening us to the personal life of the mind [esprit]," it "tends to take its place," in a statement that seems to warn us against the inflexibility of mere decoding (*ASB* 213; *CSB* 180). While conceptually, one would imagine (and Proust does) that the broadening of focus that occurs with the indirect gaze correlates with our ability to complicate as well as deepen the way we understand a text, it remains to be seen whether there is empirical evidence to warrant his idea. Is it true that mere decoding of words compromises the value of reading, and that interpolations and associations of the kind that occur in defocused reading are of crucial importance? Is it indeed important not merely to stick to the letter on the page, but to allow space for "diverse perceptual mental representations"?[20] What do scientists tell us?

An ambitious study by Michael Posner and his team shows how a directed reading gaze correlates with a form of cognitive rigidity: it found that once a target word such as *bear*, for example, is identified, upon prompting, as a dangerous animal, the result, as confirmed in PET scans, "is strong interference so that the likelihood of detecting a simultaneous target [i.e. another word belonging to the same category] is reduced."[21] Furthermore when primed with another related word, the reader overlooks any *semantic* flexibility that might exist within the target word: the "activation of alternative meanings of the same word tend to be suppressed," the authors declare.[22] The direct gaze of reading, intently fixated on decoding a specific lexical unit, thus seems to favor inflexibility as semantic play and unconscious associations.

In *Le nouvel inconscient* (see note 20), building on Posner's research, Lionel Naccache examines the indirect gaze, demonstrating how unconscious processes at work in subliminal reading correlate with cognitive flexibility, and, beyond, conceptual nimbleness. His results yield precious insights for the literary field, by offering in the scientific realm a first model for the metaphoric and metonymic generation of meaning that preoccupied structuralist thinkers such as Jakobson and Genette, as well as de Man, the poststructuralist. Naccache analyzed responses to individual words and demonstrated, through masked priming, how, for the unconscious reading gaze, a word like *bear*, which the direct gaze might limit to a dangerous animal, can reclaim its several semantic associations.[23] He describes these as "abstract mental representations that work silently but steadily to encompass an abundance of unconscious combinations."[24] His experiments involving subliminal reading reveal, at a demonstrable empirical level, what happens to meaning making when attention and focus are relaxed. They outline the first elements of what a process of generation of new meanings based on natural unconscious semantic associations might be like, with "abstract mental representations" replacing what in literature is called "figures." Though these experiments depend, in their methods, on visual promptings, they reveal – through these "directed" reading exercises involving spatial as well as very finely tuned temporal frameworks – how "conceptual knowledge finds its articulation."[25] Unaware of the stimulus with which it is presented (because of masked priming), the conscious reading mind is "distracted," in the experiments described by Naccache, into reinventing or perhaps even creating a new conceptual architecture of the world it inhabits.

To reiterate the pattern: whereas the direct gaze demands inflexibility at its point of focus, the indirect gaze, by contrast, nurtures flexibility – here the semantic flexibility – of a word's polysemous associations, as if allowing it to exist in an overdetermined, enriched state. Although the text beyond the eye's focus proves indiscernible to the *conscious* eye, a reading gaze is attending, all the while, to this dark periphery and taking it in – that is enfolding or embracing a potentially ever-growing context surrounding it. And as the literal gaze of the defocused eye, Naccache's subliminal reading gaze appears closely to prefigure the indirect reading gaze that Proust envisions on a macro level. The distracted, highly receptive child reads with all senses, taking in the phenomenal world that surrounds the text, before shaping it, imperceptibly over time, into the preserve of memories – parallel to the way in which the memory and imagination, as metaphorical gazes of the mind at work during the immediate experience of reading, quietly continue to reshape the narrative on the page.[26] From both perspectives, scientific and literary, the underlying assumption remains that the associative networks activated in situations of defocused reading will encourage semantic as well as conceptual growth.

This continual ability to reinterpret and reveal anew what has (or perhaps even *hasn't*) been consciously registered seems to be, at least in part, what interests Proust about the states of defocused attention that find their way into his writing. These might come about because a person is daydreaming, or because he is falling asleep, or because he is reading a book – or, as in the first scene of the *Recherche*, because he is falling asleep *while* reading a book. For Proust, there exists a subtle alliance between such experiences, an alliance that is suggested poetically in the overture of his fiction, in the way that the experience of falling asleep and the experience of reading coalesce and become confused within the narrator's somnolent mind: "my eyes closed so quickly," he explains, "that I did not have time to tell myself: 'I'm falling asleep.' And half an hour later the thought that it was time to look for sleep would awaken me; I would make as if to put away the book which I imagined was still in my hands, and to blow out the light" (1: 1; 1, 3).

What these defocused states of attention have in common is how they activate the indirect gaze, a gaze which for Proust is alone in possessing the power of *full* revelation – whether it reveals the wealth of imaginative possibilities inherent within the walls of a familiar room or, as in the preface to Ruskin, whether it discloses the entire world existing in all its rich and vibrant life just beyond the focus of his reading gaze. "There are perhaps no days of our childhood which we lived so *fully*," he writes, "as those we thought we had left behind without living them: the days we spent with a favorite book" (*ASB* 195, trans. mod.; *CSB* 160, our emphasis). Or again, we might think of another early scene of childhood reading from the *Recherche*, in which the buzzing housefly sensed in the periphery of the hero's reading reveals to him not merely the outside world that surrounds his reading, but as he insists, "the *entire panorama* of summer, which my senses," he continues, "if I had I been out walking, could have tasted and enjoyed only piecemeal" (1: 114; I, 82, our emphasis). All of these cases bring us back to the experimental situation in which a word, under the indirect gaze of the unconscious mind, is capable of revealing its full semantic potential.

* * *

But what of the red book then? It is part and parcel of Proust's compelling thesis, reminding us that the book we hold and touch holds a much richer promise than merely the words it carries – the promise of the creative generation of new meanings and, therefore, of a richer attunement to an outer reality. Nancy offers his own philosophical articulation of what Proust has shown us, when he speaks of

> the Idea of the book . . . as containing nothing less than its own proliferation, its multiplication, and always . . . the silent or eloquent advice . . . that is an invitation to throw it away, to abandon it. In fact reading does not lead to more reading, but to everything else, to what is sometimes called action and sometimes experience where we rub against the illegible real.[27]

Taking another look, both near and distant, at the exquisite and evocative pages of the *Recherche* built around the closed volume of a boy's bittersweet childhood, we wish to privilege the book's aesthetic potential – in returning to the claim that *Champi* contains as well as nourishes "writing." Proust's *tâtonnements* have led him to choose, with unerring flair, the very object, *François le Champi*, which could play the role of a transitional object that inspires creativity. What the object with its reddish cover promises is indeed not merely memories – or if memories then in their prospective, future oriented qualities – so that a passionate encounter with a book can become creative as well as instructive. For this to happen, however, the sweet honey of Sand's words had to be forgotten, for fear of halting the hero's progress towards becoming a narrator and author of his own created story.[28] What lies inside the red cover – a mental universe that Proust can only describe figuratively and spatially – helps the child cross the threshold to a world that lies beyond its pages and words: a world made of "wonder" and "rich illuminations" (6: 288, trans. mod.; IV, 466).

While the Proustian experience of the red book is naturally couched in the recognizable terms of aesthetic modernity, its meaning may well extend to other spheres and speak to our present moment. Proust's allegory elucidates a process of understanding that begins at the prompting of a book, yet reaches far beyond in triggering the vital work of imagination and memory – a work that occurs, as Naccache helped us see with the analogue that the science of reading provides, *subliminally*. As the child opens a book, it finds not only words, but a first alphabet made of images such as "houses and lakes," a "bee" and a "grandfather's clock," "a brisk wind and a bright sun" as well as "happy memories" and, even, a "calendar," and of course "Combray," where it heralds the birth of a writer. It is, in other words, the crucial instrument of a "spiritual" or, we would say *mental optics* that nourishes our intellectual, as well as creative relationship to the world. The first lesson in reading, in *Du côté de chez Swann*, takes place when a maternal figure brings a book to the child, and the last, when Proust reminds us, in closing this episode in *Le Temps retrouvé*, that the mental and emotional space of a child's reading connected to the book lies in the safekeeping of an ageing bibliophile. "I was too afraid," he writes, "that the child who for the first time deciphered [déchiffra] its title in the little bedroom at Combray, the child, not recognizing its voice [accent], would not listen to its summons [appel] and would remain for ever buried in oblivion" (6: 289, trans. mod.; IV, 466).[29] If reading *between* Proust's words means being open to their contemporary accent, might we be right in hearing in their urgency not only a call to preserve a child's "sacred pleasure" of reading, but also a plea not to forget that simple object, the book – the book with its singular color, "feel," or grain, as well as all the synesthetic experiences it holds?

NOTES

1 Literally, a lesson about things, and the French version of "show and tell."

2 Jean-Luc Nancy, *On the Commerce of Thinking: Of Books and Bookstores*, trans. David Wills (New York: Fordham University Press, 2009), 41.

3 "Unreading" is the name Adam Watt gives to this gesture, in his indispensable study of Proust and reading, *Reading in Proust's* À la recherche: *"le délire de la lecture"* (Oxford: Clarendon Press, 2009). Also significant for the theoretical articulation of this piece is Garrett Stewart's analysis of "the nuances of avoided literality on the painted page" in *The Look of Reading: Book, Painting, Text* (University of Chicago Press, 2006), 64.

4 Nancy, *On the Commerce*, 3.

5 For groundbreaking interdisciplinary work on such aesthesis, see Elaine Scarry, *Dreaming by the Book* (New York: Farrar, Straus & Giroux, 1999).

6 See Evelyne Ender, *Architexts of Memory: Literature, Science, and Autobiography* (Ann Arbor: University of Michigan Press, 2005), particularly chapters 1 and 6, and also page 141.

7 Nancy, *On the Commerce*, 41.

8 We owe to Proust, writes Roland Barthes, "a comprehensive system for reading the world . . . an encounter with a concrete present [une actualité] and . . . a wisdom, a knowledge of 'life' and its language." Cited by Adam Watt, *Reading in Proust*, 157 (our translation).

9 References in this section are to the "scene of the kiss" (1: 36–58; 1, 27–43).

10 For a wide-ranging and very astute discussion of the mother's role in dispensing literacy, see the chapter entitled "The Mother's Mouth," 25–69, in Friedrich A. Kittler's *Discourse Networks 1800/1900*, trans. Michael Metteer with Chris Cullens (Stanford University Press, 1990).

11 Quoting the words Henry James uses, in *What Maisie Knew*, for his heroine.

12 "To learn by heart is to afford the text or music an indwelling clarity and life force," writes George Steiner in *Real Presences* (University of Chicago Press, 1991, 9), a book whose title, like Proust's *Adoration perpétuelle*, evokes spiritual and theological notions. While the Proustian text undeniably connects reading to the kind of interiorization implicit in "learning by heart," the phrase is not to be taken literally in our interpretation. "The book . . . comports itself as an envelope of interiority," writes Nancy (*On the Commerce*, 15).

13 Peter Schwenger, "Writing Hypnagogia," in *At the Borders of Sleep: On Liminal Literature* (Minneapolis: University of Minnesota Press, 2012), 40.

14 These are Daniel Levitin's formulations, as he summarizes his research under the (catchy) headline "Hit the Reset Button in Your Brain" (*New York Times*, August 9, 2014).

15 Here again, see Scarry, *Dreaming by the Book*.

16 Stanislas Dehaene, *Reading in the Brain: The Science and Evolution of a Human Invention* (London and New York: Viking, 2009), 12–18.

17 Later in his preface, Proust discloses the identity of this "primer," Théophile Gautier's adventure novel *Le Capitaine Fracasse* (1863), while developing his description of the transfer between inner and outer impressions that takes place when reading (*ASB* 208; *CSB* 175).

18 Deheane, *Reading in the Brain*, 15–16.

19 Figures as (a) representations or forms, in philosophy; (b) as images or outlines, in an epistemological context; (c) as part of a tropological system and thus in a rhetorical sense.

20 Quoted from page 7 of an unpublished translation (by Yulia Nazvanova, Nora Carr, and Evelyne Ender) of part of the chapter "Comprendre le sens sans en avoir conscience, mythe ou réalité?," from Lionel Naccache's *Le nouvel inconscient: Freud, Christophe Colomb des neurosciences* (Paris: Odile Jacob, 2006), 101–119. Subsequent references are to this unpublished translation. Thanks to the author for granting us permission to translate these pages.

21 Michael I. Posner, Stephen E. Peterson, Peter T. Fox, and Marcus E. Raichle, "Localization of Cognitive Operations in the Human Brain," *Science* 240:4859 (June 17, 1988), 1630.

22 *Ibid.*, 1628.

23 In Naccache's experiment involving masked priming, prior to being prompted to respond to a word clearly visible on the screen (defined as a "target word"),

the reader is exposed to another word for a time span that is shortened to such a degree that conscious apprehension of this word becomes impossible.

24 Naccache, *Nouvel inconscient*, trans. Nazvanova, Carr, and Ender, 10.

25 See "Priming," in Gregory L. Richard, ed., *The Oxford Companion to the Mind* (Oxford University Press, 2004), 754. See also Maryanne Wolf on the subject of our "interpretative responses to what we read," in *Proust and the Squid: The Story and Science of the Reading Brain*, reprint edn. (New York: Harper Perennial, 2008), 156–157.

26 We owe the articulation of this paragraph (and in fact of this whole section) to the inspired and unfinished phenomenological analysis developed by Maurice Merleau-Ponty in *The Visible and the Invisible: Studies in Phenomenology and Existential Philosophy*, trans. Alphonso Lingis (Chicago: Northwestern University Press, 1969).

27 Nancy, *On the Commerce*, 41–42.

28 "Honey" that lost its attraction in the author's case, who writes defensively in a letter of 1909, "Do not think that I like George Sand" (*Corr* IX, 225); "the book was not a very extraordinary one, it was *François le Champi*" says his narrator (6: 282; IV, 462).

29 Behind Proust's use of a *passé simple* [déchiffra] lies the idea of an event. Luc Fraisse writes: "In this dogmatic novel . . . an episode, a season, a day do no less than stage the precise moment when an intellectual enigma makes a first appearance and when, miraculously, they provide the outline to an aesthetic solution." *La correspondance de Proust, son statut dans l'oeuvre, l'histoire de son édition* (Besançon: Annales littéraires de l'Université de Franche-Comté, 1998), 185, our translation.

PART V

Creative identities

CHAPTER 15

Proust and the Marx Brothers

Elisabeth Ladenson

In the midst of all the hoopla of the centennial celebrations of Proust's work, long ago firmly canonized as a great work of modernism, the sheer strangeness of his novel tends to get lost. And of all the bizarre aspects of *À la recherche du temps perdu*, one of the oddest is hidden in plain view, in the relation between the author and his magnum opus. This is at least to some extent because – despite the book having from its inception (not without a certain measure of justification) been read as some version of an autobiography, the narrator, for instance (also with some measure of justification) routinely referred to as "Marcel" – such readings have for some decades been dismissed as theoretically naïve. Let us therefore start from the beginning: the half-Jewish, homosexual, and famously snobbish author does not merely, in the service of universal appeal, efface his own repudiated characteristics from the gentile, heterosexual, and self-proclaimedly non-snob narrator of his semi-autobiographical novel. He also takes care to distribute them among notably abject secondary characters. In particular, the work features three characters, Bloch, Charlus, and Legrandin, who incarnate, respectively, Jewishness, homosexuality (or "inversion"), and snobbery. These three characters, uncoincidentally, are also all more or less failed artists.

Discussions of art and artists in Proust's writing tend necessarily to concentrate on such familiar and relevant aspects as Vermeer's "little patch of yellow wall" and the like, when they are not dealing directly with the novel's triumvirate of artists, Bergotte, Vinteuil, and Elstir, who together cover literature, music, and painting. The novel's depictions of these artists and works, real and fictional, have been extensively mined by commentators for their *mise en abyme* implications in terms of Proust's own aesthetic vision. Much has also been made of the portrait of Swann as a failed artist, who clearly represents what happens to someone whose aesthetic sensibility and knowledge are diverted from the production not only of art but of critical work – and from Proust's early hesitations between the genres of novel and essay at the inception of what was to become the *Recherche*, we can see that he considers criticism to be an entirely viable form of artistic production. Swann never does manage to write the study of Vermeer he has been working on, or at least thinking about working on, for years: ever since the text can remember.

Swann – a Jew, but not the same sort of vulgar Jew as Bloch, figures alongside Bergotte, Vinteuil, and Elstir, in the novel's great cautionary tale, as an example of what could have befallen the protagonist if he had continued to fritter away his life in pursuit of social and erotic satisfaction without actually getting down to the business of making something: that is, if he had failed to become the narrator. All this has been discussed ad infinitum, or at least ad nauseam. What has attracted far less critical attention, in terms of Proust's take on the arts and artists, is that his novel contains, besides the successful artists Bergotte, Vinteuil, and Elstir and the dilettante would-be critic Swann, the alternative trio of less exalted, semi- or para-artistic figures, Bloch, Charlus, and Legrandin.

The extent to which these three figures are also, to greater or lesser extents, artists, has not generally been remarked upon by commentators, and indeed is downplayed in the novel itself. So intensely are these characters associated with their respective abject representative identities that it is easy to forget, for instance, that Legrandin is an apparently prolific published novelist in addition to being, in his day job, an engineer. Bloch ends up being a successful playwright, after years of trying, and after having changed his name to Jacques du Rozier (a career clearly inspired at least in part by that of the prominent playwright Francis de Croisset, né Franz Wiener). Both Legrandin and Bloch are depicted as being relatively successful writers, and yet in neither case is the work itself displayed or even discussed; its existence is merely alluded to from time to time. Legrandin is eventually revealed to be not just a snob but an invert as well. Bloch is also a snob – not merely a Jew but a vulgar Jewish parvenu (that is, the very opposite of Swann). Legrandin is depicted as the "St. Sebastian of snobbery" (1: 180; 1, 127). It seems, therefore, that we may safely conclude, both in his case and that of Bloch, that the point is not art for art's sake, but its extravagant contrary: not even art for money's sake, which is what has traditionally figured as the opposite of art for art's sake, but art for snobbery's sake. A snobbish Jew with literary pretensions is of course precisely what the young Proust was himself suspected of being, on the strength of his salon-haunting youth and flower-bedecked debut volume *Les Plaisirs et les Jours*, the fatuity of which (of both of which) was instrumental in his initial rejection by the *Nouvelle Revue Française*. André Gide made this entirely clear in a letter apologizing for not having considered *Du côté de chez Swann* seriously in his capacity as editor for the *NRF*, in which he explains that he had mistaken Proust for "a snob, a *mondain* amateur" (*Corr* XIII, 50).

As for Charlus, he too is an artist of sorts – not merely an *artiste du mal* in some Baudelairean sense, martyr to his vice as Swann is to his dilettantism, but also a "*nature*," a natural at the piano, who explains to Morel that he had been destined for a great career but abandoned music at an early age: "and everything else, for that matter," he adds, before telling his musical protégé that he must play a piece as though he had composed it (4: 555–556; III, 397–398). No explicit reason is given for the abandonment of this great potential. He seems simply to have renounced everything as his attention is entirely taken up with the management of what Eve Kosofsky Sedgwick so aptly calls his "glass closet."[1] In all three cases, these characters, artists all, are too busy incarnating their respective authorial "spoiled identities," to use the sociologist Erving Goffman's great phrase – homosexuality, snobbery, and a certain kind of Jewishness – to fully embody their art.[2] Their art, it seems, is contingent. Charlus has abandoned music among other roads not taken in a life wholly subsumed by *mondanité* and inversion-fuelled insanity. Bloch and Legrandin, who have doggedly pursued their literary careers, appear to have produced ample bodies of work the worth of which is implicitly dismissed in the novel as unworthy of depiction, presumably on grounds of middlebrow crowd-pleasing mediocrity.

Why, then, did Proust bother to make them artists in the first place? Why include this alternative trio of would-be/semi-/para-artistic figures? He takes care to endow the three emblematic figures of the vulgar Jew, the flamboyant invert, and the tormented snob, with artistic gifts and mediocre accomplishments which make of them embodiments of what the author will have managed, by dint of writing the novel, narrowly but definitively to avoid becoming. Whereas Vinteuil, Elstir, and Bergotte – heterosexual gentiles all – represent various modes of truly great artistic production, this triumvirate represents various modes of failure-by-faint-success. In other words: if Swann is what the narrator could have but did not turn into, these three all together are (among other things) the equivalent for Proust himself. Not only does the semi-autobiographical narrator belong, at least by his own account, to none of these identities, it is also noteworthy that there is no single character who embodies all three at once. Bloch and Legrandin represent two each, although differently so. The former is depicted from the start as being once a Jew and a snob. The latter, the novel's flagship snob, is eventually revealed to have been an invert the whole time (we have been given hints of this from the start in his quasi-amorous interest in the boy hero in the opening section, but by the time it is openly acknowledged, thousands of pages later, his snobbery has calmed down, subsumed by his inversion and his social ascent). Charlus is a different story. Because he is both the consummate invert and the consummate aristocrat, the Baron occupies the farthest possible point in the novel's social topography from both Jewishness and snobbery (according to the Proustian definition of snobbery, which is predicated on upward pretension rather than downward dismissal).

Of course, all this is much more complicated than what I have just suggested, by the incomplete parallelisms among these three identities, and also, especially, by the extent to which all three identities, as embodied by these characters, are themselves centrally characterized by repudiation. One learns to recognize a snob, for instance, by his energetic denunciations of snobbery and unerring "snobdar." (What Sartre says of anti-Semitism applies with even more ferocious exactitude to the snob, in Proust's world: the snob is defined by anti-snobbery.)[3] Similarly, an invert is identifiable by his hyperbolic virility, prurient interest in inversion, and encyclopedic knowledge of his fellow inverts. And accordingly, a Jew (or at least, again, a certain kind of Jew, since the novel's most famous Jew, Swann, is hardly a Jew at all) makes his presence known by his anti-Semitic tirades as well as his ability to identify members of his tribe.

It is at this juncture that the Marx Brothers intertext proves so immensely helpful in any attempt to understand the Proustian enterprise. I will readily concede that the conjunction announced in my title is a somewhat unlikely one. If one were to attempt a Venn diagram of the subject, the overlapping area would be somewhat restricted. It would contain, as far as I can tell, five elements:

1. Jewishness (indeed, the Marx *paterfamilias* was a Jew from Alsace, known accordingly as "Frenchy");
2. Relatedly, an insistent yet insistently underplayed theme of Jewishness relegated to the periphery and which in neither case – doubtless in large part because relegated to the periphery – has prevented the appeal to an improbably wide international as well as national audience, with eventual canonicity in both cases in their respective genres;
3. Humor;
4. A prominent moustache.

As for the comical aspects of Proust and the Marx Brothers, they are highly divergent in kind as well as in prominence of reputation. Proust is not primarily known as a comical author, and yet the *Recherche* is in fact very funny. The extent to which this is at once true and yet apparently somewhat counterintuitive, so great is the division of genres persisting in our culture (in the face of all evidence to the contrary), was brought home to me a few years ago when a Columbia freshman confessed to me that he planned someday to read Proust. He announced this intention in much the same rueful and slightly embarrassed tone in which he might have mentioned harboring the ambition of someday scaling the Empire State Building armed only with a grappling hook. I pulled a copy of *Swann's Way* off my shelf and handed it to him. Several months later, during the summer, I received an email reporting that he had read the volume and was planning on forging ahead to the next volume. He had just one question: he had been surprised to find it funny in parts, and wanted to know whether this was warranted or whether he had perhaps been reading the book incorrectly. I had the impression that he was prepared, if necessary, to reread the volume without finding it funny, if that was what it took to appreciate the greatness of the great work.

In short, Proust shares many strong comical elements with the Marx Brothers, even if their respective modes of humor are very different, as well as their reputations. I am sure no one has ever asked permission before allowing himself to laugh at *A Night at the Opera*. This brings me to the fifth and final element in my Venn diagram confluence. Many commentators, from Serge Doubrovsky and Gérard Genette to the contestants in the notorious Monty Python "Summarize Proust Competition," have attempted, with varying degrees of success, to render the gist of the *Recherche* in a single sentence. None, I believe, has come closer than Groucho Marx, who in a telegram to the Friars Club famously captured the very essence of Proustian psychology with the observation that he didn't want to belong to any club that would have him as a member.[4] This neo-Marxian dictum accounts for almost everything that happens over the course of the novel's 3,000-odd pages. In particular, in addition to the protagonist, it is the very motor which animates Bloch, Legrandin, and Charlus, our three pseudo- or para- or would-be artists. It is central to the workings of both inversion and snobbery, as depicted by Proust (or his narrator), in that both these phenomena are predicated on impossible desire.

Proust chooses the term *inversion* over *homosexuality*, which etymologically implies a desire for sameness. The invert, in this scheme of things, desires only those who necessarily cannot desire him; by definition, that is to say, the invert desires a heterosexual man. Similarly, the object of the snob's desire is a *mondain*, a Guermantes, for instance, who can only be repelled by the attentions of a snob. This is why when both Bloch and Legrandin at various points accuse the protagonist of being a snob he responds evasively or dismissively, but reflects that the only truly appropriate – and thus completely (socially) inappropriate – reply, which he is too polite to utter, would be the Grouchesque line "if I were really a snob I wouldn't be talking to you." Of course, just as it would (explicitly) if uttered in a Marx Brothers film, this form of fantasy response cannot avoid implicitly marking the hero as a snob. Snobbery, unlike either inversion or Jewishness, entails a hall-of-mirrors effect which makes it, I would argue, much more problematic and abject than these other two phenomena. Indeed, it becomes the ur-abject identity in Proust's world, bound up with and on some level subsuming the other two in a sort of apotheosis of unspeakable abjection. (Neither in Proust's world nor in our own can we imagine a Snob Pride parade.)

Jewishness operates somewhat differently from snobbery and inversion in the novel, while still offering many parallels. Woody Allen made Groucho Marx's club aphorism famous by quoting it in *Annie Hall* to explain his love life,[5] and, accordingly, the most obvious application in the *Recherche* involves the protagonist's ardent pursuit of what he calls "fugitive beings" ["êtres de fuite"] (5: 113; III, 599) in the erotic realm (theme song: "Hello, I must be going").[6] Nonetheless, Marx's sentiment more directly referred to the well-documented exclusion of Jews in early- to mid-century America. The Friars Club to which the telegram was addressed was (and still is) a comedians' association based in New York, most of whose members were Jews, because most comedians were Jews. In Los Angeles, the Marx family spent a great deal of time at the Hillcrest Country Club, which had been founded in response to the anti-Semitic policies at the other clubs, and which Groucho referred to as "the only country club in all of greater Los Angeles that will accept Talmudic scholars such as myself as members."[7] He also reports applying for membership at another country club, to be told that he could join on condition that he not use the swimming pool, as it would make the other members uncomfortable. His reply: "well my daughter is only half Jewish, can she wade in up to her knees?"[8]

And here we come to the great divide between Proust and the Marx Brothers. Proust's approach to the difficult and crucial subject of half-Jewishness was tellingly different. Indeed this is something he does not joke about; the author's mixed origin gives rise to an extremely vexed relation to the subject, and all humor in this regard looks remarkably like anti-Semitic humor. But of course this is hardly surprising, since it is in the nature of what is called "Jewish humor" to morph seamlessly into anti-Semitic humor, according to who is telling the joke. This is to a certain extent, of course, true of all humor, and perhaps indeed all communication, within minority groups. Members of such groups have long appropriated terms of denigration for their own ends, and the offensiveness quotient of potentially offensive jokes about particular identities depends to a very great extent on who is telling them, and to whom. Jewish humor, which is notoriously predicated on self-deprecation, is particularly implicated in this phenomenon, with the result that many, if not most, if not all, of the stories in any given anthology of Jewish humor may just as easily be construed as anti-Semitic jokes if told by the wrong humorist in the wrong context.

Proust himself plays with this problem at a number of points, most notably in *À l'ombre des jeunes filles en fleurs* when his narrator overhears a stream of invective about how the Jews are overrunning the Norman coast, complete with parodic Yiddishisms, emanating from a bathing hut on the beach at Balbec, only to find that the anti-Semite in question is none other than the hero's old friend Bloch (2: 433–434; II, 97). What exactly are we to make of this? The passage would seem to bear some odd relation to the hall-of-mirrors effect alluded to earlier in terms of snobbery, in which a snob is someone who denies being a snob. The hero denies being a snob, for instance, in a way that seems designed to exempt him from this implication, and yet, bizarrely enough, he was framed by the author himself in this regard. In 1920 the influential (and frequently quite nasty) critic Paul Souday characterized *Le Côté de Guermantes* as "mostly filled, like the three preceding [volumes], with the topic dearest to the heart of M. Marcel Proust . . . snobbery," and further observed that if the protagonist is not precisely the author, he resembles him "like a brother."[9] Proust replied with a vehemently indignant letter, insisting that Souday must know that he himself had known women like the Duchesse de Guermantes all his life, and that if he had chosen to write a novel depicting snobbery "from the inside" it was for this very reason. Snobbish authors, he added, had always tended to portray snobbery from the outside, in order to pretend that they were not themselves snobs, whereas the fact that he had written from the point of view of a snob proved on the contrary that he was not one (*Corr* XIX, 574). But of course according to his own logic, this tortured vituperation à la Legrandin (and let us not forget that it is the latter who introduces both the theme of snobbery and the logic of repudiation in "Combray" when he inveighs against snobbery and identifies it as Saint

Paul's unpardonable sin against the Holy Spirit, a reference to Paul's Epistle to the Hebrews [1: 92; 1, 67]) would itself seem to be a clear declaration of *snobitude*.

The parallel between Jewishness and snobbery in the novel breaks down at a certain point, because they are not the same sort of identities. For one thing, no one identifies as a snob; there is no positive identity. Snobbery, unlike inversion, may well be something resembling a religion, but it is in no way an ethnicity. (As for the term *race*, as in *la race des tantes*[10] [the race of the aunties], it is so elastic during this period as to lead to endless formulations on the order of *la race des bourgeois*.) But it also seems to be true that Jewishness, as embodied by Proust – not his narrator, that is, but the author in the text, or rather the author in relation to his text – ends up functioning somewhat like snobbery. Proust's letter to Souday, maintaining that the fact that his narrator is a snob is somehow proof that he himself is not, should be read not only in the context of Legrandin's later mutation but also in conjunction with the author's famous letter to Robert de Montesquiou explaining that he could not join him in anti-Semitic tirades during the Dreyfus Affair because although he himself is a Catholic like his father and brother, his mother is Jewish, with the result that he is not free to hold the opinions he might otherwise have shared (*Corr* II, 66). Of course, the pronouncement "I am not Jewish but my mother is" sharply recalls those T-shirts that used to be sold during the 1990s with the ironic slogan "I'm not gay, but my boyfriend is," given the traditional definition of a Jew. Here is the central problem for Proust (as well as his reader) in terms of Jewishness: he is not half-Jewish; rather, he is entirely Jewish because his mother was Jewish, and he is also entirely non-Jewish because he was baptized.

Proust's sense of humor seems to break down around this issue; while the novel contains a number of half-Jews (Gilberte, for starters), they are all Jewish on the father's side; no character has a Jewish mother and Catholic father. What "Jewish humor" the novel includes is delegated to members of the Bloch clan. But any discussion of this issue must acknowledge that it was no laughing matter at the time of the Dreyfus Affair. Or rather it was a laughing matter, but not for the Jews themselves. When I was in graduate school I landed the job of translating all the pun- and esoteric-reference-based cartoon captions, board-game copy, and the like for the New York Jewish Museum's blockbuster Dreyfus Affair exhibit in 1987. This thankless task[11] led me to discover that the somber episode in French history was in fact the occasion for a great deal of humor, all of it completely untranslatable, and none of it Jewish in the Marx Brothers sense.

What, then, is Jewish humor in the Marx Brothers sense, when considered in the context of Proust? Like *À la recherche du temps perdu*, films such as *Duck Soup*, *Horse Feathers*, and *A Night at the Opera* are centrally concerned with class distinctions, and it is one of the peculiarities of both these bodies of work that their protagonists, Proust's hero and Groucho's characters, S. Quentin Quayle, Otis B. Driftwood, Captain Spalding, and, especially, Professor Quincy Adams Wagstaff, president of Huxley College – hyperbolic (if nominal) Gentiles all, let us not forget – manage to gain admittance, in ways that are not entirely clear, to the most exclusive of clubs. It is what happens once they are there that is so different. Proust's protagonist is there to observe, Groucho's character to let Harpo and Chico in and then destroy the place from inside. I would like to conclude by suggesting that the unlikely couple played by Proust and the Marx Brothers is in fact represented within the *Recherche* itself, by Swann and Bloch, the decorous, assimilated dandy and his crazy, vulgar counterpart. And that finally, one of the enduring, if generally unacknowledged, appeals of the novel is the spectacle, which does indeed make us uncomfortable, of Proust in the swimming pool, perpetually wading in up to the knees.

NOTES

1 Eve Kosofsky Sedgwick, *Epistemology of the Closet* (Berkeley: University of California Press, 1990), 228.
2 Erving Goffman, *Stigma: Notes on the Management of Spoiled Identity* (Englewood Cliffs, NJ: Prentice-Hall, 1963).
3 Jean-Paul Sartre, *Anti-Semite and Jew*, trans. George J. Becker (New York: Schocken, 1948), 143.
4 Groucho Marx, *Groucho and Me* (New York: Random House, 1959), 321.
5 *Annie Hall*, dir. Woody Allen, Rollins-Joffe Productions, 1977.
6 Sung by Groucho Marx in the 1930 Marx Brothers film *Animal Crackers*, this famous song has had a robust afterlife, providing the title for a 1978 biography of Marx by Charlotte Chandler (Garden City, NY: Doubleday, 1978), as well as that of a 2012 romantic comedy film (dir. Todd Louiso, Skyscraper Films).
7 Cited in Ron Goulart, *Groucho Marx, King of the Jungle* (New York: Thomas Dunne Books/St. Martin's Minotaur, 2005), 58–59.
8 Cited in John Steele Gordon, "The Country Club," *American Heritage* 41:6 (Fall 1990), 75–84.
9 Paul Souday, "Marcel Proust: Le Côté de Guermantes," *Le Temps*, November 4, 1920. This review was later integrated to Souday's biographical essay *Marcel Proust* (Paris: Simon Kra, 1927), 29–38.

10 The title of an early draft (*Cahier* 6, 1909) of what would become the first section of *Sodome et Gomorrhe*. See the Pléiade edition (III, 919 and 1796–1797).

11 Or rather almost thankless: my name does appear in the catalogue (of which I was given a copy), buried in a huge list of names in the acknowledgements. *The Dreyfus Affair: Art, Truth, and Justice*, ed. Norman L. Kleeblatt (Berkeley: University of California Press, 1987).

CHAPTER 16

Proust, Jews, and the arts

Maurice Samuels

Different critics have labeled Proust's art "Jewish" for different reasons. It was Proust's use of *language* that appeared "Semitic" to Céline, who compared his "tortuous, arabescoid, confused mosaic" style to the Talmud.[1] For the American critic Edmund Wilson, on the other hand, the *Recherche* seemed "really very un-French and rather akin to Jewish literature" because of its *tone*, the "animated humor of the social scenes" and "the capacity for apocalyptic moral indignation of the classical Jewish prophet."[2] Hannah Arendt and other more recent scholars have called attention to the Jewish *subject matter* of the novel, especially Proust's astute rendering of the vicissitudes of Jewish social integration during the period of the Dreyfus Affair.[3]

What these commentators fail to mention, however, is that the novel itself is very much concerned with the relationship of Jewishness to art. And this relationship in the novel is highly problematic. Whereas all of the central Jewish characters devote themselves in some manner to art – Swann is a connoisseur of painting; Bloch writes; Rachel acts – there are no Jews among the novel's "real" artists, those with "genius" like Bergotte, La Berma, Elstir, or Vinteuil. As Allesandro Piperno has recently noted, Proust's Jews are dabblers and dilettantes. They are superficial and lack originality. Even worse, they use art for their own social advancement.[4] If Jewishness and art are linked for Proust, it seems to be to the detriment of the latter. Indeed, as I will show, Proust's depiction of the Jewish artist echoes some of the worst anti-Semitic stereotypes of the nineteenth century. This might seem strange in a writer whose own views on art were so shaped by his Jewish mother and grandmother and who was after all a committed Dreyfusard and a sharp critic of anti-Semitism. In what follows, I want to explore this paradox to suggest that in taking up the vexed question of Jews and art, a very specific subset of the so-called "Jewish Question" in the late nineteenth century, Proust touches on questions central to his own vexed identity as a half Jew and aspiring artist.

The debate over Jews and art first took shape in France during the July Monarchy when Jewish composers like Fromental Halévy and Giacomo Meyerbeer, and actresses like Rachel Félix, began to gain a kind of fame comparable to the Jewish bankers of the period, such as the Rothschilds. "The Jew is increasingly invasive in art as he is in commerce," wrote the Romantic author Petrus Borel in an attack on an 1844 production of *Phèdre* at the Comédie-Française starring Rachel.[5] To Borel and other anti-Semitic critics, a Jewish actress might be able to speak the words of Racine, but she could never really embody their spirit, which is fundamentally Christian. Richard Wagner, of course, would make a very similar case in his 1850 tract *Judaism and Music*, devoted in large measure to attacking the influence of Meyerbeer. "Our whole European art and civilization," Wagner writes, "have remained to the Jew a foreign tongue."[6] Wagner insists that the Jewish artist's talent expresses itself in a kind of cold virtuosity: he may be able to mimic prior artistic styles and even set current trends with dazzling ingenuity, but as an outsider to European culture, he cannot tap into its sources of true inspiration.[7] The Jew can only ever produce a kind of plagiarized, vulgarized, imitative art lacking in real depth of feeling.

Édouard Drumont recycled many of these same accusations in his best-selling 1886 screed *La France Juive* [*Jewish France*]. Historians have remembered this text for its attack on Jewish financiers, but Drumont targets Jewish artists with equal ferocity. "The Semite has no creative faculty,"[8] Drumont declares in the introduction; "In art, they [the Jews] have created no original, no powerful or touching figure, no master work; they only consider what sells."[9] The Jew is too calculating, too materialist, too self-interested to produce anything but the kind of degraded art that, to the detriment of France, has become all the rage in Parisian theaters, opera houses, and newspapers.[10] According to Drumont, Jewish composers like Meyerbeer and Offenbach are nothing but German spies whose mission it is to undermine French values with their cunning parodies and sacrilegious farces. "When did the ancestors of these men pray with ours? In what corner of what village or town are to be found their family tombs? . . . How are they attached to the traditions of our race?"[11] he asks. Like Wagner, Drumont denies that Jews can ever do more than mimic a certain Parisian jargon, producing art with a surface appeal but no depth. To create art with roots, "you have to have sucked as an infant the wine of the fatherland, be a true product of its soil."[12]

Drumont's attacks did not, however, go unanswered. In 1893, Anatole Leroy-Beaulieu, a history professor at the École libre des sciences politiques, published *Israël chez les nations* [*Israel Among the Nations*], a remarkable defense of the Jews that moves beyond the tepid liberal pieties that had constituted the essence of well-meaning French philo-Semitism for a century – the Jews are corrupt and degenerate but we Christians have made them this way – to challenge the very basis of anti-Semitic calumny.[13] According to Leroy-Beaulieu, the Jews are not corrupt and degenerate at all, or at least no more so than the French and other modern Europeans in whose midst they dwell. "Is there a Jewish spirit [un esprit juif], which is to say do the Jews have moral and social tendencies that are radically different from ours? . . . This . . . strikes me as doubtful."[14] For the liberal professor, the Jew's supposed materialism and venality is not innate, but rather the product of the democratic transformation of society. These are modern traits, not Jewish ones. And it follows from this that the supposed degradation of modern art cannot be ascribed to the Jews either. How else to explain the fact, he asks, that France has the most degraded, the most vile art of all and one of the smallest populations of Jews in Europe? True, he admits, in those especially vile and degraded genres in which France excels – such as the operetta – Jewish poets and composers are over-represented. But Jews like Offenbach, Hector Crémieux, and Ludovic Halévy are merely taking their cue from their Parisian surroundings. "Here, as usual, the Jews did not set the beat, they only joined the dance."[15]

Turning now to the *Recherche*, it seems at first as if Proust wants to enter this debate over the Jews and art on the side of the anti-Semites. Each of his artistic Jews embodies one or more of the negative qualities imputed to the race by Borel, Wagner, and Drumont. Let's start with Swann, a collector and connoisseur known for his exquisite taste, who helps cultivate the young narrator's artistic sensibilities by giving him reproductions of great paintings and praising performers like La Berma. But as the narrator realizes early on in the novel, Swann's engagement with art remains stubbornly, vehemently superficial. Not only does he not himself produce any art, he also refuses to discuss the deep meaning of a work. Even his preferences for certain artists are always qualified by imaginary scare quotes so as not to implicate himself through judgment. "He appeared unwilling even to risk having an opinion, and to be at his ease only when he could furnish, with meticulous accuracy, some precise detail" (1: 136; I, 97), the narrator observes. One can almost feel Wagner's gorge rise at the way the Jewish dandy eschews depth for superficial facts and forsakes the kind of personal engagement with art that is the basis of true originality.

The narrator explains this refusal as a reaction against the overblown Romantic sensibilities of the prior generation, but he also perceives that Swann's attitude toward art reflects a social calculation designed to ingratiate him with the highest levels of the aristocracy. The narrator remarks that "Swann's wit was highly appreciated" (1:484; I, 335) in the circle of the Duchesse de Guermantes. Swann's *esprit* [wit or spirit] is something of a mystery in the novel: the narrator refers constantly to its powers but gives very few examples of its content other than to suggest its superficial nature. Referred to as a "a man of wit if ever there was one" (2: 60; I, 463), Swann, we learn, knew how to please the Duchesse de Guermantes by using "half-artistic, half-gallant . . . manners" (1: 483, trans. mod.; I, 334). In other words, Swann trades on a kind of wit that compromises art by mixing it with *mondanité*. The narrator associates this attractive but debased and self-interested form of artistic discourse with Jewishness even when it finds expression in the Duchesse de Guermantes herself. Her own brand of wit, which is described as the mirror of Swann's, is compared to the theater of Meilhac and Halévy (1: 475; I, 328), the collaborators of Offenbach on the light operas that typify the "vile and debased" Jewish style of art denounced by the anti-Semites and even by Leroy-Beaulieu.[16] The other source of this Guermantes wit, Antoine Compagnon informs us, is that other Halévy, Ludovic's cousin, Geneviève Straus, the Jewish *salonnière*.[17]

If Swann embodies the supposed Jewish tendency toward superficiality, Bloch incarnates the Jew's vulgarity. Whereas Swann does not deign to utter an opinion, Bloch does nothing but, constantly trying to impress with the boldness of his artistic tastes and the rarity of his aesthetic sensibility.[18] The narrator makes it clear that the origin of Bloch's vulgarity lies in his Jewishness, and never more so than when he tries to hide it. This becomes painfully clear at the end of the novel, when the narrator returns to Paris after the war to find that Bloch has become a famous writer and an intimate of the Guermantes. He has by this point adopted an aristocratic pseudonym in a move reminiscent of Proust's friend, the successful Jewish boulevard dramatist Francis de Croisset, born Franz Wiener. But the narrator also makes it clear that despite his airs, Bloch never manages to shed the most unattractive aspects of his Jewish origins. At the final party in the novel, the narrator describes Bloch's face as that of "an old Shylock, waiting in the wings, with his make-up prepared, for the moment when he would make his entry on to the stage" (6: 406; IV, 545). And as many critics have remarked, even his new and supposedly aristocratic name – Jacques du Rozier – calls to mind the rue des Rosiers, the center of the most Jewish neighborhood in Paris.[19]

It is Rachel, though, who incarnates perhaps the worst traits of the Jewish artist in the novel. The narrator first encounters her working in a brothel and her subsequent rise to celebrity as an actress (6: 433; IV, 579) will forever be tainted by her origin: she embodies the prostituted nature of modern art. Driven by a venal desire for gain, hers is an art of false appearances. When the narrator first watches her on stage, in a small role, he marvels at the way the blemishes that cover her face disappear when seen from a distance. Her seductive surface thus not only conceals no Wagnerian depth but actively distorts the truth. The narrator does not fall sway to the illusion, but not so his friend Saint-Loup, who succumbs to a "need for dreams" (3: 233; II, 473) that the Jewish actress seems particularly adept at gratifying. Like Bloch, Rachel achieves astounding success by the end of the novel. In the last volume we learn that she has become "a celebrated actress" (6: 433; IV, 562), much to the horror of the truly talented Berma, whom she displaces, but this fame is presented once again as a kind of illusion deriving from the public's stubborn preference for falsity over substance.

It is not hard to see why Alessandro Piperno takes Proust's representation of the Jewish artist as proof of his anti-Semitism. In *Proust antijuif* [*Anti-Jewish Proust*], the title of which contains his thesis, Piperno notes, rightly, that "the Jewish characters of the *Recherche* possess indisputable qualities and talents," but "manifest just as many indefensible vices and connivances."[20] According to Piperno, Proust appears to illustrate Wagner's allegation that Jews can never produce real art, that they can only imitate or vulgarize, "take an artistic product and alter it by commercializing it." Swann, Bloch, and Rachel are all "mimics" of high culture according to Piperno. They are also too bent on social advancement to possess the kind of disinterestedness that Wagner sees as necessary for art. "Who are these three Jews . . . ?" Piperno asks of Swann, Bloch, and Rachel. "Alchemists of the spirit [esprit]."[21] Piperno suggests, moreover, that Wagner's allegation constituted the only real slander of the Jews that Proust took to heart, the only anti-Semitic calumny that meant something to this half-Jewish writer who was himself a highly skilled mimic and social climber, but who longed to produce a Wagnerian art from the soul.[22] For Piperno, Proust internalizes the anti-Semitism of Wagner and takes it out mercilessly on his Jewish characters, punishing them for what he fears he himself might be. By showing he knows the danger of Jewish art, Proust thereby attempts to distance himself from it.

Piperno's theory is certainly plausible. But is it true? Does Proust really side with the anti-Semites as a way to rid himself of the Jewishness he disdains and to prove his artistic bona fides? I want to suggest in the remainder of this chapter that such a reading misses the point, or rather the complexity, of what Proust has to say about Jewishness and art. It does so for several reasons. First, as Piperno acknowledges, real Jews served as models for some of Proust's genuine artist characters: Sarah Bernhardt for La Berma, for instance. Piperno also cites Bergson and Anatole France as Jewish models for the writer Bergotte even though, to my knowledge, Anatole France was not Jewish and Bergson did not write fiction.[23] Nevertheless, by sharing certain identifiable traits with their Jewish models – and perhaps as well the prefix *Ber-* in their names, Bernhardt/Berma, Bergotte/Bergson – these characters subtly imply a link between true genius and *l'esprit juif.*

Second, it seems to me that the real target of Proust's satire is not necessarily the social-climbing Jewish artists themselves, but the high society denizens who fall for them – the aristocrats' eagerness, in their boredom, to welcome the Jews as what Hannah Arendt calls a fashionable "vice."[24] Bloch and Rachel especially offer Proust a way to skewer the Guermantes who cannot wait to fling open the doors of their salons to these artistic imposters in order to show themselves superior to bourgeois taste and prejudice. The bad Jewish artists are thus only accessories to the real crime of not knowing better than to shun them. Third, I would point out that Swann, Bloch, and Rachel are hardly the only characters to use art to get ahead in the *Recherche*. Morel, for example, represents an even less sympathetic combination of artistic talent and social ambition than that evidenced by the Jews. Thus, like Leroy-Beaulieu, Proust shows corruption in art to be "modern" or "Parisian" rather than exclusively Jewish. Fourth, it also seems possible that Proust is parodying anti-Semitic discourses rather than espousing them. Indeed, Proust shows his Jewish artist characters to be themselves products of representation: Bloch is always being compared to paintings of oriental figures and Rachel is dubbed "Rachel quand du Seigneur" in reference to Halévy's opera *La Juive*, which more than any other work except maybe Walter Scott's *Ivanhoe* helped forge an image of the Jewish woman in the popular imagination. Perhaps Proust is trying to show the problem of the Jewish artist to be an effect rather than a cause, the product of a society that persists in viewing Jews through certain stereotyped optics.

Finally, and this is the major point, are we really so sure that, for Proust, the social ambition or "self-interestedness" of the Jewish artist cannot go hand in hand with true genius? Is Proust himself not proof of the opposite, that real art can in fact spring from success in a salon? Bloch and Rachel represent what the artist, Jewish or otherwise, might become if he or she lacks something that redeems worldliness and ambition, something that Proust seems intent on defining over the course of the novel. Jewishness seems to name that bad form of worldliness or ambition. But Jewishness also names its opposite. Significantly, it is Swann, the king of the Jewish dilettantes, who possesses, or who comes to possess, this redemptive quality. After a lifetime spent pursuing social success, Swann undergoes a profound change during the Dreyfus Affair, a change that involves a complete recalibration of his social being. Whereas before he had studiously avoided having an opinion on art or seemingly any other matter, during the Affair he becomes passionately devoted to securing justice for the Jewish officer wrongly accused of treason. If Proust had hinted that there was something Jewish about Swann's earlier superficiality, he clearly associates his new sincerity with Jewishness as well. Indeed, the narrator describes Swann's Jewish reawakening not only as a return to the "spiritual fold of his fathers" (3: 796; II, 868) but also as a kind of physical transformation into an Old Testament figure: "Swann had arrived at the age of the prophet," the narrator says of Swann's passion for justice and solidarity with his fellow Jews (4: 122; III, 89). Even if Swann becomes something of a "boor" ["mufle"] as a result of this newfound sincerity, his commitment belies the charges of superficiality and venality that for Wagner and company constitute the essence of the *esprit juif.*

And here we begin to see how Proust in fact comes much closer to sharing the point of view of Leroy-Beaulieu than of the anti-Semites. For Leroy-Beaulieu, after showing that there is no such thing as a Jewish influence in the arts, after arguing that the Jews cannot be held responsible either for the "depraved baudelairism" of symbolism or the vulgarity of the *opéra-bouffe*, after demonstrating that "they content themselves, these sons of Jacob, with following the fashion of the day," concedes that there might in fact be an "esprit juif" after all.[25] Leroy-Beaulieu locates it in a passionate concern for justice and a commitment to bringing it about in *this* world. "They do not lose themselves in the clouds or in the azure sky," he says of the Jew, perhaps in echo of Drumont's contention that the Aryan is a poet and dreamer while the Jew is a base materialist. But if he agrees with Drumont that what the Jew aims for is "the earth and earthly realities," Leroy-Beaulieu also argues that "his goal is the establishment of peace and the spread of well-being among men."[26] The Jew, in other words, redeems his materialism by fighting for justice. Swann's transformation into a kind of Jewish prophet during the Affair can be read almost like an illustration of Leroy-Beaulieu's thesis. It shows that Jews are capable of seriousness and of depth after all.

But Proust also performs a more cunning subversion of Wagner and Drumont than merely showing that Jews do not only devote themselves exclusively to the surface of things. He does this by showing how the surface can in fact yield a surprising form of depth. Proust writes a novel about social climbing and self-interest, a novel composed of virtuosic feats of mimicry, a novel in other words that embodies the very negative stereotypes that anti-Semites attribute to the Jews. Through an amazing alchemy, however, Proust extracts real knowledge, and true originality, from these supposedly debased ingredients. He thereby overturns the opposition on which the anti-Semites build their case against the Jews, and in the process generates a transcendent form of art. Swann, of course, never produces any art of his own. And Bloch and Rachel, despite their celebrity, never achieve the status of great artist that the novel confers on a small handful. But I would like to suggest that their creator achieves what they do not, and that he does so precisely by making room for what he labels as Jewishness in his art.

NOTES

1 "Proustian poetry, conforming in style, in origins, to Semitism!" Céline declared in a letter to Lucien Combelle dated December 2, 1943, cited in Pascal Ifri, *Céline et Proust: Correspondances proustiennes dans l'oeuvre de L.-F. Céline* (Birmingham, AL: Summa, 1996), 11–12. With the exception of citations from the *Recherche*, all translations in this chapter are by Maurice Samuels.

2 Edmund Wilson, *Axel's Castle: A Study in the Imaginative Literature of 1870–1930* [1931] (New York: Scribner's Sons, 1969), 144.

3 According to Arendt, the *Recherche* offered the most "truthful record" of the position of Jews in non-Jewish society. Hannah Arendt, *Antisemitism: Part One of* The Origins of Totalitarianism (New York: Harvest/HBJ, 1968), 80.

4 Allessandro Piperno, *Proust antijuif*, trans. Fanchita Gonzalez Batlle (2000; Paris: Liana Levi, 2007), 81.

5 Petrus Borel, "Revue dramatique," *Le Journal du commerce* (July 15, 1844), 2. Piperno draws this insight from Antoine Compagnon's *Proust entre deux siècles* (Paris: Éditions du Seuil, 1989).

6 Richard Wagner, *Prose Works*, trans. William Ashton Ellis [1850] (London: Kegan Paul, 1907), III, 84.

7 Jewish composers like Mendelssohn, whom Wagner names, and Meyerbeer, whom he does not, merely "hurl together the diverse forms and styles of every age and every master. Packed side by side, we find the formal idiosyncrasies of all the schools, in motleyest chaos." Richard Wagner, "Judaism and Music" [1850], in *Prose Works*, III, 84.

8 Édouard Drumont, *La France juive: Essai d'histoire contemporaine* [1886] (Beirut, Lebanon: Édition Charlemagne, 1994), I, 7.

9 *Ibid.*, 20–21.

10 "Along with a certain kind of infirm theater, the Jews have proven successful at painting and music (again a certain kind of painting and a certain kind of music); they assimilate its processes all the more easily because, in the current debased state of artistic levels, the mode of expression, the purely formal aspect, takes precedence over the essence of the idea" (*ibid.*, 22).

11 *Ibid.*

12 *Ibid.*
13 The impulse to blame the Christians for the Jews' supposed faults can be traced back to Christian-Wilhelm Dohm's *On the Civic Improvement of the Jews*, published in German in 1781. This line of reasoning would be popularized during the Revolutionary period in France by Mirabeau in his *Sur Moses Mendelssohn, sur la réforme politique des Juifs* (1787) and by the Abbé Grégoire in *Essai sur la régénération physique, morale et politique des Juifs* (1789). Zola would still use a version of this argument in his article "Pour les juifs" (1896). Antoine Compagnon discusses Leroy-Beaulieu in *Les Antimodernes: De Joseph de Maistre à Roland Barthes* (Paris: Gallimard, 2005), 192.
14 Anatole Leroy-Beaulieu, *Israël chez les nations* [1893] (Paris: Calmann-Lévy 1983), 259.
15 *Ibid.*, 261.
16 *Ibid.*
17 In his notes to the folio edition, Antoine Compagnon informs us that Proust's model for the "esprit des Guermantes" was his friend Geneviève Straus, née Halévy, a prominent Jewish salon hostess. Proust, *Du côté de chez Swann* (Paris: Gallimard folio, 1988), 510 (328, n. 2).
18 "You really must conquer your vile taste for A. de Musset, Esquire" ["Défie-toi de ta dilection assez basse pour le sieur de Musset"] the pretentious teenage Bloch tells the narrator at the start of the novel, even while admitting that Musset and "the man Racine" ["le nommé Racine"] did in the course of their careers manage to compose at least one well rhymed verse (1: 124; 1, 89).
19 Jonathan Freedman refers to the Jewishness of the name du Rozier in "Coming out of the Jewish Closet with Marcel Proust," in *Queer Theory and the Jewish Question*, ed. Daniel Boyarin, Daniel Itzkovitz, and Ann Pellegrini (New York: Columbia University Press, 2003), 347, as does Seth Wolitz in *The Proustian Community* (New York University Press, 1971), 205.
20 Piperno, *Proust antijuif*, 43.
21 *Ibid.*, 81.
22 Here Piperno launches into a dubious psychoanalysis of the author: "Proust takes to heart the Wagnerian and post-Wagnerian accusations of plagiarism and vulgarity, but perhaps (who knows?) they resonate secretly in a deeply submerged region of his ambiguous half-Jewish soul" (*ibid.*, 80).
23 *Ibid.*, 82.
24 "Proust describes at length how society, constantly on the lookout for the strange, the exotic, the dangerous, finally identifies the refined with the monstrous and gets ready to admit monstrosities." Arendt, *Antisemitism*, 82.
25 Leroy-Beaulieu, *Israël*, 260.
26 *Ibid.*, 279.

CHAPTER 17

"Irregular" kin: Madeleine Lemaire and Reynaldo Hahn in *Les Plaisirs et les Jours*

François Proulx

Proust's first published book, *Les Plaisirs et les Jours*, has something of a bad reputation. It is often described as a commercial failure,[1] for what appears like good reason: few copies were sold. Its subject matter (fancy Parisian soirées, wistful promenades, fateful love affairs) and material presentation (a large format featuring lavish illustrations and musical scores) give the book an "overall fin-de-siècle feel"[2] that can seem kitschy and overdone – and did so to some readers even in 1896. Two contemporary reactions are cited by many of Proust's biographers: a short satirical scene that gently mocked the book's high price, and scathing reviews by Jean Lorrain. In June 1896, Lorrain wrote a short blurb attacking Proust and Robert de Montesquiou as undeserving amateurs whose publishing debuts were enabled by society connections.[3] He redoubled his attack on Proust and his collaborators in a longer piece that appeared on February 3, 1897:

> I have come across a book . . . perpetrated by one of these [salon dwellers]. Prefaced by Mr. Anatole France, who could not refuse the endorsement of his fine prose and his signature to a dear Madame (he had so often dined there), this delicate volume would not be such a typical example of the genre had it not been illustrated by Madeleine Lemaire.
>
> *Les Plaisirs et les Jours*, by Mr. Marcel Proust: grave melancholies, elegiac apathies, subtle and elegant little nothings, futile affections, inane flirts in a precious and pretentious style, with flowers by Madame Lemaire strewn like symbols in the margins or above the chapters . . . Never has Madame Lemaire's ingenuity been so well suited to an author's talent . . . And so we find a story by Mr. Proust, titled *Amis: Octavian et Fabrice*, adorned with two she-cats playing the guitar, and another, called *Rêverie couleur de temps*, illustrated with three peacock feathers.
>
> Yes, my dear, three peacock feathers: what could possibly top that?[4]

In what follows I propose to reconsider two aspects of *Les Plaisirs et les Jours* derided by these reviews – its perceived commercial failure and its

Figure 17.1 Madeleine Lemaire, "Promenade"

"delicate" illustrations (a symptom of the volume's effeminacy, for Lorrain) – in light of the young Proust's relation to Madeleine Lemaire, the hostess and painter who in many ways launched his social and literary career. In doing so I will highlight, in Proust's short pieces collected in the book (stories, poems, meditations), the intertwined recurring themes of alternative kinship and disguise. We find both themes in the piece featuring the gaudy but seemingly innocuous bird that so amused Lorrain, the peacock.

Birds of a feather

Madeleine Lemaire's drawing of two (not three) peacock feathers illustrates a story titled "Promenade" in the section "Rêveries couleur du temps" (Figure 17.1).[5] On a spring day, an unnamed wanderer happens upon a farm, and ventures to the barnyard to pick up a few eggs:

> But who is this person in royal garb striding forth among these rustic beings? . . . this is where the peacock spends his life, a veritable bird of paradise in a barnyard, among turkeys and hens, like the captive Andromache in a crowd of slaves . . . [or] Apollo who can always be recognized, even when he plays shepherd, ever dazzling, to the flocks of Admetus. (*JS* 107–108)

The three-page story ends there: clearly the peacock is its object, and should be read as an allegory. But of what? The reference to Apollo in disguise offers a clue, since it had already appeared, in an epigraph from Emerson, at the head of the first piece of the book, "La mort de Baldassare Sylvande": "Apollo kept the flocks of Admetus, said the poets. Every man is a divinity in disguise, a god playing the fool" (*JS* 9).[6] That piece had been previously published in *La Revue hebdomadaire* in October 1895 with a dedication (not reprinted in the book) to Reynaldo Hahn, the young composer with whom Proust shared a passionate love affair between 1894 and 1896. The image of a god in disguise also recurs in a letter to Hahn from March 1896, where Proust describes his work-in-progress, the unfinished novel posthumously published as *Jean Santeuil*: "I want you to be in it at all times, but like a god in disguise that no mortal can recognize. Otherwise you would have to write 'to be torn' on the whole novel" (*Corr* II, 52). The peacock, by way of Emerson's "divinity in disguise," thus emerges as an emblem for queerness, for attachments that must remain hidden and can only be expressed publically through secret codes. Yet it makes a rather odd symbol for dissimulation, since as Proust's short story makes clear, it is in fact quite conspicuous: the wanderer immediately notices how the peacock stands out among the other barnyard denizens. Proust would develop this paradox of hiding in plain sight through the narrator's at times ornithological fascination with Charlus and other strange birds in the *Recherche*.

The peacock in "Promenade," while resplendent, is also something of an ugly duckling, looking out of place next to the turkeys and hens. Like the cygnet in Andersen's tale,[7] his unusual appearance suggests that he belongs to a different species or lineage. Surrounded by a "rustic" crowd of poultry metonymically characterized as peasants, Proust's peacock is an aristocrat – or at least dresses like one. The always reversible slippage between difference as innate (Andromache, made a slave but still the daughter of a king) and difference as performed through dress (the peacock is a "person in royal garb," not necessarily a royal person) is crucial, and informs the class and family dynamics of many of the pieces in *Les Plaisirs et les Jours*: feelings of not belonging or wanting to belong elsewhere, efforts to pretend and perform, fears of being found out. I would argue that these questions also shaped the genesis and reception of Proust's book. Did the young writer belong in the prestigious company of men of letters[8] and in the rarefied social worlds he described, or was he an impostor? To a nineteenth-century French reader, peacock feathers would have evoked a colloquial expression derived from one of La Fontaine's fables ("The Jay Decked in Peacock's Feathers")[9] that described a man – specifically, in the fable, a writer – pompously laying claim to what is not rightfully his. This is why Jean Lorrain found Madeleine Lemaire's drawing so uproariously ironic: he read it as a symbol of his own condemnation of Proust's book as a publishing sham.

In "La mort de Baldassare Sylvande" a peacock-like sartorial aspiration is attributed to the protagonist, a 13-year-old boy: "Alexis, who greatly disapproved of his father's severe and somber attire . . . dreamed of a future where, always on horseback, he would be as elegant as a lady and as splendid as a king" (*JS* 10). The boy's desire to dress differently from his father transgresses both gender and class lines. "Promenade" toys similarly with gender and class, the latter through a play on the French for "barnyard," *basse-cour*, literally the "low court" of peasants as opposed to the high court of nobility. And while the noun for "peacock" (*paon*) is grammatically masculine, the casually prancing bird is compared to a wealthy hostess in fancy dress:

> Likewise on the day of a party, moments before the first guests arrive, the lady of the house – dazzling in a dress with an iridescent train, an azure gorget clasped around her royal neck, aigrettes fixed on her head – crosses her courtyard before the marveling eyes of a crowd of onlookers gathered outside the railings, to . . . await a prince of the blood whom she will greet at the very threshold. (*JS* 107)

Is this unnamed hostess, decked in expensive finery, an aristocrat with a legitimate lineage like her awaited guest, or a social impostor wearing borrowed feathers? Is her neck "royal" by birthright, or does it only look so thanks to her glittering jewels? The story does not say. She may be Proust's discreet homage to a fellow odd bird, who could sometimes act as a mother hen: Madeleine Lemaire.[10]

A different kind of mother

Madeleine Lemaire (1845–1928) also had a bad reputation in early Proust scholarship. George Painter described her as a "tall, energetic woman with . . . hair that was not all her own [and] a great deal of rouge"[11] – in other words, a garish woman in false adornments. Disparaging her "gracefully repellent brush-drawings" for Proust's first book, he characterized her as a prolific but decidedly limited artist who "indefatigably painted her flower-pieces," echoing the oft-repeated phrase, attributed to Alexandre Dumas *fils*, that "No one, except God, has created more roses" than her.[12] Proust himself had aimed to correct this distortion in a flattering portrayal of the painter and her salon, published in 1903: "She has created no shortage of landscapes, churches, and portraits, since her extraordinary talent extends to all genres" (*CSB* 458). Most damagingly, Painter identified her, as many early readers had done, with the *Recherche*'s Madame Verdurin, the tyrannical hostess for whom art and relations are largely tools for social climbing. Philip Kolb was among the first to nuance this identification, pointing out that Lemaire's enduring "kindness, generosity and loyalty" to Proust had to be left out for the novelist to create a striking character.[13] In recent years, scholarship and exhibitions have championed a renewed interest in her life and work, challenging received ideas about her artistry.[14]

An intriguing hint of gender and marital nonconformity recurs in various accounts of Lemaire. Née Madeleine Coll, the granddaughter of a Napoleonic general, she married in 1865 and had a daughter the following year (Suzanne, known as Suzette), but her husband seems to have disappeared from her life around the time of the Commune. Many later assumed or conveniently accepted that she was a widow; Proust and Hahn playfully refer to her and her unmarried daughter as *la veuve* and *la jeune veuve* [the young widow] (*Corr* VIII, 151). Yves Uro has uncovered that Lemaire was actually divorced,[15] which was legal but still somewhat unsavory in the French Third Republic. A letter written to her by Dumas *fils* in 1871 alludes to recent "debauchery": "no doubt you have tried many things and found yourself disgusted and bored, left without what they had seemed to promise for an instant."[16] The same letter, after praising her "virile intelligence," urges her to focus on her work and her young daughter, and suggests that she pursue, instead of "the vulgarities that surround" her, "the type of strong male friendship that can complete the destiny of a woman such as you."[17] In his gossipy biography of Proust, Ghislain de Diesbach describes Lemaire as "tall and strong, somewhat virile in appearance . . . she was one of those women who, as they get older, end up resembling the man they lack."[18] While such causality is certainly questionable, it does call to mind Proust's own description, in *Sodome et Gomorrhe*, of a peculiar "type," the wife of the male invert (4: 61–63; III, 46–47). More interestingly, Madeleine Lemaire's main artistic mentor, Charles Chaplin (1825–1891), is said to have raved that "everything she paints has a touch of mustache [de la moustache],"[19] meaning a manly quality.

Whatever were Madeleine Lemaire's amorous inclinations, her salon had a reputation for permissiveness; in more contemporary terms we might call it queer-friendly. Jeanne Pouquet (who knew Proust) observes, "we find [in her salon] a great number of boys of dubious morality . . . The lot of them are always breaking up, making up, breaking up again . . . It would be comical if it were not so appalling."[20] Montesquiou, a lifelong friend of Lemaire, similarly describes her fin-de-siècle soirées as a gathering spot for a motley crowd of "great-dukes, *artisses*, hustlers, queens, posers, scenesters, swindlers," in a vitriolic satirical poem published posthumously in 1925.[21] In the *Recherche*, Swann recalls how Odette once told him that Madame Verdurin had made a pass at her, possibly as "a joke" (1: 512; I, 354). We find echoes of Lemaire's open-mindedness – as well as her alleged middling – in the Verdurin salon, where Biche whispers to Cottard: "Nothing amuses me more than match-making [faire des mariages], I've brought off quite a few, even between women!" (1: 185; I, 199). That it is not the hostess who makes this statement serves as another indication that Madeleine Lemaire should not be reduced to the despotic Madame Verdurin: Biche, of course, turns out to be the painter Elstir.

The queer-friendliness of Lemaire's salon was likely a draw for Proust, as was its relative blurring of class lines. His article from 1903 glowingly depicts the salon as a space where painters, musicians and writers naturally mingled with artistically inclined aristocrats, politicians and members of the high bourgeoisie. It was there that he met Montesquiou and, in May 1894, Reynaldo Hahn.

An illustration for the story "Un dîner en ville" (Figure 17.2) depicts members of Lemaire's circle: Montesquiou is speaking animatedly in the foreground, and Proust, easily identifiable with his heavy-lidded eyes, tilted head and signature mustache, appears to be looking at him. Proust is positioned centrally, yet slightly in the background, connoting that he is both a member and an observer of this rarefied society, like the protagonist of his story. He is seated between two women: to his right (left of the drawing) is likely Suzette Lemaire, and to his left, even further in the background and partially hidden from the viewer by another female guest, is Madeleine Lemaire. Her mouth is curled in a faint, knowing smile. Where is she pointing her gaze, and what does she see? She may be looking at the readers of Proust's book: this could be her discreet wink to us, as the illustrator and artistic godmother of the volume. She might also be

Figure 17.2 Madeleine Lemaire, "Un dîner en ville" (detail)

looking at Proust, observing him just as perceptively as he observes her dinner party.

When *Les Plaisirs et les Jours* appeared, a review by Fernand Gregh noted that Proust had "gathered around his newborn book every sort of benevolent fairy," referring to the book's many collaborators.[22] A few months earlier, in a letter to a manager at the publishing house Calmann-Lévy, Proust expressed a mix of impatience and gratitude toward his illustrator. He feared that her delay in producing her drawings would further set back the publication of the book, and asked him to urge her to finish. The letter invokes "the friendship of Madame Lemaire, who for four years now[23] has been holding me above the baptismal font of literature (where I am honored to have such a lovely godmother, but really the time has come)" (*Corr* I, 453). In French, *belle marraine* incidentally suggests an odd conjunction of "godmother" and "stepmother" or "in-law." Fairy stepmother, godmother-in-law – or perhaps godmother-outlaw, Madeleine Lemaire belongs to a series of Madeleines in and around Proust's work, all linked to the maternal and to amorous transgression: Madeleine de Gouvres, an aristocrat who hopelessly lusts for a younger man in a story published by Proust in 1896 (but not included in his book); Madeleine Blanchet, the widow who adopts and eventually marries a male foundling in George Sand's *François le Champi*;[24] and Madame de Villeparisis, the painter of roses from the *Recherche*, whose first name is Madeleine, and whose rumored past of "debauchery" is alluded to in *Le Côté de Guermantes* (3: 693–694, trans. mod.; II, 795–796). Proust, who was never indifferent to onomastics or wordplay, was surely attuned to the suggestiveness of her name: *Le-mère*, the male mother.

Queer kinship

Very few letters between Proust and the Lemaires were found by Philip Kolb,[25] who deplores, in an article from 1964, "the mystery that still enshrouds" this key correspondence.[26] In 1949 a short piece by Henri Bardac made an alluring mention of the full archive of Proust's letters to the mother and daughter over a period of twenty-five years,[27] but the fate of those letters was unclear by the time Kolb assembled his edition of the *Correspondance*, and remains so today. Luckily, many letters from Reynaldo Hahn to the Lemaires have survived,[28] including from the years 1894–1896, when Proust and Hahn were lovers. Hahn's missives help fill in the picture of the unconventional network of relations between these four artists (Suzette was a painter like her mother). They give a vivid sense of the Lemaires' role in sheltering and, in the full meaning of the word, fostering his amorous relationship with Proust. In many letters, Hahn addresses Madeleine Lemaire as an artistic but also a morally permissive adoptive parent.

In early September 1895, after staying at her seaside villa in Dieppe with Proust, Hahn writes to thank his "indulgent" hostess:

> How indulgent you are toward us, so silly, so ill bred – though we do love you, and therefore deserve your love in return. But how could we ever repay you for all your kindness toward us – what woman, what great artist would deign, as you do, to put up with the quirks and the company of two oldish young men?[29]

In a letter to Suzette from July of the same year, we see another side of the relationship between the two pairs as he defends Proust against the women's accusations of neglect:

> Marcel has written me very little, but I do not doubt him, nor should you: he worked while he was in Kreuznach, and you may be surprised, one day, to see what will emerge from this "irregular."[30]

Hahn, 20 years old at the time, likely had little idea just how right he would prove to be. I will return to his insistence on questions of debt and work in the next section; for now, I want to examine his use of a particular vocabulary, often highlighted, in his expressive epistolary style, by underlining or quotation marks.

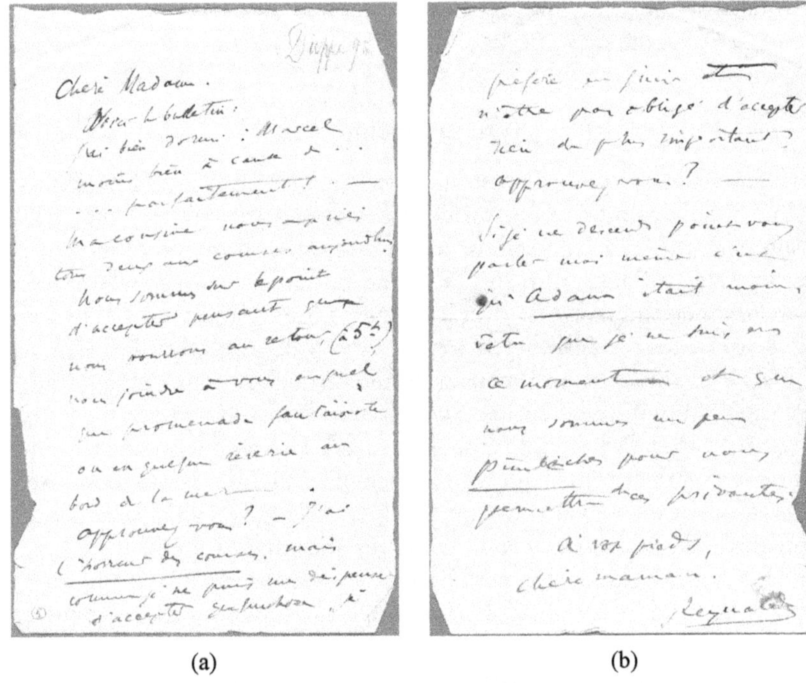

(a) (b)

Figure 17.3 (a) Reynaldo Hahn, letter to Madeleine Lemaire [August 1895], recto
(b) Reynaldo Hahn, letter to Madeleine Lemaire [August 1895], verso

Throughout his correspondence with the Lemaires, Hahn uses certain expressions or words, including "pony," his pet name for Proust, that hint at a shared set of in-jokes between the foursome. One letter (Figures 17.3a and b), written during Proust and Hahn's stay in Dieppe in August 1895, is quite daring:

> Dear Madame,
> Here is the latest:
> I slept well: Marcel less well because of. . . . . . indeed [*parfaitement*]! –
> [. . .] I dare not come downstairs and talk to you in person, since Adam wore less than I am wearing right now, and we are a bit too prissy [*pimbêches*] to allow ourselves such liberties.
>
> At your feet, dear mother.
> Reynaldo[31]

The note was written and delivered from one room to another inside the villa.[32] Explaining why Proust did not sleep well, Hahn's double ellipses invite a number of readings, the most salacious of which may well be over-readings. The elliptical formula "*. . . parfaitement*" recurs in at least two of Proust's letters to Hahn (*Corr* I 344, 436), both of which mention Madeleine Lemaire. It appears to be one of their private jokes, its full meaning unknown to us.

The last few lines are perhaps more revealing about Madeleine Lemaire's complicity with Hahn and Proust's relationship. The rare term *pimbêche*, another apparent in-joke,[33] carries an unmistakable association with femininity: Émile Littré's *Dictionnaire de la langue française* of the 1870s gives the definition "a ridiculous woman who puts on haughty airs." Not only is Hahn in the nude as he writes this letter, he camps it up for his "dear mother's" amusement.

The filial closing is a recurring feature of Hahn's letters to both Lemaires in the mid 1890s. Madeleine is addressed as *maman*, with or without quotation marks, while Proust and Hahn become "two sons and two brothers," and Suzette gets assurances of "our fraternal affections."[34] Such vocabulary is used even beyond the foursome: Montesquiou, who might be considered extended "family," for instance sends an invitation to Proust and "your brother Hahn" in July 1895 (*Corr* I, 410). This fanciful adoptive or alternative filiation is highlighted in a letter from Brittany in September or October 1895, as Hahn writes to Madeleine:

> –We have been so good these last few days, we have worked so much and taken so many hygienic and boring walks that we have barely picked up the pen to tell our legal mothers that we are not dead –. [. . .]
> Marcel will write to you tomorrow. [. . .]
> A thousand tender greetings from your two "~~pony~~" boys.
> Reynaldo[35]

In contradistinction to the legal system of kinship based on biological filiation, we discover in Hahn's letters an inventive, whimsical kinship, based on artistic and personal affinities. In this peculiar reconstituted family, two oldish, prissy, brother-like young men (with elliptical reasons for not sleeping well) find an indulgent mother and sister in a divorcée and her spinster daughter.

Kinship, a more capacious concept than "family," can be defined as "a set of practices [and] relationships of various kinds which negotiate the reproduction of life and the demands of death."[36] "Gay kinship," notes Elizabeth Freeman, often "appropriates and transforms the terminology of 'straight' kinship, emphasizing the elements of freedom, creativity, and flexibility."[37] Proust's relationship to Hahn, in its amorous phase between 1894 and 1896 but also beyond, until Proust's death, amounts to a form of queer kinship, in which the two men were not only close but akin to each other – as attested by their correspondence, with its shared private language and related or interchangeable nicknames.[38] As Rubén Gallo has shown, many of Proust's letters and drawings to Hahn indulge in fantasies of caregiving and cohabitation that gesture toward "what we would now call a domestic partnership," including fanciful imaginings of his own death.[39] Céleste Albaret described how Hahn was the only person allowed to enter Proust's apartment without being announced, and leave without being accompanied by her: not even Proust's brother was given such a privilege.[40] At the time of Proust's death, in 1922, it was Hahn who notified many of his closest or oldest friends, including Jacques Rivière and Léon Yeatman (*Corr* XXI, 535–536).

Questions of extrafamilial and fantasized kinship also traverse *Les Plaisirs et les Jours*, starting with "La mort de Baldassare Sylvande," the story Proust had initially dedicated to Hahn. As Baldassare makes a short-lived recovery from the "nervous illness" that will eventually kill him, he finds that he misses a side of himself, the "fraternal stranger" he had gotten to know when he accepted the idea of death: "he felt, waking within him, a new and still unknown natal love, like a young man who discovers he has been misled about the true land of his birth" (*JS* 20–21). The oxymoron "fraternal stranger"[41] echoes both Hahn's foreign origin (he was born in Venezuela) and the queer feeling of belonging to a different lineage embodied by the barnyard peacock in the story "Promenade." In the dedication that opens *Les Plaisirs et les Jours*, Hahn was alluded to as a "fraternal friend" on the galley proofs; Proust changed the phrase to "true friend" before publication (*JS* 912). The last story of the book opens with a woman's exclamation to her male lover: "My little tree, my little donkey, my mother, my brother, my homeland, my little God, my little stranger" (*JS* 146). A pendant to "pony," the French word for donkey (*âne*) is a homophone for Hahn. The amorous series is a declension of interchangeable, often opposite terms – brother/mother, stranger/homeland, donkey/God (recalling the citation from Emerson about Apollo guarding herds) – all related to him. In a letter to Hahn from 1912, Proust reminisces about this tender list: "I think it's in 'La fin de la jalousie' that I say, 'my homeland.' How true. How I ease my nostalgia when I set myself to thinking of you" (*Corr* XI, 198).

Bad business

Along with Jean Lorrain's barbs, the second reaction to *Les Plaisirs et les Jours* often cited by biographers is a satirical scene performed in March

1897 by a group of young writers that included some of Proust's friends. The scene stages a dialogue between Proust, Fernand Gregh, and Ernest La Jeunesse, a collaborator to *La Revue blanche*, where many of the book's pieces had appeared.

PROUST (TO ERNEST LA JEUNESSE): Did you read my book?
LA JEUNESSE: No, sir, it's too expensive.
PROUST: Alas! that's what everyone says. How about you, Gregh, did you read it?
GREGH: Yes, I cut the pages before I reviewed it.
PROUST: Did you also think it was too expensive?
GREGH: No, not at all, you certainly get your money's worth.
PROUST: Isn't that so! A preface by Mr. France, four francs... Illustrations by Madame Lemaire, four francs... Music by Reynaldo Hahn, four francs... Stories by me, one franc... A few poems by me, fifty cents... Total: thirteen francs and fifty cents, was that perhaps too much?[42]

Like Gregh's review in the *Revue de Paris*, the scene points to the excessive number of "benevolent fairies" gathered around Proust's publishing debut. This surfeit of parentage results in the birth of a strange hybrid, a veritable luxury object at a time when standard books sold for less than three francs.[43] A 1918 letter from the publisher Calmann-Lévy reports that, out 1500 copies printed, only 329 were ever shipped to booksellers (*Corr* XVII, 290). While this outcome was surely not what Proust had hoped in 1896, it did oddly reflect the book's thematic preoccupation with difference, with not fitting in. *Les Plaisirs et les Jours* lingered in the publisher's storeroom, superb and useless – like a peacock in a barnyard.

Two recently uncovered letters shed light on the particular economics of the book's creation and limited circulation. The first is from Madeleine Lemaire to Proust, perhaps in response to his complaints of tardiness passed on by the publisher:

> Dear Monsieur,
>
> If you would kindly come [see] me next Monday around four[,] I will give you all that is done for our book, ordered and numbered. You will see that I have been working!![44]

Hahn, in his letters to Lemaire, often underscores the work he and Proust have been doing, like dutiful children reporting to a watchful parent.[45] While she certainly lived in privileged comfort, Lemaire appears to have disapproved of idleness. As Virginie Greene points out, she did a considerable amount of labor for Proust's book, seventy drawings and watercolors in total.[46] A cursory glance at Proust's title (derived from Hesiod's *Works and Days*) suggests a decadent era and class where "pleasure" has replaced work. This is how most reviewers saw the book, including Jean Lorrain. Yet a more nuanced reading of the sum of the pieces reveals a potential critique of idleness. Many of the vain lovers and partygoers in the stories end up dead, while the middle section of poems about painters and musicians celebrates the enduring achievements of artists – prefiguring the divide between doomed amateurs and true creators in the *Recherche*.

In the second letter, from June 26, 1918, Proust responds with nineteen pages of sustained indignation to Gaston Calmann-Lévy's proposition of selling the remaining copies of *Les Plaisirs et les Jours* at a "very low price" – the price of a regular book, three francs (*Corr* XVII, 290). Proust reminds him that his publishing house obtained Madeleine Lemaire's drawings "gratis" ["à l'oeil"], and that she also provided "at no cost" ["pour rien"] twenty original watercolors that accompanied (and helped sell) luxury copies on Japon paper. "If, in spite of the gift of so many drawings, the book was bad business... for its publisher, it was even more so for me, since for many years it made me look like an amateur." He refutes the claim that sales have "completely stopped," since he himself has "bought up to five copies a year, twenty in total" since 1896.[47] Proust did not have a contract for the book, and received no royalties (*Corr* II, 218); as such it was never much of a commercial venture to begin with. Why would an author write a book for free, and spend his own money to purchase copies? The answer may be in Proust's use of these copies: as gifts to friends and society or literary acquaintances. Hannah Freed-Thall has proposed that we consider Proust's self-financing of *Du côté de chez Swann* as a publishing gamble that, unlike his speculation on the stock market, eventually proved to be wildly successful.[48] We might look at *Les Plaisirs et les Jours* in a related way. As it does the familial template of kinship, Proust's first book reconfigures relations of artistic production and diffusion away from what he later called the "unspeakable commercialist filth" of publishing (*Corr* XVII, 262), toward an economy of the gift. This is not to say that the book was produced leisurely or for pleasure: classic anthropology – nascent in Proust's era – argues that gifts, far from being gratuitous, are about prestige, social positioning, and establishing relations.[49] In that sense Proust's irregular book was at least partly successful, though it did not position him in quite the way he had envisioned.

Pleasures in drag

Proust famously fought a duel with Jean Lorrain on February 6, 1897, in response to Lorrain's disparaging February 3 review. Biographers now agree

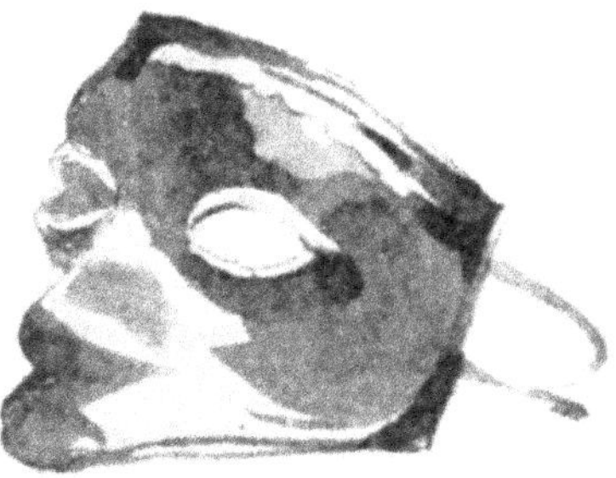

Figure 17.4 Madeleine Lemaire, "Contre la franchise"

that it was Lorrain's casual but highly insinuative mention of Lucien Daudet (the new object of Proust's affection) that prompted the confrontation. It is surprising, then, to see another reason given in older accounts from both sides. Octave Uzanne, one of Lorrain's witnesses, wrote in 1913 that "the champion of a deplorable paintress of high renown presented himself to defend her honor, after [Lorrain] rightly attacked her rather appalling works and her mercenary hobnobbing."[50] Henri Bardac, a friend of Proust, likewise wrote in 1949: "as if he had been the man of the family, Proust one day demanded reparation by arms from a writer who had spoken disrespectfully about the lady of the house."[51] Both accounts point to Madeleine Lemaire as the primary insulted party. Given her substantial contribution to the launch of his publishing career, Proust may well have felt in her debt, and paid her the gallantry of a redress. Lemaire's honor was also a convenient screen for almost all involved: Lorrain, though he had a complex relationship to visibility, was somewhat notoriously queer, and Bardac, introduced to Proust by Hahn, was also gay.[52] For Proust, playing "the man of the family" to his adoptive, nonlegal, artistic godmother amounted to a useful performance of a kind of regular masculinity.[53]

Themes of dissimulation and disguise run through *Les Plaisirs et les Jours*. In "La confession d'une jeune fille," for instance, a young female narrator states that, as she "went out more and more in society . . . no one suspected the secret crime of my life, and I seemed to all the ideal young woman" (*JS* 92). The section titled "Fragments de comédie italienne" compares Parisian high society to a troupe of actors playing stock roles from the Commedia dell'arte (Figure 17.4): "every one is quite different by nature from the character that society has found [for them] in its storeroom of costumes" (*JS* 54). Even Lemaire's salon, for all its rumored permissiveness, should not be imagined as place where guests could simply be true to their "nature" – it remains a salon, which means, as Proust's stories make clear, a space of performance. In the *Recherche*, the Verdurin salon is similarly regulated, despite its pretense of spontaneity (1: 266–267; I, 186).

In *Claudine s'en va* (1903), Colette describes an evening at Madame Lalcade's, a thinly veiled portrayal of the Lemaire salon. In her manuscript, the hostess was Madame Lapaire,[54] which both rhymes with "Lemaire" and plays with her reputation for gender nonconformity. *Lapaire* can be read as *la-père*, "the female father," while *Madame La-paire* evokes a woman with a pair, presumably of testes. In his tell-all notes on the Claudine novels, Willy confirms that the character was Lemaire, and suggests that in this final tome "Colette wanted to drag through the mud all the women with whom she had fooled around [couchotté]."[55] The soirée is actually rather tame, but it centers on a staged show: "the sad and frivolous music of Fauré will be mimed by a few *travestis*."[56] *Travesti*, in this context, should not be understood as "transvestite," a sexological term coined by Magnus Hirschfeld in 1910 and quickly adopted in English[57]: these are not drag queens performing at Madame Lapaire/Lemaire's, at least not necessarily. Rather, *travesti* in 1903 is a theatrical term more in line the broader meaning of "drag," understood as "putting on clothes that are not of one's gender or condition."[58] Seen in this light, evening dress becomes a form of drag, especially for a young bourgeois like Proust mingling with artists and aristocrats, as does playing "the man of the family." All are roles from Parisian society's "storeroom of costumes," borrowed feathers in which to parade and hide at the same time.

There are few explicit mentions of drag in the *Recherche*, including Odette's compromising portrait as *Miss Sacripant* (2: 583–584; II, 204).[59] Most male characters in drag are only paradoxically so, since they are wearing the masculine clothes of their assigned gender. It takes a trained eye, such as the hero will eventually develop, to notice that this is a form of disguise, since their true nature, according to the novel's logic of inversion, is feminine (4: 19; III, 16). A rare mention of men in female drag, in *Sodome et Gomorrhe*, appears in a particularly drawn-out preterition:

> Nor need we pause here to consider those young fools who out of childishness, to tease their friends or to shock their parents, obdurately choose clothes that resemble women's dresses, redden their lips and blacken their eyelashes . . . carried away by the same demon that urges young women of the Faubourg Saint-Germain to live scandalous lives, to defy all the conventions, to scoff at the entreaties of their families . . . (4: 31, trans. mod.; III, 24)

Figure 17.5 Madeleine Lemaire, "Mélancolique villégiature de Madame de Breyves"

Young men in shockingly feminine adornments are linked to young noblewomen with "scandalous" love lives by a common drive to outrage their parents, to flout the values of their (legal, regular) families. While there is no evidence that Proust "wore makeup or anything else suggesting drag,"[60] the comparison appears significant when one thinks back to *Les Plaisirs et les Jours*. In three of the book's stories, an upper-class female protagonist attempts to hide her dishonorable desire for a man, from her family, her domestics, or the man in question. One story, "Mélancolique villégiature de Madame de Breyves," was illustrated with a portrait by Madeleine Lemaire (Figure 17.5). Who is this figure holding a pen, with her heavy-lidded eyes, her head slightly tilted, and her left hand pressed to her cheek, in the iconic pose of the melancholic?[61] She shares many traits with contemporary photographs of the author.[62] Could Madeleine Lemaire have represented Proust in drag? "Everything she paints has a mustache," except for this intriguing drawing, which looks similar, in the position of the head and the shape of the eyes, nose, and chin, to her portrait of Proust for "Un dîner en ville" – minus the facial hair. In removing his mustache with a few strokes of her pen, Lemaire would have shown that she saw through the mask of his story. Her drawing, a visual disguise that protects a literary disguise but also potentially reveals it to the initiated, would then illustrate her role as knowing mother to a most promising irregular.

The end of Proust's romance with Reynaldo Hahn was also the end of his reconfigured kinship with the Lemaires. The "oldish" young man was growing up, and would go on to refine the strategies he learned with his first book. The economy of the gift of *Les Plaisirs et les Jours* became the self-financing of *Du côté de chez Swann*, a model that, while it was not Proust's first choice, ended up freeing him from commercial pressures. The feathers and masks of his early stories, meanwhile, evolved into a highly sophisticated disguise: the creatively liberating, temporally protean, anonymous "I" of the *Recherche*.[63]

NOTES

1 William C. Carter writes: "Although one could argue that *Pleasures and Days* was a critical success, especially for a first book, it was a publishing and public relations fiasco." *Marcel Proust: A Life* (New Haven, CT: Yale University Press, 2000), 216.

2 Nathalie Aubert, "Finding a Form: *Les Plaisirs et les Jours* to *Contre Sainte-Beuve*," in *Marcel Proust in Context*, ed. Adam Watt (Cambridge University Press, 2013), 21.

3 Raitif de la Bretonne [Jean Lorrain], "Pall Mall Semaine (Lundi 22 juin)," *Le Journal*, July 1, 1896, 6.

4 Raitif de la Bretonne [Jean Lorrain], "Pall Mall Semaine (Jeudi 28 janvier)," *Le Journal*, February 3, 1897, 2. With the exception of citations from the *Recherche*, all translations in this chapter are by François Proulx.

5 Lorrain amusingly misrepresents Proust's titles and Lemaire's drawings for added effect. In a drawing on the first page of "La mort de Baldassare Sylvande," two cats (of indeterminate gender) are lounging near a violin, not playing the guitar.

6 Ralph Waldo Emerson, "History," in *Essays* (London: James Fraser, 1841), 31.

7 On queerness and "The Ugly Duckling," see Will Roscoe, *Queer Spirits: A Gay Men's Myth Book* (Boston, MA: Beacon Press, 1995), 53–54.

8 Calmann-Lévy, the publisher of *Les Plaisirs et les Jours*, was a prestigious house: in earlier decades Michel Lévy had published Baudelaire and Flaubert.

9 Jean de La Fontaine, "Le Geai paré des plumes du Paon," in *Œuvres complètes*, ed. Jean-Pierre Collinet, Bibliothèque de la Pléiade (Paris: Gallimard, 1991), I, 152.

10 In *Jean Santeuil*, the Duchesse de Réveillon, clearly modeled on Madeleine Lemaire (who hosted Proust and Hahn at her country estate, the chateau de Réveillon), keeps peacocks in her barnyard (*JS* 462).

11 George Painter, *Marcel Proust: A Biography* (London: Chatto & Windus, 1959), 106.

12 *Ibid.*, 175 and 106.
13 Philip Kolb, "Marcel Proust et les dames Lemaire," *Bulletin de la Société des amis de Marcel Proust et des amis de Combray* 14 (1964), 122.
14 See for instance the exhibition catalog *Femmes peintres et salons au temps de Proust, de Madeleine Lemaire à Berthe Morisot* (Paris: Hazan/Musée Marmottan Monet, 2010).
15 Yves Uro, "Les Peintres de salon amis de Marcel Proust et leurs rapports avec son œuvre," unpublished doctoral thesis, Université de Paris Sorbonne 1 (2004), 195.
16 André Maurois, *Les Trois Dumas* (Paris: Hachette, 1957), 386–387.
17 *Ibid.*
18 Ghislain de Diesbach, *Proust* (Paris: Perrin, 1991), 119.
19 Uro, "Peintres de salon," 134.
20 Michelle Maurois, *Les Cendres brûlantes* (Paris: Flammarion, 1986), 40.
21 Robert de Montesquiou, *Les Quarante Bergères, portraits satiriques en vers inédits* (Paris: Librairie de France, 1925), 57.
22 [Fernand Gregh], "*Les Plaisirs et les Jours*, par Marcel Proust," *La Revue de Paris*, July 15, 1896, 457.
23 Kolb notes Proust had at this date been working toward his book for two years, not four (*Corr* 1, 454).
24 See Julia Kristeva, *Time and Sense: Proust and the Experience of Literature*, trans. Ross Guberman [1994] (New York: Columbia University Press, 1996), 6–15.
25 Kolb's edition of the *Correspondance* includes one letter from Proust to Madeleine from 1919 and a fragment from 1896, eight letters from Proust to Suzette, and two from Madeleine to Proust.
26 Philip Kolb, "Marcel Proust et les dames Lemaire," 115.
27 Henri Bardac, "Madeleine Lemaire et Marcel Proust," *La Revue de Paris* 56:8 (August 1949), 142.
28 For an overview of this corpus of letters, including valuable biographical information, see Luc Fraisse, "Un témoignage rapproché sur Marcel Proust: la correspondance inédite de Reynaldo Hahn avec les dames Lemaire," *Marcel Proust Aujourd'hui* 9 (2012), 9–29. For transcriptions of selected letters with notes and commentary, see my articles "Quatre lettres de Reynaldo Hahn à Madeleine Lemaire," *Bulletin d'informations proustiennes* 43 (2013), 23–26, and "Six lettres de Reynaldo Hahn à Suzette Lemaire," *Bulletin d'informations proustiennes* 44 (2014), 37–46. This paragraph and the next three integrate material previously published in those articles.
29 bMS Fr 219 (4), Houghton Library, Harvard University.
30 bMS Fr 219.1 (19), Houghton Library, Harvard University. The date October 1895 was added to the letter in another hand, but Jean-Yves Tadié dates the letter to late July, given its mention of Proust's trip to Kreuznach earlier that month. *Marcel Proust*, trans. Euan Camercon (New York: Viking, 2000), 217.
31 Hahn's emphasis; unbracketed ellipses are Hahn's. bMS Fr 219 (5), Houghton Library, Harvard University. Hahn likely means that Adam wore "more than" he is wearing as he writes the letter.

32 See Fraisse, "Témoignage rapproché," 14.
33 In another letter from September 1895, Hahn uses "pimbêche" as his signature. See Proulx, "Six lettres," 42.
34 *Ibid.*, 43, and Proulx, "Quatre lettres," 26.
35 b MS Fr 219 (25), Houghton Library, Harvard University. See also Proulx, "Six lettres," 38.
36 Judith Butler, "Is Kinship Always Already Heterosexual?," *Differences: A Journal of Feminist Cultural Studies* 13:1 (2002), 14–15.
37 Elizabeth Freeman, "Queer Belongings: Kinship Theory and Queer Theory," in *A Companion to Lesbian, Gay, Bisexual, Transgender, and Queer Studies*, ed. George E. Haggerty and Molly McGarry (Malden, MA and Oxford: Blackwell, 2007), 304. In this sentence Freeman paraphrases one of Kath Weston's main claims in *Families We Choose* (New York: Columbia University Press, 1991); she goes on to develop a critique of Weston's emphasis on "choice."
38 On Proust and Hahn's "lansgage," see Virginie Greene's biographical notice on Reynaldo Hahn in Marcel Proust, *Lettres*, ed. Françoise Leriche (Paris: Plon, 2004), 1240.
39 Rubén Gallo, *Proust's Latin Americans* (Baltimore, MD: Johns Hopkins University Press, 2014), 55–62.
40 Céleste Albaret, *Monsieur Proust*, trans. Barbara Bray (New York: New York Review of Books, 2003), 230; Albaret also comments that Proust and Hahn were "like young brothers" (233).
41 On this "fraternal stranger," see also Francine Goujon, "Le cryptage autobiographique dans *Les Plaisirs et les Jours*," *Bulletin d'informations proustiennes* 30 (1999), 107–110.
42 Robert Dreyfus, *Souvenirs sur Marcel Proust* (Paris: Grasset, 1926), 123.
43 Yves Sandre, "Notice" to *Les Plaisirs et les Jours* (*JS* 909).
44 Letter from Madeleine Lemaire to Proust [early 1896?], reproduced and transcribed in *Marcel Proust: L'arche et la colombe*, ed. Mireille Naturel (Neuilly-sur-Seine: Michel Lafon, 2012), 109 and 191.
45 "As Marcel told you, I have been working furiously," he writes in another letter from September or October 1895. See Proulx, "Quatre lettres," 25.
46 See Chapter 5 above, page 61.
47 Marcel Proust, letter to Gaston Calmann-Lévy, 26 juin [1918]. Sotheby's, *Livres et manuscrits*, Paris, June 19, 2014, Sale PF1403, lot 117. www.sothebys.com/en/auctions/ecatalogue/2014/livres-et-manuscrits-pf1403/lot.117.html.
48 Hannah Freed-Thall, "Proust and the Stock Market," unpublished talk, 20th/21st Century French & Francophone Studies Colloquium, March 8, 2014.
49 Marcel Mauss, *The Gift: The Form and Reason for Exchange in Archaic Societies* [1925], trans. W. D. Halls (New York: W. W. Norton, 2000).
50 Octave Uzanne, *Jean Lorrain, l'artiste – l'ami: souvenirs intimes, lettres inédites* (Paris: [E. Champion], 1913), 24.
51 Bardac, "Madeleine Lemaire," 138.
52 On Lorrain, see Painter, *Marcel Proust*, 208–209; on Bardac, see Carter, *Marcel Proust*, 605.

53 On duels in the post-Revolutionary era, see Robert A. Nye, *Masculinity and Male Codes of Honor in Modern France* (Oxford University Press, 1993).

54 Colette, *Œuvres*, ed. Claude Pichois, Bibliothèque de la Pléiade (Paris: Gallimard, 1984), I, 1390.

55 Willy, *Indiscrétions et commentaires sur les Claudine* [posth., 1962], in *L'Herne: Colette*, ed. Laurence Tacou (Paris: Éditions de L'Herne, 2011), 96.

56 Colette, *Œuvres*, I, 564.

57 Magnus Hirschfeld, *The Transvestites: The Erotic Drive to Cross-Dress*, trans. Michael A. Lombardi-Nash [1910] (Amherst, MA: Prometheus Books, 1991).

58 Émile Littré, *Dictionnaire de la langue française* (1863–1878). www.littre.org.

59 On this fictional painting, see Kazuyoshi Yoshikawa, "The Models for *Miss Sacripant*," in *Proust in Perspective: Visions and Revisions*, ed. Armine Kotin Mortimer and Katherine Kolb (Urbana and Chicago: University of Illinois Press, 2002), 240–253.

60 William C. Carter, *Proust in Love* (New Haven, CT: Yale University Press, 2006), 59.

61 See Chapter 3 above, page 35.

62 The frequently reproduced image of Proust with his hand on his left cheek was taken by the photographer Otto in 1895 or 1896. See *Proust: Du temps perdu au temps retrouvé*, ed. Gérard Lhéritier (Paris: Aristophil/Équateurs/Musée des Lettres et Manuscrits, 2010), 139.

63 See Roland Barthes, "Ça prend" (1979), in *Œuvres complètes*, ed. Éric Marty (Paris: Éditions du Seuil, 2002), V, 654–656.

CHAPTER 18

The day Proust recognized he was a great writer

Antoine Compagnon

When was Proust certain he had written a great book? When did he know he really was a great writer? There is no doubt this was his ambition from the very beginning, but in 1908, even as he definitively got back to writing, he wondered anxiously: "Presages of death. Soon, you will not be able to say all this. Laziness or doubt or impotence take refuge in uncertainty concerning the form of art. Should it be a novel, a philosophical study, am I a novelist?"[1] For a long time, he doubted that he would succeed.

By November 1913, as Proust was finalizing the promotion of his self-financed publication of *Du côté de chez Swann* with Grasset, he exuded confidence, self-assurance, even a sense of empowerment. He may have affected these feelings, since the year 1913 had begun dismally, with a string of setbacks: after Fasquelle and the *Nouvelle Revue Française* rejected his novel around Christmas of 1912, both the *Figaro* and the *NRF* declined to publish excerpts. Signs of failure dominated, public recognition seemed to be foreclosed. In these same first days of 1913, Proust decided he had enough of rejection: he would pay to be published at his own expense (*Corr* XII, 23).

True to his complex personality, Proust never contacted an editor directly. Rather, he always solicited an intermediary, and even an intermediary of an intermediary: Madame Straus had approached Calmette, director of the *Figaro*, and Calmette approached Fasquelle, as did Louis de Robert. He sought introductions and professed humility, but also demonstrated a certain indelicacy by having courted two editors at once in 1912 (Fasquelle and the *NRF*, through the intervention of Emmanuel Bibesco, Jacques Copeau, and Gaston Gallimard), with all the anxieties about confidentiality and secrecy that such a maneuver entailed. In mid February 1913 a rejection by Ollendorff was communicated to Proust in a "not very polite" letter from Alfred Humblot, the house's publishing director (*Corr* XII, 76). It was Humblot who delivered to Louis de Robert a now infamous verdict: "perhaps I am simply thickheaded, but I cannot understand why a man would spend thirty pages describing how he tosses and turns in bed before falling asleep."[2] Neither Jacques Madeleine (a pseudonym of Jacques Normand), who read the manuscript for Fasquelle, nor Humblot, who had passed on the manuscript to the playwright Georges Boyer, were amateurs; their judgments are those of professional readers. This is why the initial reception of Proust's novel must be taken seriously.

While these disappointments were no doubt trying, the year 1913 ended with the relatively successful commercial debut of *Swann* in November, and the appearance of the first favorable articles on the novel, including in England and Italy. All this added up to a generally positive reception (more than 3,000 copies were sold before August 1914) that could seem like sweet revenge. Yet this period was also marked by the departure of Alfred Agostinelli on December 1, 1913. His flight and subsequent death in May 1914 caused Proust terrible grief followed without transition by a crucial turning point in his work. The renewal of Proust's inspiration was surely spurred by these dramatic events on an immediate level (there was neither *La Prisonnière*, nor *La Fugitive* before them), but the publication of a writer's first book (and, in this sense, *Les Plaisirs et les Jours* counts for little) almost always has an effect on the work that follows. The new start of *À la recherche du temps perdu* in 1914 must also partly be a consequence of the publication of the first volume and thus, paradoxically, of the writer's triumph. Proust traversed several months marked by the extraordinary coincidence of literary success and sentimental hardship. The development of his novel owes something to both of these experiences.

Here is my hypothesis: Proust became conscious of the success of his work over the course of 1913, a year that began badly and ended in heartbreak. He made this discovery by reading his work in print, as he reviewed the proofs of his novel and corrected the Grasset galleys of "Combray," through the enormous task of rewriting he undertook in the spring and summer of that year.

Rereading oneself

Every writer experiences a shock upon seeing his work in print; it is a moment of truth, especially if long awaited. "On the day a young writer corrects his first proof," muses Baudelaire, "he is as proud as a student who has just earned his first venereal disease."[3] Reading one's proofs is a formidable test of self-recognition, akin to encountering one's double, looking out the window and seeing oneself pass by in the street, or hearing one's own story told by another. While among the Phaeacians, Odysseus hears the bard Demodocus tell a story that he recognizes as his own; he begins to weep, revealing his true identity.

Proust was highly sensitive to the experience of encountering oneself in print and to its weightiness, staging this moment memorably in *Albertine disparue* with the unanticipated publication of the narrator's article in the *Figaro*. As the narrator had sent the piece long ago, he does not expect to find it on the first page of the newspaper, and at first does not recognize himself:

> What a pity! The main article had the same title as the article which I had sent to the paper and which had not appeared. But not merely the same title, here were several words that were absolutely identical. This was really too bad. I must write and complain . . . But it was not merely a few words, it was the whole thing, and there was my signature. It was my article that had appeared at last. (6:766, trans. mod.; IV, 148)

Once the narrator clears up this misrecognition, he plays out the fantasy of his doubling from various perspectives, attempting to place himself in the position of the average reader opening his newspaper, reading himself as if he were an anonymous reader. Using his imagination, he seeks to enter every household in Paris where the paper is brought with the morning coffee, reproducing the scene of uncanny familiarity he experienced while reading himself as if he were someone else.

At this point, it is important to recall that the experience of reading the *Figaro* (and the false recognition it provokes) dates back to some of the earliest drafts, indeed to the very genesis of the novel. The scene initially appears in *Cahiers* 3 and 2, at the time of *Contre Sainte-Beuve*. In this first version of the scene, the hero's mother places the *Figaro* in his room so hastily and furtively that he immediately unlocks the secret behind her action: "I understood immediately that the article had been published."[4] Here, there is no initial mistake or delayed recognition – these belong to a later, more subtle revision, featuring the effect or the illusion before the cause, in line with the definitive Proustian aesthetic: "I opened the paper, wait a minute . . . "[5]

Proust had thus always understood that the experience of reading oneself in print was important, and – this is my hypothesis – his reading of the publishing proofs had a major impact on his novel. Let us begin by recalling the creation of the character Vinteuil in May 1913, which was the result of merging the naturalist Vington, a neighbor at Combray whose daughter is a lesbian, with the composer Berget, the creator of the famous sonata in "Un amour de Swann." The late fusion of these two shallow characters into a single one with more depth proves that the novel was working and gaining autonomy: one only had to read carefully for it to reveal its potential.

The union of two simple characters into a more complex one verifies Proust's hypothesis regarding the incoherence of the social or worldly self (Vinteuil is a timid widower, a martyred father) and the profound, sensitive, or creative self (Vinteuil is also an audacious musician of the avant-garde). Vinteuil is both a "silly old fool" and a "genius," as Proust would write, in a rare moment of satisfaction, to Lucien Daudet at the beginning of September 1913:

> Often, as you know, people say of a great artist "aside from his genius he was a silly old fool with the most narrow-minded ideas," but since they already know of his genius, they don't really imagine him to be so narrow-minded and ridiculous. Therefore I found it more striking to first show Vinteuil as a silly old fool without giving any hint that he is a genius, and in the second chapter, to describe his sublime sonata that Swann cannot for an instant imagine attributing to that silly old fool. (*Corr* XII, 259)

Proust is not being perfectly honest here, since this striking find was actually made after the fact, namely during the creative rereading performed by the "able reader"[6] that he had become upon examination of his own printed proofs.

The encounter with Bergotte

A second clue indicating that Proust became aware of the success of his novel while rereading it on the proofs emerges from the confrontation between the hero and Bergotte in "Combray," as the hero recognizes certain expressions in the great writer's prose that could have been his own. This passage is considerably transformed and amplified in the proofs. The hero, after hearing Bloch praise Bergotte's work, immediately dives in: on "the matter of Bergotte he [Bloch] had spoken truly" (1:129; I, 92). In "Combray," from this point forward, reflections on books, reading and writing, and the difficulties of creation are numerous, but it is those dealing with the meeting and the rivalry between the hero and Bergotte, fueled by a kind of mimetic desire, that interest us here. After reading Bergotte, the hero passes through a series of highs and lows regarding his own literary vocation.

Along with Elstir, another imaginary artist, Bergotte first emerged in manuscript drafts in 1910. He appears in three fragments from *Cahier* 29, though the title of the first known fragment ("Add to Bergotte") indicates that an older version must have existed, which has not reached us.[7] The character was further developed in *Cahiers* 14 and 68, the latter from 1911.[8] Nowhere, however, in any of these *cahiers* does the hero yet encounter turns of phrase that remind him of his own, a crucial experience of recognition punctuating his path to becoming a writer. That development was in fact a late invention, dating to 1913, and for this reason deserves our particular attention. The first reading of Bergotte's work simply produces an impression of originality:

> Dès les premières pages je ~~remar~~ fus sensible sans bien le distinguer – comme ~~un air~~ <des notes> qui nous charme[nt] avant qu'on ait démêlé nettement l'air qu'elles composent – à ce que je retrouvai <chez lui> une seconde fois, une troisième, ~~toujours~~ chaque fois que j'en lus, un certain arrangement des mots qui était son originalité.
>
> From the first pages I ~~notic~~ was aware, without distinguishing it clearly – like ~~an air~~ <notes> that charm us before we can clearly make out the air they compose – of something I would find again <in his work> a second time, a third, ~~always~~ every time I read it, a particular arrangement of words that was his originality.[9]

In the definitive text, this feeling remains the first to be associated with the hero's experience of the writer: "One of these passages of Bergotte . . . filled me with a joy . . . I recognized in this passage the same taste for uncommon expressions, the same musical outpouring . . . which had been present in the earlier passages without my having recognized them as being the source of my pleasure" (1:130; I, 93). In the beginning, then, there is only this somewhat passive admiration.

Following his experiences of reading, the hero begins to dream of becoming a writer. This aspiration takes shape along the Guermantes way, as he daydreams about the Duchess, near the end of "Combray." He immediately experiences powerlessness and failure: "She would make me tell her . . . about the poems that I intended to compose . . . But as soon as I asked myself the question, and tried to discover some subject to which I could impart a philosophical significance of infinite value . . . I would feel . . . that I was wholly devoid of genius" (1:243, trans. mod.; I, 170). The hero is caught in a misunderstanding: for him, the insurmountable obstacle to becoming a writer is the invention of a deep and philosophical subject. He wants to become "the foremost writer of the day" (1: 244; I, 171), but without a grand subject, he must give up this dream – "perhaps this lack of genius, this black cavity which gaped in my mind when I ransacked it for the theme of my future writings, was itself no more than an insubstantial illusion" (1:244; I, 171).

The sight of Madame de Guermantes in church intensifies his slump. Written at the beginning of 1911, *Cahier* 11 sketches out the hero's walks along the Guermantes way up to the conclusion of 'Combray" (fos. 7–26), and introduces the theme of renouncing writing (fos. 12–15).

> Elle [Madame de Guermantes] me faisait raconter le sujet des ~~romans~~ <poèmes> que je devais ~~écrire~~ <composer>. Et ce m'était un avertissement que, puisque je voulais ~~écrire~~ être écrivain qu'il était temps de penser à ce que je voulais écrire. Mais dès que je me le demandais <tâchant + <+de trouver un sujet philosophique d'une profondeur infinie [11 v°]>>, mon esprit cessait aussitôt de fonctionner, je ne voyais plus que du noir devant moi. /, <et ne me considérant pas du dehors comme une autre personne, et n'ayant pour mesurer ~~ma~~/mon ~~pensée que la~~ pouvoir intellectuel que la sensation <intime> immédiate et changeante que j'en recevais [add. marg.]> ~~Je~~ <je ne me> sentais que je n'avais pas ~~de~~ <aucun> génie, <peut-être était-ce une maladie qui l'empêchait de naître>, j'étais inquiet . . .

> She [Madame de Guermantes] asked me to tell her about the ~~novels~~ <poems> I intended to ~~write~~ <compose>. And this was a warning to me that, since I wanted ~~to write~~ to be a writer, it was time to think about what I wanted to write. But as soon as I asked myself, <attempting + <+ to find a philosophical subject of infinite profundity [11 v°]>>, my mind ceased to function, and I saw nothing but darkness before me. /, <and not considering myself from the outside as another person, and having nothing to gauge ~~my~~/my ~~thought but the~~ intellectual power except that <private> immediate and mutable sensation that I received from it [marg. add.]> ~~I felt~~ <I did not feel> that I had ~~no~~ <any> genius, <perhaps this was some affliction that did not allow it to be born>, I was worried . . . [10]

Two remarkable details emerge in this important draft: first, the reference to doubling as a condition of literary success, and by extension its absence, "not considering myself from the outside as another person," as condemnation to failure; second, the association between writing and affliction or "darkness."

Despite his lack of literary inspiration, unexpected moments of ecstasy and rapture suspend the hero's discouragement. *Cahier* 11 takes up older fragments from *Cahiers* 12 and 26, dating to 1909, where neither the theme of creative impotence nor the final revelation of the three church steeples figured, setting up the oscillation between lasting failure and fleeting happiness that would not be resolved until the scene of "Perpetual Adoration" in *Le Temps retrouvé*. In *Cahier* 26 an intense creative joy was already inspired by the vision of the church steeple, but left without resolution:

> ~~De~~ C'est de ces promenades solitaires que je fis à l'automne du côté de Méséglise que date une des lois <vraiment immuables> de ma vie spirituelle.

> Tout d'un coup tandis qu'une image passait sous mes yeux ou dans ma pensée, je sentais à un plaisir particulier, à une sorte de profondeur, qu'il y avait quelque chose *sous* elle, une réalité plus profonde.
>
> ~~From~~ It was these solitary walks I took along the Méséglise way that autumn that gave rise to one of the <truly immutable> laws of my spiritual life. All of a sudden, as an image passed before my eyes or in my mind, I felt that within a given pleasure, at a kind of depth, there was something *under* it, a deeper reality.[11]

This "law" linking sensation and spiritual life is not yet related to writing. A few pages earlier in *Cahier* 26, an early version of the famous "Gosh, gosh, gosh, gosh" (I:219; I, 153) was added to a verso, as "Gosh, how lovely!," a feeling of being overcome by a simple joy:

> Quelquefois au lieu des coups de parapluie de droite et de gauche, ~~c'était~~ l'exaltation de ma pensée s'échappait en des mots qui ne la traduisaient pas plus clairement. ~~Je criais: Zut, ou: Que c'est beau ! Je riais~~ Je me rappelle encore la première fois ~~où frappant de mon parapluie~~ où dans l'ivresse des idées que je formais, frappant d'un coup de parapluie le coude du pont vieux, je criai: Zut, que c'est beau ! en riant de // bonheur. ~~Je m'arrêtai~~ En entendant ce: 'Zut" je m'arrêtai malgré la pluie qui commençait à tomber. . . . <Je cherchai à revenir à quelques instants en arrière et à apercevoir cette idée dont le passage+> <+m'avait rendu si heureux que j'avais crié, et que je n'avais pas vue>. Et depuis je n'ai guère fait autre chose ~~dans mes meilleurs mome~~ <en un certain sens et pour une partie au moins de ce que j'ai écrit> quand j'écrivais que ~~revenir~~ d'essayer de revenir sur ces minutes heureuses où l'on crie Zut que c'est beau, et de dire ce qu'était la minute heureuse, que "Zut que c'est beau" ne dit pas . . . Dans cet ordre d'idées <même> les <petits> pastiches qu'on a lus de moi, ne sont que la continuation de l'effort qui commence sur le pont vieux.
>
> Sometimes, instead of swipes of my umbrella from right or left, ~~it was~~ the exaltation of my thought escaped in words that did not translate it any more clearly. ~~I cried out: Gosh, or: How lovely ! I laughed~~ I still remember the first time ~~when, striking with my umbrel~~la when, intoxicated by the ideas taking shape in my mind, striking my umbrella on the curve of the old bridge, I cried out: Gosh, how lovely it is! laughing with // happiness. ~~I stopped~~ On hearing this: "Gosh" I stopped despite the rain that was beginning to fall. . . . <I tried to return to a few earlier moments and to glimpse the idea whose passage+> <+had made me so happy that I had cried out, and that I had not seen>. And from that moment I have done nothing else ~~in my best mome~~ <in a certain sense and for a part at least of what I have written> when I was writing than ~~to return~~ to try to return to those happy minutes where one exclaims Gosh, how lovely it is, and to say what that happy minute was, which "How lovely it is" cannot express . . . In

> this sense <even> the <little> pastiches of mine that people have read, are nothing but the continuation of the effort that began on the old bridge.[12]

In this passage, the confusion of the author and the hero or narrator is obvious, since the profession of faith mentions those "little pastiches of mine that people have read."[13] Narrator and author are entwined throughout these pages on literary vocation, and both share the experience of failure, which legitimates the temptation to read the encounter between the hero and Bergotte autobiographically.

The innovation of *Cahier* 11, in 1911, consists in the author's reflections on literary vocation, the philosophical failure of grand ideas, and poetic revelation by way of little things, since such reflections were absent from the earlier *Cahiers* 12 and 26. The hero lacks the philosophical ideas he believes he needs in order to become a writer, and he bemoans this lack, but he also experiences moments of intense joy and exaltation ("Gosh!"), which do not, for now, lead to anything, because he does not see them as a proper subject for literary creation. Yet these intermittent exaltations are described in the very same terms as the happiness felt when reading Bergotte. Such moments are not yet linked to writing or literature, as if the misunderstanding regarding the nature of literary inspiration needed to persist.

The three church steeples

The scene of the "three church steeples" provides the revelation, separating writing from great ideas and linking it instead to little things. This final epiphany was suggested in *Cahier* 26, which simply enumerated occasions for ecstasy, much in the style of *Carnet* 1: "quelque image qui était a priori sans valeur intellectuelle, quelque clocher filant dans une perspective, quelque fleur de sauge, quelque tête de jeune fille" ["some image that was, a priori, without intellectual value, some church steeple receding in perspective, some sage flower, some young girl's head"].[14] This starting point is amplified, in 1911, by the curious insertion of the page about the three church steeples to "Combray." Here Proust takes up again an article dating to 1907, "Impressions de route en automobile," published in the *Figaro*; he attributes to the hero, still a child, the adult writer's text on the three steeples of Caen, seen while being chauffeured by Agostinelli. Later, when including this page in *Pastiches et mélanges* in 1918, he would preface it with a note: "in *Du côté de chez Swann*, it is only partially cited . . . in quotation marks, as an example of what I wrote in my childhood. And in the fourth volume (not yet in print) of *À la recherche du temps perdu*, the publication in the *Figaro* of this reworked page is the subject of nearly an entire chapter" (*CSB* 64). Proust's note attests to the connection between the page from "Combray" about the three church steeples and the experience of reading the article in the *Figaro*, much further in the novel, in *Albertine disparue*.

While the scene associates writing with the delight of little things and thus announces an alternative to failure, this conclusion nevertheless remains implicit:

> Without admitting to myself that what lay hidden behind the steeples of Martinville must be something analogous to a pretty phrase, since it was in the form of words which gave me pleasure that it had appeared to me, I borrowed a pencil and some paper from the doctor, and in spite of the jolting of the carriage, to appease my conscience and to satisfy my enthusiasm, composed the following little fragment, which I have since discovered and now reproduce with only a slight revision here and there. (1:255; I, 179)

The doctor Percepied is substituted for the tax collector of *Cahier* 11;[15] both are avatars of Agostinelli, the original driver. Here, an excerpt of the 1907 *Figaro* article is inserted, without modification, along with the following commentary:

> I never thought again of this page, but at the moment when . . . I had finished writing it, I was so filled with happiness, I felt that it had so entirely relieved my mind of its obsession with the steeples and the mystery which lay behind them, that, as though I myself were a hen and had just laid an egg, I began to sing at the top of my voice. (1: 256–257; I, 180)

An article published in the *Figaro* when the author was 36 is inserted into the novel, presented as a piece of juvenilia – the interpolation is rather strange. Why might this piece be of such importance? Why does it elicit such joy? The church steeples give the illusion that they are moving, whereas it is the traveler who is in motion. By this effect of shifting perspective, the world appears to move while the observer remains immobile. This is an ideal short piece: it is overwhelming because it contains a revelation of the essence of art. In the midst of the hero's perceived failure, it manages a small victory: it announces the hope of a triumph over creative impotence, offering a glimpse of what will come in *Le Temps retrouvé*. The piece, "a little prose poem which I had made up years before at Combray on coming home from a walk" (2: 35; I, 447), is the one Norpois will later read, at the instigation of the hero's father, when the ambassador comes to dinner. Norpois will detect in it "the unfortunate influence of Bergotte" (2: 62; I, 465).

Debating paternity

When did Proust realize he had overcome the narrator's fluctuations between chronic doldrums and rare bouts of enthusiasm, that he had vanquished powerlessness in spite of repeated failures? By November 1913 he gave the sense of already knowing this. In the novel, the prolonged motif of the vain wait for publication of the article in the *Figaro* returns like a Wagnerian theme that traverses the better part of the narrative: the childish text, inserted in "Combray" and shown to Norpois in *À l'ombre de jeunes filles en fleurs*, is sent to the *Figaro* in *Le Côté de Guermantes*, and finally published in *Albertine disparue*, when the hero no longer expects it and can no longer readily recognize it.

I would like to suggest that this realization coincided with the rereading of the galleys in the spring of 1913, before Louis de Robert and Lucien Daudet became the first readers of the proofs. In January of a year that "started badly," with "troubles and grief" (*Corr* XII, 21, 23), Proust confided to Louis de Robert that, in his dejection, he compared himself to the authors he was reading, and felt that he could no longer understand his contemporaries. "When I read a sentence where I recognize an idea or image of which I had thought, which I found odious, and of which I am aware and have the memory of having gone far beyond (I who am such a small thing)," he writes, he experiences stupefaction in seeing *La Nouvelle Revue Française* gush with admiration for the writer he harshly judged as being of little consequence, and he is astounded at the blindness of literary critics (*Corr* XII, 38). Proust cites the example of the works of Charles Péguy, to which he soon adds the name of Jacques Normand, a striking coincidence since he mentions him without knowing that Normand is the very reader whose report had caused Fasquelle's rejection of his manuscript.

Proust "recognized" in the work of some published writers, praised by critics, certain ideas or images that had occurred to him and that he had deemed unworthy of his ambitions. A similar test of recognition occurs in "Combray," during the hero's reading of Bergotte, but has the opposite effect, one of encouragement rather than discouragement:

> When, one day, I came across in a book by Bergotte some joke about an old family servant which the writer's solemn and magnificent prose made even more ironic, but which was the same joke I had often made to my grandmother about Françoise, and when, another time, I discovered that he considered not unworthy of reflection in one of those mirrors of truth which were his writings a remark similar to one which I had had occasion to make about our friend M. Legrandin . . . then it was suddenly revealed

> to me that my own humble existence and the realms of the true were less widely separated than I had supposed, that at certain points they actually coincided, and in my newfound confidence and joy I had wept upon his printed page as in the arms of a long-lost father. (I: 133, trans. mod.; I, 95)

When was this long sentence inserted into "Combray"? Might it not have been added precisely at the beginning of 1913? At that time, Proust felt himself trapped in a state of mutual incomprehension with his peers. In a letter to René Blum, whom he asked to serve as an intermediary to Grasset, he recounts all the reasons that could make a case against self-financed publication. Invoking the urgency imposed on him by his illness, he pushes all these reasons aside en masse, except for one, which he refutes in particular: "You have too much talent to pay for publication like some amateur." "This," he writes, "is true (except for the part about talent, about which I know nothing)" (*Corr* XII, 80). We should read the parenthesis as meaning "I do not know if I have any talent." This essential and humble term, *talent*, is a word the writer uses often to designate his own literary ability or inaptitude.

Over the course of 1913 Proust underwent the same perplexities about his aptitude for literary pursuits as the hero of "Combray." To Louis de Robert, in February 1913, he confesses his qualms in restrained form: "And while you have not yet read the full work I want you to know that you have recommended something that is not unpublishable. But will it ever be published?" (*Corr* XII, 87). In response, Louis de Robert encourages him in vain, as Bloch does in the novel: "Take heart; you will triumph in the end and you will taste the pure glory that comes from on high, that which we all hope for and you deserve, one of the best among us" (*Corr* XII, 89). Robert would later convey a friend's response to a mention of Proust: "'Ah, Marcel Proust!' she says to me, '*The man who has so much talent*!'"(*Corr* XII, 169). Talent, yet again.

In the second half of June, Proust sends the second proofs of nearly the whole of "Combray" to Louis de Robert, who soon responds: "I am still in admiration . . . *Cut nothing*, it would be a crime . . . so many original insights, so many observations of such surprising accuracy and truth!" (*Corr* XII, 219). He then sends the third version of the proofs to Lucien Daudet, though not without hesitation: "I am afraid to commit a 'roumestanerie' by offering you this, and, in the end, it must bore you to death" (*Corr* XII, 255) – meaning an offer made to be refused, as in Alphonse Daudet's *Numa Roumestan* (1881). Daudet responds quickly, and Proust writes in return: "what you call your admiration for my book is a product of your great kindness towards me. And perhaps this prodigious kindness has never been so manifest as in this quick reading and prompt reply" (*Corr* XII, 256–257). Proust still has doubts about his achievement, and refuses to believe in this "admiration" – Louis de Robert and Lucien Daudet use the same word, which is as pertinent as "talent" – because it came too rapidly to seem real.

Lucien Daudet showed the proofs to his mother, Alphonse Daudet's widow, eliciting Proust's gratitude: 'I am very happy about what you have told me of your mother's favorable opinion" (*Corr* XII, 266). Without going through Lucien, he thanked Madame Daudet for her reading of the proofs, playing on the word itself: "I can think of no 'proof' of mettle [épreuve] more formidable and penetrating than this one" (*Corr* XII, 272). A curious twist follows this reading: Madame Daudet – due to susceptibility or writerly vanity – believed that she had recognized in "Combray" an image that she thought Proust must have borrowed from her. This forced him to explain the accidental resemblance by referring to the very page from "Combray" where the hero recognizes himself in Bergotte, a page that Madame Daudet herself had mentioned in noticing the encounter, which confirms that this page was indeed one of those that struck Proust's first readers: "as in those pages to which you allude with such generosity, I reassured myself by thinking of Bergotte's vast reflections, so I drew confidence from my admiration for you . . . admiration is a small proof of resemblance" (*Corr* XII, 272). In all modesty, without presuming to "equal" Madame Daudet, Proust justifies the "resemblance" she believes to have found by invoking his own "admiration," and without giving more details. To Lucien, he explains further: "Madame Daudet may be certain that if there was an encounter, there was never any plagiarism; even if I had known her piece[16] before writing this page (in fact written years ago), I would have been incapable of introducing anything that did not come from me" (*Corr* XII, 258). The pages of *Cahier* 14 where the sentence in question appears,[17] significantly reworked, indeed date back to the spring of 1910.

In any case, this incident concerning an imaginary encounter and hypothetical plagiarism shows that the reading of the proofs by the Daudets, mother and son, was attentive and meticulous. Coming after Louis de Robert's reading and before that of Jean Cocteau, who was likely the third reader of *Du côté de chez Swann* before its publication (as mentioned in a letter to René Blum [*Corr* XXII, 295]), this reading gave Proust the "proof" he needed. He subsequently displayed confidence and determination: his letter to René Blum, in early November 1913, discusses a strategy for the publication of excerpts, articles, and advertisements in the press.

Bergotte *en abyme* in "Combray"

The minor quarrel over paternity with Madame Daudet confirms the importance of the pages about reading Bergotte in "Combray," as well as the importance of the notion of "encounter" – to use Proust's term – or of "recognition." These pages are heavily reworked in the Grasset proofs; the passage underwent so many corrections that Proust had to remove *placard* 15 from the set of galleys now at the Bibliothèque nationale de France and insert it in the other set of galleys now at the Bodmer Foundation,[18] where this *placard* features numerous handwritten additions. The episode was more succinct in the two typescripts, known as D1 and D2, that Proust sent to the Fasquelle (D1) and the NRF publishing house (D2) in the fall of 1912.[19] Therefore, the passage was developed in two distinct steps: first, at the beginning of 1913, on typescript D2 (it is absent from D1), when the typescript was returned by the NRF, before Proust sent it to Ollendorff, or once Ollendorff returned it, before he sent it to Grasset; second, on the Grasset proofs, in April or May 1913.

The development of these pages stems from the idea that the hero wants to know Bergotte's opinion about every possible thing. We read in the definitive text:

> Convinced that my thoughts would have seemed pure foolishness to that perfected spirit, I had so completely obliterated them all that, if I happened to encounter [*rencontrer*] in one of his books something which had already occurred to my own mind, my heart would swell as though some deity had, in his infinite bounty, restored it to me, had pronounced it to be beautiful and right. (I: 132, trans. mod.; I, 94)

Entirely absent from typescript D1, the idea of a fortuitous, accidental "encounter" between one of the hero's thoughts and one of Bergotte's appears in typescript D2, but in a minimal form, as we will see, and without the important development that follows in the definitive text, which was therefore added later:

> It happened now and then that a page of Bergotte would express precisely those ideas which I often used to write to my grandmother and my mother at night, when I was unable to sleep, so much so that this page of his had the appearance of a collection of epigraphs for me to set at the head of my letters. Even in later years, when I began to write a book of my own and the quality of some of my sentences seemed too inadequate to persuade me to go on with the undertaking, I would find their equivalent in Bergotte. But it was only then, when I read them in his pages, that I could enjoy them; when it was I myself who composed them, in my anxiety that they should

> exactly reproduce what I had perceived in my mind's eye, and in my fear of their not turning out "true to life," how could I find time to ask myself whether I was writing was pleasing! But in fact there was no other kind of prose, no other sort of ideas, that I really liked. (1: 132–133, trans. mod.; 1, 94–95)

Thus, this essential passage, which brings the hero and Bergotte closer, was absent from the two typescripts, D1 and D2. However, a short, rudimentary version can be found in a handwritten note on the verso of a page from D1.[20] This late idea for an addition, never added to D2, was therefore jotted down at a moment when Proust had D1 on hand but not D2, a situation that occurred in March and April 1913, when D2 was at the printer's.[21]

The brief note explicitly links the experience of the encounter with Bergotte to the reading of the famous article in the *Figaro*, which again confirms the profound link between these two episodes:

> I will say when I read the article [in the *Figaro*] that I read it as I used to read Bergotte. When I say that I find in Bergotte thoughts similar to my own; like things I had sometimes tried to write [en écrire],[22] I enjoyed them more than if it had been I who had written them; or, rather, I enjoyed them only when it was he[23] who had written them, for as long as it was me [lui qui les avait écrites, car tant que c'était moi], like a cook who has no time to be a gourmand, I learned only what I thought, what I wrote was similar to what I perceived, I was afraid that it was not that, that it was not good, I had no time to stop to see if it was pleasant . . . Yet, as soon as I read one of Bergotte's books, without a qualm, without effort, less severe towards him than towards myself, I found, all of sudden, in the things that I loved, a joy like that of a cook who doesn't have to cook for once, but can instead just eat, and thus find the time to be a gourmand.[24]

This canvas, including the comparison with the off-duty cook, would be reused and incorporated in the galleys,[25] which, as we have seen, necessitated the exchange of a BnF *placard* with a Bodmer *placard*. The amplified version appears on a *papier collé* over column 2 of *placard* 15:

> Even a bit later when ~~I tried to write~~ I ~~wanted to begin~~ began ~~a book it to which I~~ to ~~write~~ <compose> a book, ~~and aban several~~ <certain> phrases that I wrote and that did ~~not suffice~~ not seem to me good enough to encourage me to finish it, it happened that ~~when~~ I found ~~again later~~ <sometimes their> equivalent in Bergotte's work . . . when all of sudden I found them in the work of another, that is to say, without ~~a qualm~~ having a qualm, I // let myself finally experience the taste that I had for them, like [a] cook who not having to cook for once ~~can in that of others~~ finally finds the time ~~to eat~~ to be a gourmand.[26]

This addition was elicited by the remark, which follows in the definitive text, on the hero's words about Françoise or Legrandin that he sometimes rediscovered in Bergotte's work. It is therefore indeed this addition, absent from D1 and appearing on a *papier collé* folded onto the right margin of D2, that seems to have played the generative role in the comparison of the hero and Bergotte. That remark – which would be only slightly different in the definitive text (1: 133; 1, 95, cited on pages 261–262) – is thus the earliest point in this sequence: composed on the Bodmer galleys, it is displaced and stuck onto *placard* 15. The bottom of column 2 is cut and pasted at the top of column 3.[27]

To sum up: there was no trace of an "encounter" with Bergotte, of the hero's recognition of his own words in Bergotte's books, at the stage of *Cahiers* 29, 14, and 68, which sketch the hero's reading of the writer at Combray. All that can be found in those *Cahiers* is an incidental remark on Bergotte's use of "noble words," on his "solemn music" to describe "a familiar scene that became, by contrast, all the more comical," a remark illustrated by a quotation from Anatole France.[28] In those *Cahiers*, the narrator emphasized the writer's burlesque or heroic-comic poeticizing of simple things, and focused on the comic effect of this "noble language applied to vulgar things."[29] At that stage, the lesson learned from Bergotte related exclusively to his incommensurate way of speaking about ordinary life. Such is the originality of Bergotte's language, to which the hero is sensitive. Starting in the typescripts, this distance between lowly things and refined words becomes a particularity that the hero finds in his own writings. Such a characterization could just as well be applied to the way the narrator describes Françoise's kitchen as "a little temple of Venus" (1: 98; 1, 71), or to his grandiloquent image of Legrandin, "St Sebastian of snobbery" (1: 180; 1, 127).

Talent and genius

It is therefore credible to see the brief insertions made in the typescripts, and then their significant amplification in the galleys, as signs of the great writer's late recognition of himself. Indeed a parallel and equally essential addition follows a little further in the galleys, at the end of the section concerning Bergotte, concerning the writer's fans:

> I also noticed <~~something else~~> in the way Swann talked to me about Bergotte some ~~another~~ something that on the other hand was not particular to him, but ~~just as in all other circles~~ on the contrary, common to all fans

> of Bergotte at the time, ~~to some circle~~ in every circle . . . Like Swann, they said of Bergotte: "He has a delightful mind, so individual, he has a way of his own of saying things which is a little far-fetched, but so agreeable. You never need to look for the signature, you can tell his work at once." But none of them would have gone so far as to say: "He's a great writer, he has great talent." They did not even credit him with talent at all. They did not do so, because they did not know. / We are very slow to recognize in the peculiar ~~face~~ <~~mind~~> <physiognomy> ~~that a~~ of a new writer, the model which is labelled "great talent" in our museum of general ideas. Precisely because this physiognomy is new, we can find in it no resemblance to what we call talent. We say instead: originality, charm, delicacy, power; and then one day, we realize that it is precisely all this that adds up to talent.[30]

This remarkable passage, also absent from the manuscript as well as from the typescripts,[31] is thus also an addition to the Grasset galleys in April or May 1913, and it would change little in the definitive text. It attests to the writer's reflection about himself and his work, and to his realization of his own importance (more so than his "originality, charm, delicacy, power"), which he names "talent." As we have seen, the word occurs frequently in Proust's letters from 1913, to designate a writer's worth (it is also the word used by Louis de Robert's friend). The hero's rivalry with Bergotte and the narrator's meditation on the delayed recognition of Bergotte's talent are indeed inventions of 1913, in the typescripts and galleys, developed at length and carefully reworked on *placard* 15 in April and May 1913.

The passage is striking, and it was duly noted by the first readers of the novel, who applied it to Proust himself. It is cited, for example, in one of the best early reviews, that of Lucio D'Ambra, published in *La Rassegna contemporanea* on December 10, 1913. D'Ambra predicted that Proust would be considered equal to Stendhal in fifty years' time: "Still, no one would dare to say: 'He is a great writer, he possesses a very great genius.' They would not even say that he had genius. They did not say it because they did not know it."[32] The pages about Bergotte were immediately read as a *mise en abyme* of Proust's destiny, a commentary by Proust about the reception of his own book, a writer's reflection on the resistance that originality encounters before being recognized, "talent" being the word chosen by Proust to designate this value.

Let us conclude by returning to the leitmotiv of the article in the *Figaro* and to the fantastical scene in *Albertine disparue* that serves as its culmination. There, the scene concerns reading as if one were another; earlier, in "Combray," we saw the hero reading the other, Bergotte, as if he were reading himself. The crucial theme of doubling recurs in both scenes. We remember that the beginning of Proust's handwritten note on a verso of typescript D1, the first version of the development about Bergotte, linked the two passages: "I will say when I read the article that I read it as I used to read Bergotte."

My initial hypothesis was therefore not overly audacious. The amplification of the "encounters" with Bergotte, and the reflections on "talent," confirm that it was while correcting the Grasset galleys in April and May 1913, after many failures, disappointments, doubts and setbacks, that Proust, confronted with the shock of reading himself in proofs, became definitively aware of his own talent, of his greatness as a writer. This is further confirmed by the last allusion to the *Figaro* article in *Albertine disparue*, after the hero's disappointing visit to the Duke and Duchess of Guermantes, who have not seen the article. Attesting to the essential link between these two passages and the encounter or rivalry of the hero with Bergotte, the conclusion of the leitmotiv, characteristically delivered with some irony, is this:

> Two days later <in the morning>, I found myself rejoicing at the thought that Bergotte was a great admirer of my article, which he had been unable to read without envy. But a moment later my joy subsided. For Bergotte had written me not a word. I had simply wondered whether he would have liked the article, fearing that he would not. As I was asking myself the question, Mme de Forcheville had replied that he admired it enormously and considered it the work of a great writer. But she told me this while I was asleep: it was a dream. Almost all our dreams respond thus to the questions which we put to ourselves with complicated statements, stage productions with several characters, which however have no future.[33]

The passage appears in the fair copy of the manuscript as a marginal addition, but it had been so reworked in the typescript that it became illegible, and its transcription in the original edition of *Albertine disparue* in 1925 rendered it unrecognizable. It was important to restore it, because it shows to what extent Proust, like the narrator, desired to be recognized as a "great writer."

NOTES

1 *Carnet* 1, fos. 10v–11r, in Marcel Proust, *Carnets*, ed. Florence Callu and Antoine Compagnon (Paris: Gallimard, 2002), 49–50.

2 Cited in Louis de Robert, *Comment débuta Marcel Proust* (Paris: Gallimard, 1969), 9.

3 Charles Baudelaire, *Œuvres complètes*, ed. C. Pichois, Bibliothèque de la Pléiade (Paris: Gallimard, 1975), 1, 694.

4 *Cahier* 3, fo. 5r; see also Marcel Proust, *Contre Sainte-Beuve*, ed. Bernard de Fallois (Paris: Gallimard, 1954), 95.
5 *Cahier* 3, fo. 27r; see also Proust, *Contre Sainte-Beuve*, 95.
6 Michel de Montaigne, "Various outcomes of the same plan" (*Essays*, Book I, chapter 24), in *The Complete Works: Essays, Travel Journals, Letters*, trans. Donald M. Frame, Everyman Library (New York and Toronto: Alfred A. Knopf, 2003), 112.
7 The three fragments from *Cahier* 29 are dispersed in the Pléiade edition: (1), fos. 41r and 42r (I, 1027–1030); (2), fos. 47 to 51 (I, 781–783 and I, 1030–1032); (3), fos. 58 to 65 (I, 784–788).
8 *Cahier* 14, fos. 51 to 54 (I, 788–790) and fos. 66–85 (I, 758–766); *Cahier* 68, fos. 39r–50r.
9 *Cahier* 14, fo. 52r (I, 788).
10 *Cahier* 11, fos. 12r–13r (I, 878). The symbols < > enclose additions. The symbol / follows a punctuation mark that was struck through. The symbol + is used by Proust himself to indicate an addition written in a different location (that location is given in brackets). Marginal additions are signaled with [add. marg.], in English [marg. add.].
11 *Cahier* 26, fo. 15r (I, 839).
12 *Cahier* 26, fos. 9v–10v (I, 835–836).
13 Proust published pastiches based on the Lemoine Affair in *Le Figaro* between February 22 and March 21, 1908.
14 *Cahier* 26, fo. 16r.
15 *Cahier* 11, fo. 14r (I, 879).
16 A verse from the poem "Juin," published in a collection that appeared in May 1913. Julia Daudet, *Les Archipels lumineux* (Paris: Lemerre, 1913), 27.
17 *Cahier* 14, fo. 63r and 64r.
18 Anthony R. Pugh, *The Growth of* À la recherche du temps perdu*: A Chronological Examination of Proust's Manuscripts from 1909 to 1914*, 2 vols. (University of Toronto Press, 2004), II, 664. The set of galleys at the BnF was given the call number NAF 16753. The Bodmer proofs for "Combray" were published as Marcel Proust, *Du côté de chez Swann: Combray, Premières épreuves corrigées,* 1913, ed. Charles Méla (Paris: Gallimard, 2013).
19 BnF call numbers NAF 16730 and NAF 16733, respectively.
20 Typescript D1, fo. 138v, T1030. Sections of D1 and D2 were given page numbers 103a–u, from the Sunday reading scene to the development on Bergotte (1: 116–139; I, 83–99), attesting to a late montage, reworking elements from *Cahier* 68, fos. 39–50. See the Pléiade edition (I, 1078–1079), and Pugh, *Growth*, 636.
21 The Pléiade edition (I, 95, var. *a*), signals that this addition is absent from D1 and D2, and figures on the second set of proofs. The edition provides a transcription of the note added to D1 outlining the addition (I, 1147, n. 1).
22 Here, the Pléiade transcription omits "*en écrire*," signaled as "illegible."
23 Here, the Pléiade transcription jumps to "*moi*."
24 See Pléiade (I, 1147, n. 1), but my reading of the manuscript note is different, as signaled above.

25 See Pugh, *Growth*, 664.
26 *Du côté de chez Swann: Combray, Premières épreuves corrigées*, placard 15 (April 12, 1913), columns 2 and 3 (n.p.).
27 See Pugh, *Growth*, 664.
28 *Cahier* 29, fo. 48r; see Pléiade (1, 782).
29 *Cahier* 14, fo. 53r; see Pléiade (1, 789).
30 *Du côté de chez Swann: Combray, Premières épreuves corrigées*, placard 15 (April 12, 1913), column 5 (n.p.). See also the definitive version (1: 136–137; I, 97–98).
31 See Pléiade (1, 98, var. *a*).
32 Lucio d'Ambra, "Cronaca di Letteratura Francese," *La Rassegna Contemporanea* 6 (series 2):23, December 10, 1913, 822–824.
33 *Cahier* XIV (NAF 16721), fo. 33r. See also the definitive version (5: 799; IV, 171).

Bibliography

Unless otherwise stated, works in French are published in Paris.

WORKS BY MARCEL PROUST

À la recherche du temps perdu, ed. dir. J.-Y. Tadié, 4 vols., Bibliothèque de la Pléiade (Gallimard, 1987–1989).

Against Sainte-Beuve, trans. J. Sturrock, Penguin Classics (Harmondsworth: Penguin, 1988).

Cahiers 1 à 75 de la Bibliothèque nationale de France, ed. dir. N. Mauriac Dyer (Turnhout/Paris: Brepols/Bibliothèque nationale de France, 2008–).

Carnets, ed. F. Callu and A. Compagnon (Gallimard, 2002).

Comme Elstir Chardin . . . , postface S. Pierron (Altamira, 1999).

Contre Sainte-Beuve précédé de *Pastiches et mélanges* et suivi de *Essais et articles*, ed. P. Clarac and Y. Sandre, Bibliothèque de la Pléiade (Gallimard, 1971).

Contre Sainte-Beuve, ed. B. de Fallois (Gallimard, 1954).

Correspondance, ed. P. Kolb, 21 vols. (Plon, 1970–1993).

Du côté de chez Swann, preface and notes by A. Compagnon (Gallimard [folio], 1988).

Du côté de chez Swann: Combray, Premières épreuves corrigées, 1913, ed. C. Méla (Gallimard, 2013).

In Search of Lost Time, trans. C. K. Scott Moncrieff, T. Kilmartin, and A. Mayor, revised by D. J. Enright, 6 vols. (New York: Modern Library, 2003).

In the Shadow of Young Girls in Flower, trans. J. Grieves (Harmondsworth and New York: Penguin, 2002).

Jean Santeuil, précédé de *Les Plaisirs et les Jours*, ed. P. Clarac and Y. Sandre, Bibliothèque de la Pléiade (Gallimard, 1971).

Lettres: 1879–1922, ed. F. Leriche with C. Szylowicz, preface and afterword by K. Kolb, biographical notes by V. Greene (Plon, 2004).

Lettres à Reynaldo Hahn, ed. P. Kolb (Gallimard, 1956).

Lettres à une amie: recueil de quarante-et-une lettres inédites adressées à Marie Nordlinger 1889–1908 (Manchester: Éditions du Calame, 1942).

On Art and Literature, 1896–1919, trans. Sylvia Townsend Warner (New York: Carroll & Graf, 1997).

On Reading Ruskin: Prefaces to La Bible d'Amiens *and* Sésame et les Lys *with Selections form the Notes to the Translated Texts*, ed. and trans. J. Autret, W. Burford and P. J. Wolfe (New Haven, CT: Yale University Press, 1987).
Les Plaisirs et les Jours (Calmann-Lévy, 1896).
Ruskin, J., and M. Proust, *Sésame et les Lys*, précédé de *Sur la lecture*, intro. by A. Compagnon (Editions Complexe, 1987).
Ruskin, J., *La Bible d'Amiens*, trans., preface and notes by M. Proust (Mercure de France, 1926).

Manuscripts are available online at gallica.bnf.fr. A detailed inventory is available at www.item.ens.fr/index.php?id=578147

OTHER WORKS

Abbate, C., "Music: Drastic or Gnostic?," *Critical Inquiry* 30 (2004), 505–536.
Addison, J., *Remarks on Several Parts of Italy*, 2nd edn. (London: J. Tonson, 1718).
Albaret, C., *Monsieur Proust*, trans. B. Bray (New York: New York Review of Books, 2003).
Allen, W., dir., *Annie Hall*, Rollins-Joffe Productions, 1977.
Ambra, L. de, "Cronaca di Letteratura Francese," *La Rassegna Contemporanea* 6(series 2):23 (December 10, 1913), 822–824.
Apollinaire, G., "La vie anecdotique," *Mercure de France*, April 1, 1917, no. 451, 557–561.
"Zone," trans. R. Shattuck. *The Yale Anthology of Twentieth-Century French Poetry*, ed. M. A. Caws (New Haven: Yale University Press, 2004).
Arendt, H., *Antisemitism: Part One of The Origins of Totalitarianism* (New York: Harvest/HBJ, 1968).
Aristotle, *De anima*, trans. Hugh Lawson-Tancred (Harmondsworth: Penguin, 1986).
Aubert, N., ed., *Proust and the Visual* (Cardiff: University of Wales Press, 2012).
Baldwin, T., *The Picture as Spectre in Diderot, Proust, and Deleuze* (London: Legenda, 2011).
Bales, R., *Proust and the Middle Ages* (Geneva: Droz, 1975).
Bardac, H., "Madeleine Lemaire et Marcel Proust," *La Revue de Paris* 56:8 (August 1949), 137–142.
Barthes, R., *Œuvres complètes*, ed. É. Marty, 5 vols. (Seuil, 2002).
Batchelor, J., *John Ruskin: No Wealth but Life* (London: Chatto & Windus, 2000).
Baudelaire, C., *Œuvres complètes*, ed. C. Pichois, Bibliothèque de la Pléiade (Gallimard, 1975).
Bedriomo, E., *Proust, Wagner, et la coïncidence des arts* (J.-M. Place, 1984).
Belting, H., *An Anthropology of Images: Picture, Medium, Body*, trans. T. Dunlap (Princeton University Press, 2011).
Blanc, C., *Les Beaux-Arts à l'Exposition Universelle de 1878* (Librairie Renouard, 1878).

Blanchot, M., *The Book to Come*, trans. C. Mandell (Stanford University Press, 2003).
Borel, P., "Revue dramatique," *Le Journal du commerce*, July 15, 1844.
Bretonne, R. de la [J. Lorrain], "Pall Mall Semaine (Jeudi 28 janvier)," *Le Journal*, February 3, 1897.
"Pall Mall Semaine (Lundi 22 juin)," *Le Journal*, July 1, 1896.
Brown, P., *Venetian Narrative Painting in the Age of Carpaccio* (New Haven, CT: Yale University Press, 1988).
Butler, J., "Is Kinship Always Already Heterosexual?," *Differences: A Journal of Feminist Cultural Studies* 13:1 (2002), 14–44.
Callu, F., with A. Angremy, eds., *Catalogue des Nouvelles acquisitions françaises du département des Manuscrits, 1972–1986, nos. 16428–1875*, (Bibliothèque nationale de France, 1999).
Carbone, M., "Composing Vinteuil: Proust's Unheard Music," *RES: Anthropology and Aesthetics* 48 (2005), 163–165.
Carter, W. C., *Marcel Proust: A Life* (New Haven, CT: Yale University Press, 2000).
Proust in Love (New Haven, CT: Yale University Press, 2006).
The Proustian Quest (New York University Press, 1992).
Chaleil, F., ed., *Gustave Moreau par ses contemporains* (Éditions de Paris, 1998).
Colette, *Œuvres*, ed. C. Pichois, Bibliothèque de la Pléiade (Gallimard, 1984).
Collier, P., *Proust and Venice*, trans. D. Fink (Cambridge University Press, 1989).
Compagnon, A., *Les Antimodernes: De Joseph de Maistre à Roland Barthes* (Gallimard, 2005).
"Le 'profil assyrien' ou l'antisémitisme qui n'ose pas dire son nom: les libéraux dans l'affaire Dreyfus," *Études de langue et littérature françaises* (Université de Kyoto) 28 (1997), 133–150.
Proust Between Two Centuries, trans. R. E. Goodwin (New York: Columbia University Press, 1992).
Connelly, J., *Music in Marcel Proust's* À la recherche du temps perdu (Hingham, MA: Orris Publishing, 2013). www.proust-ink.com/proust_playlist.pdf
Coutts, H., *The Art of Ceramics: European Ceramic Design 1500–1830* (New Haven, CT: Yale University Press, 2001).
Cusack, C. M., "Hagiography and History: The Legend of Saint Ursula," in *This Immense Panorama: Studies in Honour of Eric J. Sharpe*, ed. C. M. Cusack and P. Oldmeadow (Sydney: School of Studies in Religion, University of Sydney, 1999).
Daudet, J., *Les Archipels lumineux* (Lemerre, 1913).
Dehaene, S., *Reading in the Brain: The Science and Evolution of a Human Invention* (London and New York: Viking, 2009).
Deleuze, G., *Proust and Signs: The Complete Text*, trans. R. Howard (Minneapolis: University of Minnesota Press, 2000).
Deleuze, G., and F. Guattari, *A Thousand Plateaus, Capitalism and Schizophrenia*, trans. B. Massumi (Minneapolis: University of Minnesota Press, 1987).
Derrida, J., *Writing and Difference*, trans. A. Bass (University of Chicago Press, 1978).

Dias, N., *Le Musée d'Ethnographie du Trocadéro, 1878–1908: anthropologie et muséologie en France* (Éditions du CNRS, 1991).

Diderot, D., "Letter on the Deaf and Dumb, For the Use of Those Who Hear and Speak," in *Selected Writings*, ed. and intro. by L. G. Crocker, trans. by D. Coltman (New York: Macmillan, 1966).

Salons, ed. J. Seznec and J. Adhémar, 4 vols. (Oxford: Clarendon Press, 1963).

Diesbach, G. de, *Proust* (Perrin, 1991).

Disdéri, E., *Essai sur l'art de la photographie*, ed. F. Masanès (Séguier, 2003).

Dreyfus, R., *Souvenirs sur Marcel Proust* (Grasset, 1926).

Drumont, E., *La France juive: Essai d'histoire contemporaine* (Beirut, Lebanon: Édition Charlemagne, 1994).

Emerson, R. W., "History," in *Essays* (London: James Fraser, 1841).

Ender, E., *Architexts of Memory: Literature, Science, and Autobiography* (Ann Arbor: University of Michigan Press, 2005).

Finlay, R., *The Pilgrim Art: Cultures of Porcelain in World History* (Berkeley: University of California Press, 2010).

Flat, P., *Musée Gustave Moreau: l'artiste – son oeuvre – son influence: 18 héliogravures hors texte* (Société de l'Édition Artistique, 1899).

Fraisse, L., *La correspondance de Proust, son statut dans l'oeuvre, l'histoire de son édition* (Besançon: Annales Littéraires de l'Université de Franche-Comté, 1998).

"Un témoignage rapproché sur Marcel Proust: la correspondance inédite de Reynaldo Hahn avec les dames Lemaire," *Marcel Proust Aujourd'hui* 9 (2012), 9–29.

Freedman, J., "Coming out of the Jewish Closet with Marcel Proust," in *Queer Theory and the Jewish Question*, ed. D. Boyarin, D. Itzkovitz, and A. Pellegrini (New York: Columbia University Press, 2003).

Freeman, E., "Queer Belongings: Kinship Theory and Queer Theory," in *A Companion to Lesbian, Gay, Bisexual, Transgender, and Queer Studies*, ed. G. E. Haggerty and M. McGarry (Malden, MA and Oxford: Blackwell, 2007).

Freud, S., "Das Unheimliche," *Imago* 5 (1919).

Frizot, M., ed., *Femmes peintres et salons au temps de Proust, de Madeleine Lemaire à Berthe Morisot* (Hazan/Musée Marmottan Monet, 2010).

Gallo, R., *Proust's Latin Americans* (Baltimore: Johns Hopkins University Press, 2014).

Gamble, C. J., *Proust as Interpreter of Ruskin: The Seven Lamps of Translation* (Birmingham, AL: Summa Publications, 2002).

"Zipporah: A Ruskinian Enigma Appropriated by Marcel Proust," *Word & Image* 15:4 (1999), 381–394.

Gandelman, C., "The Drawings of Marcel Proust," *Adam International Review* 40:394–396 (1976), 21–57.

Garner, P., *Émile Gallé* (London: Academy Editions, 1976).

Garnier, F., *Le langage de l'image au Moyen Âge: Signification et symbolique* (Le Léopard d'Or, 1982).

Gastaldi, A.-L., and Ivanoff, P., eds., *Marcel Proust, une vie en musiques* (Archimbaud/Even & Arts/Riveneuve, 2012).

Gautier, T., *Italia: Voyage en Italie*, ed. M.-H. Girard (La Boîte à Documents, 1997).

Gibbon, E., *The Letters of Edward Gibbon*, ed. J. E. Norton (London: Cassell, 1956).

Gibhardt, B. R., and J. Ramos, eds., *Marcel Proust et les arts décoratifs: poétique, matérialité, histoire* (INHA/Classiques Garnier, 2013).

Girard, R., *Deceit, Desire, and the Novel: Self and Other in Literary Structure*, trans. Y. Freccero (Baltimore: Johns Hopkins University Press, 1965).

Gleick, J., "Quiet Clay Revealed as Vibrant and Primal," *New York Times*, May 5, 1987.

Goethe, J. W., *Italian Journey, 1786–1788*, ed. T. P. Saine and J. L. Sammons, trans. R. R. Heitner (New York: Suhrkamp, 1989).

Goffman, E., *Stigma: Notes on the Management of Spoiled Identity* (Englewood Cliffs, NJ: Prentice-Hall, 1963).

Goncourt, J., and E., *Arts et artistes* (Hermann, 1997).

Gordon, J. S., "The Country Club," *American Heritage* 41:6 (fall 1990), 75–84.

Goujon, F., "Le cryptage autobiographique dans *Les Plaisirs et les Jours*," *Bulletin d'informations proustiennes* 30 (1999), 103–126.

Goulart, R., *Groucho Marx, King of the Jungle* (New York: Thomas Dunne Books/St. Martin's Minotaur, 2005).

Greene, V., and C. Szylowicz, "Le miroir des images: étude de quelques dessins médiévaux de Proust," *Bulletin d'informations proustiennes* 28 (1997), 7–29.

Gregh, F., "*Les Plaisirs et les Jours*, par Marcel Proust," *La Revue de Paris*, July 15, 1896.

Hamilton, P., and R. Hargreave, *The Beautiful and the Damned: The Creation of Identity in Nineteenth Century Photography* (Burlington, VT: Lund Humphries, 2001).

Hamon, P., *L'ironie littéraire: Essai sur les formes de l'écriture oblique* (Hachette Supérieur, 1996).

Harkness, N., and M. Schmid, eds., *Au seuil de la modernité: Proust, Literature and the Arts* (Oxford and New York: Peter Lang, 2011).

Heerman, V., dir., *Animal Crackers*, Paramount Pictures, 1930.

Hewison, R., *Ruskin On Venice: The Paradise of Cities* (New Haven, CT: Yale University Press, 2009).

Hilton, T., *John Ruskin: The Later Years* (New Haven, CT: Yale University Press, 2000).

Hirschfeld, M., *The Transvestites: The Erotic Drive to Cross-Dress*, trans. M. A. Lombardi-Nash (Amherst, MA: Prometheus Books, 1991).

Hodson L., ed., *Marcel Proust: the Critical Heritage* (London: Routledge, 1997).

Hughes, E. J., "The Primitivism of Françoise," in *Marcel Proust: A Study in the Quality of Awareness* (Cambridge University Press, 1983).

Hulme, F. E., *The History, Principles, and Practice of Symbols in Christian Art* (New York: Sonnenschein, 1910).

Ifri, P., *Céline et Proust: correspondances proustiennes dans l'oeuvre de L.-F. Céline* (Birmingham, AL: Summa, 1996).

Ireland, C., "Confronting Evil, Embracing Life: Two Truncated Harvard Conferences Prove Surprisingly Relevant after a Cave-dark Week," *Harvard Gazette*, April 23, 2013.

James, H., *What Maisie Knew* (Oxford University Press, 1996).

Jankélévitch, V., *Music and the Ineffable*, trans. C. Abbate (Princeton University Press, 2003).

Jarocinski, S., *Debussy: Impressionism and Symbolism*, trans. R. Myers (London: Eulenburg Books, 1976).

Jaurès, J., "L'affaire Panama. Le devoir du gouvernement," discours parlementaire, February 8, 1893. www.assembleenationale.fr/histoire/jaures/discours/panama_08021893.asp

Johnson, T., "Marcel Proust et Gustave Moreau," *Bulletin de la Société des Amis de Marcel Proust* 28 (1978).

"The Painter and his Art in the Works of Marcel Proust," Ph.D. thesis, University of Wisconsin, 1964.

"Proust and Giotto: Foundations for an Allegorical Interpretation of *À la recherche du temps perdu*," in *Marcel Proust: A Critical Panorama*, ed. L. B. Price (Urbana: University of Illinois Press, 1973).

Karpeles, E., *Paintings in Proust: A Visual Companion to In Search of Lost Time* (London and New York: Thames & Hudson, 2008).

Kato, Y., *Étude génétique des épisodes d'Elstir dans À la recherche du temps perdu* (Tokyo: Surugadai-Shuppansha, 1998).

"Proust et Manet: à propos des 'Notes sur Manet' de Jacques-Émile Blanche," *Gallia: Bulletin de la Société de Langue et Littérature Françaises de l'Université d'Osaka* 39 (1999), 1–8.

Kittler, F., *Discourse Networks 1800/1900*, trans. M. Metteer with C. Cullens (Stanford University Press, 1990).

Gramophone, Film, Typewriter, trans. G. Winthrop-Young and M. Wutz (Stanford University Press, 1999).

Kivy, P., *Authenticities: Philosophical Reflections on Musical Performance* (Ithaca, NY: Cornell University Press, 1995).

Kleeblatt, N. L., ed., *The Dreyfus Affair: Art, Truth, and Justice* (Berkeley: University of California Press, 1987).

Klibansky, R., E. Panofsky, and F. Saxl, *Saturn and Melancholy* (London: Nelson, 1964).

Kolb, P., "Marcel Proust et les dames Lemaire," *Bulletin de la Société des Amis de Marcel Proust et des Amis de Combray* 14 (1964), 114–151.

Kristeva, J., *Time and Sense: Proust and the Experience of Literature*, trans. R. Guberman (New York: Columbia University Press, 1996).

Kugler, F., *A Hand-book of the History of Painting* (London: John Murray, 1842).

La Fontaine, J. de, "Le Geai paré des plumes du Paon," in *Œuvres complètes*, ed. J.-P. Collinet, Bibliothèque de la Pléiade (Gallimard, 1991).

Landes-Ferrali, S., *Proust et le Grand Siècle* (Tübingen: Gunter Narr Verlag, 2004).
Lassels, R., *The Voyage of Italy* (Vincent du Moutier, 1670).
Leonard, D. R., "Proust et Ruskin: réincarnations intertextuelles," *Bulletin d'informations proustiennes* 24 (1993), 67–82.
Le Pichon, Y., *Le Musée retrouvé de Marcel Proust* (Stock, 1990).
Leroy-Beaulieu, A., *Israël chez les nations* (Calmann-Lévy, 1893).
Levitin, D., "Hit the Reset Button in Your Brain," *New York Times*, August 9, 2014.
Lhéritier, G., ed., *Proust: du temps perdu au temps retrouvé* (Aristophil/Équateurs/Musée des Lettres et Manuscrits, 2010).
Mâle, É. *L'art religieux du XIII*[e] *siècle en France. Étude sur l'iconographie du Moyen Âge et ses sources d'inscription*, new edition, revised and augmented (Armand Colin, 1902).
Religious Art in France of the Thirteenth Century, trans. Dora Nussey (London: J. M. Dent and New York: E. P. Dutton, 1913).
Malraux, A., *Picasso's Mask*, trans. J. Guicharnaud (New York: Holt, Rinehart & Winston, 1976).
Marx, G., *Groucho and Me* (New York: Random House, 1959).
Maspero, G., *Guide to the Cairo Museum*, trans. J. E. and A. A. Quibell (Cairo: Printing-office of the French Institute of Oriental Archaeology, 1910).
Life in Ancient Egypt and Assyria, [no translator credited] (New York: Appleton, 1892).
Mauriac Dyer, N., "Dessins," in *Dictionnaire Marcel Proust*, ed. A. Bouillaguet and B. G. Rogers, (Champion, 2004), 297–298.
Mauriac Dyer, N., and K. Yoshikawa, eds., *Proust aux brouillons* (Turnhout: Brepols, 2011).
Mauriac Dyer, N., K. Yoshikawa, and P.-E. Robert, eds., *Proust face à l'héritage du XIXe siècle: tradition et métamorphose* (Presses Sorbonne Nouvelle, 2012).
Maurois, A., *Les Trois Dumas* (Hachette, 1957).
Maurois, M., *Les Cendres brûlantes* (Flammarion, 1986).
Mauss, M., *The Gift: The Form and Reason for Exchange in Archaic Societies*, trans. W. D. Halls (New York: W. W. Norton, 2000).
May, G., "Chardin vu par Diderot et par Proust," *PMLA* 72:3 (June 1957), 403–418.
McCauley, E. A., *A.A.E. Disdéri and the Carte de visite Portrait Photograph* (New Haven, CT: Yale University Press, 1985).
McDonald, C., *The Proustian Fabric: Associations of Memory* (Lincoln: University of Nebraska Press, 1991).
Melnick, D., "Proust, Music, and the Reader," *Modern Language Quarterly* 41 (1980).
Merleau-Ponty, M., *The Visible and the Invisible: Studies in Phenomenology and Existential Philosophy*, trans. A. Lingis (Chicago, IL: Northwestern University Press, 1969).
Migeon, G., *Le Caire* (Laurens, 1909).
Miguet-Ollagnier, M., *La Mythologie de Marcel Proust* (Besançon: Presses Universitaires de Franche-Comté, 1982).

Molmenti, P., and G. Ludwig, *The Life and Works of Vittorio Carpaccio*, trans. R. H. Hobart Cust (London: John Murray, 1907).

Montaigne, M. de, *The Complete Works: Essays, Travel Journals, Letters*, trans. D. M. Frame, Everyman's Library (New York: Alfred A. Knopf, 2003).

Montesquiou, R. de, *Les Quarante Bergères, portraits satiriques en vers inédits* (Librairie de France, 1925).

Roseaux pensants (Bibliothèque-Charpentier, 1897).

Mortimer, A. K., and K. Kolb, eds., *Proust in Perspective: Visions and Revisions* (Urbana and Chicago: University of Illinois Press, 2002).

Murakami, Y., "Gomorrhe 1913–1915: survivance de l'affaire Dreyfus dans le Cahier 54," *Genesis* 36 (2013) 79–88.

Murat, L., "Les souliers rouges de la duchesse, ou la vulgarité de l'aristocratie française," in *D'Après Proust*, ed. P. Forest and S. Audeguy (Gallimard/NRF, 2013).

Naccache, L., *Le nouvel inconscient: Freud, Christophe Colomb des neurosciences* (Odile Jacob, 2006).

Nancy, J.-L., *On the Commerce of Thinking: Of Books and Bookstores*, trans. D. Wills (New York: Fordham University Press, 2009).

Nattiez, J.-J., *Proust as Musician*, trans. D. Puffett (Cambridge University Press, 1989).

Naturel, M., ed., *Marcel Proust: L'arche et la colombe*, (Neuilly-sur-Seine: Michel Lafon, 2012).

Newark, C., and I. Wassenaar, "Proust and Music: The Anxiety of Competence," *Cambridge Opera Journal* 9 (1997), 163–183.

Newark, T., *Émile Gallé* (Secaucus, NJ: Chartwell, 1989).

Norton, C. E., and Ruskin, J., *The Correspondence of John Ruskin and Charles Eliot Norton*, ed. J. L. Bradley and I. Ousby (Cambridge University Press, 1987).

Nugent, T., *The Grand Tour*, 3rd edn. (London: J. Rivington, 1778).

Nye, R. A., *Masculinity and Male Codes of Honor in Modern France* (Oxford University Press, 1993).

O'Brian, J., *Degas to Matisse: The Maurice Wertheim Collection* (New York: Harry N. Abrams/Harvard University Art Museums, 1988).

O'Daley, G., *Augustine's* City of God (Oxford University Press, 1999).

Oriol, J., *Femmes Proustiennes* (EST, 2009).

Orledge, R., *Debussy and the Theatre* (Cambridge University Press, 1982).

Ortel, P., *La Littérature à l'ère de la photographie: enquête sur une révolution invisible* (Nîmes: Chambon, 2002).

Osma, G. de, *Mariano Fortuny: His Life and His Work* (New York: Rizzoli, 1985).

Painter, G., *Marcel Proust: A Biography* (London: Chatto & Windus, 1959).

Paredes, L., *Sèvres Then and Now: Tradition and Innovation in Porcelain, 1750–2000* (London: Hillwood Museum, 2009).

Pauset, E. N., "Proust musicologue? Le positivisme ambigu ou: de sentir pour écrire à sentir est écrire," *International Review of the Aesthetics and Sociology of Music* 40 (2009), 63–79.

Pemble, J., *The Mediterranean Passion: Victorians and Edwardians in the South* (Oxford: Clarendon Press, 1987).

Perley, N., "The Language of an Unknown Country: Intratextuality in Proust's *In Search of Lost Time*," *Nineteenth-Century Music* 36 (2012), 136–145.

Piperno, A., *Proust antijuif*, trans. F. Gonzalez Batlle (Liana Levi, 2007).

Posner, M. I., S. E. Peterson, P. T. Fox, and M. E. Raichle, "Localization of Cognitive Operations in the Human Brain," *Science*, n.s. 240:4859 (June 17, 1988), 1627–1631.

Prestwich, P. F., *The Translation of Memories: Recollections of the Young Proust* (London: Peter Owen, 1999).

Prieto, E., *Listening In: Music, Mind, and the Modernist Narrative* (Lincoln: University of Nebraska Press, 2002).

Proulx, F., "Quatre lettres de Reynaldo Hahn à Madeleine Lemaire," *Bulletin d'informations proustiennes* 43 (2013), 23–26.

"Six lettres de Reynaldo Hahn à Suzette Lemaire," *Bulletin d'informations proustiennes* 44 (2014), 37–46.

Pugh, A. R., *The Growth of* À la recherche du temps perdu: *A Chronological Examination of Proust's Manuscripts from 1909 to 1914*, 2 vols. (University of Toronto Press, 2004).

Rhodes, D., and R. Hopper, *Clay and Glazes for the Potter* (Iola, WI: Krause Publications, 2000).

Richard, G. L., ed., "Priming," in *The Oxford Companion to the Mind* (Oxford University Press, 2004).

Ripa, C., *Iconologia* (1593–1603), ed. P. Buscaroli, preface by M. Praz (Milan: TEA Arte, 1992).

Robert, L. de, *Comment débuta Marcel Proust* (Gallimard, 1969).

Roddick, A., and E. Klarich, "Arcillas and Alfareros: Clay and Temper Mining Practices in the Lake Titicaca Basin," in *Mining and Quarrying in the Ancient Andes: Sociopolitical, Economic, and Symbolic Dimensions*, ed. N. Tripcevich and K. J. Vaughn (New York: Springer Verlag, 2012).

Roscoe, W., *Queer Spirits: A Gay Men's Myth Book* (Boston, MA: Beacon Press, 1995).

Rouillé, A., *La Photographie: entre document et art contemporain* (Gallimard, 2005).

Rubin, W., ed., *"Primitivism" in 20th Century Art: Affinity of the Tribal and the Modern* (New York: Museum of Modern Art, 1984).

Rudorff, R., *The Belle Époque: Paris in the Nineties* (New York: Saturday Review Press, 1973).

Ruskin, J., *The Works of John Ruskin*, 39 vols., Library Edition, ed. E. T. Cook and A. Wedderburn (London: George Allen, 1903–1912).

Saint-Simon, L. de R., duc de, *Mémoires complets et authentiques du duc de Saint-Simon, sur le siècle de Louis XIV et la Régence* (H.L. Delloye, 1840).

Sand, G., *Lettres d'un Voyageur* (Brussels: Meline, Cans, 1838).

Sartre, J.-P., *Anti-Semite and Jew*, trans. G. J. Becker (New York: Schocken, 1948).

Scarry, E., *Dreaming by the Book* (New York: Farrar, Straus & Giroux, 1999).

Schéfer, G., *Chardin: biographie critique* (Laurens, 1904).

Schlicht, M., *La Cathédrale de Rouen vers 1300: Portail des Libraires, portail de la Calende, chapelle de la Vierge* (Caen: Société des Antiquaires de Normandie, 2005).

Schulz, J., *The New Palaces of Medieval Venice* (University Park: Penn State University Press, 2004).

Schwenger, P., "Writing Hypnagogia," in *At the Borders of Sleep: On Liminal Literature* (Minneapolis: University of Minnesota Press, 2012).

Sedgwick, E. K., *Epistemology of the Closet* (Berkeley: University of California Press, 1990).

Simmel, G., *The Philosophy of Money*, ed. D. Frisby, trans. T. Bottomore and D. Frisby (London and New York: Routledge, 2004).

Small, C., *Musicking: The Meanings of Performing and Listening* (Middletown, CT: Wesleyan University Press, 1998).

Sollers, P., *L'Œil de Proust* (Stock, 1999).

Souday, P., *Marcel Proust* (Simon Kra, 1927).

Spottiswood Mackin, S., *A Society Woman on Two Continents* (London: Transatlantic, 1896).

Steele, V., *Paris Fashion: A Cultural History* (New York: Berg, 2001).

Steiner, G., *Real Presences* (University of Chicago Press, 1991).

Stendhal, *Life of Rossini*, trans. R. N. Coe (New York: Criterion Books, 1957).

Stewart, G., *The Look of Reading: Book, Painting, Text* (University of Chicago Press, 2006).

Strickland, D. H., *Saracens, Demons and Jews: Making Monsters in Medieval Art* (Princeton University Press, 2003).

Sullivan, C. A., "Classification, Containment, Contamination, and the Courtesan: The Grisette, Lorette, and Demi-Mondaine in Nineteenth-Century French Fiction," Ph.D. thesis, University of Texas at Austin, 2003.

Szylowicz, C., "Les dessins dans les lettres de Marcel Proust à Reynaldo Hahn," in *Cher ami... Votre Marcel Proust: Marcel Proust im Spiegel seiner Korrespondenz: Briefe und Autographen aus der Bibliotheca Proustiana Reiner Speck*, ed. J. Ritter and R. Speck (Cologne: Snoek, 2009), 44–57.

Tacou, L., ed., *L'Herne: Colette* (Éditions de L'Herne, 2011).

Tadié, J.-Y., *Marcel Proust*, trans. E. Camercon (New York: Viking, 2000).

Proust et le roman (Gallimard: 1971).

"L'univers musical de Marcel Proust," *Revue de Littérature Comparée* 67 (1993).

Tadié, J.-Y., with F. Callu, eds., *Marcel Proust, l'écriture et les arts* (Gallimard/Bibliothèque nationale de France/Réunion des Musées Nationaux, 1999).

Tarde, G., *The Laws of Imitation*, trans. E. C. Parson (New York: Henry Holt, 1903).

Thédenat, H., *Pompéi: Histoire – Vie privée* (Laurens, 1910).

Uro, Y., "Les Peintres de salon amis de Marcel Proust et leurs rapports avec son œuvre," doctoral thesis, Université de Paris Sorbonne I, 2004.

Uzanne, O., *Jean Lorrain, l'artiste – l'ami: souvenirs intimes, lettres inédites* ([E. Champion], 1913).

Valazza, N., *Crise de plume et souveraineté du pinceau: écrire la peinture de Diderot à Proust* (Classiques Garnier, 2013).

Vasari, G., *Lives of Seventy of the Most Eminent Painters, Sculptors, and Architects*, ed. E. Blashfield and A. Hopkins (New York: Charles Scribner's Sons, 1896).

Wagner, R., *Prose Works*, trans. W. A. Ellis (London: Kegan Paul, 1907).

Warmus, W., *Émile Gallé: Dreams into Glass* (Corning, NY: Corning Museum of Glass, 1984).

Watt, A., ed., *Marcel Proust in Context* (Cambridge University Press, 2013).

Reading in Proust's À la recherche: *'le délire de la lecture'* (Oxford: Clarendon Press, 2009).

Wilson, E., *Axel's Castle: A Study in the Imaginative Literature of 1870–1930* (New York: Scribner's, 1969).

Wolf, M., *Proust and the Squid: The Story and Science of the Reading Brain* (New York: Harper Perennial, 2008).

Wolitz, S., *The Proustian Community* (New York University Press, 1971).

Yoshikawa, K., "Proust aux expositions," in *Proust et les moyens de la connaissance*, ed. A. Bouillaguet (Presses Universitaires de Strasbourg, 2009), 207–218.

Proust et l'art pictural (Champion, 2010).

"Vinteuil ou la genèse du septuor," in *Études proustiennes*, 3 (Gallimard, 1979), 289–334.

Index

Lightning Source UK Ltd.
Milton Keynes UK
UKHW022112221218
334458UK00018B/393/P